THE FORGIVENESS
OF NATURE

Graham Harvey is the Agricultural Story Editor of *The Archers*. His first book, *The Killing of the Countryside*, won the 1997 BP Natural World Book Award.

ALSO BY GRAHAM HARVEY

The Killing of the Countryside

Graham Harvey

THE FORGIVENESS OF NATURE

The Story of Grass

VINTAGE

Published by Vintage 2002

2 4 6 8 10 9 7 5 3 1

First published in Great Britain in 2001 by
Jonathan Cape

Vintage
Random House, 20 Vauxhall Bridge Road,
London SW1V 2SA

Random House Australia (Pty) Limited
20 Alfred Street, Milsons Point, Sydney
New South Wales 2061, Australia

Random House New Zealand Limited
18 Poland Road, Glenfield,
Auckland 10, New Zealand

Random House (Pty) Limited
Endulini, 5A Jubilee Road, Parktown 2193,
South Africa

The Random House Group Limited Reg. No. 954009
www.randomhouse.co.uk

A CIP catalogue record for this book
is available from the British Library

ISBN 0 099 28366 2

Printed and bound in Great Britain by
Cox & Wyman Limited, Reading, Berkshire

To Annie

Grasses are the greatest single source of wealth in the world.

Agnes Chase, *First Book of Grasses*

Of all things the most common, grasses are the least known.

J. C. Mohler, *Grasses in Kansas*

You shall also know that your descendants shall be many,
And your offspring like the grass of the earth.

Job, 5:25

The basis of human proliferation is not our own seed but the seed of grasses.

Evan Eisenberg, 'Back to Eden'

Songs like the grass are evergreen:
The giver
Said 'Live and be' – and they have been,
For ever.

John Clare, 'Song's Eternity'

Contents

Acknowledgements

There's something about the idea of grass that can suddenly take hold of you. It happened to me as a farming student back in the 1960s, the realisation that within the commonplace there dwells the truly extraordinary. By then I must have spent a good deal of my life walking on it, sitting on it, working and playing on it. But only now did I start to grasp its amazing gifts and possibilities.

Most of those who guided me on this present journey have shared the same fascination with the world of grass. Dai Hides – a good friend from university days and himself a life-long enthusiast of grassland – has been, as always, unstinting in his help and encouragement. I also owe much to his former colleagues at the Institute of Grassland and Environmental Research in Aberystwyth. Their studies continue to reveal the potential of this too-often neglected national resource.

An early visit to the Kent home of botanist Geoff Chapman got my own researches off to a flying start. Formerly of Wye College, Geoff has written eloquently on the subject of grasses and their biology. He is one of those admirable scientists who somehow manage to combine an infectious enthusiasm for the subject with a scrupulous academic rigour.

Philip Grime of Sheffield University is another such scientist. Giving generously of his time and knowledge, he did much to advance my understanding of the secret contests and rivalries that drive the plant kingdom. Grassland ecologists Richard Jefferson and Heather Robertson of English Nature were equally helpful in revealing the intriguing social life of grasses, as were their colleagues Simon Leach and Brian Johnson from English Nature's Taunton office.

In delving into our agrarian past I was fortunate to receive assistance from Richard Moore-Colyer of the University of Wales. Like the best historians, he combines scholarship with a refreshingly open mind. I am grateful to Cledwyn Fychan for introducing me to the fascinating history of the summer pastures and to the Wiltshire archivist Nancy Steele for sharing her researches on water meadows.

Former adviser Gwyn Jones, one of the post-war champions of upland livestock farming, provided some fascinating glimpses into this significant chapter in modern agrarian history, while my friend Lucy Large gave me invaluable advice on art history. In my home county of Somerset, Wayne Bennett at Dillington House provided a fresh and challenging insight into the British Neolithic.

At the start of this journey my accumulated knowledge of sports turf development would have fitted onto a smallish seed packet. If now I have succeeded in telling some part of this momentous story credit must go to a handful of patient professionals who helped me enormously. I am particularly indebted to Peter L. K. Dury, whose own deep knowledge and pioneering spirit has played a part in that revolution. I am grateful for the help and encouragement of staff at the Sports Turf Research Institute, West Yorkshire, whose own contribution to contemporary sport is widely acknowledged.

My understanding of parkland and its importance in cultural life was enhanced by staff of the Milton Keynes Parks Trust, particularly Ian Richardson and Rai Darke. I am equally grateful to my friend Malcolm Bole for his valuable research. Staff of the Meat and Livestock Commission were also generous with their help and support. I am happy to acknowledge the particular assistance of librarian Neil Hudson.

Finally I must mention Pascal Cariss, the editor of this volume. His input has been, as always, invaluable.

In addition to those owed special thanks are countless others who have helped – most of them unwittingly – in the writing of this book. They are the hundreds of farmers, scientists and naturalists I've met in my years as a farming journalist. All have generously shared their knowledge and enthusiasm. To them I say a heartfelt: 'Thank you'.

Graham Harvey
August 2001

1   *The Enduring Passion*

In 1863 the artist Édouard Manet outraged Parisian society with a picture that Émile Zola was later to hail as his greatest work. In a sun-splashed woodland clearing two fully dressed men lie semi-recumbent on the grassy sward. Beside them sits a nude woman, her ivory skin contrasting starkly with the dark hues of the forest edge.

It is a scene with echoes of a painting by the sixteenth-century artist Giorgione. In *Concert champêtre* naked and contemporarily dressed figures are seen in a Venetian landscape. But in Giorgione's work all are fully absorbed in their own world, a fictional world remote from the viewer.

In Manet's picture – *Le Déjeuner sur l'herbe* – the naked woman defies convention by staring unashamedly out of the picture. There is no modest lowering of the eyes as demanded by polite, nineteenth-century society. Instead the viewer is drawn reluctantly into her world. Her gaze is disturbing because it strips away the comfort that this is a remote and fictional place. By her stare the woodland glade is made an extension of our own reality just as the viewer is made an extension of hers.

When it appeared at the Salon des Refusés, Manet's picture

with its uncompromising stare challenged contemporary views on decent behaviour and sent shock-waves rumbling through Parisian society. This assertive young woman, sitting beside her rumpled clothes and the spilled contents of a picnic basket, had turned the smart Salon set into voyeurs.

In placing such a provocative figure on a turf Manet was acknowledging a profound truth. Somewhere deep within the human psyche, grass is indelibly linked with freedom, with a flouting of convention, with a cocking of snooks at the established order. Over the centuries image-makers have used the green sward to denote a spirit of independence. It has become a sort of visual shorthand suggesting robust individualism and lives uncluttered by social niceties.

Today grass is seen as the great escape. Whether it is an afternoon on the golf course or ninety minutes of kicking and sliding in the local Sunday soccer league, grass is a release from the ordinary. It may be a picnic on a roadside verge or a motorway rest area. For some it will be a sun-lounger on the lawn, or a lunch-time sandwich in the park by the office on a sweltering summer's day.

To step on to a turf is to step out of the everyday; to break with the humdrum and the tyranny of routine. Grass represents liberty. It is the universal opt-out from the confinement of civilisation and regulation. By stepping on to the grass we temporarily reject the ordered world of human affairs and take a brief walk along the edge of the infinite.

The appeal of grass runs deep. You have only to watch the excitement of small toddlers playing outdoors on the lawn. Out here the normal rules are relaxed. Out here it is fine to shout and scream and throw the toys about. No one seems to mind. There is a new freedom to jump and roll about, to splash wildly in the inflatable pool, to abandon for a while the tedious laws of existence. And through it all to feel the cool, soft caress of grass leaves between bare toes.

It is a heady amalgam of the sensual and the spiritual, this anarchic world of grass; a formative experience that will never be forgotten. Primary teachers see it every year – the barely contained explosion of excitement when youngsters are allowed to play on the school field for the first time after the winter. The games they play are the games they played yesterday on the hard tarmac playground – football, handball, skipping and tag; the running, screaming, roughing-and-tumbling of kids everywhere. But when they are played outside, on the soft, green turf, they are imbued with a new joy, a greater abandon.

Years later many will experience the same collision of longing and sensuality when they lie with a lover in the park on a summer night. To make love on grass is to embrace the wild and the untrammelled, to brush against the great forces of the infinite as Laurie Lee did on his magical night beneath the hay wagon with Rosie, his first love. Grass is a reminder that we have a history older than our lives. We come from some faraway place, and that soft, green vegetation beneath our bodies has made the journey with us. When we touch it, when we walk on it and play on it, lie on it and make love on it, that is when we feel intensely alive.

The world's grasslands – the class of vegetation characterised by the grasses, the Poaceae – occupy almost a quarter of the earth's land surface. It is the vegetation of open spaces, of wide, rolling plains; the landscape of light and heat, of burning sun and biting winds, of distance and emptiness and broad, open skies. Above all it is the landscape of dryness. All the world's great natural grasslands are arid. If they received more rain they would disappear under forest trees.

Vast areas of wild grassland once circled the earth on either side of the equator. North America contained the prairies, a great, rolling sea of grass stretching in a wide belt across the continental heartland from the forest edge of Canada to the Gulf Coast of south-eastern Texas. The grasslands of the American plain were mirrored in the steppes of Eurasia stretching eastwards from the European plain, around the southern Urals, as far as the foothills of the Altai Mountains in Mongolia; reaching down from the forest edge of northern Europe and Siberia to the semi-deserts of the Caspian Sea region and central Asia.

In the southern hemisphere the pampas grasslands of Argentina ran from the tall prairie bordering the River Plate to the short grass country of Bahia Blanca, stretching across the south to the foothills of the Andes Mountains. In South Africa the grasslands of the veld extended from the eastern interior Cape Province northwards to the Limpopo River. Further to the north and east the grasslands were dotted with trees and shrubs making them more like tropical savannah. The remaining great area of grass was in South Island, New Zealand, where the 'tussock' grasslands occupied no less than sixty-five thousand square kilometres on and around the Canterbury Plains.

In addition to these 'true' grasslands the drier regions of the planet supported immense areas of savannah, a vegetation characterised by grasses and sedges, but with a scattering of trees and shrubs. Savannahs range from those dominated by tall grasses and sparse tree populations, such as the 'elephant grass savannah' of central Africa, to those of meagre vegetation like the 'desert grass savannah' or 'orchard steppe', landscapes dominated by drought-resistant grasses and a few pinched trees and shrubs. This is the vegetation that fringes the Sahara and Kalahari deserts and covers broad stretches of Australia's dry northern states, the sparse, dusty grassland that clothes the drier regions of the Deccan in India and the Mexican Plateau in north America.[1]

Grasslands comprise one of the four great terrestrial habitats or *biomes*, the others being forest, desert and tundra. Their poor innate productivity make them harsh places to live. Civilisations grow up in lush river basins and on fertile alluvial plains, on soils that are rich in plant nutrients and where irrigation water is plentiful. Sometimes the soils of grasslands are inherently fertile as on the American prairies and many tropical savannahs. But their aridity renders them unproductive in their accumulation of biomass, the biological opposites of the tropical rain forest with its extravagant and colourful growth.

Those who inhabit the wild grasslands are nomadic peoples, following their flocks and cattle herds from grazing ground to grazing ground. They travel because on grasslands the earth's bounty is too slight to sustain them in one place. Until the invasion of an industrial society with its mass transport systems fuelled by fossil energy, there were no great cities on the steppes or on the windswept prairies. From the dawn of mankind grasslands were places of movement and of liberty. Like the modern child playing in the park, the peoples of grass were free to live by their own rules, unencumbered by the trappings and diktats of 'civilised' society.

American writer Richard Manning, who sensed the spiritual relevance of grassland even in a modern state, dismisses the 'crown-of-creation fallacy': the idea that human history works as a kind of progression beginning with hunter-gatherer nomads and ending with cities.[2] Nomads are not nomads because they lack the technology, skills or intelligence to become farmers. The record suggests otherwise. Nomadism is a condition dictated by the land.

> Nomadism implies motion, not a random motion of the nomads' choosing, a wanderlust, but a motion dictated by the conditions of the land. Nomadic economy is based on wild grass too thin to support pastoralism, the fixed pastures of domesticated animals, or the commons that grew up in conjunction with settled agriculture. Pastoralism, the intensive raising of domestic stock, is an intermediate step between farming and nomadism. The nomadic economy is extensive rather than intensive. Nomads follow animals following grass.[3]

In the northern steppes – the great sweep of plain and plateau extending from Hungary to Manchuria below the northern forest – peoples who had embraced agriculture as it spread from western Asia, later abandoned it in favour of the nomadic existence.[4] Though they retained their traditional skills of tent-making, wagon-building and metal-working, they chose a life of movement, following their grazing herds from pasture to pasture. These were not arbitrary journeyings but an annual cycle of seasonal migrations from exposed summer pastures to sheltered river valleys for the winter.

In the eastern steppes, the land of the Mongolian herders, each tribe or clan would return to their traditional pastures year after year.[5] The pattern was altered only when the expansion of the flock or herd obliged the tribe to search out new grazings, or when another nomad group forced them off their traditional pastures. It was a life of mobility and constant change made possible by the tent or *yurt*, constructed by stretching circular layers of felt over light, wooden frames. Today most Mongolians still prefer the nomadic life even though village settlements have been available since the time of the Soviet regime.

The nomadic tribes that traversed the broad grasslands of the American prairies were not herders of livestock but hunters of the great migratory herds of bison. According to the writer and traveller Bruce Chatwin, the hunter cannot truly be called a nomad. The word derives from the Greek *nomos* – a pasture. Thus the true nomad is a mobile pastoralist, the owner and breeder of domesticated animals.

But like the nomads of the steppes, the tribes of the American plain carried their own form of portable dwelling, the *tipi*, made from tanned buffalo hides sewn together and stretched across long cedar poles. These were transported on dog sleds as the hunters followed the bison herds along their timeless migration routes, killing them by herding them into compounds or by driving them over cliffs at 'kill sites'. Nomads or not, the tribes of the Great Plain are made to pay the same tribute of all the peoples of grassland – constant mobility. And, like all peoples of grassland, they are rewarded with the same great blessing of liberty.

The world of grass had another gift for the nomads, one that would increase their wealth and enrich their lives, making them lords of the open plains. With it they were able to enlarge their cattle herds and sheep flocks so they could support bigger families. They would spend more of their time in craft work, and would make their daily lives more comfortable by carrying with them domestic goods. At times they would bring terror to the settled people of the city.

In AD 376 news reached the far-flung Roman garrisons on the Danube that a fearsome and unknown army of mounted bowmen had overrun the Gothic kingdom of what is now Romania and were threatening the mighty empire of Rome. These devilish warriors from somewhere beyond the Volga spread panic throughout Europe, thundering across the dusty summer turf on their sturdy steppe ponies, loosing wave after wave of arrows with unnerving accuracy. Yet these were a nomadic, pastoralist people with no settled homes, no kings and, according to the contemporary historian Ammianus Marcellinus, no knowledge of agriculture.

'No one ever ploughs a field in their country or touches a plough handle,' he wrote of the fearsome Huns. 'They are ignorant of home, law, or settled existence, and they keep roaming from places in their wagons. If you ask one of their children where he comes from, he was conceived in one place, born far away and brought up still farther off.'[6]

The transformation of these wandering herders into the most terrifying fighting machine of the Old World was brought about by equitation and the horse. The first people to ride wild horses probably lived around six thousand years ago on the western edge of the Asiatic steppes in what is now Ukraine.[7] Across those same grasslands rode the Huns on their ponies descended from a strain of the 'cold-blooded' northern horse that survives to this day in Mongolia. It is named the Przwalsky after a Russian colonel who travelled in the region.[8]

The Huns brought up their children to value animals more than human life. Young boys were sat upon sheep almost before they could walk. From the animal's back they learned to loose off arrows at birds and rats. By the time they reached early manhood they had total command of their horses and could shoot arrows with deadly accuracy even at full gallop. Bruce Chatwin wrote: 'The Huns, we are told, bought, sold, slept, ate, drank, gave judgement, even defecated without dismounting.'

Grassland demanded mobility of those who would make their home in its vast, rolling empire. But it also gave them an animal that would make their motion quick and sure so they would become rulers of that land. The broad swathe of steppe grassland which stretched unbroken from Hungary to Manchuria gave birth to a progression of nomadic peoples – the Scythians, the Sarmatians, the Magyars and the Mongols. They passed their tented lives in constant motion from pasture to pasture, following the seasonal ebb and flow of the grass tide, trading their meat and their leather for silks and grain and, on occasion, terrorising the world of settlement and civility with their daunting cavalry assaults.

So enraged was the Chinese emperor Wu-ti, who ruled in the second century BC, that he devoted much cunning and treachery to procuring the perfect weapon to defend his vast territory against the uncivilised nomads. The object of his fury were the Hsiung-nu, a warlike, nomadic people – ancestors of the Huns – who constantly raided China's northern border. The emperor had heard tales of the 'heavenly horse', a legendary 'hot-blooded' strain that was said to sweat blood and to have descended directly from heaven.[9] Possession of it would give him control of his borders. Such was the power of the horse in the world of the open plain. Those with the greatest mobility were rewarded with riches and power.

Horse culture came late to the American prairies. The prehistoric horse had become extinct following the sinking of the land bridge across the Bering Strait. But as if to fulfil its destiny the horse returned to the Great Plain, reintroduced from Spanish stock brought over to Mexico by the conquistadores in the sixteenth century. There it transformed the lives of prairie nomads as it had revolutionised life on the Eurasian steppes. The tribes of the plain could now cover greater distances and hunt over a wider area. No longer did they need to herd bison toward fixed 'kill sites'. They could dispatch them with precision from horse-back, at first using the bow and arrow, then later the European rifle.

With the horse-drawn travois replacing the dog sled, tribal groups were able to carry more food and household possessions. There was now time for creative activity, for skin painting and beadwork. Ceremonial and ritual such as the sacred Sun Dance began to play a prominent part in tribal life. The bison culture of the prairie nomad blossomed just as the Europeans were about to cut it down with their railroads, their homesteads and their barbed wire.

Like the nomads of the steppes, the Plains Indians took to the horse as if they had been waiting for it for a thousand years. The

American artist George Catlin described the extraordinary horsemanship of the Comanche people.

> Amongst their feats of riding there is one that has astonished me more than anything: a stratagem of war, learned and practised by every young man in the tribe; by which he is able to drop his body upon the side of his horse at the moment he is passing, effectively screened from his enemy's weapons as he lays in horizontal position behind the body of his horse, with his heel hanging over the horse's back; by which he has the power of throwing himself up again, and changing to the other side of the horse if necessary. In this wonderful condition, he will hang whilst his horse is at fullest speed, carrying with him his bow and his shield, and also his long lance of fourteen feet in length, all or either of which he will wield upon his enemy as he passes; rising and throwing his arrows over the horse's back, or with equal ease and with equal success under the horse's neck.[10]

The former foot nomads – peoples including the Kiowa, Crow, Blackfoot, Plains Cree, Sarcee, Assiniboine and Arapaho – quickly embraced the horse culture and for a time flourished. Others such as the Cheyenne and Teton-Dakota – tribes which had been at least partially agricultural before the coming of the horse – now abandoned their settlements and took to the plain. Whatever their origins, the horse nomads shared a common way of life, following the buffalo herds across the wide grasslands. It was a society that celebrated martial values yet believed in democracy and sexual equality. It was a society that produced happy, well-adjusted children. It was a free society. For the American nomad an age-old trek across the prairie ended with a final, furious gallop across the blazing grassland.

I was born upon the prairie, where the wind blew free and there was nothing to break the light of the sun. I was born where there were no enclosures and where everything drew a free breath. I want to die there and not within walls. I know every stream and every wood between the Rio Grande and

the Arkansas. I have hunted and lived over that country. I
lived like my fathers before me, and, like them, I lived
happily . . . So, why do you ask us to leave the rivers, and the
sun, and the wind, and live in houses? Do not speak of it
more . . . we only wish to wander on the prairie until we die.
               —Parrawasamen (Ten Bears), *Comanche*.[11]

The city child's game on a grass lawn is light-years from the
last ride of the Plains Indian. Yet both are responses to a single
compelling urge, the unspoken demand of grass made since the
dawn of mankind – the irresistible impulse for motion. Some
claim that the long, loping stride is an evolutionary adaptation –
unique to the hominids – for covering distances across open
savannah. Without such a bipedal walk there might have been
no development of the manufactory hand, it is argued, and
without that, no enlarged brain.

Bruce Chatwin observes that human babies show an instinctive appetite for movement. Often they scream for no other
reason than that they cannot bear to lie still. 'A crying child is a
very rare sight on a nomad caravan, and the tenacity with which
nomads cling to their way of life, as well as their quick-witted
alertness, reflects the satisfaction to be found in perpetual
movement. As settlers we walk off our frustrations.'[12]

It was on grassland that human beings acquired that appetite
for movement. At some time between one and two million
years ago, an ancestor of humans abandoned the ancient forest
home and made a new life on the dry, grassy plain. No one can
be sure exactly when and how the transition took place, but
members of the species *Homo erectus* clearly possessed a number
of physical attributes that were well suited to life out on the
open savannah. For a start they walked on two legs, a habit that
gave them an upright posture as their name implies. This is
likely to have given them a real advantage in a country of tall
grasses.

Not that this was anything new. An earlier hominid,
Australopithecus afarensis, made famous by the skeleton Lucy, was
known to share the two-legged gait.[13] But *afarensis* was scarcely
more than one metre tall, not much of an advantage in the tall-

grass country. *Erectus* had become far taller, approaching the height of modern humans. It also had a bigger brain – about one-fifth bigger than that of its immediate ancestor, *Homo habilis*. Perhaps because of this the hand tools made by the later hominid showed a new level of skill and sophistication. Males seem not to have been much bigger than females, a characteristic taken by some as an indication that co-operation between males had begun to replace competition. *Homo erectus* was equipped for a degree of social interaction.

Life out on the plain was taxing. For the quick and cunning hunter there were rich pickings to be had among the myriad herbivores. But the risks were as high as the potential rewards. Out here in the open there was no hiding place from the large carnivores – the lions, leopards, wolves and hyenas that stalked the savannah grassland. There had been dangers enough in the forest, but at least among the trees and tangled undergrowth there were places of refuge, escape routes, the chance of being missed. Out on the endless savannah there were none. The game was more intense; for the losers the end was swift. This was life in the fast lane.

But the tall upright ape appears to have flourished. Archaeological sites associated with *Homo erectus* have revealed the remains of sizeable building structures.[14] Others show evidence of the mass killing of elephants and baboons, deposits reminiscent of those found at relatively modern bison 'kill sites' on the American prairies. Some archaeologists have even suggested that these were the result of dozens of hunters acting co-operatively, the original version of the popular management exercises in male bonding and survival skills.

Whatever the truth of these deposits, there is no doubt that *Homo erectus* multiplied on the dusty savannah grassland. Fossil evidence shows that at least one other hominid species inhabited that dry African plain, yet it was *erectus* that went on to produce human beings, the Internet, Handel's *Messiah* and Cruise missiles. Sometime between one million and 700,000 years ago the progenitor of liberated woman and modern man migrated from Africa to colonise the warm, temperate regions of Mediterranean Europe and Asia. The first hominid to be found outside Africa, it went under a number of aliases including Java Man and Peking Man.

By 300,000 years ago the species had made a home on the arid steppe grasslands and the cold, northern forest, eventually leaving its mark on Britain. It was *Homo erectus* that gave rise to the steppe nomads – the Huns and the Mongols – and, via the Bering land bridge, to the tribal nomads of the American prairies. Not for another 200,000 years or more would there be the great cultural explosion that marked the emergence of modern human beings. In the Upper Pleistocene period the intelligent hominids developed the techniques of social hunting on the tundra grasslands. In the south of France the so-called 'Cro-Magnon Man' – a collection of fossil skeletons – was discovered in a rock shelter along with pierced seashells, animal teeth and remnants of necklaces and bracelets, the sort of body adornments that might now be seen on the beach at St Tropez.

But this early model of *Homo sapiens*, the body made for a Calvin Klein ad, was devised, refined and tested on the dry savannah and the icy tundra. Like the horse and the hyena it was first and foremost a creature of grass. And somewhere inside that bubbling broth of consciousness, reason and emotion, it still is.

Every year an outburst of football passion marks the end of the season and the beginning of summer – the English soccer Cup Final. The venue is the old Wembley Stadium, the twin-towered icon of England's post-war sporting life and scene of a host of cultural extravaganzas such as the 'Feed the World' concert. The year 2000 saw the last Wembley final before redevelopment. The competing teams were Chelsea, 'the Blues', with their glittering array of world stars and smart, West End address, and Aston Villa, the plain, honest, hard-working team from the West Midlands, who had failed to lift the trophy for more than forty years.

With just minutes to go until the kick-off the two sides line up nervously in the cavernous Wembley tunnel as the chanting and roaring of the crowd gushes around them like a torrent down a storm drain after a sharp summer downpour. Some smile and talk and share a joke with team-mates. But most stand silent, locked in private thought, frozen at the prospect of their imminent trial beneath the glare of the sun. Suddenly the walls around them seem comforting and safe, like the tall forest canopy, secure and enfolding. Can that early tribal group have felt something of the kind as they gathered at the woodland edge summoning the will to take their first, uncertain steps on to the open plain?

On the pitch the shadows are gone. Out here, under the sky, there is space and freedom. This is the grassy plain, the place of speed and opportunity, the environment that made the species successful, this tall, upright ape with the unusually large brain. Far away the stands with their ranks of bellowing fans recede in the consciousness. Like the teeming forest, they are now far off. Here is where the players can be truly themselves; here is where they can show their hard-won grace and skill, like the Comanche horseman lying horizontal on the flank of his galloping pony, and the mounted bowman of the steppe loosing his arrows with pinpoint accuracy. Grassland is their place of destiny, the place they become fully alive, fully human.

It can be no coincidence that so many great competitive team sports are played on grass. Soccer has been a game for the green turf since the medieval villagers took to the nearest level stretch of common pasture for their savage game of 'fote-balle'. As early as 1175 the monk William Fitzstephen, writing of London life, described the Shrove Tuesday entertainment in which 'all the youth of the city go to a flat patch of ground just outside the city for their famous game of ball'.[15] An annual game of primitive football is still played on Shrove Tuesday in the Derbyshire village of Ashbourne.

By the early seventeenth century football was being played on grass by students at Oxford and Cambridge universities. A century later the boys of Eton School were playing their notorious wall game on a grass pitch. When the split came between the ball-dribbling and ball-handling forms of football, the rugby version – allegedly resulting from an incident at Rugby School – maintained the custom of playing on turf.

Ireland shares the British tradition of folk-football extending back to the unruly village contests and later formalised in the games of field caid and cross-country caid. But the efforts of the

Gaelic League led to the development of purely Irish games, Gaelic football and hurling, both of them played on grass.[16] The first cricket matches were played on grazed pastureland, much of it uneven and tussocky. In search of a smoother surface, some of the early players opted to play in churchyards. In 1622 six Sussex men were prosecuted for playing on consecrated ground. Though the origins of hockey lie shrouded in pre-history, the modern form of the game was developed by cricketers at Teddington who played it on the 'outfield' using a cricket ball.

For all of these games grass is the chosen surface. No doubt many of the reasons are purely practical. In fast contact games a hard surface is unwise. The toll in injuries would be too high. The violent, inter-village encounters of the Middle Ages would have led to wide-scale slaughter had they been played on cobbles. Those early amateurs sought nothing more than a soft, level area without too many obstructions, and the best they could come up with was the communal pasture. No one has yet devised a better surface.

In 1981 the London soccer club Queens Park Rangers installed a sand-filled synthetic pitch in their stadium. The players started to sustain friction burns and the kind of jarring injuries that result from playing on surfaces with poor shock absorbency.[17] Nor did the innovation do much to improve the quality of the game. The plastic surface caused the ball to bounce half as high again, and when it started rolling it didn't stop until it ran up against the advertising boards at the edge of the pitch. Synthetic playing surfaces have improved in the intervening years. Even so the English Football League decided to ban artificial pitches for the professional game, having carried out its own investigation.

The surface that has been played on for a thousand years is still the favourite of sports stars. With luck the rugby three-quarter felled by a bruising tackle from an eighteen-stone forward will get up with nothing worse than a thick layer of mud on his strip. That is how the players like it. They are also keen that the ball should roll and bounce the way it always has done. Not that there is anything intrinsically wrong with a high bounce if that were the way the ball had always behaved.

However, to introduce it now would be to change the nature of the game, and nobody is keen to do that.

All are sound, sensible reasons for wishing to play on the familiar turf. But might there be another, less rational basis for this attachment to grass? Could it be that like the toddler on the lawn and the school child on the playing field, sports stars are happier playing on a living, green sward? Richard Manning writes of feeling a 'rush of freedom' on encountering an open vista of grasslands.[18] He believes it to be a racial memory of a time when human beings first learned to run among those wide open spaces. Sociologists speak of the 'biophillia effect': the way a good environment appears to improve social behaviour. Research evidence also shows that regular – or even occasional – contact with nature reduces stress, anxiety and aggression. After a few minutes in a green space, heart rate, blood pressure and muscular tension all begin to fall.[19]

The association of human beings with grasses has been close and long-lasting. No other plant family has played such a dominant role in the advance of the human species. Grasses supply most of the carbohydrate energy in human diets through the major grain crops – rice, maize, wheat, oats and barley sorghum – together with sugar cane. Then there are the proteins and fats supplied as meat and dairy products from the animals that graze pastures or feed on the conserved products of grassland such as hay and silage. A large proportion of dietary protein and fat comes from grazing animals.

But the contribution of grass to human well-being is not limited to the food it supplies. Since the first pastoral peoples began herding cattle, sheep and goats, their cultural activity has been bound up with the grasslands that supported their livestock. Food crops seldom require continuous attention from the farmers that plant them. Human intervention is usually limited to fixed periods of the seasonal cycle such as harvest time. Livestock, by contrast, demand frequent attention from their human minders. Cows, goats and dairy sheep need regular milking; animals kept for their meat, hides and wool must be protected from predators and moved on to fresh pastures.

Throughout history pastoral and farming peoples have spent

long periods of time on grassland. Their wealth, prosperity, even their survival, was bound up in their animals. And it was the green turf that sustained them. The pastoral landscape came to represent security, independence and plenty. The pasture field and the hay meadow were familiar, comfortable places to be. Small wonder that those whose lives depended so heavily on grass should devise games and pastimes to play on it.

In Britain grassland is not the natural vegetation as it is on the dry savannah. At this latitude forest is the climax, or stable, vegetation. Grasses flourish only in those places that are too high or too exposed for tree growth, or where wild herbivores are constantly nibbling the young saplings before they can become established. For thousands of years after the ending of the last ice age the British Isles were covered with natural forest, the *wildwood*. But since prehistoric times the occupants of these islands have been busy clearing it for cultivation or converting it to that more favoured landscape of human beings, the open landscape of grass.

The hunter-gatherers of the Mesolithic (9,000–4,000BC) are likely to have congregated at the woodland glade, if only for deer and wild cattle attracted by the grazing. These sun-dappled clearings in the dense, dark forest may have come to represent feasting and plenty. Could they also have been places for rest and relaxation, for domestic tasks such as trimming animal skins and fashioning bone ornaments; places for games and for love-making? Certainly they would have been favourite play areas for the children.

Later came the people of the Neolithic (4,000–2,400BC), Britain's first farmers, combining a knowledge of cultivation and cropping with a powerful urge to pastoralism. Using fire and stone axes, they cleared large areas of forest, converting much of the chalk landscape to open grassland. Though they established cultivated plots and tended them from time to time, there is little evidence of permanent settlements in Britain. These were a semi-nomadic people, herding their cattle and sheep from pasture to pasture like the nomads of the steppe. Their monuments litter the countryside: burial mounds and barrows, henges and stone circles, causewayed enclosures and long cursus earthworks; places of feasting and bartering, sex and social display; places of ceremonial and ancestor worship set in a wind-blown landscape of rippling grasses.

The Anglo-Saxon invaders who followed the Romans to Britain knew the worth of a productive grass meadow, probably because they needed good grazing for their ox teams. Some cattle enthusiasts were so adept at choosing the best sites for their meadows or *hamms* that they bequeathed their names to the villages that later grew up around them.[20] Passenham or Passa's hamm and Wappenham or Waeppa's hamm commemorate two of seventeen in the county of Northamptonshire alone, sites that one thousand years later were some of the best beef-fattening pastures in the country.

In village Britain many growing settlements put grassland at the very heart of their little communities. The triangle, circle or rectangle of grass that formed the village green became the centre of civic and social life for centuries. In Domesday times the lord of the manor or his bailiff dispensed justice on the communal turf, chopping off a thieving hand or hanging a goat-stealer from the village oak tree as the villagers looked on in squirming fascination and their geese grazed unconcerned on the lush grasses.

During the Middle Ages the men of the village practised their archery on the green, using longbows cut from churchyard yews. Village greens trained the English armies like Henry V's 'band of brothers' who defeated a French army of more than twice their number at Agincourt 'upon St Crispin's Day' in 1415. Hugh Latimer, Bishop of Worcester under Henry VIII and later burnt at the stake by Mary, recalled being taught by his father 'how to draw, how to lay my body in my bow, and not to draw with strength of arm as other nations do, but with strength of body. I had my bows bought me according to my age and strength; as I increased in them, so my bows were made bigger and bigger, for men shall never shoot well unless they be brought up in it.'[21]

There were gentler pastimes, too. On May Day the men of the village would bring a tall birch sapling from the wood and set it up on the green. There the 'May pole' would be garlanded with flowers before the village girls danced around it in a timeless ritual of fertility. In Wales the green or *twmpath chwarae* was the traditional venue for dancing to the fiddle or harp, though wrestling, bowling and throwing the stone or beam were other popular May pastimes.[22] Grassland seemed the natural place to celebrate the return of spring, and not just for the formal village activities. In 1583 the puritan moralist Philip Stubbes was scathing in his condemnation of sexual revelries that took place on the night before May Day. He had heard it from 'men of great gravity and reputation, that of forty, threescore or a hundred maids going to the wood overnight, there have scarcely the third part of them returned home again undefiled'.[23]

Greens also became centres for rural trade following the granting of royal licences for markets and fairs. Itinerant traders carried their wares from village to village, bringing news and gossip as an additional, under-the-counter offering. On feast days the bigger fairs often attracted exotic entertainers – conjurers and acrobats, jugglers and balladeers, trainers of performing monkeys and fearsome dancing bears. The village grassland was the focus of commerce and amusement, a culture that still finds its echoes in travelling fairs and car boot sales.

When industrialisation emptied the villages and smothered green fields beneath marching ranks of grim back-to-back houses, the rural refugees sought escape from their squalid surroundings in a new form of communal grassland. The first of the great urban parks were laid out on the design principles of the eighteenth-century private estate. But they became places for the people, village greens reset in the smoke-blackened landscapes of industrial Britain. They were the 'green lungs' of the city; places for exercise and social interaction; places where people, herded by capitalism into the 'dark, satanic mills', could become once more, for a moment, what they had been born to be – nomads of the open, grassy plain.

Human beings were conceived and born on to grassland. As a species we passed our childhood and adolescence in grassy places. When we learned to reconstruct our environment we surrounded ourselves with the vegetation that made us feel at ease with ourselves. We draped it across the hills and cast it upon the fields. We took it into the city and spread it around our homes. We played on it, we fought on it, we loved and died on it. 'All flesh is grass', the Bible says. But in some mysterious way, so too are our minds and our hearts. We are creatures of grassland and we will not let it go.

2 People of the Grass

In September 1991 Erika and Helmut Simon, a German couple holidaying in the Italian South Tyrol, discovered the nut-brown skull and upper torso of a man protruding from glacier ice below the Alpine peak called the Finailspitze. Assuming him to have been the victim of some earlier climbing accident, they reported the grisly finding with its location, then got on with enjoying the remaining few days of their holiday.

But when the Simons finally returned to their home in Nuremberg they found a posse of journalists waiting to interview them. The corpse they had stumbled upon high in the Alps had been no modern-day accident victim. Misfortune had claimed this man's life more than five thousand years ago. Subsequent carbon dating of body tissue fragments and associated plant fragments revealed a date between 3,300 and 3,200BC.[1] The corpse in the glacier had been a man of the later Neolithic.

In the received wisdom of prehistory the people of the Neolithic were the world's first farmers. In landscapes peopled by wandering hunter-gatherers they developed a new pattern of living based on the growing of crops and the herding of domesticated livestock. They were the creators of settled agriculture, the essential precursor of towns and cities, industrialisation, big business, world wars, space travel and the Internet. They were the spiritual founders of western civilisation and democratic capitalism, or so we like to believe.

But the man in the Alpine glacier was no settled agriculturalist. His equipment seemed better suited to a person spending prolonged periods away from his home settlement. For one thing he carried a backpack, a basic frame made from a hazel rod and some short larch wood boards, the whole construction lashed together with cords made from grass stems which had been twisted together.

In a belt pouch or 'bumbag' of calf leather he carried three flint implements for working on hide, bone and wood – a smoothing and scraping implement, a pointed tool for punching holes and a fine blade for delicate work such as the fashioning of arrow shafts. The pouch also contained a piece of tinder and a bone awl with a needle point for sewing or body tattooing. Attached to the belt was a small flint-bladed dagger held in a scabbard of plaited bark and grass cord, together with a firelighter – a piece of ignitable tinder-fungus dusted here and there with minute grains of tell-tale pyrites.

Among his other equipment was an axe with a blade of pure copper, a bone-tipped 're-touching tool' for putting a fine edge on flint blades, a grass string net for fishing or trapping birds, and a pair of tubular, birch-bark containers, one of which had been insulated with maple leaves for carrying hot embers. Their owner was equipped with a full tool kit for travel and survival far from any supporting community. At the time he died he was working on a new longbow of yew and a set of fresh arrows for his quiver.

The ice man's clothes seemed equally suited to a life of movement and self-reliance. His upper garment of fur had been expertly stitched together with fine threads made from animal sinews. But a few seams had been hurriedly and inexpertly repaired using grass threads, presumably by the wearer during a long sojourn away from his native settlement. His leather-soled shoes, held on with straps, included uppers made of grass cord netting beneath which dried grass had been stuffed for warmth and insulation. As an over-garment he wore a long cloak made from plaited grasses, an item that would double as a water-repellent raincoat or ground-sheet.

Archaeologist Konrad Spindler, author of *The Man in the Ice*, suggests that this was a shepherd who spent long periods herding sheep and goats between summer grazings in the mountains. High grasslands above the treeline of the Otztal Alps are known to have been used for pasturing livestock since at least 4,000BC. Spindler's theory is that the ice man was part of the Neolithic settlement in the Val Venosta, to which he returned each autumn in time to help with the grain harvest.

In the Alps the Neolithic life style was clearly not one of settled agriculture, at least not for the whole community. For many it was a semi-nomadic existence spent moving livestock from pasture to pasture in a regular seasonal pattern, a form of transhumance still practised in many Alpine regions today.

In Britain, where grass will grow for much of the year, the notion of Neolithic people as farmers may be even more illusory. The British archaeological record contains little to indicate the Neolithic as the cradle of agriculture. For a start there are few signs of a 'domestic architecture': preserved remnants of permanent dwellings that might be expected to accompany a way of life centred on mixed farming. A few pits here and there, the postholes from a building, an assortment of household débris – these are the only indications of farmsteads.

So far no one has found remnants of large, wooden longhouses like those built by the first farmers on the loess plateaux of northern Europe, and in which people lived with their livestock for at least part of the year. Nor is there evidence of organised field systems, though the Ceide Fields of County Mayo show that they had been established in Ireland.

For those wedded to the idea of a Neolithic agriculture in Britain it is simply a matter of time before the evidence is found. 'They will turn up, perhaps not on the present land surface and probably not in the "classic" field areas, but buried beneath the erosion deposits in a lowland English valley; or just out of sight below the rim of a bog or marsh.'[2]

But it is equally possible that the reason why the farmsteads and field systems have failed to appear is that they do not exist. Perhaps in Britain the Neolithic did not mark the start of a settled agriculture. For some archaeologists the evidence of stone tools and their associated débris, together with the record of animal bones and carbonised plant remains found at known Neolithic sites points in an entirely different direction.

Far from being settled tillers of the soil, Britain's first farmers may have been semi-nomadic, a pastoral people, moving their herds of cattle and sheep across a landscape they had opened up to grassland. Their diets, like those of the hunter-gatherers they succeeded, were largely made up of the wild foods of the forest – hazelnuts, crab apples, blackberries, wild raspberries, sloes and hawthorn berries, supplemented with the meat of domesticated animals and possibly dairy products.

Cereals were grown – emmer wheat, *Triticum dococcum*, einkorn wheat, *Triticum monococcum*, along with naked and hulled barley, *Hordeum vulgare* var. *nudum* and *Hordeum vulgare* – but these may have had a largely symbolic value, making little contribution to the everyday diet.

These were no 'dirt farmers' caught up in a ceaseless round of tillage and sowing, weeding and harvesting. Certainly they had their 'garden' plots, small islands of cultivation amid the open pastures and towering forests. But they were not tied to them in the way that settled farmers are bound to the land. They might tend them for a season and then move on, perhaps returning to them in a year or two. Or they might plant them in the spring, then abandon them until harvest time, leaving the hardy sown species to battle it out with the weeds.

With their cattle, sheep and pigs they moved across the countryside in a complex pattern governed by the seasons and their understanding of terrain. They were a people bound to a landscape rather than to land, playing out their lives on a broad stage. This was the antithesis of agriculture, with its dedication to place and permanence. For the Neolithic herders there were no boundaries, no walls, no concept of possession and occupation to divide them. They were free to traverse a landscape partially cleared of forest and made safe by ancestral bones and a network of monuments in earth and stone – their cairns and barrows and causewayed enclosures.

It was a life style never to be repeated in recorded history. With the coming of settled agriculture in the Bronze Age the people of Britain became for ever reliant on the constant working and re-working of the same fields. But for a moment in time – a mere millennium or two – they were neither servants of the land nor its dependents, neither masters of nature nor its victims. Like Native Americans they lived in harmony with nature, at one with the cosmos. And, as on the American prairies, their way of life was sustained by grassland. This was no prelude to civilisation. It *was* a civilisation.

On a bright June morning the towering chalk massif of Hambledon Hill rises steeply above the Dorset countryside, its summit bearing the deep folds of a huge Iron Age hill fort. The sides of the hill are draped with chalk grassland, its fine flowerheads trembling in the light summer breeze – slender sheep's fescue and red fescue, *Festuca ovina*, *F. rubra*, crested hair-grass, *Koeleria cristata*, the beautiful quaking grass, *Briza media*. Among them glow the flowers of midsummer, bright horseshoe vetch, the bee orchid, fragrant squinancy-wort, the golden lady's bedstraw.

Away to the south the chalk downlands rise and fall like an ocean swell. No longer are they clothed with the grasslands that still find refuge on the Iron Age fortress of Hambledon. The flowing chalklands of southern Britain are now spread with the crops of industrial agriculture – wheat, barley, oilseed rape – sustained by agrochemicals, husbanded by giant machines.

Modern, high-output farming is seen as one of the triumphs of western civilisation, supporting great cities and a vast industrial edifice, freeing the mass of the population to work in manufacturing and service industries. Society is proud of its achievements, convinced of the superiority of settled agriculture with its ordered fields and strong belief in possession and ownership.

The idea that Britain's first farmers established settlements and laid out ordered field systems appeals to our sense of perma-nence, of the countryside always having been like it is today. It confirms the supremacy of the western social model, particularly when those early colonists can be seen to have dominated the earlier hunter-gathering tradition. We need to believe that the Neolithic farmers succeeded because their methods were superior, the methods we employ today. Unfortunately such notions blind us to an earlier triumph of British agriculture, the triumph of grass-farming and the particular form of freedom that went with it. It was a freedom we were never to find again.

The accepted view of the Neolithic is that a technically advanced society supplanted a primitive one. It appeals to our sense of progress and the belief that things generally get better. Certainly the initial spread of agriculture in Asia seems to have been at the expense of hunter-gathering traditions.

The earliest firm evidence for agriculture stems from the western 'fertile crescent', principally a 'core area' of the southern Levant and the middle Euphrates Valley in Iraq. Here the remains of domesticated cereals – barley, einkorn wheat and emmer wheat – and pulses and flax have been recovered from archaeological sites and radiocarbon-dated to between 10,000BC and 8,500BC.[3] By the end of this period these 'founder crops' of Neolithic farming had spread across an area from western Iran to Turkey, while domesticated goats and sheep had appeared at sites in the Taurus and Zagros Mountains.

As it spread across central Asia, Neolithic agriculture seems to have been adopted as a fully developed 'package' of agro-pastoral production. There is little evidence of its slow integration into an existing hunter-gatherer tradition. The new culture was often linked to an expansion of settlements and the introduction of pottery, as on the piedmont of southern Turkmenistan where rectilinear mudbrick architecture, pottery and domesticated sheep, goats and cereals all appeared together at around 6,000BC.

The first Neolithic communities to cross the Alps and Carpathians were the Bandkeramic groups who colonised a vast area of Europe.[4] They formed settlements and practised a system of intensive, small-plot horticulture and cattle-raising, seeking out sites on deep loess soils close to watercourses. But by the time the Neolithic arrived in Britain the cohesion of the

Bandkeramic culture had begun to break down. Even so many archaeologists have accepted the model of settled mixed farming as the most likely explanation of the British Neolithic. The new culture was assumed to have quickly obliterated the old.

Somehow the 'farming kit' – the material package which included seed corn, sheep, goats and, possibly, domesticated cattle – was brought across from mainland Europe and taken up in many parts of the country. No one knows whether this early form of technology transfer was the result of a mass immigration of pioneer farmers from the Continent or by a process of 'acculturation' by coastal communities in Britain who acquired the stock and techniques by making periodic trips across the Channel.

Log boats and rafts had long been used by hunter-gatherers of the Mesolithic. They were a common means of getting around areas of marshland and swampy water such as the low-lying Somerset Levels. The stretch of water that then separated Britain from mainland Europe was little more than a broad swamp, so there was likely to have been a constant traffic across it.

In the orthodox view the mixed farming habit had become well entrenched in Britain by around 4,000BC.[5] Archaeological studies in the Avebury area of Wiltshire suggest that some land had already been cleared for arable cultivation when the first long barrows were constructed from about 4,100BC. The ground beneath one of them, the South Street long barrow, was found to be heavily scored with the marks of a ripard, an early form of plough. This is taken to mean that the land had been under intensive cultivation before the barrow was built.

An alternative explanation is that the marks were produced by some ceremonial which preceded construction of the barrow – a ritual breaking of the turf on what was to be a sacred site. But the idea of a settled agriculture proved too strong.

Roger Mercer, who led a team excavating the Stepleton Spur enclosure, part of the Neolithic earthwork complex on Hambledon Hill, had few doubts:

By the time the earliest major funerary monuments were being built in southern and northern Britain, substantial areas of the lighter, more tractable soils, particularly on the chalk but probably also on our river gravels and on the unrivalled fertility of the loams and brickearths of south eastern England, had been broken in to arable cultivation. Bordering such clearances were, probably, areas of depleted forest where cattle and pigs were grazed. Clearances of this kind are witnessed in the fossil pollen record over a very wide area of Britain.[6]

The people of these islands had apparently bought into the whole package – they had become mixed farmers. In the course of a few centuries they had given up the nomadic life style of the hunter-gatherer, abandoned their 'benders' – their huts built of supple branches and animal skins – and settled down to till their cereal plots.

The inferred move to a settled agriculture was linked to a host of other cultural changes. The archaeological record began to reveal evidence of pottery, a clear sign to many that the travellers had now become home-lovers. A wooden trackway buried deep within the peat on the Somerset Levels, and dated precisely to the year 3,807BC – the early Neolithic period – was found to have a broken pot filled with hazelnuts nearby. Hunter-gatherers were supposed not to make pots. This was clearly a settled farming community.

The dating of the trackway, the Sweet Track, named after its discoverer, Raymond Sweet, an employee of the Eclipse Peat Works, was carried out by a process known as dendrochronology. The pattern of growth rings on the timbers used in the trackway's construction were compared with a standard reference set covering more than 7,000 years. The distinctive ring 'signature' of the timbers from the peat can be read like a bar code to give a precise measure of when the trees were felled.

The sheer volume of timber used in the 2km track, along with the techniques used in its construction, suggest a degree of woodland management which some have linked to the clearance of land for arable.[7] The sides of the track were strewn with flint flakes characteristic of the 'farmers' flint technology' which produced broad, long blades very different from the small and delicate flints used by the hunter-gatherers.[8] The British Neolithic was presumed to have been a time of settlement just as it had been in central Europe, when a growing population took up mixed farming, clearing land for grazing and, more importantly, for growing cereals.

Writing of Wessex Barry Cunliffe observes: 'Small plots of arable land produced wheat and a little barley, areas of pasture carved from the forest or created from disused arable provided pasture for sheep and at times for cattle, while the all-important forest, never far away, yielded ample browse for cattle, pigs and goats.'[9] Looked at from 215 generations later it is an idyllic picture, a Britain of farmsteads and small settlements, of animals and crops augmented by the wild fruits of the forest.

Even the record of pollen cores appears to support this view of small-scale, mixed farming. Sometime around 4,000BC the pollen produced by elm trees showed a dramatic fall, an event known as the 'elm decline'. One explanation is that early farmers stripped the branches from elm trees to provide winter fodder for their cattle. Or it may be that elms were more common on the light, free-draining soils that were the first to be cleared. It may even be the result of a prehistoric epidemic of elm disease. Whatever the cause, the tree's sudden decline is taken as further evidence of a farming revolution in the Neolithic.

Why a nation of nomadic foragers should, in a short space of time, cease travelling and settle down to a lifetime of tilling the soil has not been satisfactorily explained. The hunter-gatherer life style is easily dismissed as brutish, hazardous and beset with food insecurity. But in the landscape of the later Mesolithic, food was likely to have been plentiful. At around 4,000BC most of Britain was still covered by forest; birch and pine in the highlands of northern Scotland, and a mixture of oak and hazel in the uplands of England and Wales. Across lowland Britain the forest was largely of lime, hazel and oak, interspersed with pockets of ash, elm and beech.[10]

Through these dense woodlands, whose canopy was frequently 15m high, roamed red deer, wild boar and aurochs, the large wild cattle, browsing the forest leaves and grazing in the sunlit glades where trees had fallen. Hunting bands armed with throwing spears and bows and arrows were able to take them with little risk to themselves.

They had also begun modifying the environment to facilitate hunting and collecting, using fire to clear stretches of forest and create new glades in the forest canopy.[11] Grasses and herbs would quickly colonise these areas, along with an under-storey of shrubs. Deer, wild cattle and pigs drawn to the 'artificial' grazings would present an easy target for the hunters. There is some evidence that Mesolithic groups actively herded deer. They had used dogs – domesticated wolves – since the early Mesolithic period.

The newly created glades would also encourage food-bearing species such as bramble, blackthorn, hazel and hawthorn. Even weed species like fathen, knotgrass, chickweed and annual knawel contributed to the diet of the hunter-gatherer.

Forest clearance selected those trees and shrubs with rapid powers of regeneration, among them hazel whose nuts were a particularly important food item. Hazel coppices freely and its root stocks are rarely destroyed by fire. It is possible that the Mesolithic foragers used fire and the flint axe to create and maintain hazel groves that they could return to year after year.

Given such abundant food sources it is difficult to see why the nomadic life should have been so quickly abandoned in favour of a settled one. While the image of the little farmstead surrounded by its cultivated plots may look appealing from our twenty-first-century vantage point, the reality is very different. Even today the life of the subsistence farmer is one of unremitting toil. By contrast hunter-gatherers, even those in harsh environments, are rarely engaged in a ceaseless search for food. On the contrary, they frequently enjoy a great deal of leisure.

The traditional explanation for a cultural shift of such magnitude is material necessity. Rising populations or perhaps some climatic change may have induced the switch to settled agriculture, or so it is argued. The new way of life would have produced surpluses and supported greater numbers of people.

But if food was short why not clear more virgin forest? Why

not create more open glades to attract deer and establish more hazel groves? Why give up the life style of your ancestors when the alternative is the dreary, back-breaking grind of cultivating the soil? Why forsake the mobile for the sedentary, the open for the enclosed, the wild for the tame?

A better explanation might be that the Neolithic revolution led not to the establishment of agriculture, but to the establishment of a form of nomadic pastoralism. Rather than apply the entire mixed farming package from central Europe, the hunter-gatherers simply adopted those parts of it which suited their own mobile way of life. They cleared more forest and created new grazings just as their forest-dwelling forebears had learnt to do. But they stocked them with the new domesticated cattle.

Though they sowed land with wheat and barley in the more fertile areas, they were not tied down by their cultivated plots. Instead they would return to harvest them after a seasonal absence. They still retained the mobility of their ancestors, moving in and out of cultivation as easily as they herded their cattle from one grazing to the next. Their cropping of the land was sporadic and fitted round the demands of a nomadic livestock husbandry, hence the absence of evidence for farm-steads or hamlets in the archaeological record.

Alasdair Whittle has coined the term 'tethered mobility' for the Neolithic life style, one in which groups moved across the landscape in set patterns and returned to fixed points.[12] Groups may have fluctuated in composition, with members separating and coming together at appointed moments in the temporal round. It was a way of life a world apart from subsistence farming.

The Neolithic in Britain certainly produced the island's first farmers. But they were not the growers and cultivators of the standard textbooks. They were predominantly graziers, livestock raisers. Beneath the great Wessex monuments of Silbury, Durrington Walls and Marden there is evidence of maintained grassland,[13] a clear indication that by the later Neolithic areas of open landscape had been created on the chalk uplands. These early farmers had made the momentous discovery that the soils and climate of this land were supremely well suited to the growing of grass, a characteristic that was to shape the destiny of the island's people through the next 4,000 years of its history.

Just to the west of Cranborne Chase, Hambledon Hill guards the lush valley of the River Stour and the Blackmore Vale. Excavation of the Neolithic earthworks suggests that they comprised three enclosures protected by a series of ditches and banks designed to encompass the entire hilltop, an area of some fifty hectares, making it the largest enclosed Neolithic site in Europe.

Huge numbers of animal bones have been recovered, principally of cattle. Their general condition suggests that the occupants ate well but wastefully.[14] Whole, articulated joints of meat were found to have been partially consumed and then thrown away. The less attractive parts of the animal were simply discarded untouched.

The whole assemblage conjures up a picture of extravagant and wild feasting. Perhaps this was the indulgence of a privileged hierarchy? Alternatively it may have been an exuberant celebration by a whole people well supplied with food and at one with their environment.

A study of the sex and age ratios of the Hambledon Hill bones showed that most were from female cattle. The implication, according to Tony Legge's report on the site, is that the herd was managed principally for milk production rather than for meat.[15] It was a culling pattern not dissimilar to that of a modern dairy farm. Could it be that the people who roamed with their livestock across the first grasslands cleared from the wildwood were dairy farmers?

Early objectors to the theory argued that to digest milk the early Neolithic population would first need to develop a biological tolerance for lactose. However, yoghurt, cheese, butter and ghee are largely free of the milk sugar and so might have provided useful proteins even for those individuals who had not yet adapted to a diet containing lactose.[16]

The female cattle killed at Hambledon Hill represented the surplus from herds based at other, as yet undiscovered, Neolithic sites, perhaps on the low-lying, marshy grasslands of Blackmore

Vale, Thomas Hardy's 'Vale of Small Dairies'. Wetland areas like this were the most productive ecosystems, rich in aquatic life and wildfowl, an unrivalled source of protein. Here the travelling hunter-herders could fish using their grass nets, and shoot ducks and waders with their flint-headed arrows.

The lush marsh grasslands made ideal grazing areas, particularly in summer when the water table was low. Down here the herbage was more nutritious than on the thin, poor downland soils. And when the marsh grazings became too wet – or needed to be set aside for hay – the cattle and sheep could be herded back up to the hill pastures by their resourceful and self-reliant minders, like the Alpine shepherd in the ice.

From time to time the cattle herds were brought to the hilltop enclosure and other causewayed enclosures for slaughter, probably as part of a ceremonial or ritual which included communal feasting. Their remains – particularly the heads, hooves and hides – were treated with considerable care, sometimes being buried with human bones as part of funerary deposits.

The ditches of these enclosures were filled with the débris of feasting, the bones of cattle, sheep and pigs together with pieces of broken pottery. At Hambledon Hill the ditches of the main enclosure contained parts of human skeletons at all levels, including skulls which appeared to have been placed in the ditch bottoms soon after they had been dug.[17] Most of the remains were disarticulated: they were no longer complete skeletons but scattered single bones and parts of skeletons such as limbs and torsos.

Many of the bones bore the teeth marks of dogs, an indication that they had been left exposed for a time before burial. This suggests the practice known as excarnation – the exposure of bodies to the elements so that the fleshy parts can decay.[18] It is a practice associated with Neolithic tombs from Wessex to the Orkneys. Bodies were often exposed at one site before being bundled up and transported to a tomb elsewhere, a process which usually resulted in the loss of smaller bones.

Roger Mercer describes the main enclosure at Hambledon Hill, at least in its initial phase, as 'a gigantic necropolis'. The hilltop, he says, was little more than a vast, reeking cemetery, whose silence was broken only by the din of the crows.

It seems likely that people gathered at causewayed enclosures in large numbers to feast in memory of the dead. These were special sites, perhaps associated with hierarchies or religious leaders. Beef seems not to have been an everyday food item. The usual staples were the wild plants and fruits of the forest supplemented by a small amount of cultivated cereals, along with pig meat, mutton and probably dairy products.

Feasting on cattle flesh was an event that took place at particular times and seasons. It was restricted to sacred places such as causewayed enclosures, places dedicated to the ancestors. Such sites also acted as regional centres. They held a special significance for a mobile and often scattered people. Here the travellers could gather for celebration and ritual, for marriage and feasting, and for the exchange of prestige objects such as polished stone axes. It was a time for reinforcing the values and beliefs underpinning the semi-nomadic way of life.

For the Neolithic was not a prescription for mixed farming, nor a blueprint for the production of cereals or pigs or sheep. It seems more likely to have been a set of ideas and beliefs, a body of knowledge – some of it arcane, shamanistic and magical – which inspired new forms of relationship and behaviour. More than anything it was a social glue that held scattered groups together and produced a form of cultural homogeneity that became expressed in particular styles of pottery and monument.

Because it was rooted in ideas rather than bags of seed corn the farming revolution of the British Neolithic was unlikely to have duplicated the central European model with its settled smallholdings. The earlier people of the Mesolithic may already have adopted some of the new materials. Equally, some of their own skills and practices were retained into the new age. Techniques for clearing forest and opening up grasslands continued as the herds of domesticated cattle and sheep ranged across an increasingly open landscape.

The most obvious signs of Neolithic activity in modern Britain are the hundreds of earth and stone monuments which still brood over the countryside. First to be built were the causewayed enclosures like Hambledon Hill, with their strange interrupted ditches making them singularly ineffective at either keeping animals in or aggressors out. Contemporary with them are the earthen long barrows of the south and east, and the megalithic tombs and long cairns of western and northern Britain.

A little later in the Neolithic period came the linear enclosures known as cursus monuments, parallel ditches with internal banks 100 metres apart and extending up to ten kilometres. The greatest of them, the Dorset Cursus across Cranborne Chase, is estimated to have involved half a million man hours of labour. Finally, in the late Neolithic, came the henges, along with the stone and timber circles found from the Orkneys to the south coast.

Many explanations have been put forward for this vast human investment in the construction of monuments. Some suggest that they were built by dominant social groups whose position had somehow come under threat. Their works loom over the landscape as a warning to challengers. Others interpret monuments as a sign of confidence, a mark of conspicuous wealth, proof of the success of settled agriculture.

In his book *Rethinking the Neolithic* Julian Thomas speaks of 'the inscribed landscape' – the idea that monuments represent landscape features that can be interpreted or 'read' in a similar way to print on the page.[19] Our experience of the space around us provides us with an identity, a sense of who we are. We acquire it by moving through that space, either in a single, unique act or by some repetitive motion ordered by the seasons or the diurnal cycle of day and night.

Nomadic pastoralists moving their cattle across open grassland or from forest glade to forest glade see themselves in ways very different from those of farmers continuously cultivating their plots of land. Monuments modify people's interpretation of space and time, and hence the ideas they develop about their own identities. They are a means of social control, of inculcating the ideas of a dominant group. A society like that of the British Neolithic, engaged in structuring a landscape through the building of monuments, is helping to 'create' identities and shape group consciousness just as billboards do today.

But what was the social message the tomb builders and ditch diggers were trying to impart? Without doubt it had much to do with the dead and with ancestors. Neolithic burial rituals were complex and protracted, though there were usually two stages. First, the bodies were exposed for defleshing, usually on some sort of timber platform. Later a long mound was piled over them. The burial site had become another monument in the landscape.

Bodies were usually buried collectively, with the remains of many individuals being incorporated in the tomb or grave together,[20] an indication that there were no rigid hierarchies or paramount leaders in Neolithic society. In death the individual was of no consequence. The well-being of the group depended on the generalised body of ancestors, whose remains were ceremonially returned to the earth beneath a tumulus or the filled ditch of a causewayed enclosure.

For settled farmers with concepts of private property, kin groups are important. The rewards from a farm which has been handed down from generation to generation are due, in part, to the efforts of those who went before. But for a rootless people regularly moving around a landscape they neither own nor permanently occupy, the presence of ancestors at fixed points on the journey gives them a sense of belonging, a link with the land.

In this open, boundless world monuments become the 'way stations' on an endless seasonal round, reinforcing the collective beliefs of the group, limiting the infinity of the space they move in, linking them to a time stream by giving them a history. Monuments mark the boundaries – of the past and present, of life and death, of wild and tame, of the human and the infinite.

Were they simply an ostentatious display of wealth, the indulgence of a comfortable agricultural society which, like other early civilisations, had gathered a surplus? It seems more likely that they were a statement of faith by a pastoral people learning for the first time how to modify and control their own environment.

What were they like, those early farmers, the first exploiters of Britain's grasslands? Anatomical studies on bones from West Kennet suggest they were only marginally shorter than people today.[21] They were also of similar build. They suffered badly from disease: arthritis, particularly of the back, was almost universal in people over twenty-five, perhaps as a result of carrying heavy loads. Many children died in infancy, so the average death rate was as low as thirty, though some individuals may have lived to well past fifty.

They were probably a gregarious people with few notions of private space or the internal world of self, those trappings of assertive individualism that so colour modern, industrial societies. The development of oval barrows, cursus monuments and henges in the later Neolithic suggest a people increasingly preoccupied with space and with the great dualities of inclusion and exclusion, the open and the enclosed, the bounded and the boundless. For the most part they lived as integrated members of groups that would sometimes coalesce into larger gatherings, brought together at some preordained point in the seasonal round, perhaps in response to a particular astronomical alignment.

The wide range of Neolithic artefacts found beside the Sweet Track in Somerset includes an exquisite axe-head of polished green jadeite originating in the region of the Alps. These were not a parochial people. They maintained complex networks of trade routes extending not only across Britain, but deep into Continental Europe, continuing links with older societies from which they had sprung. Like most peoples of grassland theirs was an open, mobile society.

They may even have conducted a trade in people. For semi-nomadic groups of herders, crossing and re-crossing sparse upland grazings, there are limits to the numbers of children that can be supported and carried. Seasonal gatherings at sacred sites gave the Neolithic pastoralists an opportunity to pass on surplus infants to groups inhabiting more productive areas such as river valleys and lowland marshes. The seasonal gathering was also a chance to conceive a new child, perhaps for adoption at next year's festivities.

These were sophisticated people with advanced language skills and an intellectual capacity equal to our own. The concept of fertility was well understood; indeed it was central to their culture and social organisation. A carved ash figure found beneath a Neolithic trackway at Westhay on the Somerset Levels represents a hermaphrodite (having both male and female attributes). Perhaps it was fashioned as a child's doll or a fertility symbol. Or it may have been whittled as an idle pastime by some bored shepherd or cattle herder with time to spare.[22]

This was not a society worn down with toil and the constant struggle to make a living. All that was to come with settled agriculture. These were people who adorned their bodies with jewellery, made toys for their children and enjoyed feasting and celebration. There is even evidence of a drug culture. Henbane, *Hyoscyamus niger*, a plant producing hallucinogenic effects when taken in small amounts, has been associated with Grooved Ware pottery, a style used in the Neolithic and found particularly at ritual sites.[23] Some archaeologists have also suggested that barley was grown principally for the purpose of brewing beer.[24]

It was a way of life linked intimately with the land. Like Native Americans the people of the Neolithic would have had a profound knowledge of the wild plants and animals around them, and of their uses as food items, craft materials and medicines. Like the man in the glacial ice they would have known which grasses to weave into their weather-proof cloaks, to twist into cord for fishing nets, or to stuff into their shoes for insulation. Like him they would have employed a range of natural medicines such as the birch fungus antiseptic he carried on his wrist.

Livestock were central to this way of life. Starting with the powerful and aggressive wild ox or auroch, *Bos primigenius*, which stood up to two metres high at the shoulder, these first farmers bred a smaller, more manageable domestic beast for herding across their open grazings. Selective breeding may have meant no more than the killing and eating of the larger, meatier animals first, leaving the smaller animals to mate. But it was effective enough to reduce dramatically the size of cattle.

Of all Neolithic livestock, cattle were the most valued,

perhaps as a repository of wealth or alternatively as a mark of prestige. They were also prized as sources of fertility, their dung lifting the productivity of cultivated plots. It is likely that Neolithic people understood the link between livestock and the bounty of the earth. They had discovered the key to civilisation and the industrial society five thousand years before it was manifest.

The ritual placement of cattle bones in burial sites used for human remains suggests a spiritual relationship. People whose well-being is bound up with livestock have been known to attribute souls to their animals. So it may have been with the wandering tribes of the British Neolithic as they herded their cattle like fellow travellers, crossing and re-crossing the landscape.

Slowly through the third and early second millennia BC this mobile life style came to an end. The first widespread evidence of continuous field systems and settled cultivation appeared on mainland Britain in the Bronze Age, with the Dartmoor reaves and the 'Celtic fields' of Wessex. Linear dykes stretching over several kilometres formed the templates for land division within which field systems were constructed.

The reasons for the change can only be guessed at. It may have been the pressure of population growth. For all its toil and drudgery, settled cultivation produces more food from a given area than pastoralism, and so will support a greater number of people. With too many cattle ranging over the upland grazings their productivity would have fallen as soils became impoverished.

Alternatively the decline of pastoralism may have come about through the rise of powerful hierarchies and emerging concepts of property and land ownership. Whatever the causes, settled farming now became the dominant culture, setting Britain on its momentous path to ownership and exclusion, enclosure and dispossession, industrialisation and urban living, to factory farming and genetically modified foods. With the ending of the Neolithic the nation was bound for civilisation.

But for a brief time in our pre-history – for perhaps a couple of millennia – the land of Britain was occupied by a people who, like the nomadic Native American tribes of the Great Plains, had no concept of private ownership. They moved freely about a landscape they themselves had constructed and embellished with their monuments, a landscape they occupied by right of living in that place, a landscape made legitimate by the bones of their ancestors.

It would be unwise to idealise their way of life as some form of early socialist utopia. Life was generally brutal, uncomfortable and dangerous. But it is equally foolish to saddle these people with our own cultural ideas. It seems unlikely that they were the inventors of field system and farmstead, of hearth and home. They were not the originators of a model rural settlement that was to last for 6,000 years.

The Neolithic way of life seems unfamiliar to us with our ideas of place and permanence. Yet it combined social obligation with freedom in ways rarely seen in modern industrial societies. Its heritage remains in the monuments that still litter our landscape, a reminder of an alternative life style.

There is another heritage of that far distant time. Those remote people bequeathed to us their genes; their blood still courses through the veins of modern Europeans. We also share a social inheritance, a predilection for particular styles of living – a desire to unpick the ties that bind us to one place, the urge to travel, a delight in space and mobility, a liking for the companionship of animals and, above all, an irrepressible lust for freedom.

The Neolithic left us with an indelible impression of what it means to be free. This was not to be the last time in the story of Britain that the concept of freedom would be linked to a culture founded on grassland.

3   Travellers on the Wind

G rasses – the Poaceae – evolved almost seventy million years before the appearance of human beings. Yet the fortunes of the two families are inextricably linked. Grasses are the great colonisers of the plant kingdom, the early occupiers of disturbed soils, homesteaders looking for places to settle and form communities. They are natural opportunists, exploiting change.

Human beings are the creators of change. They bulldoze the forests and level the ground with their machines. They plough and till and turn the soil. They score and scrape, dig and excavate, shaping and reshaping the landscape in a restless search for immortality. But in their endless pursuit they make kings of the little plants that drape the bare earth in green.

Botanist William Chaloner uses the fairy tale form to describe the opportunities open to the Poaceae in the late Tertiary period.[1] Already the great, natural grasslands of savannah and prairie were supporting vast populations of mammals. But to further their advance the grasses needed a benefactor, a fairy godmother, to clear the forests and prepare the ground for new growth, to curb competitive plants and shrubs, and to transport their seed around the world.

Enter *Homo sapiens*, exactly on cue. The glory days were here. At once the aggressive hominids set about clearing the forests and creating vast, open tracts of pastureland for grazing their cattle and sheep. Some grasses they chose as their staple foods, changing them by selective breeding and planting them in the most fertile soils. Wheat, rice, maize, sorghum, millet, sugar cane were to be their great food crops: all are grasses. The leafier species they carried into their cities to green the open spaces and provide a living surface on which to play and exercise and trade.

The Poaceae with 10,000 species and the Hominidae with just one member species had become families of mutual dependence.[2] In the language of history human beings are said to have domesticated the grasses. But in the language of ecology the grasses might as easily be said to have domesticated the hairless apes.

Grasses were well adapted to exploit the environmental turmoil set in train by *Homo sapiens*. From out of the angiosperms – the flowering plants – evolution had produced a group that was versatile and highly mobile. They had abandoned the practice of laying down woody tissue each year as a means of securing permanence. Instead they opted to move quickly into the reproductive phase in their life-cycle, so speeding the rate at which they could colonise new ground. They had chanced their survival not on strength and durability, but on speed of occupation. It was an adaptation that would make them the most successful plant group on the planet.

In its early growth stages the grass plant consists of a collection of shoots or 'tillers', each made up of leaves growing from the base. No stem is visible. The true stem, at this stage highly compressed, lies hidden beneath the layers of tightly rolled or folded leaves. Active growing points – at the stem tip and at the bases of the leaves – are close to the ground surface and well protected from stomping hoofs, grinding molars and the whirling blades of rotary mowers.

The leaves themselves may be crushed, sawn off or burned

brown in a blazing prairie sun. But from countless little engines of growth buried deep beneath the tattered remnants of foliage, the first shoots of the new turf are already being formed. With the passing of the grazing herd and the coming of the rain the grassland community is able to renew itself and continue with the job of reproduction and taking over the world.

With their protected growing points, grasses are able to thrive under extreme conditions almost anywhere plant growth is remotely possible. Only two flowering plants have been found to penetrate the Antarctic circle. One of them is a grass, the hair-grass *Deschampsia antarctica*.[3]

The Victorian botanist and director of Kew Gardens Sir Joseph Hooker was amazed to discover sheep's fescue, *Festuca ovina*, that stalwart of low-lying English meadows, growing at a height of almost 5,500 metres in the Himalayas.[4] He was equally incredulous when, during frosty weather in Yoksun, Sikkim, he found semi-tropical grasses including millet *Panicum miliaceum*, and a large bamboo surviving at a height of nearly 1,700 metres.

Species of grama grass of the genus *Bouteloua*, which migrated from Central America to the North American plains, are known to flourish at heights of 300 metres on the prairies and more than 2,000 metres in Arizona, enduring extremes of temperature ranging from 38 degrees to minus 40 degrees centigrade.[5] Bermuda grass *Cynodon dactylon*, a species originating in tropical Africa, has now spread around the world, chiefly because of its tolerance of extremes of climate and soil acidity. In America it proved 'explosively aggressive', ousting many local species.[6] It also travelled as far north as Britain, establishing itself at Marazion Bay in Cornwall and Studland Bay in Dorset.[7]

The record for survival under harsh conditions must go to Lalong grass, *Imperata cylindrica*, which has been found growing in a volcanic fumarole in Java.[8] There it thrives in the swirling, steam-laden, sulphurous clouds, an innocent at the entrance to Hades.

The other great competitive advantage of the Poaceae arises from the sheer diversity of their sexual habits. Although the grass stem, or culm, is initially enfolded within its layers of leaves, at some point early in the plant's life-cycle it is ready to flower. It then begins to elongate so rapidly that the central tissue is torn apart and it becomes hollow. Rising above the mass of foliage, it prepares to form the flowerhead that will cast millions of tiny pollen grains on to the wind.

The flowers of the grass plant are fairly nondescript structures. They are born on structures called spikelets, each of which is protected by two leathery scales. There are no brightly coloured petals, no sweet scents to waft on the cool evening air. These are wind-pollinated plants; they have no need of cheap tricks to lure insects. But there is little in nature more beautiful than the delicate flowerhead of quaking grass, *Briza media*, trembling on a summer breeze. Nor have structural engineers come up with anything which, weight for weight, is stronger and more flexible than the slender cylinder of cellulose and lignin that holds it aloft.

Like other flowering plants, the grasses carry all the necessary tackle for run-of-the-mill sexual reproduction. Typically their flowers contain three pollen-producing stamen, two styles ending in light, feathery stigmas, and an ovary containing a single ovule. Though the flowers of most grasses are hermaphrodite the Poaceae possess a highly advanced 'incompatibility mechanism' to prevent self-fertilisation. The female receptor organ, the stigma, is able to recognise and reject pollen grains produced on the same flower.

Such a sophisticated system for screening out the wrong partner would seem to indicate a plant family strongly committed to sex. In the flowering plants mating takes place when a male gamete containing half the usual chromosome number fuses with the egg cell, itself containing half the normal chromosome complement. The resulting cell is diploid – it possesses a double set of chromosomes. The embryo so formed is endowed with character traits from both parents, conferred when the genes are re-assorted.

Grasses take a number of other measures to safeguard this conventional sexual union and reduce the chance of self-pollination. Some species separate male and female sexual organs between different parts of the same plant. Maize, the most extreme example, carries male, pollen-producing tassels at the tip of the stem while developing female flowers – later to become corn-on-the-cob – in the angles between leaf and stem. Some species, such as buffalo grass, *Buchloe dactyloides*, locate the two sets of sexual organs on different plants, making the all-female lawn at least a theoretical possibility, though sexing the seeds might prove something of a headache.

But to view the grasses as steadfastly heterosexual would be wrong. In matters of reproduction this family is distinctly pragmatic. Between them the species making up the Poaceae possess an extraordinary array of reproductive strategies, some of which appear freely interchangeable, others downright contradictory. Despite possessing a system designed to prevent self-fertilisation, many species have flowers which remain closed throughout the season, making cross-pollination impossible and self-fertilisation inevitable.[9] Annual grasses, in particular, make frequent recourse to 'selfing'. It allows them quickly to colonise a new habitat without waiting for a sexual partner to arrive on the scene.

In wheat plants the florets never open. Inbreeding is the norm, though this seems to have led to no noticeably deleterious effects. The prairie grass, *Bromus unioloides*, is more promiscuous, opening its florets whenever the days are short and the soil moisture level high. Under these conditions cross-pollination is apparently a risk worth taking. But in the long summer days, and under arid conditions, it keeps its florets firmly closed, making reproduction a distinctly family affair.

Many grasses have adopted the curious habit of apomixis, which also precludes cross-pollination and genetic reshuffling. Though the plant forms seeds, their embryos are not the result of fusion between male and female gametes. In some species a megaspore mother cell fails to produce the haploid female gamete, with a single set of unpaired chromosomes: the normal precursor to sexual reproduction. Instead the embryo develops directly from the diploid mother cell. In other species the embryo develops from a cell originating in the nucellus, the tissue surrounding the megaspore.

In neither process is there a reduction of the normal diploid cell to produce a gamete. Nor is there a fusion of nuclei from two separate parents. Apomixis is a form of vegetative reproduction giving rise not to a genetically new plant, but to the clone of a single parent. The process results in an apparently normal seed – the little package of embryo and nutrient-rich endosperm that is the product of sexual crossing throughout the plant kingdom. However, the seed is a fraud. Instead of a unique individual it will grow a rejuvenated copy of the old.

In an even stranger manifestation of the process, sexual fusion is mimicked simply as a way of triggering the development of an embryo. Again no genetic re-assortment takes place. One of two male gametes developed by the pollen tube approaches the egg but fails to fertilise it. Instead it fuses with one of the associated polar nuclei to form the cell that will later develop into the endosperm. Once more the embryo itself develops from the diploid mother cell.

Apomixy may seem an odd habit for a group of plants seemingly committed to sexual reproduction. Each summer the grasses throw up their flowerheads and fill the air with pollen grains. Thousands suffer the misery of hay fever because of this restless drive for sexuality, change and renewal. At the same time many species have distorted the sexual process to turn it into little more than a form of cloning. The risks and opportunities of cross-pollination are abandoned in the interests of rapid colonisation.

Quite apart from apomixis, the grasses possess a battery of methods for reproducing themselves without genetic change. In many species new tillers growing in the leaf axils – the angle between leaf and stem – burst through the enveloping leaf base to form side shoots. Growing out horizontally above the ground as stolons or below ground as rhizomes, they put out new roots and shoots at regular intervals. These little outgrowths will be the new plants, identical to their parents, yet colonising new ground as the 'umbilical' is severed and they become separate individuals.

A few grasses have developed the extraordinary habit of growing miniature clones of themselves on the spikelet – part of the flowerhead, and normally the bearer of the sexual organs. In a variant of sheep's fescue known as viviparous fescue, *Festuca vivipara*, sex is abandoned altogether and the flowers are replaced by tiny green plantlets, genetic copies of the parent. After a while these drop to the ground, put down roots and grow as independent plants.

Together the grasses are able to marshal a battery of reproductive methods to suit changing conditions. It is their sheer versatility at duplicating themselves that has made them the great colonisers of the plant kingdom. They thrive because they are not stuck in any one reproductive rut. Sometimes they mate, sometimes they clone themselves. Theirs is a pick-and-mix life style, but it is one that has given them global success.

Grasses are equally versatile in the ways they prepare the next generation for independent life. Casting seeds into a potentially hostile environment is always going to expose them to risk, but the parent plants make sure they will not start to grow until conditions are favourable. Seeds are rarely primed for germination from the moment they are shed. Most enter a dormancy period that will be broken only by some particular environmental event such as a sequence of high or low temperatures.

Even then germination does not take place until a further set of environmental 'triggers' have kick-started the process. The grass seed is genetically programmed to remain inactive in the same way that a computer program is protected by a password. The environmental 'password' is specific to the individual grass species, perhaps even to a local strain or *ecotype*.

In temperate regions like Britain, winter annual grasses will only germinate at low temperatures. But this cannot happen until their dormancy has been broken by a spell of high summer temperatures. Should the summer prove unseasonably cold, the seeds will still not germinate. They have been programmed to begin their life-cycles in the autumn.

By contrast, perennials and summer annual grasses need a period of cold weather to break their dormancy. Their seeds will not germinate in the autumn because temperatures are too low. But once they have been through their essential cold-weather conditioning they will germinate at these same low temperatures. They are genetically programmed to start growing in spring.

The parental controls persist even after the ending of dormancy. Species such as couch, *Agropyron repens*, tufted hair-grass, *Deschampsia caespitosa*, and smooth-stalked meadowgrass, *Poa pratensis*, need darkness and an alternating temperature in order to germinate. Since the daily temperature variation in the soil is lower at greater depths, these seeds have an in-built means of depth-detection.[10] Some seeds, like those of great millet, *Sorghum halepense*, become less sensitive to temperature fluctuations as they get older. Even though they may have been buried too deeply to have much hope of survival, they will eventually germinate. Nature has given them a sporting chance.

To most sports ground managers the ubiquitous annual meadowgrass is public enemy number one. This little interloper finds a way of invading even the best-managed turf. It is the supreme colonist of disturbed ground. When an area of turf becomes badly worn, *Poa annua* is usually the first grass to move in and occupy the space. It does it by sensing a change in the daily amplitude between day and night temperatures.

Bare soil shows a wider spread of maximum and minimum temperatures than soil under vegetation. This is the trigger for seeds of annual meadowgrass to germinate. Within two months new plants are shedding a fresh generation of seed on to the bare patch. More ground has been won for the empire of *Poa*.

Grass species vary in the environmental conditions they need for germination. The seeds of some marsh species must be flooded with water before they can be induced to grow, while metal-tolerant species germinate best when they are bathed in mild solutions of mercury, lead, cadmium and other noxious poisons. In arid regions the seeds of drought-tolerant species may require six days of continuous rainfall to stimulate germination.[11]

Grasses are wanderers – plants of movement, exploiters of new lands; plants of invasion, conquest and occupation. Their stock of reproductive strategies fits them for this life style of mobility and change. So does the genetic lock on germination, the gateway to life in a different, possibly a hostile, place. But first the plant has to get there.

Grass seeds are rarely cast off naked by the parent plant.

Usually they are enclosed in some modified part of the flowering structure, the spikelet. Its form provides many species with a mode of transport, a means of carrying their genes to a new world of opportunity. A number of grasses produce 'plumed' seeds whose flight through the air is improved by tufts of fine, silky hairs.

When American entomologists used aircraft to investigate insect flight paths, they were amazed to capture seeds of vaseygrass, *Paspalum urvillei*, at a height of 1,200 metres.[12] Introduced into Louisiana from South America early in the nineteenth century, this species is now commonly found from Virginia to southern California. The reedgrass *Calamagrostis epigeios*, whose plumed seeds are ideally equipped for flight, is one of the most widely distributed grass species, being native to Europe, Africa and India.[13]

The seeds of a grass known as water-pink, *Spinifex squarrosus*, which grows on sandy shores in India, Burma and China, are spread by the detached flowerhead as it blows along the ground. Once the seeds have ripened, the flowerhead forms a light, spiky ball that rolls across the land, sometimes bounding into the air, and all the time shedding seeds. With a fair wind behind it this natural seed distributor moves so fast that 'a pursuing fox terrier has difficulty keeping up'.[14]

Many grasses use animals to disperse their seeds. The leathery glumes which enclose the flower may be modified to form a hook that will catch in the fur of mammals and the feathers of birds, so stealing a ride across the land. The small-burr-grass, *Tragus racemosus*, succeeded in colonising much of Australia by back-packing on the country's sizeable population of sheep.[15] A species known in Malaysia as 'cloth-spoiling grass', *Centotheca lappacea*, found in India, China, Australia and Africa, owes its widespread distribution to the stiff, reflexed spines on its seeds, enabling them to cling tenaciously to furs and textiles.[16]

An early nineteenth-century resident of Ascension Island described the landscape changes that followed the arrival of a new grass, *Enneapogon mollis*, probably introduced as seed clinging to the plumage of birds.[17]

It first appeared to windward of the plain which the wide-a-wakes (sooty terns) frequent during their periodical visits, and has spread from there by the prevailing south-east trade wind to the Garrison three or four miles on. It has quite altered the appearance of Garrison and the intervening country . . . It is climbing up the craters and turning them from red to green hills.[18]

Some grasses are not averse to the guts of animals. Scientists in central Spain successfully germinated the seeds of fifteen grass species from the dung of rabbits, deer and cattle.[19] The greatest number of dung-germinated seeds were of the traveller and colonist annual meadowgrass.

This grass travels . . . in a variety of ways. Its spikelets may be blown about, the grains remaining enclosed in the glumes which act as wings. They are also carried by rain-wash along paths and roadsides and even streets. The way in which this species may spring up between flags or cobblestones justifies its name of causeway-grass. *Poa annua* is one of a number of grasses found in birds' nests in willows near Cambridge. In the Himalayas, Hooker found it on a path leading from Walloong to Wallanchoon at 3,700 metres. He concluded that man or the yak must have imported this little wanderer from the north.[20]

Human beings have been the unwitting couriers of seed. When the early American colonists imported livestock from 'the old country', the ships that had carried them were cleared of hay and manure before the return voyage. It was not long before native British grasses began to grow along America's eastern seaboard.[21] More sinister was the appearance of African grasses such as Guinea-grass, Bermuda-grass and molasses-grass which had been used as bedding for slaves.

The American grass red-top, *Agrostis alba*, was introduced into New Zealand by Nova Scotian immigrants, who filled their mattresses with hay before setting out on their journey. When they discarded the mattresses in New Zealand, the seeds germinated, and the American grass quickly became wide-spread.[22] The Jamaican grass known locally as 'pianograss', *Themeda arguens*, is thought to have been introduced by a British civil servant in the days of the Empire. When he was relocated from south-east Asia, he lined the packing case of his piano with the grass, which subsequently became naturalised in the West Indies.[23]

Grasslands encircle the earth, making up a quarter of the world's vegetation cover. They clothe the plains of North America, the vast steppes of Asia, the dry velds of Africa, and the pampas and savannahs of South America. They fringe the polar regions and drape the high plateaux of great mountain ranges. Their roots plumb deep marshes and bind the shifting sands of seashore and desert dune. And now they share in the adventure of the city, greening suburbs and the urban heartland.

Grasses are the bedrock of human civilisation. As Evan Eisenberg wrote in *Back to Eden*: 'The basis of human proliferation is not our own seed but the seed of grasses.' And just as grasses have been central to human progress, so humans have aided the advance of the Poaceae, clearing forests, turning the soil, causing the very disturbance that allowed these tenacious plants to gain new footholds and grow in strength.

Yet the grasses flourished on this planet a full 70 million years before the appearance of *Homo sapiens*. Though the fossil record is far from clear, palaeobotanists take the view that grasses emerged in the Cretaceous period (135 million to 70 million years ago) when flowering plants were becoming the dominant vegetative form, displacing the gymnosperms, the group which includes the ferns and conifers.

In the mild, sub-tropical climate of the Jurassic (180 million to 135 million years ago) the rainfall supported dense forests of tree ferns, maidenhair trees and towering pines and firs. Then during the Cretaceous the flowering plants or angiosperms – meaning enclosed seeds – rapidly gained supremacy, transforming the landscape and spreading across the land surface of the planet.

Palaeontologist Robert Bakker attributes this dramatic change to the appearance of new forms of herbivorous dinosaur. The early Cretaceous saw the emergence of wide-mouthed, ground-feeding animals such as the brontosaur and the stegosaur, which replaced the taller browsers of the Jurassic.

Close grazing benefited those low-growing plants that had acquired the knack of fast reproduction, namely the flowering plants. And the biggest winners were the grasses. With their flexible life styles and talent for rapid multiplication they were well placed to gain maximum advantage from the feeding habits of the new animals. Admittedly the fossil record supporting this theory is scanty. The evidence is largely circumstantial and relates to the present distribution of the Poaceae.

Since the five great subfamilies are found in all the continental landmasses except Antarctica, the likelihood is that they evolved before the fragmentation of the original landmass. According to the continental drift theory of German meteorologist Alfred Wegener, the world's continents were joined at the start of the dinosaur age, about 230 million years ago. By the end of the Cretaceous the super-continent of Pangaea had begun to break up. A plant group evolving after this time could not have achieved the world-wide distribution of the grasses, or so the argument goes.[24]

But while the grass subfamilies are represented on all major landmasses, individual genera are more restricted. It seems that evolution within subfamilies took place after the continents had separated. The Cretaceous remains the most likely period for the appearance of grasses even though the first pollen finds are linked to the ensuing epoch, the Palaeocene, beginning sixty-five million years ago.[25]

Early evidence of a grass spikelet – the flowering branch – turned up in an Eocene deposit in western Tennessee. From the same period came fossil evidence of seed dispersal by animals, the process known as epizoochory. A mammalian hair preserved in amber had the seed of a bamboo still attached.[26] It seems that by the end of the Eocene period thirty-eight million years ago the grasses had already become a diverse family.

In north-western Kansas a Miocene site, bizarrely named 'Minium's Dead Cow Quarry', has proved to be a rich repository of fossil grasses. So well preserved were the fragments of leaf that cell structures could be discerned from the intact vessels revealed in cross sections. To palaeobotanist Joseph Thomasson it was like finding 'a fossilised rabbit that still had its eyelashes'.[27]

But the most remarkable feature of the site was the close association of animal and plant remnants. The findings paint a vivid picture of the American plains seven million years ago – a land of fertile, sub-tropical grasslands teeming with large mammals such as rhino, elk and the early ancestors of the horse. The site also sheds light on another milestone of grass evolution – the emergence of an alternative chemical pathway for photosynthesis.

Modern grasses make use of two distinct biochemical processes for the reduction of carbon dioxide – the so-called C_3 and C_4 pathways. In photosynthesis light-energy absorbed by chlorophyll molecules powers the production of carbohydrate, releasing oxygen and water. The basic carbon reduction cycle is common to all grasses.

But some species known as C_4 grasses have an additional mechanism for taking up carbon dioxide molecules and transforming them temporarily into organic acids with four carbon atoms. These are carried to specialised cells where they are broken down to deliver extra carbon dioxide into the normal carbon reduction cycle. The plant has found a way of boosting the 'feedstock' supplied to the photosynthetic process.

C_4 grasses are more efficient and faster-growing than the primitive C_3 grasses. They are often better adapted to extremes of heat and sunlight and so are more commonly found in the tropics. Sugar cane, a C_4 grass, will fix carbon at up to twice the rate of the best wheat variety, though wheat is likely to perform better at cooler latitudes.[28] Many an American home-owner has watched in despair as his fine lawn of Kentucky bluegrass has been colonised and spoiled by the aggressive C_4 species crabgrass.

The leaf structures of C_4 and C_3 grasses are very different. The vessels of a C_4 leaf are surrounded by a characteristic wreath-like pattern of cells which enable them to separate energy-producing and energy-consuming chemical processes. Unlike the leaves of C_3 grasses they are able to store carbon dioxide. As a result they can close their pores during periods of extreme heat to save water.

Until the excavation of Minium's Quarry scientists had little idea when the C4 pathway evolved in grasses. But Joseph Thomasson's work at the site convinced him that by seven million years ago the separation of the two photosynthetic types had already taken place. In fact, the split could have taken place very much earlier, perhaps in response to a more arid climate than that of the Miocene.

The Kansas evidence supports the view that the American plains were heavily stocked with big game. The open sub-tropical grasslands carried huge herds of zebra, rhino, antelope and horses, all of which left their record in the sediment along with the fossil remains of the grasses on which they fed.[29]

The endless plains of prairie and steppe; the dry, dusty savannah – these have been the realm of grasses for as long as grasses have existed. It is the testing landscape evolution has fitted them for: exposed, burned by a relentless tropical sun or chilled by a penetrating polar wind. It is a harsh, unforgiving domain, but one which the Poaceae have colonised and made their own.

The common ancestor of the grasses was almost certainly a flowering plant of the lily family, the Liliaceae, adapted for life at the forest edge. The primitive flower structure of many tropical grasses suggests that the family originated deep in the forest. Yet unlike forest flowers which are insect-pollinated, the Poaceae are clearly adapted to wind pollination, a strategy that would have been doomed to fail in the sheltered forest heart. The forerunner of the grasses had been prepared for life in the open.

The move was not a total success. One early subfamily of the Poaceae, the bamboos, quickly retreated back into the forest. The bamboos returned to the elaborate flower structure typical of forest plants, combining this with the woody habit adopted by perennial shrubs and trees. In evolutionary terms it was not a particularly smart move. Seldom have the bamboos succeeded in a forest environment.

Across the world it is the woody dicotyledons that are the lords of the forest – the broadleaved oak, ash and beech of the temperate zone, the teak and mahogany of the tropics, the mighty conifers of fir, cedar and redwood. The bamboo forest is a rarity; in the hierarchy of vegetation types little more than a curiosity.

While the bamboos were retreating back into the forest another group of early grasses was venturing into the open. Botanists consider the subfamily Arundinoideae to be relatively primitive. Its members have unspecialised flowerheads and largely represent the earlier C3 form of photosynthesis.[30] They are thought to have dominated the tropical grasses for a while, but at a later stage in grass evolution they were ousted by the more efficient C4 species that now hold sway in the tropics.

The Arundinoideae include a number of well-known grasses, among them ornamental pampas grass, *Cortaderia seleana*, and common reed, *Phragmites australis*, used for thatching and for making screens.[31] Lesser known members are a group of Australian 'resurrection grasses', which have the ability to green up rapidly after rainfall. They belong to the genus known as *Micraria*, which is almost unique in arranging its leaves in a spiral around the stem. These grasses have adopted a moss-like growth habit, clinging tenaciously to rocky outcrops where there is virtually no soil and where they are subject to alternate periods of drought and flood.

Some members of the subfamily spread to cooler temperate regions of the northern hemisphere where a few survive to this day. But evolution produced a more advanced subfamily better equipped to thrive in a cold climate, the Poodeae. This group has been spectacularly successful in colonising temperate areas. They have also made a huge contribution to the well-being of mankind, counting among their number the crop species of wheat, barley and oats as well as a range of grazing, sports and amenity grasses.

The two other great subfamilies – the Chloridoideae and the Panicoideae – dominate the dry, open landscapes of the tropics and sub-tropics. Relying chiefly on C4 photosynthesis, the Chloridoideae have made a speciality of drought-tolerance, establishing themselves in arid tropical areas and thriving under the most extreme conditions. Like the Arundinoideae they include among their number a clutch of 'resurrection grasses'.

Rangeland grasses in the group include the North American buffalo grass and the African Rhodes grass, *Chloris gayana*, a common resident of the central uplands. Two cereal varieties – the Ethiopian t'ef, *Eragrostis tef*, and the African finger millet, *Eleusine coracana* – also belong to this subfamily.

The subfamily Panicoideae are less at home in extreme tropical regions, choosing instead to inhabit those parts of the tropics that are neither too dry nor too wet, neither too hot nor too cold. The group includes such important food crops as sugar cane, *Saccharum officinarum*, Japanese millet, *Echinochloa crus-galli*, sorghum, *Sorghum vulgare* and maize, *Zea*.

The adaptation to life in the open has been hugely successful for the grasses. In the world of vegetation they are the pioneer corps, the occupying troops of disrupted habitats. They are the Roman legions of the plant kingdom pushing out the limits of empire from their homeland at the forest edge. But they have enlisted some powerful help along the way.

In the early 1930s American palaeontologists reconstructed the skeleton of a small, arch-backed animal that had been dug up in the Big Horn Basin in Wyoming.[32] Standing about 35cms tall, the creature was equipped with four toes on the forefeet and three on the hindfeet, all of them ending in hoofs. Behind the toes was a broad pad like that of a dog's paw to spread the animal's weight and allow it to move more easily on soft soil like that of a tropical forest floor.

Dating back to the Eocene epoch about sixty million years ago, the skeleton belonged to *Eohippus*, the Dawn Horse, now viewed as the forerunner of the modern horse as well as related species like the zebra and the ass. The development of the *Equidae*, the horses, is a remarkable example of co-evolution. Before the arrival of human beings to speed the advance of the grasses, these two families, the *Equidae* and the Poaceae, were mutually dependent.

Grasses need the grazing animal. Though they are robbed of a great deal of foliage, they are freed from the competition of shrubs and trees. Close-grazing eliminates the first shoots of woody perennials which, if allowed to establish, might come to dominate the open landscape, particularly in areas of high rainfall. In return for their service the grazers are assured of a plentiful supply of fresh, green vegetation, constantly replenished from growing points beyond the reach of grinding molars.

Unlike the teeth of the modern horse, those of *Eohippus* were short-crowned, more like the dentition of pigs and monkeys. They were well suited to browsing on the soft, succulent leaves of forest shrubs. Dappled markings provided the Dawn Horse with the ideal camouflage for its forest setting. But they were not going to be of use to its descendants.

By the middle Oligocene, about thirty million years ago, the *Equidae* had produced a new variant, the larger *Mesohippus*. Standing about 45cms high, this animal had longer legs than its early ancestor, and the number of toes on its forefeet had been reduced to three. The array of teeth included early pre-molars or incisors, capable of chopping and grinding actions, and adapted to a wider range of vegetation. *Mesohippus* appeared at a time when the climate was becoming more arid. Areas of forest and jungle were giving way to grassy savannahs characterised by tall, clump-forming grasses, shrubs and scattered trees.

In the Miocene, the epoch of the first identifiable grass fossils, the scrubby savannah was itself giving way to more open grassland. This was the territory of *Merychippus*, a tall horse-like creature measuring a full 90cms at the shoulder. While the three toes remained, most of the weight was now borne on the middle toe, the other two becoming almost vestigial. The neck had lengthened, allowing the animal to feed at ground level and also to raise its head higher for a longer view across the dangerous open prairie.

The teeth were now high-crowned with a protective layer of enamel and a heavy cement filling to reduce the wear of grinding hard, silica-laden grass leaves. *Merychippus* had also developed better eyesight and heightened senses. The forest browser was becoming the alert and fleet-footed wanderer of the plains.

Throughout the Pliocene – beginning seven million years ago – grasslands continued their advance across the land surface of the planet. In North America where the first 'true' horse was to develop, forest and savannah were in steep decline. On to these grassy plains galloped *Pliohippus*, the prototype of *Equus*. Standing more than a metre high at the shoulder, the animal had a single hoof controlled by a powerful leg ligament, the 'springing' foot that gave the later equids their efficiency of movement. This was ancestor to the herbivore group which included the zebras, asses and the hemoinids, the 'half-asses', as well as horses.

Over a period of a million years, ending with the close of the Ice Age in 9,000BC, the first horse, *Equus caballus*, together with its near relatives, spread outwards across existing land bridges to South America, Asia, Europe and finally Africa. With them went the grasses, colonising the great land masses alongside their hoofed partners in occupation, the grazing animals.

Somewhere around 10,000 years ago the horse disappeared from North America, its niche being filled by bison and sheep crossing from Europe via the land bridge across the Bering Strait. The reasons for the disappearance of the American horse are obscure, though they were probably connected with climatic changes taking place at the end of the glacial period, perhaps exacerbated by the over-hunting of early humans. *Equus caballus* came close to extinction elsewhere in the world. Its survival may have been the result of domestication by those same over-hunting humans.

The horse was not the only herbivore whose evolution was synchronous with that of the grasses. The steppe grasslands of Asia and North America were also grazed by vast numbers of bison, elk, woolly rhinoceroses and mammoths. All had developed the toughened, grinding teeth to deal with phytoliths, the silica granules in the epidermal cells of grass leaves. But the horse was perhaps the most extraordinary evolutionary companion of the grasses, if only because its survival seems so unlikely.

In *The Nature of Horses*, Stephen Budiansky muses on the 'improbability' of the modern horse.[33] Here is an animal whose very size would seem to put it at a disadvantage. Many herbivores of equivalent stature eat copious quantities of high-quality green material. Carnivores of similar weight such as the polar bear and the lion will get through up to forty kilograms of meat in a single meal.

Yet the horse thrives on a diet of grasses with a protein content below that required by almost every other large herbivore. And while ruminants like cattle and sheep need to rest after grazing, the horse can simply eat and run. More than that it has the strength and stamina to sustain a gallop of nearly seventy kilometres an hour.

Somehow grasslands produced an animal that is swifter, more intelligent and more efficient as an energy converter than any comparable creature on the planet. But that was only the start. The grasses were about to begin a partnership with an even more remarkable creature.

4   A Plot of Dreams

It could just be the most cosseted turf in England. On the surface it looks ordinary enough – a few highly bred ryegrass varieties sown into a soil that is almost pure sand. But these particular grasses have been given a little heavy-duty support in the form of polypropylene strands implanted, like human hair at a transplant clinic, deep into the ground.

Then there's the underground air-circulation system, a kind of air-conditioning for grass. A blower connected to ducts beneath the surface draws air down through the turf to remove water, or blows air upwards to keep the roots warm. The two-way flow stops the grass getting waterlogged at times of heavy rain and freezing during frosts. The aim is to keep grass growing strongly even under conditions that are hostile.

This 'high-dependency' turf covers the pitch at London's Upton Park stadium, the home of West Ham football club. Soccer pitches are not exactly the ideal places to grow grass: twenty-two star performers kicking and sliding their way through ninety minutes would be punishment enough at any time of year. But in the average British winter it's lethal. This is the time when farmers take their cattle off grass and shut them up inside. They know that heavy trampling on a rain-sodden turf will destroy it. Yet the beautiful game chooses just this moment to unleash its onslaught of flailing studs and gouging heels.

In the summer of 1998 West Ham applied their £800,000, high-technology antidote to the annual round of pitch despoiling. Now the players can display their skills on a surface that remains unchanged through the season, neither becoming too soft in wet weather nor turning to stone during freeze-ups. At Upton Park complaints about the state of the pitch have become as rare as the dislodged divot.

Football evolved as a game for playing on grass. But in Britain, the home of the sport, the traditional playing surface at many grounds was mud. By Christmas there was precious little grass left, especially around the goal area. Though players came on to the field wearing their team colours, a couple of sliding tackles were enough to convert them to a standard strip – a fatigue kit of mottled brown.

Not that mud-bath soccer was without its own peculiar fascination. While it seldom rewarded skill it often revealed character. On the most notorious pitches a team of determined local sloggers stood a sporting chance against the highest-paid stars of the league. But a handful of talented ground managers are beginning to change all that. Using modern, highly bred grass varieties and the latest turf technology, their aim is to put playing skills back at the centre of the action. The modern game is being re-invented – not in club boardrooms, but in the cluttered yards of the ground staff.

Soccer changed dramatically in the second half of the twentieth century, becoming a faster, sharper game, more demanding of players, less forgiving of mistakes. As a spectacle it grew beyond measure. Here was a true test of human skill and courage, rich in incident, drama and excitement. In part this was the result of improved player fitness. But it could not have happened without a transformation of the playing surface. The pace of the modern game owes as much to the ground staff as it does to the players.

Steve Welch, grounds manager for Nottingham Forest, looks

over the club's City stadium pitch with the satisfaction of an artist studying a newly finished canvas. The turf stretches away before him, bright green, even, unblemished. Nowhere is there a mark or indentation, nowhere a brown wheal of bare earth; just a smooth, unbroken surface of velvet stretching across to the far stand. And this is late April, almost the end of the season. By now the pitch has withstood a full programme of games, and one of the wettest springs on record.

Walking on this turf is a strange experience. The first surprise is its sheer strength. It feels firm, solid, yet more yielding than either tarmac or concrete. It has a resilience, a bounce, a sense of the ground pushing back under your feet so you feel an urge to break into a run. The closest sensation is that of walking across a sprung wooden dance floor, except that this one is softer, as if the boards have been covered with a thick pile carpet.

Steve Welch crouches down in the clipped turf and tugs at a handful of grass. Nothing tears. Nothing comes away in his hand. He says: 'They're locked solid. That's what makes it such a durable surface. You can scar the turf – say with a sliding tackle – but the turf won't break. It stays in place – there's no divot. So even at the end of the season the pitch still looks good and plays well. That's what makes this job satisfying. We're making a real contribution to football.'

This is the language of a new breed of sports ground manager – the professionals who look after grass. They bear no resemblance to the old stereotype, with his cloth cap and trenchcoat, trudging along behind the mower. Turf managers are highly trained, ambitious and mostly young. Steve Welch was appointed head groundsman at his former club – Leicester City – at the age of only twenty. Within three years of taking his present job he had initiated a major renovation of the City ground pitch, making it one of the best playing surfaces in the league.

The new turf technology has given ground managers control over the pace and style of modern sports, if not the outcome of matches. In the past there was little they could do to maintain a firm, grassy surface for the length of the playing season. Spike aerators might improve drainage and help to get oxygen down to the roots, but when the weather turned wet on the day of the big game, transforming the top few centimetres of the pitch into a quagmire, they were virtually powerless. The elements – earth and water – dictated the action and sometimes the result.

In a modern turf, however, the 'root-zone' – the twenty centimetres or so below the soil surface – is made up chiefly of sand, reinforced with plastic fibres. The sand allows water to drain away easily while the fibres add cohesion and strength. At the City ground tiny polypropylene fibres are simply mixed in with the sand. Other 'root-zone' strengthening systems use pieces of polypropylene mesh, each about the size of a pack of playing cards. Thousands are mixed into the sand-rich growth medium. There they interlock to support the 'root-zone', creating a stable, three-dimensional structure. As the grass roots develop, they entwine with the mesh to form a deep, firm root system.

The seed mixtures sown into this artificial soil are mostly varieties of perennial ryegrass, *Lolium perenne*, the first grass to be sown as a crop by British farmers. Known in the seventeenth century as red darnel or ray-grass, it has played a central role in livestock farming down the ages.

When town youths crowded on to the nearby pasture field for their rowdy game of football, the chances are they played on a turf containing ryegrass. It was probably a component of the narrow pitch used in the Eton wall game, at least until the sheer intensity of use reduced it to dust or mud. Almost certainly grounds like the Oval – established for cricket and later used for rugby and football in winter – will have contained the grass, particularly in the early days when summer mowing was carried out by sheep.

But the varieties used in modern soccer grounds have little in common with agricultural varieties. These are the thorough-breds of the ryegrass stable, as finely prepared for the big match as the twenty-two players in their team strips. With names like Verdi, Allegro, Barlinda and Dancer, they have finer leaves and grow more slowly than the old farm varieties, well able to tolerate frequent mowing. More important, they are bred to withstand the particular punishment of the soccer field with its skidding boot heels and crushing studs.

Ground managers use a battery of technical aids to keep the high-performance thoroughbreds in peak condition. There are under-soil heating pipes, sand-bands to speed drainage, and computer-controlled sprinkler systems for night-time irrigation. The dazzling displays of football's contemporary heroes can only occur because ground staff have first created the stage.

But the ground manager's new status comes at a cost. The modern sports turf with its pedigree grasses is like the highly tuned athlete. To keep performing well it needs careful management, and sometimes intensive physiotherapy. Pitch preparation is no longer a simple matter of mowing and marking out the white lines.

After each game at the City ground, Steve Welch and his team walk the entire surface repairing any minor damage. The new 'root-zone' reinforcement systems may have largely consigned divots to history, but after a tough match the turf will bear its inevitable scars and blemishes, the tell-tale marks of conflict. These must be carefully restored and smoothed out by hand, a job that can take several days.

The pitch then gets a thorough grooming. Every square metre is meticulously brushed – once more by hand – so the flattened grass stands erect ready for the mower. Laid grass is at greater risk from disease. The flattened foliage blocks the flow of air between leaf blades, producing hot-spots of high humidity, the ideal conditions for fungal infection.

Between matches the pitch is mowed – by hand-mower – to a little over an inch. This is longer than the players want to see it. To them a close-cropped turf means more accurate passing and a faster ball. But to Steve Welch a scalped turf spells danger. Without sufficient leaf area to trap sunlight and produce sugars through photosynthesis, the grass will stop growing and become weaker. Like all athletes, its needs must be recognised and met. When the pitch is below par the standard of game will suffer, too.

'This patch of grass is a living entity. We have to understand its essential requirements – for light and oxygen and soil nutrients – and provide them. I also believe in doing as much as possible of the regular maintenance work by hand. We use tractors only for aeration with the vertical tine machines. We'll even use hand forks for the routine treatment around the goal areas during the winter months.

'Tractors put unnecessary pressure on these highly bred grasses. Even ride-on mowers will have an effect. There's the weight of the operator combined with the weight of the machine compressing these living plants. We have to avoid it. They get enough punishment during a game without us adding to the damage.'

Ground managers can be as protective of their pitches as team coaches of players and club directors of a full trophy cabinet. That rectangle of turf – created at high cost to the club – becomes a kind of bargaining chip. Ground managers argue in its defence against the conflicting interests of players who want to display their skills, managers who need results, and chairmen who are seeking glory days for their clubs. It is a tussle from which the grass sward and its minders often emerge as winners.

Though this is not a match day, dozens of primary school pupils have begun filing into the front half dozen rows of the City ground stand. Today the club is playing host in an 'outreach' to the local community. It is a chance to introduce a new generation of fans to the special atmosphere of the big stadium. The youngsters are excited, a little bewildered and clearly fascinated by this bright, green stretch of grass. Steve Welch has seen that look before.

'People see this pitch and they're impressed,' he says. 'Maybe they compare it with the lawn at home, or the patch of grass around the flats. They know immediately this is something special. It adds to the thrill of the place, it's part of the promise. They know they're going to see good football here. That's what my job's all about.'

In Britain good football and a fine turf belong together. In drier climes, bare ground, baked hard by the sun, creates a playing surface that is fast and true. Skills are rewarded and games are often filled with incident. Not so in soggy Britain. Here the mild, wet winters produce mud, slow games and mediocrity. To shine in a northern European climate soccer's young superstars need a carpet of close-cropped grass to show off their talents. They need it as the fashion model needs the catwalk and the racing driver needs the track. Without that rectangle of fine turf their skills are worthless.

Though they might not care to acknowledge it, today's young football heroes owe some of their stardom to turf grass scientists and ground managers. Few have any knowledge of the conditions endured by an earlier generation of players. Coventry City manager Gordon Strachan began his playing career at Dundee. He recalls the 'nightmare' of having to play at Greenock Morton when the tide was high in the nearby River Clyde. The water would back up in the drains around the ground, turning the pitch into a mudbath. Strachan once lost his boot in the mire, then suffered the added indignity of not being able to find it again.[1]

In conditions like these there was little chance to exploit a talent, to develop an aptitude for ball control. The champions of those days were the tough, dogged, boot-it-and-run merchants; the army of sloggers who substituted stamina and fortitude for real skills. The pitches they performed on made them the players they were, just as today's firm, flat sports fields have produced a new breed of ball-control wizards. Given the way the game developed, that earlier generation of stars could have been no different.

Football has always taken its character from the turf it was played upon. When town youths flocked to open spaces for their disorderly, and sometimes violent, game of 'fote-balle' as early as the twelfth century, the places they chose were on farmland, mostly the common grazings. The only pitch preparation was summer grazing by sheep. By the early sixteenth century the game had become a mainly winter pastime, as Alexander Barclay observed in one of his pastoral poems.

> The sturdie plowman, lustie, strong and bolde
> Overcometh the winter with driving the foote ball.[2]

Until 1790, the pupils of Winchester College played their football on St Catherine's Hill, a prehistoric earthwork outside the college grounds. In 1810 the Chapter of Westminster School directed 'that Jonathan Green's bill of £3. 1s. for marking out ten acres of ground in Tothill Fields as a play-ground for the Westminster scholars, and for the use of his team of horses and plough two days, viz. the 28th and 29th of August last to mark the said piece of ground with a deep furrow, be paid.'[3] In industrial Sheffield six men of Norton, dressed in green, and six men of Sheffield, dressed in red, played a football match at Bent's Green. It lasted for three days.

In those early days the game was as rough and unstructured as the playing surface. As farmers took their cattle off pastures at the start of winter to stop them being reduced to the consistency of plum pudding, so the young men of towns and public schools were crowding on to the grass in pursuit of their savage sport. On many waterlogged grasslands the effect was catastrophic.

Skill played little part in this primitive form of football. Rules were minimal, and the cloddy, mud-covered arena allowed for little accurate passing or sustained movement of the ball. The attributes required of players in this mêlée of flailing boots and arms were physical strength, aggression and sheer guts. Like Barclay's ploughman these early stars were 'lustie, strong and bolde'. For the urban dweller toiling in a dark, satanic mill, or the schoolboy confined by the tedious round of classroom lessons, football became the great escape – the square of grass represented freedom.

The wild, lawless game was overwhelmingly tribal – the re-enactment of a drama three million years old in which *Homo erectus*, mankind's early ancestor, left the African forest to colonise the wide, open plains of sub-Saharan grassland. These tail-less, upright apes, not particularly well-adapted to life in the forest, found themselves in a terrain that suited them. Open grasslands were places of freedom and movement, places to hunt, places to dominate. They were the cradle of human societies, so it is hardly surprising that they should be the places chosen by men for their great sporting adventures.

By the end of the nineteenth century football – and football pitches – were becoming better organised. The great divide had taken place between the foot-dribbling game that was to become soccer and the handling game, the forerunner of rugby and American football. The basic rules of soccer – established at Cambridge University in 1846 – had been refined in a series of meetings which led to the creation of the Football Association. At the same time breweries and other businesses had begun investing in the new clubs.

On the pitch, surface markings to indicate the playing area were introduced in 1882. Over the next twenty years they were extended to include goal areas, a half-way line and an eighteen-yard line. Clubs seeking suitable sites for their new grounds were often forced to accept places that were far from ideal – uneven and sloping land, overgrown wasteland, disused quarries and gravel pits.[4] Cardiff City made use of a glass-strewn rubbish tip in the development of Ninian Park.

Methods of pitch construction were primitive by modern standards, with little thought given to the creation of healthy growing conditions for grass. Industrial waste materials such as mining spoil, ash and clinker were widely used for building up playing areas. Some clubs even made use of rubbish. Pitches were carefully levelled by hand rake or with the aid of horse-drawn scrapers. Finally they were topped with soil and sown down to grass.

Few of the pioneer constructors gave much thought to getting the drainage right, though by the turn of the century circular tile drains were widely used in farming. Where regular-sized industrial clinker or hard ash was used to build up the foundations of a new pitch, its drainage characteristics were good. Unfortunately many contractors were content to use fine fly ash, subsoil or mixed wastes for the foundations, materials that made waterlogging almost inevitable.

Bradford's Valley Parade ground – built originally as a rugby ground – was completed in 1886 at a cost of £1,400.[5] Construction work included the levelling of a steep hillside followed by the building up of layers of ballast, ashes and topsoil. Finally the entire pitch area was laid with turf. But despite the complexity and cost of the work there is no record of drain installation.

Poor drainage in the foundations compounded the drawbacks of ordinary topsoil as growing medium. Soils contain clay whose fine particles provide structure. In a well-structured soil clay particles are joined together in the form of aggregates, opening up airways through which water can quickly drain away. Air is able to penetrate the soil profile, stimulating biological activity, while grass roots can grow down through the profile in search of moisture and nutrients.

But the clay aggregates break down when the soil is made to carry too much traffic, particularly when it is saturated. The characteristic 'crumb' structure of a well-managed soil is lost, and the upper horizon becomes compacted. Water and air can no longer pass through, growth stops and the vegetation starts to die. Continued traffic will turn the whole area into a lifeless sea of mud.

With poorly drained subsoils there was not much ground-keepers could do except open up the turf by spiking it. Right up to World War Two the only short-term treatment for a waterlogged pitch was a small army of ground staff armed with hand forks. From the 1930s onwards spiking machines were gradually introduced, though it was not until 1980 that the Dutch Verti-Drain machine offered a real alternative to the hand fork.

Not even the most sophisticated machine could remedy the real malaise of British football which was seated not in the 'root-zone', but deep down in the subsoil or the industrial ballast. Solid metal tines might open up a compacted turf, but this was of little use if there was nowhere for the water to go. Mud remained a characteristic feature of the British game for the best part of a century.

While most of the big competitions were limited to the British Isles, nobody in the game seemed too worried. The odd encounter between two legendary sides at a venue more reminiscent of a Great War battlefield than a sports pitch charged the contest with added excitement. A near-quagmire makes the result even more unpredictable.

But in 1953 there came a turning-point in the British game. The England side – unbeaten on their home turf of Wembley – were taken apart by Hungary, champions of the 1952 Olympics. Ferenc Puskas and his fleet-footed warriors from the grassy Hungarian plain outplayed and outmanoeuvred the home side with their flair and teamwork. Like the fearsome Huns who had galloped across the steppes to challenge the Roman empire, the Hungarians took on the inventors of football in their own citadel and left them bewildered and demoralised. By half-time they had fired four into the English net. At the final whistle they had notched up six.

The home game looked fine when both sides were from the British Isles. But when the home sides faced European or South American opposition their weaknesses became all too apparent. Why was it, the public began to wonder, that British football heroes seemed so slow and ponderous when pitted against the Brazilians, the Argentinians, even the Italians? The answer was obvious. These southern sides had developed their game on surfaces that were dry, fast and true. In their hot, arid lands they had no need of grass on the pitch. It was an optional extra. But in a cool, damp climate a good turf was essential. Yet British football grounds seemed designed to kill it off.

In a west Wales glasshouse, plant breeder Danny Thorogood gently shakes the inverted polythene bag containing the flower heads of two perennial ryegrass plants. His careful action encourages the release of pollen grains so that each plant fertilises the other in a process known as 'controlled hybridisation': the deliberate crossing of two selected plants. Though the whole operation takes place in an enclosed glasshouse, the polythene bag provides an extra defence against contamination by stray pollen grains.

Dr Thorogood breeds amenity grasses at the Institute for Grassland and Environmental Research, a cluster of glasshouses and laboratory blocks folded into the Cambrian hills near Aberystwyth. Among his objectives are a range of ryegrass varieties better suited to the harsh regime of a modern, professional football pitch with its punishing fixture list. Until the 1970s the varieties used on football pitches were chiefly those which had been bred for agriculture. But farmers want grasses that will grow quickly, especially at high levels of fertiliser nitrogen. Since they take their cattle off in winter and put them into sheds, they have little need for varieties that will form a tough, wear-resistant turf.

The breeders of sports turf varieties have different aims. They want grasses that will produce a mass of shoots – or tillers – at the base. Not for them the 'open' grass sward of the silage field. Their idea of good grassland is one in which densely packed tillers form a strong, 'closed' turf, well able to withstand the stamp of studded boots. They also want varieties with fine, slow-growing leaves. Farmers are mainly interested in production. For them wide, sappy leaves are fine just so long as they grow back quickly after grazing or cutting for silage.

But the soccer pitch must look smooth and even, like soft velvet, an aesthetic achievable only with fine-leaved grasses. Ideally it should not need mowing too often. Most important of all, it should be tough enough to take a hammering. Wear tolerance, the turf technologists call it – the kind of wear inflicted by twenty-two fit, young athletes wearing boots. Football inflicts heavy punishment on grasses at the time when they are at their most vulnerable. In winter the light intensity is low so grasses are unable to photosynthesise fast enough to produce all the sugars they need for growth.

The development of the superstadiums has further weakened pitches. Wrap-around stands with roofs that block out the sun have made winters even darker down at the level of grass. In Cardiff's Millennium Stadium light levels fall so low that the loss of sugars through respiration outstrips the plant's ability to produce them by photosynthesis. Shoots die and the turf becomes thinner, less able to withstand the wear of an international rugby game.

The Cardiff pitch is constructed in modular form. The idea is that when a section of turf is showing signs of wear-and-tear, the module can be removed and replaced by a fresh one. But the exchange is a slow process, and it isn't cheap. In Holland the designers of superstadiums have come up with even more radical solutions. So bad are the growing conditions in the Ajax stadium in Amsterdam that the pitch is ripped up and re-seeded no less than five times a year. At the Vitesse stadium in Arnhem the entire pitch is built on rollers. After a match it is rolled out through a detachable section of the stand for a spell of recuperation in the wind and sunshine.

In the northern European winter grasses slow their rate of metabolism and enter a semi-dormant state. Yet clubs arrange a punishing programme of fixtures over an ever-lengthening season. Modern pitches have to withstand a continuous sequence of matches from August right through to early May. The West Ham ground at Upton Park will host about seventy matches in a full season. The old agricultural grasses would never have survived such a harsh schedule. Modern sports grasses have to be tough to survive. And the breeders are out to make them tougher still.

At the heart of modern soccer there is conflict between the demands of the sport and the needs of a living plant community – the grasses of the pitch. Ground staff struggling to maintain a healthy, growing turf are involved in an exercise in damage limitation. They know the more top growth there is on a turf, the better will be its resistance to wear. For this reason they don't like mowing the grass too short. A scalped turf spells danger. Without sufficient leaf area to trap sunlight and produce sugars through photosynthesis, the grass will stop growing and become weaker.

Players take a different view. They want the pitch shaved as close as a billiard table. This is the kind of surface that will show off their skills to best effect, and produce fast, exciting football. A turf with too much top growth slows the ball and deadens its bounce. Ground staff have to reconcile these two conflicting aims each time they take the mower to a pitch. They are walking a tightrope between dull games and a weakened turf. But the plant breeders reckon they have a solution.

If they can come up with varieties which produce masses of tightly packed shoots, the established turf will have plenty of top growth even at low cutting heights. Even clipped short this denser sward will have enough green leaf to make the most of poor winter light. It should continue to thrive when shaved close enough to keep the players happy.

Hard-wearing grass strains are those which channel a high proportion of their sugars into the formation of buds for new shoots rather than into leafy growth. To the breeders a dense mass of shoots makes for a wear-resistant pitch. They are constantly searching for new ryegrass strains that will deliver the goods.

At Aberystwyth they have developed a machine to measure the ability of new grass varieties to soak up physical punishment. The hand-operated contraption applies a studded roller to the small, experimental squares of turf in an action which mimics the tread of soccer boots. There is even a 'differential slip' mechanism to imitate that distinctive assault of the soccer field, the sliding tackle.

Through careful selection and crossing the grass breeders have started to transform the lush, leafy ryegrasses of the farm into the leaner, tougher stars of the soccer pitch, as characteristic of the modern game as lightweight boots and the chequered ball. Starting with the old farm varieties, they first have to pick out individual plants which seem to be well-endowed in the character traits they are looking for – a high density of shoots, fine leaves, the habit of slow growing and resistance to fungal diseases like red thread. These top performers are then used as 'studs' in breeding programmes aimed at creating better varieties.

Wild grasses provided the breeders with their basic genetic stock. Grasses grow everywhere in Britain: on roadside verges, in woodland clearings, in riverside meadows and across broad sweeps of open moorland. In every habitat the grass population adapts to local conditions. Plants well suited to the local conditions thrive and multiply at the expense of those that are poorly suited to the site. So when the grass breeders go out in search of new material, they concentrate on sites that are likely to encourage the genetic traits they are looking for.

In their quest for the tougher strains of perennial ryegrass they searched in places where the indigenous grasses were already subjected to harsh treatment. They dug up plants from well-worn footpaths and roadside verges; from commons grazed smooth by rabbits, and from playing areas trampled almost bare by children's feet. Any patch of ground where grasses had received sustained punishment and yet had managed to survive was a promising site. One of the first amenity ryegrasses was bred from plants collected in New York's Central Park. Bred at Rutgers University in New Jersey, the variety was marketed under the name Manhattan.

In Britain, parts of Romney Marsh in Kent have proved fruitful sources of new genetic stock. Over centuries these marshland grazings had acquired an unrivalled reputation as prime fattening pastures. Some had been heavily stocked with sheep and cattle for a thousand years or more. This punishing regime had produced ryegrass strains tough enough to withstand regular trampling. The breeders harvested the results of centuries of natural selection. Exposed sites such as clifftop grazings have also produced tough, wear-resistant grasses.

These wild genes were used in breeding programmes along with genetic material from earlier, forage varieties. They produced a new generation of ryegrasses highly adapted to the rigours of the football pitch. Dutch grass breeders were quick to the market with a family of low-growing varieties. But by the end of the millennium the turfgrass performance charts were topped by a variety bred at Aberystwyth. Aberelf combined wear resistance with many of the features that make good lawns – fine leaves, a high density of shoots and the ability to withstand regular close mowing. In the sports field it was one of those rare grasses that satisfied both the ground staff and the players.

A new variety from the Institute for Grassland and Environmental Research is no novelty. The very name Aberystwyth was once synonymous with the best grass strains. Originally part of the University of Wales, the Institute was founded in 1919 as the Welsh Plant Breeding Station. Its founder and first director, the legendary Professor George Stapledon – who was later knighted – founded a dynasty of highly productive forage grasses and sparked a renaissance in Britain's pastoral economy during the depressed years between the two world wars. Now the institute has a programme to raise the standard of sports and amenity grassland. Having helped to feed the nation, the plant breeders are now concerned to raise its cultural well-being.

Danny Thorogood takes a practical view of his role in modern culture. He is content to be a breeder of grasses that will stimulate a fast, skilful, entertaining style of football. But he believes that a highly functional turf should also have an aesthetic value. Like the classic eighteenth-century garden, it should be a delight to the eye as well as an inspiration to the spirit.

Looking across the flawless turf of the Nottingham Forest ground it is easy to understand what he means. Even at the end of the playing season it remains a green oasis in the built environment of stands and terracing and concrete. It is a living thing, an enigmatic thing, at the same time serene and charged with expectation.

Together plant breeders and ground managers have created a flawless and durable turf, using just a handful of élite grasses. But it thrives only with the aid of some expensive technology and a battery of inputs, from fertilisers to pesticides. It also demands the constant attention of its human minders to cut it, roll it, brush it and generally carry out a continuous programme of manicure. The hallowed turf of the sports field must be served by its own priestly caste.

5   Turf Doctors

Steve Birks, head groundsman at Trent Bridge, England's oldest county cricket ground, has his own form of stress therapy. When the pressure of the job gets too much he climbs aboard a ride-on mower and heads off to cut the outfield. A gentle drive beneath empty stands, with the sweet smell of new-mown grass in the air, is the perfect antidote to tension. Out here on the bright green turf he can forget the cares of the day.

The idea that looking after a patch of turf is a relaxing, stress-free occupation is about as wide of the mark as the myth that comedians are happy, fun-loving people. Modern sport is big business. And the biggest bucks of all ride on the great national team games played on grass pitches. When the ground is in poor shape the quality of the game takes a dive, or so the theory goes. And when playing standards slip the sport's income is likely to suffer.

In August 2000, the England cricket team routed the West Indies at Yorkshire's Headingley ground in under two days, the first time it had happened for eighty-eight years. The English players were jubilant. So were their fans. They had watched a thrilling match, the kind they would be talking about for years. To them it did not matter that the game had ended three days short of its scheduled time span.

Cricket's administrators took a different view. They calculated that three lost playing days would cost them a fortune at the turnstiles. More serious still, it would make the sport's sponsors more reluctant to put their names to lucrative hospitality deals for the final day or two of future test matches. The blame for the débâcle was laid on the standard of the pitch, and indirectly on the groundsman.

'England may have won, but the men who run English cricket ought to be concerned,' wrote the *Sunday Times* cricket correspondent with appropriate gravitas. 'They will not cultivate world-class players on cabbage patches.'[1] England's former captain Michael Atherton joined in the attack. Writing in the *Sunday Telegraph* he said: 'Make no mistake, this was a poor Test match pitch. The players, however, are not surprised any more as the days of good Test pitches in England are long gone.'[2]

This is the kind of criticism that sends Steve Birks and his fellow ground managers off to mow the outfield. Blaming the pitch for cricket's ills has become a popular pastime. Batsmen do it when they fail to score runs. Bowlers do it when they're not taking wickets. Administrators do it when they decide a game is not producing the excitement and entertainment it ought to. Getting caught in the middle puts groundsmen under stress.

'Sometimes there's so much hassle it's as if you're dealing with a nuclear weapon not a cricket pitch,' says Steve Birks. 'Looking after the ground is easy. The hardest part of the job is dealing with the people. Everyone seems to want something different – the players, the club, the English Cricket Board. And when something goes wrong it's us who get the blame.'

At Somerset's county ground at Taunton, head groundsman Phil Frost shares his sentiments. 'To hear some people talk you'd think we went out of our way to produce duff pitches. The press are partly to blame for this idea. It's true that sometimes a pitch isn't everything it might be. But if the weather's bad there's not a lot we can do about it no matter what technological support we've got. We try to produce the best pitches we can in the circumstances. That's all we can do.

'A lot depends on the sun. Sunshine puts pace in the wicket, dull weather slows it down. Give us three weeks of cold, dull weather and we'll start to hear complaints about the slowness of the pitch. But give us a dry summer so we can control the water that goes on and we'll produce a wicket that bowlers can bowl on and that batsmen can score runs on. It's as simple as that. There's only so much the groundsman can do. We're not gods.'

In an age when sport has become a religion it is perhaps not surprising that they should be treated that way. In the national team games of cricket, soccer and rugby the trappings of organised religion are everywhere. The great sporting stadiums are modern cathedrals echoing with the hymns and ritual chants of ecstatic worshippers. Before the roaring fans is the hallowed turf, the setting for the spectacle that will rouse them to a fervour of passion and excitement.

When a famous pitch is to be replaced or renovated hundreds will bid to buy a square of the sacred sward. Some will even choose to have their ashes scattered on it when they die. In such an atmosphere it is easy to see how the people who tend the turf might come to be viewed as a sort of priestly caste, gifted with powers to decide the outcome of games. And it has to be said that the groundsmen themselves have helped to foster the myth.

In the past cricket pitches were blatantly prepared to favour the home side. Dave Bridle, former head groundsman at Gloucestershire's Bristol ground, recalls the post-war years when almost every ground had its own characteristic wickets. In Derbyshire, for example, pitches were noted for their lush, grassy surfaces, a characteristic which did not please Gloucestershire's clutch of spin bowlers.

'Derbyshire had a reputation for pulling men out of the pits, putting cricket boots on them and getting them to bowl fast. Those green pitches didn't suit our spinners at all. But put them on our home grounds at Bristol or Gloucester and it was a very different story. Our pitches were drier with a lot less grass, just right for our spinners. On the Cheltenham ground, which has lighter soil, they used to say if we could win the toss we would have the game sewn up by tea-time on the second day. The pitch wouldn't stand up to a longer game.'

In the early 1980s the Trent Bridge groundsman, Ron Allsopp, regularly prepared 'green' wickets to favour the team's star pace bowlers, Richard Hadlee and Clive Rice. In 1981 Nottinghamshire carried off the county championship after winning every one of their home games. One press report spoke of a visiting team having to take on the combined skills of Hadlee, Rice and Allsopp.

Such obvious partisanship from ground staff is no longer allowed by the England and Wales Cricket Board – the ECB – which controls the sport. Nowadays the board demands the kind of pitches that will sustain a four-day game right up until late in the final afternoon. Playing surfaces of the sort that produce innings collapses or huge run totals are shunned. Head groundsmen have to hand in pitch reports for all first-class matches. These must include details of when the pitch was rolled and watered. To prevent overnight watering the pitch has to be protected by raised covers for the forty-eight hours preceding a four-day match.

At the start of the game, soil cores are taken from the pitch and sent away for analysis. Among the parameters measured are the density and moisture content of the soil, and the total weight of root. Meanwhile umpires carry out their own inspections, marking each pitch for pace, and penalising those that fail to meet the board's minimum standards. It is all very scientific. But not everyone agrees that it will produce better cricket.

Phil Frost certainly has his doubts. 'Star players are paid a lot of money by their clubs. They are the players who will bring in the crowds. That makes them key assets of the clubs. If a side's strength happens to lie in its seam bowlers, say, why shouldn't the ground staff prepare a pitch that will help them show their skills to maximum advantage? That's what the crowd wants to see.

'It takes a lot of skill to prepare a pitch for home advantage. You've got to know your square. It doesn't always work anyway. In 1993, when we were playing Yorkshire, we prepared a pitch for our seamers and Darren Gough came and bowled us all out. But by doing away with home advantage you take some of the entertainment value out of the game.'

The keepers of England's cricket grounds are an independent, self-reliant bunch with clear ideas about how best to look after their own particular stretches of turf. Most feel an instinctive loyalty to their own county sides. This makes them unhappy about applying any kind of formula or 'blueprint' handed down by the games authorities for some universal standard – an all-purpose pitch that will behave in the same way at any ground in the country and under all conditions.

'The ECB tells us to produce the driest, hardest surface possible, but every county is going to try for a pitch that will help the home team,' says Dave Bridle. 'It's a fine line because you're aware that you could lose points for an unsuitable surface. In practice it's easier for a head groundsman to help seamers than spin bowlers. For seam bowlers all you need do is leave the wicket a little more damp than it ought to be. For spinners you need a dry, bare wicket with footmarks and other edges to accentuate the turn.

'Some people put on spiked cricket boots and tramp around where the ball will pitch at a spin bowler's length. Or they'll scrub the turf with wire brushes and yard brooms to try and remove the grass and leave the surface dusty. You can get a striped effect like a zebra crossing – bare and dusty where the spinners pitch close to the batsman and green further back where the seamers pitch.'

While such extreme manipulation of pitches may be uncommon, ground staff can come under intense pressure to give an advantage to the home side, particularly towards the end of the season when clubs are chasing trophies. Ground keepers know there are limits to what they can do to secure a particular result. Grass management is not a precise science. Any stretch of turf is influenced by a thousand factors outside the control of ground staff. Club executives rarely grasp this point. They want the home side to win and they expect their groundsmen to shorten the odds.

Phil Frost has his own routine for preparing a pitch to ECB standards. It is based on an intimate knowledge of the Taunton ground built up over more than twenty years. Three weeks before a match he will put out the stumps, mark out the pitch, then drench the area for three hours or more using a hand-held hosepipe. Afterwards the area is covered overnight with a sheet so that the water can soak down to ten centimetres or more.

After that it is all a matter of the judicious use of the heavy roller, normally for twenty minutes every other day. Rolling is a key activity in cricket pitch preparation. It compresses the upper soil layers to produce a playing surface that is hard, dry and fast. Taken to excess it can weaken grass tillers and lead to the loss of top growth. Devising the ideal pitch programme – involving a range of rollers from the half-tonner to the big three-tonner – means balancing a number of key factors including cutting height and soil moisture content.

Juggling all the elements to achieve a good playing surface is a process that takes both experience and intuition. To get it right groundsmen have to understand the character of the turf and the qualities of the soil it grows on. They walk their own particular turf constantly, getting to know its character and behaviour – the way it responds to rain and irrigation, to rolling, aeration and cutting. After a while they come to know, almost by instinct, when to send in the mower or the heavy roller, when to turn on the irrigation system. Like all intuitive skills it is not easily explained. It is what gives the turf keepers their air of mystery, their supposed power to influence the outcome of matches, a power most would say was exaggerated.

Sports authorities are intent on taking this mystique out of ground management, to take control back to the centre. They are determined to make it all a matter of hard science. In cricket the ECB has put up the funds for a major investigation into the science of pitches. Carried out by the Sports Turf Research Institute at Bingley in Yorkshire, the study aims to find out how soil structure and the type of grass affect a moving cricket ball.

There are machines to measure the hardness of the surface, and the bounce of balls dropped from standard heights. A rotating drum device is used to simulate the action of a spinner, while a pendulum apparatus is helping the scientists measure friction between the ball and playing surface. Stroboscope photography using digital cameras has been developed to follow the speed, angle and direction of the ball after it has hit the pitch.

Many groundsmen view these developments with a distinct lack of enthusiasm. In part this is self-preservation. An all-purpose formula for pitch preparation would take much of the skill out of their job. In future it could be carried out by a competent technician given a bit of training. But alongside this runs a genuine concern about what it will do to the game.

Modern ground management techniques are already making pitches more consistent in their playing characteristics. The use of high-clay soils such as 'Surrey loam' have begun to iron out differences between grounds. A number of clubs use the technique of hollow tining to strengthen the structure of their pitches. A specialist machine removes a series of small diameter soil cores across the cricket square. The chosen replacement loam is then 'agitated' into the holes, changing for ever the playing characteristics of the pitches.

The latest scientific study could take this trend to its ultimate conclusion. First-class grounds everywhere might be forced to adopt the standard pitch. This would almost certainly lead to uniform playing styles and more predictable results. While this might suit sponsors and television companies keen to see games 'go the distance', the sport would become far less exciting.

In lawn tennis the scientific construction of playing surfaces has progressed even further than in cricket. The result, according to many fans of the sport, has been a dulling of the spectacle, a fall in the entertainment value of the game. At the international level matches are characterised by a surfeit of high-speed 'ace' services and a dearth of entertaining rallies. Before the evolution of the modern playing court – flat and rock hard – the bounce of the ball was slower and less predictable.

At Wimbledon, Britain's premier lawn tennis venue, courts are constructed on strictly scientific principles. The soils used have a clay content of exactly 22 per cent, giving them powerful cohesive qualities and ensuring a high degree of surface hardness, as measured by the Clegg impact soil tester. The grass mixture for the turf is made up of 70 per cent perennial ryegrass and 30 per cent slender creeping red fescue.

The actual varieties are selected for their resistance to the characteristic wear and tear of the tennis court – the scuffs and skids made by tennis shoes during a four-hour tussle for the men's singles championship. Long before varieties are sown in the turfs that will later be laid down at Wimbledon, they are tested for wear-resistance and other traits at the Bingley research station.

Eddie Seaward, head groundsman at Wimbledon, has spent a working lifetime watching sports grass technology slowly take over from human intuition. He is resigned to the change. 'Between my generation and the next we'll see the revolution. I can walk out on to a court and say that it needs rolling. I can see it with my eyes and feel it through my feet. The younger ones, the college-trained ground keepers, they are the ones who need all the data to make their decisions. It's up to this generation to develop the data which will allow them to take over in the future.

'There are other advantages in having everything defined and laid down. It gives you something solid when you're having to talk to the press or a club committee. The data has to be more reliable – and certainly more intelligible to outsiders – than the groundsman's opinions and intuition. That's what makes a technological future inevitable. At the same time we must not lose sight of what it's all about. It's the grass we're interested in, not the gismos.

'There's a cricket ground in Australia where the head groundsman was backed by all the computers, monitors and technical aids imaginable. Yet out on the grass the standard of the playing surface was going downhill. He had taken his eye off the ball and got lost in the wonders of the technology. In the end he lost his job. While the science may be inevitable let's not deceive ourselves into thinking of it as an end in itself. It's only a tool, that's all.'

At Wimbledon there is still a place for human intuition, particularly in preparing pitches for play, then repairing them at the end of a tough season. In the run-up to the season Eddie

Seaward has developed a precise pattern of mowing and rolling to bring the thirty-four grass courts to prime condition. Afterwards, with the courts showing signs of wear, he has a battery of measures for restoring them. These include 'spiking' them with jets of super-pressurised water to allow air down to the roots, and scarifying them to rip out the 'thatch' of dead and dying leaves.

Through the winter the courts also get a daily brushing with a 'drag brush', which fluffs up the grass leaves to keep air circulating between them, so reducing the risk of fungal disease. 'It's like brushing your hair,' says Eddie Seaward. 'Somehow it seems to make it grow stronger.'

No fewer than thirteen full-time staff are engaged in keeping the courts in peak condition. The annual Wimbledon tournament is the only grass court event of the four 'grand slam' championships on the tennis circuit. So why not abandon this costly and eccentric playing surface and opt for hard courts? Eddie Seaward is convinced there is nothing to match grass. He explains: 'The joy of this job is that you see the contribution you are making to good tennis. When the ball is coming through fast and bouncing true the players can really show off their skills. That's why they like Wimbledon.

'It may take them a couple of days to adjust after the French clay court championship. The ball is slightly lower on grass, and faster because there's less friction, so players' reactions have to be sharper. But they enjoy the challenge of a faster game. They also like the fact that grass is kinder on the body – there's less jarring than on a hard surface.

'Some people now argue that the game's too fast on a good grass surface. Apparently it needs slowing down. There are too many aces and not enough rallies. On a hard surface it's the very opposite – the game seems to be too slow. All I know is the grass tournament adds tremendously to the popularity of this game.'

Like ground staff everywhere, Eddie Seaward takes a pride in his grass. During the redevelopment of Wimbledon's famed Centre Court immediately after the 1997 tournament, dozens of eight-wheeler trucks were driven to and fro across the hallowed turf. It was the only way to remove the builders' rubble. But the playing surface was so hard that the massive tyres left no ruts, not even a small indentation, says Eddie with obvious delight.

He tells a story to highlight the mythic nature of the Wimbledon turf. Before the start of one famous Centre Court battle, an American spectator was overheard discussing the playing surface. 'No way is that grass – it's got to be artificial,' the spectator was telling a fellow tennis fan. Eddie invited the sceptic to step over the boundary fence and check the surface for himself. The incredulous visitor ran his fingers through the close-cropped leaves. 'That is incredible,' he muttered. 'I never would have believed it.'

Like all those whose working lives revolve around grassland of one sort or another, Eddie Seaward knows the personalities of all his swards. The Wimbledon courts have the same species composition, the same clay-rich soils, the same day-to-day management. Yet each has its own distinctive personality. While all are fast in play and true of line, each has its particular subtleties and idiosyncrasies.

Sports ground managers know these character traits and how to manage them. They understand the life of grass in the way that the downland shepherd knew when to move his flock to the lowland and the marshland grazier knew when to transfer his cattle to firmer ground. The knowledge of grassland is part of Britain's rural heritage. In pastoral districts it was passed from generation to generation until powerful corporations turned farming into an industrial process driven by fossil fuel. Now the guardians of the sports turf are helping to keep the tradition alive.

Growing up on a mixed farm in Monmouthshire, Dale Gleed was an inheritor of that tradition. For a while when he left school he worked on the family farm. Then he went off to college to study first agriculture, and later sports ground management. After a lengthy period at Eastbourne's Devonshire Park, he now runs the grass courts at Nottingham Tennis Centre, the busiest tennis venue in Britain. It is a job which, for all the modern scientific aids, still calls on that older knowledge.

One of his biggest headaches is dealing with invasive grasses, particularly meadow-grasses, the genus *Poa*. The grasses sown on the Nottingham courts are dwarf perennial ryegrasses and creeping red fescue. But the venue has proven as attractive to the meadow-grasses as to the international players who are drawn to the Nottingham Open.

Smooth-stalked meadow-grass is the chief interloper. Its bluey-green leaves lie like dark shadows amid the brighter greens of ryegrass and fescue. This is the American Kentucky bluegrass, once widely used as a sports grass. Nowadays it cannot compete with modern perennial ryegrasses in its ability to withstand hard punishment. It also comes under attack from leaf spot, a fungal disease that kills off foliage. Once established in the meadow-grass, the disease will go on to infect ryegrass, causing extensive damage to the sward.

Then there is the enemy of ground staff everywhere, the ubiquitous annual meadow-grass. 'I've heard it said that cockroaches would be one of the few organisms to survive a nuclear war,' says Dale Gleed. 'But I've got no doubt that *Poa annua* would be out there, too. I've seen it on some of the best golf greens in the country. Maybe they can tolerate it. But on the tennis court it's too shallow-rooting to take the wear. Otherwise we'd learn to live with it.

'It's a very competitive species. Once it has got a hold it puts all its energy into producing seed. The lower you cut it, the more it seeds.'

Science offers no simple solutions to the invasion of the meadow-grasses. Chemical sprays are as likely to damage the grasses you want to keep as those you want to get rid of. Specialist machines for cutting through the turf and weakening the weed grasses are unusable in wet weather. A series of wet springs gave the meadow-grasses a strong boost in the late 1990s.

Dale Gleed uses a more subtle strategy, one with its roots in an older grassland tradition. He is not looking for the 'quick fix'. From his knowledge of the turf he has created instead a management programme that encourages the favoured grasses and discourages the rest. He is prepared to use the full range of techniques, from mowing and rolling to sprays and fertilisers, but in a pragmatic way, as the weather allows. And if patches of smooth-stalked meadow-grass still persist, it need not be a disaster.

'Professional tennis players are not too concerned with the look of the court,' he says. 'What they expect is a surface that produces a good, consistent, even bounce. They get that here, which is why the place is so popular. Grass courts are not the easiest to manage. But when they're good there is no more exciting surface for tennis.'

Managing a sports ground has a lot of stresses. There are no hard and fast rules, no right and wrong courses of action. And the weather can disrupt even the best-planned grassland management programmes. When mistakes are made the results are evident for all to see. Dale Gleed worries less about the job than he used to. After all, he has experienced it all before – the sudden downpour, the flooded court, the frustration of not being able to get on court to deal with a weed grass infestation.

But it is no nine-to-five occupation. During the season they are on your mind constantly, those neat rectangles of grass.

Steve Braddock, head groundsman at Arsenal Football Club, considers the care of a sports turf to be more a way of life than a job. He is candid about his own feelings for that bright green pitch. 'It's easy to get very protective of your beloved grass. When you lavish so much care and attention on an area of grass you come to respect it more than anyone. Then you see fans who reckon they're entitled to tear chunks out of it as souvenirs. It really makes you want to weep.'

The pitch at Arsenal's Highbury ground is considered to be one of the finest in the English premier division. Like his opposite numbers around the country, Steve Braddock has no fail-safe formula for producing a top-class playing surface. For him it is simply a matter of knowing the turf – its particular strengths and idiosyncrasies – then coming up with a day-to-day management programme that suits its character.

'By personality I'd have to say I was a cautious person,' he admits, 'the kind of person who leaves home, walks to the end of the street, then has to go back to see that the front door's closed. I don't like taking a gamble. Once I've found a system that gets results I'll stick with it. This can get me into trouble sometimes. People might call me over-cautious. For example, I might go to the expense of verti-draining the pitch even in a dry summer. But I know it works. I know it produces the results. So I'll do it, even if it makes me unpopular.'

When he was interviewed for the job of head groundsman back in 1987 the club's managing director told him: 'We don't want much from you – only the best pitch in the Football League.' It is a message he took to heart. Since coming to Arsenal he has won the league's Groundsman of the Year Award no fewer than five times. The award is based on the assessment of referees together with nominations from visiting teams. It represents the professionals' verdict on the quality of a playing surface. There are few clubs with a pitch record to match that of Arsenal.

Two years after he took the job the 'cautious' Steve Braddock initiated a radical programme of reconstruction. The entire pitch was dug up, and drains and under-soil heating pipes were laid across the playing area. The trenches were back-filled, first with gravel, then with a layer of sand. Finally a mixture of sand and topsoil were spread on top for the 'root-zone'.

For the groundsman who disliked taking a gamble it was a bold undertaking – the construction of a pitch built largely on sand; light, free-draining but lacking the cohesion to support the concentrated boot-pressure of a twelve-stone soccer star in full flight. The missing element was grass, or more precisely the grass roots that would bind the whole unstable structure together and transform it into a firm and durable playing surface.

The pitch was seeded with a commercial mixture of perennial ryegrasses. The actual varieties were of little concern to Steve Braddock. In his view modern varieties are all much the same. The only variation is in the marketing message. But whatever they are they need the right soil conditions for germination and fast growth. At Highbury the newly sown seeds are covered for a week to protect them from pigeons and to keep warmth in the ground. Once established, the turf is then given a dose of quick-release fertiliser to kick-start growth. After that the policy is to treat the grass mean.

'I like to treat grass as I would treat a human being,' he says without embarrassment. 'OK, people might say I'm off my head. The experts might call it rubbish. But if you give human beings too much to eat and drink they get lazy, and it's the same for grasses. If there's too much fertiliser and water around they won't bother to put down roots. All the roots will stay near the surface.

'That's why I don't believe in putting the sprinklers on until the young turf is starting to turn a bluey-brown colour from lack of moisture. It encourages the plants to put down roots in search of water and nutrients. You end up with a well-developed root structure which gives a firm, hard-wearing surface. In the playing season the aims are different. The players want a soft surface to play on so we'll water the turf more often. But in the summer months the aim is to make the grass work harder. It's not what the experts recommend but it seems to work here.'

Steve Braddock's definition of the ideal football surface is one with a good covering of grass, soft enough to take boot studs, and mown to a length that will allow the ball to run fast and freely. This is the kind of pitch the Arsenal players turn out on at every home game. After each match the ground staff carry out a comprehensive repair job to make good damage to the turf. The first step is to replace the divots, those slivers of turf ripped like flesh from the turf by sliding tackles and skidding studs. Where the divots still have root attached they are grafted back on to the bared surface, their edges stitched on to undamaged grass by small areas of re-seed.

After that the pitch is lightly brushed to remove torn foliage, aerated with spikes, lightly watered if the weather is dry, and finally mowed twice by cylindrical mowers working in two different directions. This post-match intensive-care programme does for the Highbury turf what the club physio does for its stable of talented players – it keeps the ground in top playing condition. Under Steve Braddock's management the north London pitch has become almost legendary, with its deep network of drains and sand-rich subsoil bound together by a mesh of hungry, probing roots.

Not that this stops the players complaining. 'They like to

have a whinge,' he says ruefully. 'The ground is too soft or the grass is too long. Usually it's that the ground is too hard. They never stop to think about the weather conditions we're up against. How am I supposed to go out there and soften the pitch when there's a force-ten gale blowing? There's not much point in watering if half the stuff's going to end up in the stand.

'The effect of the pitch on a game can get exaggerated. With so much money in the game players are looking for reasons why they're not performing up to their full potential. The pitch is a good scapegoat. Obviously if a pitch is so bad that you can't push the ball two yards in front of you without getting bogged down in the mud it will influence the result of the game. But whatever the state of a pitch it's the same for both sides, that's the important thing to remember.'

6 Battleground

John James Ingalls, United States senator from Kansas in the 1870s, left few memorable utterances on the politics of his time. But in an address published in the *Kansas Magazine* he had a thing or two to say about grassland.

> Grass is the forgiveness of nature – her constant benediction. Fields trampled with battle, saturated with blood, torn with the ruts of cannon, grow green again with grass, and carnage is forgotten. Streets abandoned by traffic become grass-grown like rural lanes and are obliterated . . . It invades the solitude of deserts, climbs the inaccessible slopes and forbidding pinnacles of mountains, modifies climates and determines the history, character and destiny of nations.

The senator's vivid prose was penned in celebration of bluegrass, which dominated the ranges and pastures of his home state. The object of his praise was not a native species but a refugee from the Old World, an émigré from Britain where it is known as rough-stalked meadow grass. The early colonists brought it over in their seed mixtures, then discovered that it thrived in the local conditions.

But the senator's 'benediction of nature' is seldom the gift of any one species. Grasses rarely thrive as isolated plants. They are destined for life in community, growing in densely packed swards in company with other species, both grasses and non-grass plants. It is not so much the grasses as *grasslands* that deck a quarter of the earth's land surface in green. It is grassland that reclaims the shell-pocked battlefield and the wheel-rutted farm lane; grassland that transforms the muddy square of earth into the stud-firm soccer surface; grassland that turns a dreary back yard into a magical playground for toddlers.

In temperate regions grasslands are never a natural habitat. Left to themselves they would soon be overcome by forest from which they have escaped. They are entirely the creation of animals, fashioned by grinding molars of herbivores or the whirling blades of the mower that mimics them. Under this harsh treatment grasses appear to lose their individual identities. It is as if they are subsumed into the greater organism which is the meadow, lawn or sports pitch. The green sward takes on a personality of its own.

The turf-forming grasses produce clusters of shoots or tillers from the base of the plant half hidden at the soil surface. These tillers sprout new leaves and send down additional roots. As foliage is stripped away by grazing animals or the mower, replacement tillers appear at the plant base. But instead of expanding upwards they grow out laterally, staying close to the ground. The plant has responded to constant mowing or grazing by changing its shape, or growth habit.

The tightly packed plants develop a dense mat of intertwined shoots just above the soil surface. Below ground the mass of fibrous roots from neighbouring plants merge to form a fine, tangled mesh just below the surface. Together the above-ground mat and the below-ground root mesh form the characteristic 'turf' of the grazed pasture and closely tended lawn or sports field. In mature grassland this surface is tough and resilient, well able to withstand the skidding boot and the stomping hoof.

Many common turf grasses – including the fine-leaved brown top, *Agrostis tenuis*; creeping fescue, *Festuca rubra* subsp. *rubra*; and the meadow grasses *Poa pratensis* and *Poa trivialis* – send out runners or stolons, or underground shoots, or rhizomes. At regular intervals these horizontal 'stems' throw up clusters of new tillers and put down fresh, fibrous roots. In this way the ground is colonised by a new generation of plants, each one a clone of the parent. Successful plants are able to expand their territory and extend their influence on the wider turf.

In mature grassland ageing tillers are constantly dying just as new, replacement tillers are sprouting and growing. Eventually the turf ceases to function as a collection of independent plants. It looks and acts like a single organism – an amorphous mass of tillers and leaves, some related to their neighbours, some not. Like the citizens of a collective state, individual plants lose their separate identities and become anonymous units of the great turf. It is the dream of green keepers and lawn enthusiasts everywhere – the perfect surface; homogenous, even, durable.

When grassland is treated in a consistent way over a long period, plants can survive almost indefinitely through cloning. Classic experiments carried out on hill grazings in northern England – grazings that had never been ploughed in all history – showed that natural clones of red fescue can spread over great distances and survive as a genotype for hundreds of years.[1] Like the giant Californian redwoods, a clutch of grass tillers growing in an ancient hay meadow may contain a thousand years of history in the genes.

Another group of grasses has found a rather different method of securing immortality. These are not subsumed into the turf: they stand apart from it. Known as tussock or *caespitose* grasses, they are able to build long-running dynasties while remaining close to their place of origin. Unlike the turf-forming grasses they develop no creeping stolons or rhizomes. Instead new 'families' of tillers develop inside the encompassing leaves of the established plant.

Under this protection they put down their own roots and eventually form a new generation of plants clustered around the parent. As the 'family group' expands outwards, so the diameter of the tussock increases. Eventually a 'hollow crown' is formed at the centre with a circle of thriving plants gathered around it, each genetically identical to the parent. Like a village community the tussock grows slowly. The process takes about sixty years for tufted hair-grass, *Deschampsia caespitosa*. In other species it may be even longer.[2]

The leaves and stems of caespitose grasses are usually coarser and tougher than those of the turf-forming grasses. This makes them slower to decompose as the old tillers die and new ones replace them. Decaying vegetation accumulates between tillers so that the tussock begins to project upwards as well as outwards, eventually rising several inches above the surrounding soil surface in a form of monumental architecture that does not go down well with ground keepers.

Like a powerful business empire the ageing tussock exerts a growing influence on the surrounding area. It begins to gather and monopolise nutrients within the soil, denying them to potential competitors. While the tussock grasses have no underground rhizomes in which to store essential elements, they manage somehow to accumulate and hold them in the soil surrounding their roots. Plant scientists have found far higher concentrations of nitrogen and organic carbon below the roots of caespitose grasses than in the soil between them.[3] They tie up essential raw materials so they are no longer available to other plants seeking to colonise the area.

In the community of turf-forming grasses the competition between species is intense. A sown stretch of grassland – lawn, sports pitch or pasture – will contain only a limited number of grasses, all of them slugging it out for space. An intensive grass ley, sown and managed for silage or grazing, may contain just one species – perennial ryegrass, *Lolium perenne*. The British Isles are home to around 160 different grass species, either indigenous or naturalised. But the numbers that will thrive on any one site are strictly limited.

Every grass species is adapted to a particular set of soil and climatic conditions. A site that fails to provide those conditions will not keep the species for long. An acid soil is unlikely to support a turf containing lime-loving 'calcareous' grasses. A boggy site will seldom attract those grasses which 'like to keep their feet dry'.

The more fertile the soil, the fewer the species it is likely to contain. Highly fertile soils are quickly dominated by a few aggressive species, particularly perennial ryegrass and cocksfoot, *Dactylis glomerata*. Most farmers spread their grasslands with artificial fertilisers encouraging these fast-growing species to take over. But where fertility is low, as on the thin chalk soils of the southern downland, the aggressive grasses have no opportunity to smother their neighbours with their flamboyant growth. A greater number of grasses and other plants are able to survive, as the nature writer W. H. Hudson observed a century ago.

This turf is composed of small grasses and clovers mixed with a great variety of creeping herbs, some exceedingly small. In a space of one square foot of ground, a dozen or twenty or more species of plants may be counted, and on turning up a piece of turf the unnumerable fibrous interwoven roots have the appearance of coconut matting. It is indeed this thick layer of interlaced fibres that gives the turf its springiness, and makes it so delightful to walk upon.

In every stretch of grassland, from the suburban lawn to the endless, rolling prairie, each member plant is constantly striving to expand its territory, to occupy a little more space at the expense of its neighbours. Above the ground leaves jostle for supremacy, for their place in the sun as the miniature forest of vegetation grows ever more dense. Below ground the struggle is even fiercer with neighbours frenetically putting out adventitious roots in a bid to grab the lion's share of moisture and soil nutrients.

Yet for all their jousting and manoeuvring, the plants making up a turf will eventually arrive at a truce. In mature grassland – an old meadow, a rugby pitch, a churchyard or a village green – the members have grown to tolerate each other. Each will have found its own individual niche, one that differs marginally from those of its neighbours. Its roots may be drawing soil minerals from a slightly greater depth, or the odd arrangement of its leaves may enable it to trap sunlight without shading from the plants on either side. Though competition continues, it is at a relatively low level. The turf will have taken on its own distinctive personality.

Plant ecologists classify grasslands according to their dominant or characteristic species. No system can be wholly accurate since every turf has its own unique combination of plants. Nor can the botanical make-up be more than just a momentary snapshot of a scene that is in constant flux. The struggle for survival continues. Every day there are winners and losers. Even so it is possible to identify broad types of grassland which have their own characteristic species.

Those growing on soils formed from a parent rock of chalk or limestone are known as calcareous grasslands. Not surprisingly their residents are the calcium-loving species or *calcicoles* (from the Latin *calx*, meaning chalk, and *colo*, to inhabit). Among calcareous grasslands are the species-rich swards of the southern chalkland, some dominated by the hardy sheep's fescue, *Festuca ovina*, and meadow oatgrass, *Avenula pratensis*.

Other downland swards have the fibrous upright brome, *Bromus erectus*, or the unpalatable tor grass, *Brachypodium pinnatum*, as their indicator species. But while these key plants are common, dozens of others – both grasses and herbs – share this sparse environment. In summer a host of bright flowerheads tremble in the gentle breeze – kidney vetch, *Anthyllis vulneraria*; common rockrose, *Helianthemum nummularium*; the purple clustered bellflower, *Campanula glomerata*; small scabious, *Scabiosa columbaria*, and pale fairy flax, *Linum catharticum*.

Grazed hard by sheep or rabbits, these are Hudson's springy turves, 'so delightful to walk upon'. They were the haunt of Richard Jefferies, another observer of the southern downland, who wrote 'the air came softly up from the wheat below, the tips of the grasses swayed as it passed sighing faintly; it ceased, and the bees hummed by to the thyme and heathbells'.[4]

On the Carboniferous limestone of Derbyshire, Yorkshire and Cumbria the grasslands are characterised by blue moorgrass, *Sesleria albicans*, with its short, slender rhizomes, and the prostrate form of slender bedstraw, *Galium sterneri*. This is the land of wild thyme, *Thymus praecox*, rockrose, *Helianthemum chamaecistus*, lady's bedstraw, *Galium verum*, and eyebright, *Euphrasia nemorosa*, with its delicate, two-lipped flowers.

In the Cotswolds Jurassic limestone produces grasslands characterised by the two grasses upright brome and tor grass growing together. In an earlier time H. J. Massingham wrote of the Cotswolds that 'everywhere, ahead, behind, by the sides of the track and climbing the northern slopes, the innumerable company of grasses sways and sibilates its responses to the chant of the wind'.[5]

Acid grasslands, with their *calcifugous* or lime-hating plants, are often thought to be poorer in their species content than calcareous grasslands. In fact they may have as many or more species per square metre as the most valued chalk grassland.

On light soils in dry, lowland areas acidic pastures are often dominated by sheep's fescue and common bentgrass, *Agrostis capillaris*, along with the wild herb sheep's sorrel, *Rumex acetosella*, with its rust-coloured flowers and arrow-shaped basal leaves. It is these three species which characterise many grasslands of the Norfolk brecklands, Britain's richest surviving reserve of flower-rich acid meadows and pastures. They are also characteristic of the open heath grasslands of parts of the New Forest.

In wetter areas acid grassland is dominated by the graceful wavy hair-grass, *Deschampsia flexuosa*, the tussocky perennial with its slender, spreading flowerhead carrying the shining purple or silver spikelets. This beautiful grass is characteristic of acid soils in heathland and moorland areas, often growing in close proximity to purple flowering heather, *Calluna vulgaris*, both in the hills and lowlands. The last major grassland type of acid soils is found mostly in upland areas of northern and western Britain and is characterised by a trio of species – sheep's fescue, common bentgrass and the mat-forming heath bedstraw, *Galium saxatile*, with its spear-shaped leaves and delicate white flowers.

Despite their ill-deserved reputation for being species-poor, acid grasslands harbour a large number of rare or scarce grasses and wildflowers, including the tufted grey hair-grass, *Corynepho-rus canescens*; wild gladiolus, *Gladiolus illyricus*, with its startling crimson flowers; the oddly named smooth rupture-wort, *Herniaria glabra*; breckland thyme, *Thymus serpyllum*; the prostrate perennial knawel, *Scleranthus perennis prostratus*, and the delicate, blue-flowered spring speedwell, *Veronica verna*, found locally in East Anglia.

Neutral or *mesotrophic* grasslands – those on soils that are neither acid nor lime-rich – include the classic, flower-rich hay meadows of lowland England. Dominated by the grass crested dogstail, *Cynosurus cristatus*, and the perennial common knap-weed, *Centaurea nigra*, with its striking purple flowers, the traditional hay meadow is home to many of Britain's most beautiful and treasured wild flowers. Among them are the bright yellow rattle, *Rhinanthus minor*; dyer's greenweed, *Genista tinctoria*; the tall-standing common meadow rue, *Thalictrum flavum*; meadow saxifrage, *Saxifraga granulata*, throwing up its clusters of white summer flowers, and the exquisite snake's head fritillary, *Fritillaria meleagris*, hanging its purple lantern head over the spring sward.

The flower-rich hay meadow is a masterpiece of the pastoral arts. Like the great cathedrals, its construction has taken a century or more. Like them it is the handiwork of generations of unknown crafts people – the shepherds and stockmen who grazed the autumn growth, knowing exactly when to bring on the animals and when to take them off again; the scythesmen who laboured in the summer heat to harvest the sunlight locked up in the sugars of fresh, green leaves; the army of women who raked and turned the drying foliage, finally pitching it high on to the harvest wagon.

Richard Mabey encountered his first traditional hay meadow on a dull day in north Oxfordshire. He was surprised by the vividness of 'this brilliant field lapped with layers of colour and movement – yellow hay-rattle, red betony, purple knapweeds and orchids, the swaying cream umbels of pepper-saxifrage, and butterflies so dense and vibrant above the flowers that it was hard to tell them from the heat-haze'.[6]

In northern England the neutral hay meadows, which are

concentrated in the valley grasslands and river banks of the Pennine dales of Swaledale, Wharfedale and Teesdale, have their own special glory. Here the dominant grass is the early flowering sweet vernal grass, *Anthoxanthum odoratum*, whose dried leaves impart the smell of new-mown hay to a winter cattle yard. Wood crane's-bill, *Geranium sylvaticum*, with its lobed leaves and purple flowers is the second characteristic species.

Like the southern hay meadows, those of the north have their own particular floral gems. Among them are the powerfully aromatic perennial spignel, *Meum athamanticum*, and a trio of rarer variants of the common lady's-mantle, *Alchemilla vulgaris*, with its small yellow-green flowers.

Neutral grasslands subjected to seasonal flooding take on a wholly different but equally vibrant character. Here the dominant species are the early-flowering grass meadow foxtail, *Alopecurus pratensis*, and great burnet, *Sanguisorba officinalis*, with its tight, egg-shaped flowerhead. Damp, alluvial meadows also support a profusion of characteristic wild flowers including ragged robin, *Lychnis flos-cuculi*; the charming, pink veined bog pimpernel, *Anagallis tenella*; marsh valerian, *Valerian dioica*; the rare narrow-leaved water-dropwort, *Oenanthe silaifolia*, and the snake's head fritillary.

Traditionally managed grasslands with their characteristic groupings of flowers and grasses are bright jewels of the landscape, places of colour and life, places that celebrate the sheer exuberance of nature. They are also becoming increasingly scarce. Most of Britain's grasslands are no longer classified as species-rich plant communities. They have been agriculturally 'improved'. They now belong to the vast group of grasslands that are dominated by that Attila of the grass kingdom, perennial ryegrass, either on its own or in association with that other warlord of the fertile soils, crested dog's-tail.

Intensive agriculture has taken a heavy toll of Britain's glorious pastoral inheritance. The plough, the crop sprayer, land drains and the fertiliser spreader have each played a part in the destruction of species-rich grasslands. Over the past half century or so these have disappeared at a faster rate than tropical rainforests.[7] By 1984 the total area of unimproved grassland in England and Wales was estimated at just 3 per cent of the area it occupied in 1930.[8] And the destruction has continued.

Worcestershire, a county once rich in traditional hay meadows, lost more than one-third of them during the 1980s, with a further one-third being subject to severe damage.[9] Dorset lost 60 per cent of its species-rich neutral grasslands over a six-year period in the mid 1980s,[10] while a 1995 survey of neutral grasslands in Berkshire showed that half had been damaged or destroyed during the previous decade.[11]

England now possesses less than 20,000 hectares of botanically rich neutral grassland, most of it dispersed in tiny pockets of less than twenty hectares.[12] Flood plain meadows, including those which support the last surviving colonies of such rare treasures as the snake's head fritillary, occupy less than 1,500 hectares of the English lowlands. Chalk and limestone grasslands are slightly more plentiful, with a little under 40,000 hectares, though they remain a rare habitat. The extent of species-rich acid grassland is estimated at between 10,000 and 20,000 hectares, making it an even more scarce resource.

The plant communities that make up grasslands, particularly those of high species diversity – the flower-strewn meadows of popular imagination – are precarious associations. They have grown up over centuries in response to a host of environmental conditions – the type of soil and parent rock, the aspect of the site, the height and fluctuation of the water table. They are also heavily influenced by the activities of people.

Grasslands are semi-natural ecosystems – they cannot survive without the intervention of grazing animals, usually under the control of humans. Grasslands are in a state of flux. Small and localised changes in soil acidity or the height of the water table will enable some species to gain ground at the expense of others. But so long as the changes are slow and contained, the overall character of the community is unlikely to be drastically altered. The damp, alluvial meadow continues to produce its annual crop of snake's head fritillaries while it remains damp and alluvial.

The human input must stay constant, too. The alluvial

meadow is species-rich only because its year-round management has been constant over generations. Each year the
meadow is shut up for hay in mid February and mowed
sometime in July. Once the hay has been carted off the meadow
is opened up for grazing. On 'lammas land' the grazing might
well begin on old Lammas Day, 12 August. It is this time-
honoured pattern of management as much as the constancy of
the water table movement that keeps the familiar flowers of the
meadow appearing at their allotted time.

But any change in conditions will set off a new round of
Darwinian struggle and conflict within the grassland ecosystem.
It may be the result of climatic change: perhaps a run of wet
seasons leading to local waterlogging in a dry meadow. Or the
surface of a pasture may be 'poached' by a period of intensive
physical wear – perhaps the hoofs of grazing animals churning
up the sodden turf after a prolonged period of rain. More
commonly there may be an abrupt and catastrophic change in
the level of fertility as the farmer applies a heavy dressing of
nitrogen fertiliser.

Whatever the nature of the disturbance the old order is upset,
the established hierarchy is undermined. Suddenly there are new
opportunities to ascend the pecking order. Grasses and other
plants that have barely hung on in the sward may now increase
in number. 'Invading' species, their seeds blown in from
elsewhere, may have a chance to germinate and gain a foothold
in this once-hostile territory.

The botanical make-up of the grassland turf will alter. The
changes may be small and subtle. Or they may transform the turf
beyond recognition. This has been the fate of Britain's
twentieth-century inheritance of unimproved grasslands. At the
turn of the century flower-filled meadows flourished across the
countryside. By the end of it they survived as a handful of
scattered remnants, secreted away in nature reserves like
museum pieces, a reminder of a glorious past. And the chief
cause of their destruction has been the bag of chemical fertiliser.

In 1856 John Bennet Lawes, a Hertfordshire landowner and
manufacturer of fertilisers, enlisted the help of the scientist
Joseph Henry Gilbert in setting up an experiment on the

manuring of grassland. Their aim was to find out how chemical fertilisers and organic manures could change the productivity of a hay meadow. They divided the meadow into plots and applied a range of fertiliser treatments to each of them, carefully recording the hay yield. But changes to the species composition of the grassland were so dramatic that the two researchers concluded that the experiment was of greater interest to 'the botanist, vegetable physiologist, and the chemist than to the farmer'.[13]

The experiment, now known as the Park Grass Experiment, still continues today at Rothamsted experimental station, making it the longest-running ecological study in history. The results over almost a century and a half mirror the changes that have taken place throughout pastoral Britain.

In general the greater the output from a given fertiliser treatment, the lower the species diversity – the number of species in the sward.[14] Fertiliser nitrogen was particularly damaging. Only plots receiving nitrogen at the lowest level continued to display the floral diversity of the original meadow.[15] Plots receiving artificial nitrogen at higher levels quickly assumed the monotonous characteristics of the modern perennial ryegrass monoculture.

Lawes and Gilbert's classic experiment graphically demonstrates how chemical fertilisers strip wild flowers from the meadow. No less than 85 per cent of grassland now receives nitrogen fertiliser at an average rate of 160kg of nitrogen per hectare each year,[16] more than enough to knock out most meadow flowers. This is why the grasslands of Britain, while remaining green enough, are seldom speckled with the bright flowers of summer.

Across the length and breadth of the country 'improved' pastures are dominated by the same two species – perennial ryegrass and crested dog's-tail. This is the bog-standard production turf that underpins modern livestock farming, the engine that drives the pastoral economy. It may have started as an alluvial pasture in the valley of a northern river or as a species-rich hay meadow on the clay lands of Buckinghamshire or Northants. But following a dressing or two of a compound fertiliser containing the three major plant nutrients – nitrogen, phosphate and potash – it has adopted the same dull guise of 'everyturf'. It does its job admirably, exploiting the raised fertility to grow more leaf and so intercept the sunlight more efficiently, thus increasing the biomass. It grows more beef and puts milk in the bulk tank far faster than the traditional, mixed-species turf. But compared with the life and vibrancy of the flower-strewn meadow, it is a bland and lacklustre thing.

The very existence of species-rich plant communities is something of a scientific conundrum. At first sight Darwinism would seem to rule out the possibility. Under a given set of conditions the component species of a meadow, a fine lawn or a sports turf might be expected to compete for share of available resources – mineral nutrients, water, light, carbon dioxide – so that successful species would come to dominate and finally replace the poorer competitors. Darwinism ought to produce monocultures. And yet it seldom does.

Single-species vegetation almost never occurs in nature. Even in fertile sites at least a handful of species manage to co-exist. On the thin, hungry soils of a chalk downland a square metre of turf may contain a hundred or more species, each maintaining its place in the sun over years, perhaps even over centuries.

Plant ecologist Professor Philip Grime of Sheffield University has refined a theory to explain why plant communities – including grasslands – take the forms they do. They are the result of a series of 'strategies' adopted by the individual plant species to deal with the three main forces acting upon them – competition, stress and disturbance.[17]

Competition takes place between neighbouring plants as they try to capture the same units of light, nutrients, water and ground space. When allowed to produce a result, this battle for scarce resources would, in true Darwinian manner, determine the composition of the sward. In theory, at least, the habitat should become occupied by a single species, even by a single plant. But such unbridled competition never takes place. There are two other forces helping to shape the final outcome.

First, the physical environment imposes stress on plants. This may take the form of shortages – of water, nutrients or light, through shading. Or it may be caused by low temperatures or the presence of soil toxins. At the same time physical damage to the vegetation produces disturbance. This may be due to grazing animals, plant pests or diseases, or to such human assaults as trampling, mowing, scuffing and cutting up divots.

Together stress and disturbance intervene to end competition before it can produce a result. It is as if the floodlights failed at a soccer match, or the pitch was rocked by an earthquake. On an impoverished downland soil, the stress imposed by a general shortage of plant nutrients limits the competition and stops any aggressive species becoming dominant. The turf retains its rich mixture of slow-growing grasses, herbs and flowering plants.

On a heavily fertilised meadow the stress of nutrient shortage has been eliminated, and as a consequence competition between neighbouring plants is fierce. A vigorous, fast-growing species like perennial ryegrass has the resources it needs to increase biomass and dominate the sward, crowding out less competitive species. Farmers like their grasslands to be productive. But in the natural world productivity and species richness are rarely compatible, so flower-filled meadows vanish from the land-scape.

Evolution has equipped the flowering plants with a range of mechanisms for dealing with the forces that act upon them. Philip Grime suggests three main *strategies*, each with a particular set of character traits. Plants exploiting habitats that are regularly subject to disturbance are known as *ruderals*. They are characterised by rapid life-cycles, with high growth rates at the seedling stage and an early onset of flowering. Their seeds mature quickly and are given a high priority for plant nutrients, even when the parents are suffering from a shortage.

This emphasis on reproduction makes the ruderals remarkably adept at colonising disturbed land. They are short-lived, ephemeral, the risk-takers of the plant world, staking everything on the chance to occupy a disrupted habitat. They include a string of hated arable weeds – mayweed, *Matricaria matricarioides*; chickweed, *Stellaria media*; knotgrass, *Polygonum aviculare*, and groundsel, *Senecio vulgaris*, plants with an almost legendary talent for taking over bare land. Among grasses with a talent for carving out new territory is the ubiquitous annual meadow grass. With its short generation interval and habit for frequent flowering, it quickly builds up a stock of durable seeds in the soil 'bank', an ideal base from which to launch an invasion.

However, the ruderals are markedly less successful at establishing themselves on undisturbed habitats. By channelling all their energies into producing flowers and seeds they are rarely able to develop the extensive root and shoot systems needed to thrive in productive, stable habitats.

The lords of undisturbed land are the group known as *competitors*. Given fertile soils and stable habitats, these high flyers of the plant kingdom are able to build mighty empires. Frequently growing tall, they quickly spread outwards both above and below ground, securing for themselves an ever bigger share of the available resources. In Britain the most aggressive competitors include the fast-growing rosebay willow-herb, *Chamerion angustifolium*, and stinging nettle, *Urtica dioica*. But when these taller herbs are removed there are a clutch of grasses to take on the mantle – perennial ryegrass; cocksfoot, *Dactylis glomerata*; tor grass, *Brachypodium pinnatum*, and common bent, *Agrostis tenuis*.

Competitors are the big players, the species equivalent of the FTSE top one hundred companies, dedicated to the job of monopolising whatever resources are going. These are active foragers, constantly replacing their leaves and fine roots to recreate their above-ground and below-ground architecture so as to capture more of the available light and soil nutrients. In energy terms it is a costly life style. Maintaining a sizeable empire can mean delaying seed production, so this group are not the fastest at snatching opportunities offered by ground disturbance. But while resources remain plentiful these are the plants that corner the market.

Finally there are *stress-tolerators*, plants adapted to habitats where the essentials of life – light, water and nutrients – are in short supply, or where growing conditions are tough. Competitors would not do well here. But however hostile the environment there are plants adapted to survive, even thrive. On lime-rich soils cowslip, *Primula veris*; crested hairgrass,

Koeleria macrantha, and the beautiful quaking grass, *Briza media*, are characteristic stress-tolerators, while on acid soils well-adapted species include the mat-forming heath rush, *Juncus squarrosus*, and mat grass, *Nardus stricta*, with its wiry, grey-green leaves and flowerhead, a one-sided spike.

These plants are slow-growing and persistent, the dogged tortoises of the ecosystem rather than the flamboyant hares. Their particular skills lie in gathering nutrients from soils where they are in short supply, and then hanging on to them at all costs. Unlike the competitors they take time to produce new leaves and shoots. But having acquired them they keep them for a long time.

The foliage of stress-tolerators is sometimes spiked with silica or laced with toxic alkaloids, making them unappetising to grazers from sheep to leaf beetles. In fertile environments they are quickly outstripped by the more aggressive competitors with their constantly changing leaf architecture and foraging root systems. But where the pickings are meagre it is the competitors that go under and the stress-tolerators that survive.

In every patch of grassland, from the hillside pasture to the inner-city recreation ground, the three groups of plants are slugging it out for dominance. Where the soil is poor or the grass heavily shaded by trees or high buildings, stress-tolerant species are likely to reign supreme. In areas of intense disturbance – around the goal-mouth of a soccer pitch or on the bowler's run-up to the wicket – the ruderals have the best chance of flourishing. And in those favoured areas where fertility is high and disturbance minimal, the competitive species have a field day.

In practice few species can be said to belong wholly to one or other group. Most plants share characteristics of all three functional types. Their relative proportions will give each species its own particular strengths. A plant may be highly competitive yet have a level of stress tolerance built in. Another might be adapted for colonising disturbed land while remaining competitive enough to benefit from fertile conditions.

In every turf the same tussle is taking place. The challenge of lawn owners, ground-keepers and farmers is to understand the ecology of grasslands, the endless drama of the Poaceae played out on a brown earth stage in the bright glare of sunlight. They must know their characters – the leading actors, the supporting roles, the bit players and the extras. And they must devise a plot that will bring out the star performers.

When the aim is a velvet turf that is smooth and even – a bowling green, cricket square or the classical ornamental lawn – the stars are likely to be those grasses that produce a dense mat of leaf close to the ground surface, principally the bents and the fescues. They include species like red fescue, *Festuca rubra*; chewings fescue, *Festuca nigrescens*; common bent or browntop, *Agrostis capillaris*, and creeping bent, *Agrostis stolonifera*, fine-leaved species from among those farmers used to call 'bottom grasses', the ones that remain leafy close to the soil.

To make sure they flourish the gardener or green-keeper must keep the fertility high. Fine-leaved varieties like these need to replace damaged tissue quickly or the smooth, dense surface will be lost. Frequent close mowing is another management essential if the sward is not to be taken over by coarser, competitive species such as perennial ryegrass or crested dog's-tail.

In the first half of the twentieth century farmers would include a number of fine-leaved species in their grazing mixtures. Their aim was to give the pasture 'bottom', strengthening it with a thick mat of leafy growth at the base. This made it tougher, harder wearing and less susceptible to damage by treading hoofs. Nowadays production is all that matters. And when it comes to production, that supreme competitor perennial ryegrass knows no equal.

Under conditions of high fertility perennial ryegrass is unmatched in its ability to push out fresh foliage and forage ever further with its hungry root system. Grazing cattle may crush it with their hoofs and tear away leaves with their tongues. The chomping jaws of sheep may slice off the top growth at ground level. Yet as long as the soil remains fertile this flamboyant grass will keep growing back, throwing up new foliage, shading out poorer competitors, and capturing an ever greater share of whatever soil nutrients are going.

In the sports world perennial ryegrass is also the choice of groundkeepers looking after pitches for the great winter-season games. No grass is better adapted to absorb punishment and recover fast. But even champions have their limits. When a divot is physically gouged out by a sliding boot or flailing hoof to leave a patch of bare, exposed soil, the unrivalled growth and repair capacity of the grass is of little use. In the jargon of ecologists the site has been severely disturbed. And in the wings an audacious understudy is waiting to upstage the star.

Annual meadowgrass is the opportunist *par excellence*. Its seeds lie dormant in soils everywhere, waiting for the moment to strike. Bare soil provides the trigger. In sunlight it warms up quicker than the foliage around it, producing a temperature gradient which is the signal for germination. The seed springs back to life pushing out an embryonic first root, the radicle, and a shoot, the coleoptile.

Within weeks the meadowgrass plant has completed its life-cycle, scattering a new generation of seeds on to the turf. There they will lie, perhaps for years, like a terrorist cell that has gone to ground, patiently awaiting a new moment to strike.

Where there is little physical disturbance a competitive species like perennial ryegrass holds sway. But where there is physical damage there comes an opening. At that moment the advantage swings from the great competitor to the accomplished exploiter of disturbed habitats, the *ruderal*. While change spells disaster for some species, it opens up undreamt-of opportunities for others.

In the unfolding drama of grassland the part played by humankind is pivotal. The plants in the sward may battle it out for supremacy, each mobilising its own adaptations and attributes to take advantage of some aspect of the environment. But it is the actions of gardeners, groundkeepers and farmers which set the rules of the game. They are the manipulators of the action, the storyliners of the drama.

In a species-rich, lowland grassland it may be the dryness and neutral, non-acid condition of the soil which determines the potential cast list. But it is the farmer's decision to graze it with cattle and sheep that decides who the winners and losers will be.

It is grazing that allows the low-growing perennials autumn hawkbit, *Leontodon autumnalis*, and creeping jenny, *Lysimachia nummularia*, to thrive; grazing which prevents the more competitive grasses crested dog's-tail and Yorkshire fog, *Holcus lanatus*, from becoming so rampant that they crowd out everything else.

In damp fen meadows it is grazing that prevents the tussock-forming purple moor-grass, *Molinia caerulea*, from overwhelming the delicate carnation sedge, *Carex panicea*, and glaucous sedge, *Carex flacca*. Grazing animals can get their tongues round and teeth into the upright grasses more easily than the low-growing species, so they harvest a greater proportion of the dry matter they produce. Thanks to the intervention of the farmer the species balance is shifted, and more species survive in the pasture. This is why mowing for hay or grazing with livestock is essential to the maintenance of flower-rich grassland.

Fields, lawns and grassy places are proving grounds for the plant kingdom, with individual species nudging and jostling for some competitive advantage. It is a game gardeners and groundkeepers know well. Though they seldom achieve exactly the turf they want, the clever operators manage to turn the game their way.

7 *The Endless Plain*

When the early American settlers pushed westwards in their bid to tame the continent they were pulled up short by the boundless ocean of grass at its heart. Nothing in their culture or experience had prepared them for this.

For two hundred years their forebears had grazed their cattle on the stream-side pastures and woodland clearings of New England. Later they had driven through the Allegheny Mountains carving farms out of the forest as their ancestors had done on the Atlantic coast.

They had established range beef enterprises on the western edge of the Virginia settlements and south across the Appalachians on the upland pastures of the Piedmont, marketing the finished cattle in Charleston and even as far away as Baltimore and New York. By the end of the eighteenth century they had occupied the small grass prairies of Ohio and Indiana, at least those that were close to the rivers. And they had begun to settle the grasslands and clearings of the oak forests of Michigan, Wisconsin and Illinois.

But confronted by the real prairies they paused. For a people whose lives had been framed by forests and woodlands this seemingly endless expanse of open grassland was disturbing. How was a living to be made in a landscape of nodding flowerheads and harsh, relentless winds?

Trees were an integral part of the pioneer economy, providing timber for cabins and furniture, game as a prime source of meat, and shelter from the fierce winter storms. What future could there be on land too poor and arid even to grow trees? On their early maps the settlers labelled it 'The Great American Desert', and for a while they backed off.

Thomas J. Farnham, a lawyer from Vermont, travelled from Illinois to Oregon in 1839. He later wrote of the plains region that it was 'burnt and a desert, whose solemn stillness is seldom broken by the tread of any other animal than the wolf or the starved and thirsty horse which bears the traveler across its wastes'.[1]

But this was not a desert. In the continent's arid heartland the forces of sun, wind and fire had combined to create an assemblage of plants which made these open lands a powerhouse of life. Over thousands of years evolution had honed this dry grassland into a vast engine of increase, capturing the random energy of the sun and sending it coursing through the myriad creatures of the plain – elk and pronghorn; prairie dog, grey wolf and grizzly bear; mountain plover and peregrine falcon.

Most impressive of all were the herds of bison, the great monarchs of the prairie. In the 1860s, before the white settlers arrived, there were an estimated sixty million roaming the plains, shaking the earth with their thunderous hooves and scoring deep paths in the earth as they followed their traditional migration routes.

When one of the bigger herds was on the move a rider on horseback might take days to pass or intersect the animal tide. The writer Mari Sandoz retells the experience of Colonel Richard I. Dodge near Fort Dodge – later Dodge City – in Kansas.

At least twenty-five of the thirty-four miles were through one immense dark blanket of buffaloes – countless smaller bunches come together for their journey north. From the top of Pawnee Rock, Dodge could see six to ten miles in most directions, all one solid mass of moving animals. Others who saw the herd reported that it was twenty-five miles wide and took five days to pass a given point – probably fifty miles deep. Dodge estimated that there were about four hundred eighty thousand in the one herd: perhaps a half million that he saw himself on that single day. With those that others observed beyond Dodge's sight but still of the same herd, it was estimated at from four million to twelve million counting fifteen head per acre for the former number. This was the great southern herd.[2]

The American pioneers overcame their prairie phobia. With inducements from the federal government the 'homesteaders' moved on to the plains, gouging out the deep turf to build their sod houses. With the settlers came the railroad companies, their trains bringing sharp-shooters to slaughter the bison and carrying away the skins and tongues to booming markets back east.

With the new steel ploughs – courtesy of the John Deere Company – the prairie farmers began tearing apart the work of a thousand years of sun and fire, planting the cleared land with corn and wheat. In a little more than fifty years it was all over. The great American grassland, which had been sustained by fire, died in a billowing, black cloud that rolled across the nation's heartland turning day into night and bringing traffic to a halt.

The 'smoke' was prairie soil swept away in the dust bowl winds of the 1930s. In March 1935, the geology department at the University of Wichita recorded five million tons of dust suspended over thirty square miles of the city.[3] The huge cloud darkened the streets of Washington D.C. just as Congress began to consider setting up a soil conservation service.

Before the arrival of Europeans the great American grassland stretched in a continuous garment from the forest edge of Alberta and Saskatchewan in Canada to the Gulf Coast of south-east Texas; from the foothills of the Rockies to the middle west plains of Illinois and western Indiana, pushing slim fingers into the dark woodlands of Ohio.

It was a biological powerhouse, rich in wildlife and with a productivity no modern farming system could match. Yet Americans waged a ceaseless war on this priceless asset, and now it has all but disappeared, its life snatched by the quick cut of steel or slowly sapped by overgrazing. Today the original prairie grassland survives in a few tattered remnants preserved as curiosities in nature parks and cemeteries, a painful reminder of past glories. John Ernest Weaver laments its passing.

So gradually has the prairie been conquered by the breaking plow, the tractor, and the overcrowded herds of man, and so intent has he been upon securing from the soil its last measure of innate fertility, that scant attention has been given to the significance of this endless grassland or the course of its destruction. Civilised man is destroying a masterpiece of nature without recording for posterity that which he has destroyed.[4]

Prairies, like all grasslands, bear the strong imprint of place. The community of grasses and plants that make up any patch of turf are there because of the soil and topography, the climate and the hydrology. Its botanical composition is as revealing as the flavours of a vintage wine.

The character of prairie grassland is shaped largely by the Rockies, the multiple waves of mountain peaks that stretch from Canada through the western states of Montana and Wyoming down to Colorado and New Mexico. It was the uplifting of the Rockies sixty million years ago that formed the great plain and determined the kind of vegetation which would grow there.

At that time the mid continent was occupied by a shallow inland sea. But the forces that threw up the mountains created a gentle east-to-west slope over 800 miles causing the water to drain slowly into the Mississippi valley. On to the drying surface came a steady stream of sediment, washed out from the mountains over numberless millennia. Mixed with rubble from continental glaciers together with *loess*, a wind-borne dust of silt, sand and clay, it was to form the deep prairie soil.

The mountain ranges also changed the climate. Their high peaks blocked the flow of moist air from the Pacific, creating a vast rain shadow across America's heartland. Arid conditions favour the dominance of grassland over forest. All was now in place for the emergence of a vast empire of grass.

While the Rockies gave birth to the prairies it was fire that nurtured and sustained them. Lightning bolts from the rumbling summer storms frequently set the grasses ablaze, leaving the prairie winds to chase flames across the open plain, sometimes for hundreds of miles. Fire posed no threat to the grasses. With their active growing points held close to the soil surface they were unharmed by the burning kiss as it passed by on its journey of judgment. But shrubby species perished leaving the grasses to rebuild their leafy canopy unchallenged.

Across the millennia fire visited every part of the prairie grasslands at least once each decade, rejuvenating the grasses and changing the botanical make-up of the turf. Long before the white settlers came, native Americans were using the 'red buffalo' for their own purposes.

According to William Least Heat-Moon they

used it as a white man would plow to bring forth sweet and nutritious new grasses, or as a scythe to open up a route over the prairie, or as a horse to dislodge deer or drive bison for harvesting, or as a cake of salt to draw the beasts within arrow range, or as a telegraph to send a message with smoking grasses. Indians, recognising the bond between flame and prairie, seemed to understand in a symbolic way how fire shaped the grasses and plants, how a green beauty rose and evolved from wet clay as if the master hand of fire turned a potter's wheel.[5]

Under the influence of fire, grazing and an arid, mid-continental climate the continental heartland developed three distinct types of grassland. The wetter, easternmost region, watered by more than fifty centimetres of rain each year, became the land of tallgrass, the 'true' prairie. Here the dominant species were the tall-growing Indian grass, *Sorghastrum nutans*; switchgrass, *Panicum virgatum*, and the legendary big bluestem, *Andropogon furcatus*, which stretched 'as high as a horse'. In a good season they would grow two centimetres a day and reach a height of four metres; a swirling, rippling sea of grass glinting wine-coloured, bronze and green in the summer sun.

Far to the west, in the immediate rain shadow of the Rockies, shorter species clothed the dusty land – buffalo grass, *Buchloe dactyloides*, and blue grama, *Bouteloua gracilis*, which grow no higher than thirty centimetres. Nature's response to arid conditions is to produce low-growing vegetation. In high rainfall areas forest rules; in the near-desert of the west, short-grass species cover the plains.

Between the short grasses and the true prairie ran a broad band of mixed prairie whose eastern edge followed roughly the line of the one hundredth meridian extending through central Texas, Oklahoma and Kansas, across Nebraska and the Dakotas into southern Saskatchewan and Alberta. In the mixed-grass prairie the short-grass species of buffalo grass and blue grama are combined with mid-height species such as little bluestem, *Andropogon scoparius*; needlegrass, *Stipa comata*; side-oats grama, *Bouteloua curtipendula*, and western wheatgrass, *Agropyron smithii*.

The mixed prairies of the great plains were the chief grazing grounds of the vast buffalo herds which played their part in maintaining the short-grass condition. The sod-forming species of buffalo grass and blue grama made up the bulk of vegetation, together forming a tight mat-like turf. But so long as the prairie was not overgrazed, little bluestem held its own, shining bright green in spring and taking on a red-brown hue in summer.

While the broad divisions of tallgrass, short-grass and mixed-grass prairies held true across the great sweep of the American heartland, there were many variations. Big bluestem, the dominant grass in low-lying areas of the true prairie, ranged far to the west along valleys and ravines, often in association with little bluestem.[6] The long-leaved prairie dropseed dominated many of the drier uplands, its foliage bleaching white in winter. In the bottomlands that accompanied the rivers flowing through tallgrass country a coarse-leaved species known as prairie cordgrass or sloughgrass, *Spartina pectinata*, often emerged as the dominant grass, producing foliage so dense that other species were shaded out. From early times native Americans used the leaves for thatching their lodges. Later the pioneer settlers used the grass to cover haystacks and corn cribs. The writer David F. Costello has strong memories of the species.

My father called it 'rip gut' grass because the sawtooth margins of the four-foot-long coarse leaves could cut bare arms and hands like razor blades. He regularly cut sloughgrass for hay, and the intertwined stems and leaves clung so closely together in the stack that only a strong man could lift a pitchforkful. When the stacked hay settled it had to be cut with a hay saw.[7]

While the grass species contributed most to prairie biomass, they were outnumbered four or five to one by forbs: the wild flowers and herbs that filled out these species-rich habitats. An intact piece of tallgrass prairie might contain as many as four hundred different plants, most of them non-grass species. They occupied the spaces between grasses, boosting soil fertility by bringing up nutrients from deeper in the soil, and, in the case of legumes, by 'fixing' nitrogen from the air.

Like the low-growing shrubs in a forest, these were the 'understorey' of the grassland ecosystem, flowering early before the dominant grasses had grown enough to shade them out, or later in the season when grass growth had slowed down. Their sequence of flowering from spring through until the autumn was one of the glories of the prairie landscape.

The flowers of the prairie tell the story of America – the yellow blooms of the compass plant, whose vertical leaves face east and west to catch the sun; rattlesnake master, with its spiky leaves and golf ball-like flowerhead, said to cure snakebite; and the nitrogen-fixing leadplant, with its silver-green leaves, known by native Americans as the buffalo bellow because its purple, finger-like flowerheads appeared in the animal's rutting season.

From April through to September the prairie wildflowers bloom in a sequence that splashes bright colour across the ever-changing hue of the grasses – downy gentian; the strawberry-like prairie cinquefoil; prairie lousewort; the delicate prairie rose; Sullivant's milkweed; the orange-flowered Indian paint brush; prairie smoke, with its fruiting head trailing down-covered filaments like shards of flame and wisps of smoke; showy goldenrod, and the fiery red brands of prairie blazing star.

It was the very diversity of its plant life that made the prairie grassland so productive, as Charles Darwin predicted in the *Origin of Species*.[8] Plants of different genera exploit a variety of ecological niches at the same site, so together they make fuller use of the available resources. Because their leaf structures differ they are able to intercept more of the incoming sunlight. A low-growing perennial plant with prostrate leaves will pick up some of the energy lost by a taller-growing grass with narrow, erect leaves.

Though dozens of plants grow in close association, their life-cycles and flowering dates differ. Just as some species are growing vigorously and expanding their leaf architecture, others have begun to die back. The rich mix of plant types ensures that at any time in the growing season the maximum amount of solar energy is being captured and bound in carbohydrates.

Below ground a similar process is taking place. The various species develop a variety of root systems, each drawing moisture and minerals from a particular part of the soil profile. Buffalo grass, one of the dominant grasses of the arid, short-grass country of the high plains, sends down a network of fine roots to a depth of about a metre and a half. On the true prairie big bluestem reaches down two metres, while on the dry plains switchgrass roots may go down three metres. But the perennial prairie herb false boneset sends down a gigantic taproot to a depth of four metres or more. The roots of some prairie plants reach down as much as ten metres in their quest for moisture, a few of them even exploiting the groundwater.

In this way the prairie grasslands make the most of whatever soil moisture is available, particularly on the dry upland plains. At times of severe drought the shallow-rooted grasses may suffer, their foliage dying back. But the deep-rooted perennials survive, sustained by their foraging root networks. When the rains return the grasses re-establish themselves from seeds lying dormant in the soil or by regeneration from underground stems or rhizomes. It is the very diversity of species which makes the prairie grasslands so resilient.

Prairies have another means of securing their survival, one with huge benefits for mankind. They are able to build up in the top few centimetres of soil a vast reservoir of fertility, a store of nutrients and water to power production without the need for fertilisers or irrigation.

For all its flamboyant foliage, much of the life of prairie plants takes place below ground. A square metre of tallgrass may have an underground network of roots and root hairs which, placed end to end, would stretch twenty miles. Two-thirds of the plant biomass of prairie grassland is, like much of an iceberg, out of sight. The dense rooting network formed by grasses is constantly being renewed. Roots decay and die, their functions being taken over by young replacements. The discarded roots are broken down and incorporated into the general stock of organic matter by the activities of free-living bacteria and other soil microorganisms.

Their ultimate chemical destination is a group of complex carbon compounds known collectively as *humus* or *humic acid*, and created by the action of soil bacteria and protozoa. Humus is the power-pack of life. It is the bridge between living matter and dead matter, a subterranean carbon exchange taking in the exhausted and decayed, reprocessing it, and finally recycling it as building materials for new life. The myriad molecules that are together known as humus exhibit an extraordinary range of structures and life histories. A single molecule may contain as many as 20,000 individual atoms. Some humic acid molecules are as old as Stonehenge. Others split apart within minutes, releasing carbon and other minerals into the water-borne life of the soil.

Humus has many other benefits. It is able to bind soluble forms of mineral so they are not washed out of the soil during rainstorms but are held on the molecular surface. From here they can be taken up by plant roots to enter the dance of life. Humus retains water and so provides plants roots with moisture even in times of drought. And its molecules improve the physical structure of soil, binding together clay, silt and sand particles to form crumbs or aggregates, opening it up to roots and air, maintaining the productivity of the planet.

Every terrestrial organism ultimately ends up in humus: animals, birds, insects and plants, as well as the myriad life forms of the soil – earthworms, nematodes or roundworms, ants, millipedes, fungi and bacteria. Humus is the starting point of fertility and civilisation. It builds populations and cities. And grassland, especially long-established grassland, has a rare ability to create it.

Forest, that other great producer of biomass, replenishes soil organic matter from above. Most of it comes from leaves falling on the forest floor. These decay and build into a loose, crumbly layer which gradually becomes incorporated into the top few centimetres of soil through the action of earthworms and other organisms such as millipedes and harvester ants.

But the decaying roots of grasses produce humus throughout the soil profile. Fertility comes ready mixed and placed in precisely the right position for growing plants to use. Since grasses take up higher levels of minerals – particularly calcium – than forest trees, the humus they return to the soil is richer, a near-perfect growing medium. This is why the unbroken prairie supported such an abundance of life.

Stretching in a wide band from Alberta and Saskatchewan to southern Texas are a group of soils known as the black earths or *chernozems*. Deep brown or black in colour, they once covered the western edge of the true prairie and the eastern section of the mixed prairie. Their colour was entirely due to their humus content – without it they would have been pale grey. These were typical prairie soils, rich in organic matter, productive, durable, not remotely like the poor desert soils the early American pioneers supposed them to be.

Writing in *The American Grass Book* of 1953, Sellers Archer and Clarence Bunch recognised the true worth of the prairie: 'Grass is the only soil builder of any consequence among the

natural vegetation that originally covered this continent. Grass is
that indispensable form of plant life without which civilisation,
as we know it, would not exist.'

The organic matter content of those fertile prairie lands was
typically 10 per cent, though it could rise as high as 15. Not all
came from decaying roots. As with forest trees the grasses of the
plain bequeathed their dead and dying leaves to the soil. But
before returning to the earth they still had a part to play in
securing the future of the grassland community from which they
had come.

Prairie grasses such as buffalo grass are known as 'sod-
forming' grasses – they spread by putting out surface runners
which together form a dense matted turf. On to this mat fall the
decaying leaves that are constantly being replaced by new
growth. After a few seasons a thick layer of plant débris builds
up on top of the root mat. This insulating layer helps to hold in
moisture, covering any bare ground and reducing evaporation
on the hot, dusty plain.

Grasslands made this desert bloom. Over the millennia they
created an exceptional growing medium – twenty centimetres
of fertile earth, dark with organic matter, lime-rich, friable and
crumbly in texture. In an arid environment it made the most of
every drop of rain, binding it to soil humus, holding it within
the root-zone. Only rarely did rainwater percolate through to
the subsoil, taking with it valuable plant nutrients. In many parts
of the prairie the subsoil remained permanently dry.

This twenty centimetres of fertility produced an extravagance
of life. The first residents were creatures of the soil – millipedes,
seed-collecting harvester ants with their mighty hills, earthworms, burrowing gophers, and prairie dogs with the labyrinth
of tunnels that make up their 'towns'.

North America is home to five prairie dog species. The
black-tailed prairie dog alone has more than 130 different
vertebrate species associated with it, many of them predators.[9]
They include prairie falcons, golden eagles, ferruginous and
swainson's hawks, badgers and coyotes. Smaller animals like
cottontails and deer mice frequently take up residence in the
prairie dogs' tunnels. They are joined by dung beetles, rove

beetles, burrowing owls and slithering heaps of hibernating rattlesnakes.

The sheer profusion of prairie life is evidence of the energy-transforming power of grasslands. From the booming, strutting displays of the prairie chicken to the melodic song of the meadowlark, soaring above a nest hidden deep in a tussock of prairie grass, or the golden eagle with its two-metre wing-span gliding effortlessly in a cloud-flecked sky – all owe their existence to the capture of sunlight by a rippling sea of blue grama and buffalo grass.

Among its teeming insect populations the prairie has its heroes and its villains. Tumblebugs, the ball-rolling dung beetles that bury their manure pellets in the earth before eating them, are usually considered heroes. They aerate the soil and stimulate root growth, speeding the breakdown and rebuilding of humus acid molecules.

The defence case for grasshoppers is more difficult to sustain. Each state of the prairie region lays claim to at least a hundred species.[10] In 1818 vast hordes wiped out the crops of settlers who had ploughed the prairie in Minnesota's Red River Valley, while in the 1870s the damage caused by the Rocky Mountain grasshopper was considered a national catastrophe. Even so most rangeland grasshoppers are selective, having their own distinct food preferences. The spotted bird grasshopper devours stiff goldenrod and coralberry, seldom resorting to grasses.

A host of insects from leafhoppers to butterflies play a part in pollinating the prairie flowers. The bright-coloured soldier beetle feeds on goldenrod flowers and in doing so aids in their reproduction. The migrating monarch butterfly seeks out milkweeds, while the great spangled fritillary produces larvae that eat the leaves of violet. However, most of the pollination is carried out by bees. Though the honeybee was introduced by European settlers, more than a thousand native species were found on the central plain.[11]

The life of the prairies is made up of species beyond measure; a mingling of life styles; a frenzy of fighting and feeding, of mating and dying, played out to the song of the wind and the grasses. But it was the immense, wandering herds of buffalo that showed the true productive power of this ecosystem.

The American buffalo, *Bison bison*, whose ancestors crossed from Asia across the land bridge that once connected Alaska to Siberia, weighed up to a ton and stood nearly two metres high. At the peak of their population, their combined weight was greater than that of the entire human population of the United States and Canada today. And it was the prairie grasslands that sustained them, along with fifty million pronghorn antelope, five million prairie dogs, elk, deer, plains grizzlies and buffalo wolves.

The prairies also nourished an army of unseen grazers. A single square metre of prairie soil contains over five million plant-eating nematodes, the roundworms. These creatures munched their way through an even greater tonnage of vegetation than the bison.

Without fertiliser or irrigation – in a climate where rainfall is low and unpredictable – the prairie grasslands supported a biomass greater than that of modern, intensively managed croplands. But nineteenth-century America had another plan for the prairies. Not long after the Europeans arrived, the plains began to echo to the crack of the high-powered Sharps repeating rifle and the ring of the steel-bladed John Deere plough ripping through root systems. Within three generations the great grasslands had gone.

In *Grassland*, a powerful elegy for the prairies, Richard Manning finds an eighteenth-century vision for the American West set out in a Virginian country estate called Poplar Forest. This was once the retirement home of Thomas Jefferson, one of the nation's founding fathers. According to Manning, the layout clearly reflects his thought process. 'It is a monument to geometry, with houses and gardens laid out as cleanly as on a draftsman's table. Geometry stood at the center of Jefferson's notion of harmony. The gardens at Poplar Forest are a reorganisation of life to conform to geometry's lines.'[12]

Jefferson never saw the great American grasslands, but he was bent on sacrificing them to his geometrical vision. Manning sees him as the true founder of the West, if only because it was he who made the 'Louisiana Purchase', the 1803 acquisition from France of a vast territory west of the Mississippi. The deal had been no isolated act. It was the centre-piece of a plan which the founding fathers believed would produce the perfect democracy.

Jefferson accepted what has been called 'the agrarian myth' – the idea that family farms are good for democracy. In his view the ideal farmer was the yeoman, the independent property-owner with just enough land to support his family without having to employ others or to work for wages. Such people, he believed, were the bedrock of a free society and a bulwark against tyranny.

As he himself wrote in a letter of 1785: 'Cultivators of the earth are the most valuable citizens. They are the most vigorous, the most independent, the most virtuous, and they are tied to their country and wedded to liberty and interests by the most lasting bonds.'

The supreme rationalist constructed his new democracy by dividing up the wild prairies like a chess board. It came to be called the Jeffersonian grid – the rectilinear cadastral survey – as laid out in the Land Ordinance of 1785. Working from navigators' lines of latitude and longitude, the government divided the land into blocks of thirty-six square miles, which were called townships. These were further divided into sections of 640 acres, and quarter sections of 160 acres. Into this grid yeoman farmers were to be dropped like chess pieces, an instant democracy constructed according to strict mathematical principles.

The architects of the scheme believed that 160 acres was exactly what a yeoman would need to support his family. The land was initially put on sale at a dollar an acre, but speculators quickly moved in, buying up whole sections and selling them on at a handsome profit. To stop them the government passed the Homestead Act in 1862, allowing settlers to claim sections for nothing so long as they had worked them and lived on them for five years.[13]

America's wild heartland had been redesigned like a country estate in the Old World. At a time when English landscape designers were striving to bring the natural world into the garden, the New World's founding fathers were trying to turn the wilderness into a kitchen garden. As Richard Manning notes, it was somewhat optimistic.

> The whole scheme assumed a uniformity of nature in harmony with the democratic ideal. The creation, like a good government, was everywhere equable, benign and even-handed. The land was assumed to be democratic. That is, there was no such idea as ecosystem or habitat. The agrarian myth could not conceive of the aridity that was particular to the West. The lands in question were vacant not only of yeoman but of particular conditions and therefore particular knowledge, a blank slate needing only lines, plows and bags of European seeds. Aboriginals were not nomads because of aridity, but because of ignorance.

As an inducement to railway companies driving new routes across the prairies the government gave them townships on either side of their tracks. The companies could sell this land and so raise more money for railway building. They responded by mounting huge poster advertising campaigns, not only in the eastern states but throughout Europe. Thousands were attracted by the lure of cheap land.

Their numbers were swelled by thousands of former slaves fleeing the southern states for the chance of a better life on the plains. With them came war veterans from the Union and Confederate armies, the restless misfits of conflict desperately searching for stability and permanence. On to the prairies they surged, this strange assortment of people united in hope, a nation within a nation, hacking out the age-old turf to build their sod houses, ploughing, sowing and harvesting a different kind of grass – wheat and maize.

With fortitude they bore the retribution of the plains – blistering summer heat and bone-chilling winter blizzards, cruel droughts that withered their crops, fire and failed rains, plagues of grasshoppers that stripped every square centimetre of vegetation. The railways brought in buffalo hunters, dealing out slaughter from the windows of their coaches, pausing only when their rifle barrels overheated. Later the trains brought steel ploughs and mechanical reapers, wind pumps and barbed wire, and the new Turkey Red wheat variety which was tough enough to withstand the harsh, prairie winters.

They harvested bumper crops and a thousand years of fertility. During the next thirty years grain yields fell by three-quarters and the level of soil organic matter was halved. The 'sod busters' had brought an extractive industry to the grasslands, robbing the rich, dark soils of their wealth and shipping it around the world to bring ruin to farmers in the Old World.

The arrival of ranching on the plains brought with it the same culture of over-exploitation. In the early nineteenth century the towns and cities of the east and north had been supplied with beef from great Longhorn herds driven overland from Texas. When the railways came to the West cattle towns sprang up, among them Abilene, Dodge City and Wichita, places where the Texan drovers could meet northern dealers safe from the attention of rustlers, angry homesteaders and hostile tribes.

But the cattlemen quickly realised that it was easier to rear their stock on the plains rather than risk the dangerous drives from Texas. They bought up land along the rivers, giving them control of water sources while allowing their cattle to roam freely across the open range. In just twenty years from 1860 the number of cattle in the state of Kansas rose fifteen-fold to one and a half million, while those in Nebraska leaped from just thirty-seven thousand to more than one million.[14]

The ranchers swapped their fierce, hardy Longhorns for the more placid British breeds – the Shorthorn, Hereford and Aberdeen Angus – whose tender, fatty meat suited the palates of northern city folk. The ranchers used the newly invented barbed wire to fence off and appropriate public land – almost half the land in the eleven western states is publicly owned. They then stocked these federal lands so heavily that the once-rich grasslands were grazed practically to dirt.

The buffalo had grazed and moved on. Prairie grasses were given a chance to recover and salt away food reserves in the root system, an insurance against the next assault on their leaves and stems. But English cattle – heavily stocked – selected the most palatable species, and continued to graze the regrowth as soon as it appeared. The plant was forced to draw on root reserves with no chance of recovery, and so was slowly weakened.

Under this new pressure the palatable species were quickly depleted to be replaced by less palatable plants. Species like the livestock favourite, sideoats grama, and blue bunch wheat grass, *Agropyron spicatum*, once the dominant grass of the short-grass prairie along the northern Rockies, went into steep decline. Unpalatable species such as cheatgrass, *Bromus tectorum*, sagebrush and tumbleweed thrived under the new regime.

In this way the subtle and rich species mix that made up the prairie grasslands was eroded. The network of underground roots – along with the moisture and nutrient-holding humus – was weakened and destroyed. The grinding molars of European cattle destroyed the ancient turf as effectively as the steel-bodied plough.

Much of the capital for these big-business ranches came from investors in England and Scotland. In 1879 the British Parliament sent two MPs to look at the beef-raising potential of Texas range-land. Their report on the great kingdom of grass sparked a British invasion from the Texas panhandle up to Canada.

> Edinburgh drawing rooms buzzed with stories of the bonanza. Staid old gents scarcely knowing the difference between a steer and a stone cow discussed the bonanza over port and snuff as they warmed their knees. Young aristocrats hungry for adventure, particularly if a little wild and an embarrassment at home, had no trouble tapping the family exchequer for investment. The western cattlemen were only too happy to unload their holdings at fancy prices to such investors. As always in a profit-hungry time, swindlers flourished. Paper companies put out attractive prospectuses and handsome stock certificates. Without an acre of land or a solitary Longhorn steer they raked in the money like a croupier in a boom town.[15]

A Scotsman, J. S. Tait, issued a brochure on *The Cattle-fields of the Far West*, in which he estimated the possible profits at between 33 and 66 per cent. In the early 1880s dozens of ranching companies were set up with Scottish and English capital. They included Bay State Land, the Prairie Cattle Company, the Texas Land and Cattle Company of Dundee, Powder River, Swan Land, and Lord Tweedmouth's Rocking Chair Ranche, known by the local Texas cowboys as 'Queenie's Cow Outfit' because of its supposed link with Queen Victoria.[16]

Those investors who were not ruined by swindles, prairie fires and the great 'die-ups' of cattle in harsh western winters, shipped their beef back to Britain in the new refrigerated ships, depressing the market for cattle farmers in their own country.

In time the mining of the prairie lands brought its own savage retribution. The dust bowls of the mid-1930s – when the degraded soils of the plains literally blew away – were blamed on drought. But the prairie grasslands had always been subjected to periodic droughts.

The living turf was not simply a carpet laid over the land, but an intimate bond between root and soil that helped sustain the planet. The settlers and the ranchers broke that bond and raised an angry storm cloud of dust as their retribution.

Today America's heartland is occupied by over-grazed range lands and overworked crop lands. The prairie crops are still sizeable, but only because they are dosed with artificial fertiliser and pesticides, and because the government spends billions of dollars irrigating them. Prairie grasslands once gave mankind their spectacular products free of charge, courtesy of the sun and soil. They can do so no longer. We must now buy the prairies' output with an annual tribute of fossil fuels. To Richard Manning it makes little sense:

American agriculture, with all its technology, subsidies, and labor, supports a population of forty-five million cattle in the plains states, the same area that held fifty million bison without any of these. In many ways, though, cattle themselves provide a way to hide surplus grain. There is no need to feed grain to grazers. The bison that were the basis of the traditional plains economy ate no corn, nor did the Mexican cattle that grazed the grasslands for three hundred years. The habit of fattening cattle on grain is just that, a habit. As a result, we eat fatter meat and the heart-stopping cholesterol it contains. Seventy per cent of the grain crop of American agriculture goes to the livestock that replaced the bison that ate no grain, and one wonders, what is agriculture for?[17]

The white settlers had not been the only ones to claim the bounty of the prairies. There had been another way, the way of the nomad. The north American continent was first occupied nearly 12,000 years ago when Palaeolithic hunters followed the herds of bison, mammoths, camels and American horses across Beringia, the broad, flat plain that then connected Alaska and Siberia. The Clovis people, as they were later called, hunted their prey using flint-tipped spears.

By the time the first Europeans arrived at the edge of the Great Plains, they were shared by two types of tribal society. Along the banks of the major rivers were the settled peoples, including the Mandan, Pawnee, Kansa, Iowa, Missouria and Hidatsa tribes. Living in large, earth lodges, they grew crops of maize, beans, squashes and sunflowers, occasionally venturing on to the plains for meat to supplement their diet.

The plains themselves were inhabited by a small group of foot nomads, including the Blackfoot, Plains Cree and Assiniboine nations. Carrying their skin lodges with them, they formed loosely organised bands to hunt bison. These they trapped in wood stockades or killed by driving over cliffs as at the world heritage site Head-Smashed-In Buffalo Jump in Alberta, Canada. The plains nomads embraced a meat culture, eating an extraordinary range of buffalo parts, including most of the internal organs, the blood, testicles, marrow and foetus.[18] No part of the animal was wasted. Skins were used for clothing, containers and tipis. Horns, bones and hair became the materials for a variety of arts and crafts.

From earliest times the great American grasslands supported these two contrasting cultures. At the more temperate fringes of the plain were the settled agrarian peoples, while at its arid heart wandered the nomads. When the Europeans arrived they carried the concepts of settlement and transformation out on to the prairies, and in doing so destroyed them. But not before the nomads had had their moment of heady and glorious freedom.

The lives of the plains nomads were transformed by the re-introduction of the horse. Though the native American horse had long been extinct, the animals were brought back to the continent in the seventeenth century by Spanish ranchers in what is now New Mexico. As horses found their way northwards through trade and by theft, the plains peoples took to them as though they had been born partners. By the early eighteenth century they were being used by the Pawnee, Missouri, Oto, Kansa and Ponca tribes.

The coming of the horse led to a late flowering of plains culture. On the dry, open grasslands the horse was the route to freedom and power. Such was the allure of this new way of life that tribes like the Cheyenne, Crow and Dakota gave up the settled life of farming to become fully-fledged mounted hunters.

But the renaissance of the plains culture was not to last long. By the end of the nineteenth century the culture of the Plains Indians had been swept away in a flood-tide of white settlement. The buffalo had been all but wiped out; the ceremonial, trade and social structures of their hunters had been eliminated. The idea of industrialism was now to shape the prairie landscape.

Might the meeting of the old Americans and the new have produced a different outcome? Richard Manning thinks so. By the early nineteenth century European traders – particularly the French – had begun trading seriously in the softened buffalo robes (skins) used for centuries by the nomadic tribes. These were not tanned hides. Instead they had been treated with the animal's brain tissue, then pounded and softened like buckskin. Until the development of a tanning industry in the east, these buffalo robes found a keen demand in the growing American cities.

According to Manning the trade created 'a stable hybrid culture, a model of successful integration of Europeans into the nomadic culture of the plains ... It was stable, both in the economic sense and in the environmental sense. It was appropriate technology.'[19]

But the promising hybrid was overwhelmed by the powerful new concept of democracy and the equally powerful drive of industrialism which underpinned it. Native Americans enjoyed the true freedom of nomadic peoples, especially after the arrival of the horse. At the Medicine Lodge Treaty of 1867 the Yamparikas Comanche Paruasemena lamented: 'You said that you wanted to put us upon a reservation, to build us houses and make us medicine lodges. I do not want them. I was born upon the prairie, where the wind blew free and there was nothing to break the light of the sun. I lived like my fathers before me, and like them I lived happily.'

In place of Native Americans the Washington government sent homesteaders, pioneer farmers dropped into an open landscape to fulfil the dream of a land-owning democracy. But it was to prove a flimsy thing out there on the arid soils of the Great Plains.

The precisely drawn quarter section was wholly inadequate to sustain a family. On the prairie, as on the high plains of the west, the survivors were not yeoman farmers, but big agri-business combines and wealthy ranchers. And they only hang on with the help of substantial inputs of agrochemicals and fertilisers, heavy subsidies from urban taxpayers, and a vast transport infrastructure of railways, airlines and shipping companies to bring in the inputs and haul the end products to market.

Two academics from Rutgers University – Frank and Deborah Popper – found that 140,000 square miles of the Great Plains, with a non-Indian population of about 400,000 people, had been fiscally insolvent since the land had been taken from the Native Americans more than a century ago. They concluded – in the words of the Native American writer Ward Churchill – that it was impossible

to maintain school districts, police and fire departments, road beds and all the other basic accoutrements of 'modern life' on the negligible incomes which can be eked from cattle grazing and wheat farming on land which is patently unsuited for either enterprise ... Without considerable federal subsidy each and every year, none of these counties would ever have been viable. Nor, on the face of it, will any of them ever be. Put bluntly, the pretence of bringing Euroamerican 'civilisation' to the Plains does little more than place a massive economic burden on the rest of the United States.[20]

The Poppers suggest that the 150-year-old experiment on the prairies should be abandoned. The land should be returned to the bison herds which had occupied it 'before the West was won'. It took the British somewhat longer to destroy the fertility of their own grasslands. But they got there just the same.

8 *The Golden Fleece*

It's hard to find sheep in the fields around the small Hampshire village of Damerham. Not surprisingly, there seem to be plenty of horses about. This is, after all, classic pony paddock country. In some of the larger pastures cattle graze contentedly in the summer sunshine. And a field adjoining the minor road to the satellite hamlet of Martin has a sizeable population of outdoor pigs.

But sheep are decidedly scarce. There are none to graze the marshy grasses that border the meandering river; none to wander across the steeper land stretching up towards the chalk downland. In a meadow opposite the eleventh-century church, set amid its mossy headstones, a bunch of curious bullocks crowd around the gate. But most of the fields are in arable crops, the legacy of a quarter-century rule from Brussels.

Eight centuries ago sheep were everywhere in this quiet corner of England. The annual harvest of wool was so great that some of it had to be stored in that same little church to await the arrival of a merchant from Flanders or Italy. Much of the wool belonged not to the local lord of the manor, but to the villagers, the peasants. In the thirteenth century this small feudal community was at the centre of a social and economic revolution, one that was to shape the destiny of the island kingdom. It was a revolution rooted in England's lush, green pastures.

Damerham's part in the making of a nation is revealed in a medieval tax document. The 'assessment roll' – dated 1225 – was drawn up to help with the taxing of 'moveables' on a number of local ecclesiastical estates. Damerham, together with nearby Martin, belonged to the great estate owned by Glastonbury Abbey. Under the manorial system of the Middle Ages the 'unfree' tenants or *villeins* were required to carry out regular work on the lord's land, the *demesne*. Though they held land of their own, their obligation to provide labour services for the landlord often meant they had insufficient time or energy to develop their own holdings. Nor in a largely cashless society did they have the money to invest in livestock or additional land.

Instead most remained in servility, using their own holdings of a virgate – typically thirty acres – or half virgate for little more than subsistence. A few twelfth-century landlords had begun to waive customary labour services in return for rent, but such moves toward a cash economy were far from common. This is what makes the achievement of the Damerham villagers so remarkable.

The thirteenth-century tax document showed that 138 tenants at Damerham and Martin together owned a flock of almost 4,000 sheep, seven times larger than that of their great landlord, the Abbot of Glastonbury.[1] When names on the roll are compared with those on other abbey records it is clear that among the larger flock owners were a number of ordinary villeins of the manor. In Damerham village itself, twenty customary tenants grazed sheep on the manor pastures, the sizes of their small flocks ranging from ten to fifty-eight animals.

Despite the power of the medieval lords and the great ecclesiastical estates, ambitious peasants had found a way to build up capital, to accumulate property that might be handed on to their heirs. They had begun to chip away at the rockface of feudalism, asserting their individualism and hunger for freedom. They were able to do it because of a thriving international trade in wool. A form of proto-capitalism was taking shape out in the open fields and pastures, the wastes and the woodlands where most of the population of England still lived and worked.

In the Middle Ages English wool was highly sought after by the cloth makers of Flanders and Italy. By the fourteenth century they had become so dependent on it that when the supply was interrupted, thousands of Flemish weavers went hungry. Annual exports averaged more than 5,000 tons, worth two and a half times the country's total peacetime revenue.[2] Not surprisingly, the wool trade dominated England's commercial and political life.

Kings taxed it to finance their wars with the French and the Scots. Capitalist financiers made and lost fortunes speculating on it. A new merchant class grew wealthy by controlling it, leaving their imprint in the brasses and stained glass of great 'wool churches'. Parliament used it to curb the monarch's tax-raising powers, while out in the country peasants used it to break free of their landlords.

Wool and its riches impinged on all aspects of national life. As a mark of its importance, the Lord Chancellor chose to sit himself down on a woolsack, while a wealthy merchant had engraved on the windows of his new house: 'I praise God and ever shall, it is the sheep hath paid for all.'[3]

That merchant might equally have written his lines in praise of grass. The hardy medieval sheep may have shown a remarkable ability to survive in harsh conditions – from the rainswept fellsides of Yorkshire to the bleak downlands of southern England. But it was the faculty of grass communities to grow and thrive in such places that underpinned the wool trade. England's first engine of wealth was driven by her grasslands, and they in their turn were maintained by the sheep whose chomping jaws prevented a reversion to scrub.

The rural landscape of the Middle Ages was very different from the ordered field patterns of modern-day England. Blocks of cultivated land stood out like islands in an ocean of forest and moorland, marshland and waste, much of which had been burnt by the Saxons, the Danes and latterly the Normans. Yet wherever grass might be induced to grow, the medieval flock-owners – large and small – turned out their sheep.

On the bleak 'white moors' of the north and west, dominated by the inedible mat grass, *Nardus stricta*, with its tough, wiry leaves and impenetrable mat of decaying foliage, rain-sodden sheep would scavenge for sustenance in the small, localised plant communities growing between tussocks. There they would find the slender-leaved wavy hair-grass, *Deschampsia flexuosa*, whose purple flower heads tremble with the summer raindrops.

There might be other pickings, too – the aptly named sheep's fescue, whose slender leaves were said to produce a finer wool; creeping bent, also known as fiorin; the strongly scented sweet vernal grass, *Anthoxanthum odoratum*; perhaps a small colony of common tormentil, with its yellow, four-petalled flowers shaped like a Celtic cross, or heath bedstraw, with whorls of ovoid leaves and clusters of tiny white flowers.

On wetter hills – particularly those whose underlying rocks were low in lime – the open moorland was dominated by purple moor grass or 'flying bent', *Molinia caerulea*, its bright green leaves tinged with red and purple. Its narrow, flat-bladed leaves wither and turn brown in summer, while the roots and rhizomes form a spongy peat layer up to one-third of a metre thick. On *Molinia* moors, companion grasses are rare. An occasional clump of wavy hair-grass would have offered some dietary respite, but sheep summered on the open moor were obliged to range far and wide for a living.

Down on lower slopes the grazing was better. Here a mixture of common bent, *Agrostis tenuis*, and sheep's fescue dominated the sward, its bright green hue contrasting with the dull browns of the moorland grazings. These were pastures reclaimed from forest or scrub of sessile oak and birch. Sheep thrive on the mixture of bent and fescue, particularly when it contains the leguminous bird's-foot trefoil, whose yellow, red-tinged flowers stand bright against the summer green.

Bent and sheep's fescue also dominate 'grass heaths', the sandy, drought-prone 'commons' that made up much of the medieval 'wastes'. However, their flora was usually richer and more varied than those of hillside pastures. As well as bent and the fine-leaved fescues, creeping soft-grass, *Holcus mollis*, often became dominant, spreading by means of tough, searching rhizomes which together formed a loose mat. While these 'hungry' pastures supported few sheep, their output was improved by a range of linked species, including the delicate early hair-grass, *Aira praecox*; rue-leaved saxifrage, and sheep's sorrel, with its slender, acidic leaves and tiny red flowers.

Village pastures were mostly on deeper, less hungry soils and were much prized. Sheep folded on these grasslands developed heavier fleeces with a longer 'staple' than those running on the hills and heaths, though they lost some of the fineness of wool. The best village pastures also contained bent and sheep's fescue. But there were other, more nutritious grasses – the drought-hardy cat's tail or timothy, *Phleum pratense*; tussocky cocksfoot, *Dactylis glomerata*; meadow foxtail, *Alopecurus pratensis*, and crested dog's-tail, believed by shepherds to prevent foot-rot.

On the southern chalk downs, where many of the sheepwalks had been in continuous use since Neolithic times, grassland took on a special character. Lime-rich conditions produced a unique community of grasses and herbs, particularly on the steep slopes of the escarpment. The dominant grass in the well-grazed pasture was once again sheep's fescue, this time in association with red fescue, the two species making up the great mass of foliage. But other grasses grew among them, notably the oat-grasses with their extended awns, the bristle-like projections from the flowers. Common oat-grass, *Avena pratensis*, downy oat-grass, *Avena pubescens*, and golden oat-grass, *Trisetum flavescens*, all grew on the chalk along with the shorter-growing crested hair-grass, *Koeleria cristata*, and quaking grass, *Briza media*.

Chalkland grazings were also rich in herbs, such as the aromatic wild thyme, salad burnet, small scabious, with its distinct purple flower head, purging flax, with its tiny white flowers, ribwort plantain and the umbelliferous burnet saxifrage. Herbs helped to maintain a healthy mineral balance in grazing sheep, while the firm, springy turf reduced foot ailments. Medieval flocks thrived on the chalk downs.

But the finest grazing pastures of all were on the marshes. While an acre of chalk grassland might carry, on average, one or two sheep, an acre of the best marsh pastures in the fenland or on Romney Marsh might carry a dozen. The most productive were on deep alluvial soils in the flood plains of rivers, their fertility built up by years of seasonal inundation.

The productive perennial ryegrass frequently dominated the sward, along with rough-stalked meadow grass, crested dog's-tail and a handful of marsh-loving species. Wether sheep – the castrated males – fattened quickly on these pastures. But of greater interest to the medieval flock-owners were their heavy fleeces containing a high proportion of long-stapled wool.

So great was the demand for English wool that in the fourteenth century the sheep population reached a peak of eighteen million,[4] outnumbering the human population by as much as six to one. Pastures were at a premium and sheep grazed them all – the fellsides and the high moors, the heathlands and the downs, the riverside marshes and the coastal saltings.

On the manorial open fields they were 'folded' on corn stubble and fallow, on the demesne pastures of great lords and on the half-acre plots of the lowliest cottar. They were turned out on to the common lands, the wastes and the forest clearings. Wool was an enterprise that knew no geographic boundaries. Its production was not limited to the best land or to areas with a mild climate. Some flock owners even claimed that harsh weather produced a finer fleece.

Wool production was open to anyone who could lay claim to a pasture, whether in the hill country of isolated farmsteads, or in village England, the land of the great demesnes. Everywhere there were sheep, bred, reared and shepherded to satisfy a seemingly unquenchable demand for a basic commodity. Wool was a cash crop. It was grown for a market a long way from home. The stability of the feudal manor, with its emphasis on self-sufficiency, was being undermined by merchant venturers with Flemish and Italian names, creators of a global market.

The emergence of an overseas market broke the logjam of capital formation. In northern Europe crop-growing was a marginal activity. Never before had it taken place beyond forty-five degrees latitude of the equator. It was only conducted at all with the aid of huge amounts of capital in the form of draft oxen to provide motive power for clearing forest and tilling the soil, implements such as ploughs and harrows, harnesses for the draft animals, even storage barns for grains and fodder.

The tenant providing customary labour services to the lord of the manor had little hope of building up this sort of capital. There was no surplus beyond mere subsistence. But a lucrative overseas market for a crop produced from grass – which grew readily on the cool, damp hillsides of Britain – provided just such an opportunity. Capital, in the form of sheep, was accessible to almost anyone, from villein to lord. And to many others beside.

On a cold December day in 1132, Thurston, Archbishop of York, led a small group of rebel monks to a bleak and barren patch of wasteland in the valley of the River Skell, two miles west of Ripon. They had turned their backs on the Benedictine Order which they regarded as complacent. They were opting instead for the more spartan existence of the Cistercians as expounded by the charismatic Bernard, Abbot of Clairvaux in Champagne. They were seeking lives of austerity and asceticism, honest toil and prayer.

Here beside the tumbling waters they would build a place of worship and follow a new way of simplicity. The holy house they founded was Fountains Abbey, later to become one of the wealthiest in the north, with vast tracts of land across west Yorkshire stretching as far as Pen-y-Ghent, high on the Pennines. The life of prayer and toil created the most successful farming enterprise of the age.

The white-robed Cistercians and their lay brothers, the *conversi*, set about restoring Yorkshire after the devastation caused by William the Conqueror. They drained the marshes and cleared the forests, concentrating first on the valley bottoms with their potentially higher fertility.[5] As they created new grazings and improved the marsh grasslands, they expanded their flocks. A list of wool-producing English monasteries compiled by the merchant Pegolotti of the Italian house of Bardi showed Fountains to be the producer of 10,000 fleeces a year by the late thirteenth century, as were the sister houses of Rievaulx and Jervaulx.[6]

Even by the late fifteenth century, when many of the great landed estates had abandoned farming and leased out their demesne lands, Fountains owned at least 3,000 sheep.[7] In Monmouthshire the Cistercian Abbot of Tintern owned a flock of 2,000 wethers and 1,000 ewes whose wool was valued the highest on Pegolotti's list.[8] Its only equals were wools from the monastery of Dore and the nunnery of Stanfield in Lindsey, Lincolnshire.

The Cistercians' success with hill sheep was rapidly emulated by other landowners. The slopes of the Pennines, Cheviots and southern uplands were turned into vast sheepwalks on which abbeys, lay lords and even kings vied over the size of flocks and the volume of the annual wool crop.[9] In 1530, King James V of Scotland ran 10,000 sheep in the forest of Ettrick in competition with the flocks of the border abbeys. By this time pastoral Britain had begun to suffer from too many sheep and too few cattle for the health of its hill pastures.

Sheep are selective and close grazers. The sheer numbers of ewes and wethers on the fellsides led to an explosion in the growth of bracken and coarse grasses. The animals themselves were often half starved. Yet some quality of the soil produced on their backs the most valuable fleeces in the world. Foreign travellers marvelled at the number and size of English flocks. They had seen none like them in all Europe. The flock-owners saw no reason to reduce their numbers, even though this might lead to healthier sheep and better pastures. They feared that in some strange way it might ruin the quality of the wool.

The Cistercians were as adept at marketing the wool as they were at growing it. The holy men of Rievaulx, who had made a virtue of poverty, persuaded Henry I to exempt them from tolls. Other Cistercian houses quickly followed their example.[10] Since the privilege applied only while the wool was in monastic hands, the abbeys arranged their own transport, so exempting the buyer from tolls. They further added to their income by buying up the wool of other growers, preparing and packing it, then finally marketing it as *lana collecta*, in direct contravention of a prohibition by their General Chapter in 1157.

By the middle of the twelfth century the monks were selling 'forward', collecting payment for the fleeces of sheep as yet unborn.[11] In effect they had raised loans on security of wool, allowing them to go ahead with ambitious new buildings. In return the merchants extracted heavy interest charges. Yet, despite a ruling from the chapter general in 1181, the Cistercians continued to sell their wool ten years or more in advance. When epidemics of murrain and sheep scab ravaged flocks and ruined fleeces they were left with crippling debts.

The consequences of so reckless a strategy are poignantly revealed in an entry in the cartulary of Pipewell Abbey. The list of loans includes details of two wool contracts raised between 1314 and 1321, a period of widespread famine. On a blank page in the middle of the cartulary, and in a different hand, there appears an impassioned *cri du coeur*:

Be it remembered, beloved brethren and reverend father, that through the aforesaid recognisances and by reason of seven years of sterility and murrain among the animals, the goods of the house of Pipewell were so completely used up that the residue thereof sufficed not for the slender sustenance of the aforesaid house of monks, but sometimes they sat down in the refectory for three or four days with only black bread and pottage and sometimes they bought their bread from market to market and all this they bore patiently. Hence it is that I, the miserable sinner who once occupied the place of abbot, counsel, beg and entreat and (as much as in me lies) warn that none henceforth fall into the hands of rascals . . . [12]

H. J. Massingham wrote of the Cistercians:

To their peasants and lay brethren they were the mildest and best landlords this country has ever known. Their houses were inns, hospitals, guest-rooms, almshouses, agricultural colleges; their abbeys were shrines of peace and poverty for themselves, and of peace and plenty for others . . . The tragedy was that they exchanged a material for a spiritual wealth and the cause of that deceitfulness was their own sheep. Their farming methods, diligence, craftsmanship and power of leadership were so successful that their very virtues became the seeds of their corruption.[13]

The historical documents on medieval sheep farming are mostly concerned with the vast flocks of the demesnes, both lay and cleric. The peasant producer went almost unnoticed. On the demesnes pastoral farming was conducted on a grand scale. Many of the larger estates ran an intra-manorial system in which specialist flocks were managed by a group of manors working together. One manor would maintain the ewe flock while another looked after the wethers. A third would take care of the hoggasters or yearlings. Each flock would be in the charge of a shepherd responsible not just for the animals, but for the running of the sheep-fold.

In the Middle Ages a good shepherd was an asset beyond price. Walter of Henley, author of a thirteenth-century farming treatise, put it succinctly:

It profiteth the lord to have discreet shepherds, watchful and kindly, so that the sheep be not tormented by their wrath but crop their pasture in peace and joyfulness; for it is a token of the shepherd's kindness if the sheep be not scattered abroad but browse around him in company. Let him provide himself with a good barkable dog and lie nightly with his sheep.[14]

According to the anonymous author of *Seneschaucie*, the shepherd should be a patient man, 'not over-hasty', never absent without leave at 'fairs, markets, wrestling-matches, wakes or in the tavern'. Some contemporary writers considered lameness a useful attribute in a shepherd, since a lame man was unlikely to drive his sheep too hard.[15]

The shepherd's life was a stressful one. He faced an ever-present threat to his flock from thieves and savage dogs. During the lambing season the possibility of catastrophe seemed perpetually close at hand. All night he would toil in the bone-chilling cold of the sheephouse, caring for his ewes by the light of guttering candles. Beside him stood the pails of ewe's milk brought down from the dairy for the weakly lambs. Sometimes his efforts would be of no avail. At Collingbourne Ducis, one of the Duchy of Lancaster's Wiltshire estates, a ewe flock numbering more than 400 produced just eighty-five lambs following the deaths of many ewes from disease.[16] More than 200 lambs were still-born 'slynkittes'.

Disease was a constant worry for the medieval shepherd. The term murrain covered a wide range of endemic diseases that periodically took their toll of sheep. An outbreak in 1312 struck a flock of the Knights Hospitallers at Garway in Herefordshire. The epidemic killed one in ten adult sheep and one-quarter of all lambs. More than a century later an outbreak at Budbrooke in Warwickshire wiped out the entire flock of seventy wether sheep.[17]

The two great scourges identified by medieval writers were scab and rot. Scab first appeared in the late thirteenth century, apparently introduced with imported Spanish sheep. Almost half the 2,000-strong demesne flock on the Bishop of Winchester's Downton estate were lost following an outbreak in 1349. The shepherd's remedies included sulphur and tar, and as a precautionary measure flocks were kept off the land in autumn until the sun had purified it from the 'gelly or matty rime'.

On rot Walter of Henley's treatise is eloquent in its graphic description. Symptoms included white veins under the eyelids, wool that was easily pulled away from the ribs and a skin that would not redden when rubbed. When the November hoarfrost melted rapidly on an animal's fleece it was clearly suffering from the disease, said the writer. The cause was 'an unnatural heat'.

The standard treatment for any disease was the application of ointment.[18] From the late thirteenth century shepherds on the Winchester estates began treating flock ailments with wine, mercury and copper in the form of verdigris. By the mid-fourteenth century all had been replaced by tar and grease bought by the barrel. On the Wiltshire manor of Urchfont a regular item on the sheep-fold expenses was a payment to cover the anointing of demesne sheep and yearlings.

Despite the stresses of the shepherd's life there were lighter moments. The annual shearing feast was a regular event at many manors, and while the shepherd rarely took an active part in the work – a team of labourers were hired to help the customary tenants with sheep washing and clipping – the 'lord of the fold' was a central figure in the post-shearing celebrations.

Following the clipping of more than 1,000 adult sheep and lambs on the Wiltshire manor of Heytesbury, the receiver supervising the work authorised the spending of fifteen shillings and sixpence to cover four bushels of wheat, a quarter of barley malt for ale, a sheep, a side of beef, a pig and a calf.[19]

As a reward for his weighty responsibility, the shepherd enjoyed a number of customary rights. He was released from other manorial services and retained as a permanent member of the demesne staff, receiving a money wage. This was often supplemented with daily allowances of grain and buttermilk, together with a lamb in spring, a fleece at shearing time and a quantity of ewes' milk on Sundays between Easter and August.

He was also permitted to keep a number of his own sheep on the lord's pastures. The shepherds of Wick and Walton in the manor of Downton in Wiltshire were permitted to have the demesne flock penned on their customary acres to manure them for twelve days at Christmas.[20] At Badbury in the same county the shepherd was allowed use of the demesne plough on the third Saturday of each month in the ploughing season.

With his special privileges the shepherd stood apart from other members of the peasant community. Away in his remote sheep-fold or wheeled hut containing medicine chest and thatching tools, he might almost have been classed as a small yeoman.[21] For centuries shepherds were buried with a lock of wool so Saint Peter should know why they had failed to attend church every Sunday. Many must have been regular church-goers. Churches in rural areas were often equipped with expandable dog-tongs for removing sheep dogs that became noisy or aggressive during the service.

The shepherd was almost the sole survivor of an earlier

pastoral tradition into modern times. In popular culture he became a symbol of wisdom and constancy, a natural philosopher whose plain and honest creed was shaped during long hours of solitude. Like the peasant he had a strong sense of home and family, of vocation and inheritance. Shepherding was a family calling passed down from father to son, rarely from father to daughter. Yet shepherds embraced a broader perspective, drawing in 'a sense of the wider world from their spaces and of eternity from the skies'.[22]

In 1592 Queen Elizabeth I visited Sudeley Castle in the Cotswolds. She was greeted at the gates by a shepherd. 'These hills afford nothing but cottages, and nothing can we present to your Highness but shepherds . . . This lock of wool, Cotswold's best fruit, and my poor gift, I offer to your Highness, in which nothing is to be esteemed but the whiteness, virginity's colour, nor to be expected but duty, shepherd's religion.'[23]

Shepherds are immortalised in literature. In the Gospel story they represent the common people whose open-hearted faith brings them to devotion. 'And there were shepherds in the fields keeping watch over their flocks by night.' The 'shepherd's long arm' – his crook – has become the bishop's crosier, the very symbol of pastoral care.

The seventeenth-century writer John Aubrey, a native of Wiltshire and its chalk downs, said of the shepherd:

Methinks he is much more happy in a wood, that at ease contemplates the universe as his own, and in it the sun and stars, the pleasing meadows, shaded groves, green banks, stately trees, flowing springs, and the wanton windings of a river, fit objects for quiet innocence, than he that with fire and sword disturbs the world, and measures his possessions by the waste that lies about him.[24]

Caleb Bawcombe, W. H. Hudson's shepherd of the downs, was the embodiment of rural contentment. After a lifetime spent on the bare chalk country amid 'the tremulous bleatings of the sheep, the tinklings of numerous bells, and the crisp ringing bark of his dog', he was able to say: 'Give me my Wiltsheer Downs again and let me be a shepherd there all my life long.'[25]

By the close of the fourteenth century, demesne farming was in decline. Up to two million people had perished in the Black Death of 1348. As a result the grain price had collapsed and there was too little labour to work the manorial farms. Many owners opted to lease out their demesne lands to tenants, becoming *rentiers*. Others reduced the area in cultivation, allowing marginal land to 'tumble' back to grass. It was the reverse of the policy pursued in the twelfth and thirteenth centuries when the lords expanded their own farms, bringing new *assarts* into cultivation, and resisting pressure to lease out land.

Arable farming bore the initial impact of the agrarian slump. Some estate owners, like the Abbot of Winchcombe in Gloucestershire, opted to retain their sheep flocks until well into the fifteenth century. Sheep farming required less labour than crop growing, so ox teams were the first to go. But eventually the sheep followed and the sheep-fold fell silent. Both arable and pasture lands were leased out to tenants. Peasant flocks – like those pioneered two centuries earlier by the villagers of Damerham and Martin – were soon to blossom across the length and breadth of England.

On the Long Sutton manor in Lincolnshire – part of the great sheep farming estate of the Duchy of Lancaster – the entire demesne lands were let to the bondage tenants of the manor, the peasant farmers, to divide among themselves.[26] Sheep farming in the estate's Yorkshire and Lincolnshire manors, except for those at Pickering, had already passed into the hands of tenants. On the vast Berkeley family estates, with manors in Gloucestershire, Somerset and Essex, the centuries-old policy of farming demesne lands through reeves, or overseers, was abandoned in 1385. From then on the lands were let out to tenants, many of them at oppressive rack-rents.[27]

The changes amounted to an agrarian revolution, as Eileen Power explains in her classic, *The Wool Trade in English Medieval History*:

The typical sheep farmers of the fifteenth century were the peasantry, with a sprinkling of new men from the towns, and also, no doubt, the small squireens – the one-manor men – who sat tight; and here and there perhaps a monastic house which still produced corn for its own consumption and retained the sheep on its near-lying manors and let out the distant ones. But for the most part, on ploughland and pasture, 'Hodge rules the field'; it was the day of the small man.[28]

The flowering of peasant sheep farming led to the rise of another rural archetype, the travelling wool dealer or middleman. In their day the large estates had sold direct to the great merchants and exporters, often acting as agents for their own tenants. In the thirteenth-century world of large-scale farming there had always been a class of independent middlemen, the woolmongers, some of them villagers or villeins, but most burgesses from the towns.

While the big exporters or their agents dealt in the substantial amounts produced by the demesne flocks, they could not handle the wool from thousands of small flocks scattered all over the countryside. This is when the English middlemen came into their own. They were seldom popular with peasant farmers whose wide dispersion placed them in a weak bargaining position. The woolbrokers haggled and argued ruthlessly so that the handshake, when it came, was often sullen and resentful.

Nevertheless the small brokers were a vital part of the wool economy. They formed the vital link between small peasant flocks and the market. Many made a great deal of money. They left their imprint – the merchant's mark – on scores of churches and fine houses throughout the pastoral countryside; on tombs and monumental brasses, on ceiling beams and on stained glass.

The church at Northleach, a Cotswold town whose coat-of-arms incorporates two bales of wool, is adorned with the wool brasses of many such men – John Fortey, John Taylor, Thomas Busshe and William Midwinter, whose mark was a cross with a flying pennant standing on the letter M. In nearby Chipping Campden the house of wool merchant William Grevel is one of the finest in the town with its two-storey bow window, gothic archways and gargoyles.

In England's growing medieval towns, the wool trade laid the foundations of many a fortune made by merchants and cloth-makers. It built magnificent churches in the Cotswolds and fine medieval houses in East Anglia. In the twelfth century Henry of Huntingdon wrote of England's 'most precious wool', while two centuries later the Ordinance of the Staple spoke of wool as 'the sovereign merchandise and the jewel of this realm of England'.

It was a jewel whose substance clothed the rain-swept uplands and the fertile river valleys, and whose creator was the medieval sheep. The humble ruminant at the heart of this great trade is now all but lost, its identity obscured by centuries of breeding and genetic improvement. The eighteenth-century breeder Robert Bakewell concealed the old sheep of the Middle Ages in the guise of his New Leicester. But the modern division of sheep into closewools and longwools was already apparent in medieval England.[29]

The short-woolled sheep, the lord of poor pastures, of the high hills and moors and downland, was found along the Welsh and Scottish borders, on the Yorkshire fellsides of the Cister-cians and on the rolling chalk grassland of the south. The most renowned of the shortwools was the Ryelands, named after the tract of country stretching from the River Severn to the Welsh Marches. It was the Ryelands that grew the famous Lemster Ore, the 'golden fleece' which surpassed even the wool of the Spanish merino flocks in the production of heavy cloth.

The longwool types, on which the bulk of England's export trade was founded, came from an early version of the Cotswold breed.[30] Now almost lost through modern breeding, the Cotswold helped shape the history of English farming, leaving its imprint on the Lincolns of the heaths, the Romneys of the fertile marsh grasslands and the Leicesters which stocked the vast midlands grazings. In medieval England there was a sheep type to suit virtually every kind of terrain just as there were grassland communities to grow there. Together they provided the island kingdom with her first great, world-beating export industry.

It would be hard to overstate the importance of wool in transforming England into an outward-looking nation. While products such as wheat and cheese were regularly 'exported' from village England, wool was the one truly international commodity. And it was one that might be produced almost anywhere in the land – on the hills and on the lowlands, in large flocks and in small, by the free and the unfree. It represented the first, large-scale exploitation of the country's great natural resource, her pastoral wealth.

Wool transformed every aspect of English life. Socially it furthered the rise of the middle classes. In the countryside, tenant farmers with their growing flocks formed the stock of a new rural middle class – the yeomen farmers whose descendants would form that implacable political force, the conservative rump of the shires. In the towns the wool trade swelled the ranks of the merchant class, and for a short period in the thirteenth and early fourteenth centuries threw up a class of powerful financial capitalists, men who won and lost vast fortunes, particularly in the early stages of the Hundred Years War.

Wool also played its part in England's constitutional development. By the close of the thirteenth century the wool tax had become the main source of royal revenue, a development which coincided with the appearance of the Commons.[31] Many of the early tussles between the monarch and parliament centred on the wool tax. The skirmishing ended in compromise with the king retaining his subsidy on the crop, and parliament securing control of taxation.

But the chief and abiding legacy of this great pastoral enterprise lay in the rooting of English liberties. Grassland had always been associated with freedom, even at the time of the Normans. The England of the manor, the open fields and the demesne was the England of serfdom and constraint. But not in pastoral England, the land of small hamlets and scattered settlements, generally the high country of the north and west.

Here a tenant's wealth was measured by the numbers of his livestock, not by the area under the plough. In the pastoral economy labour services to the lord of the manor were rare.

This was an economy run on money. Into this world came merchants with open purses and a seemingly insatiable demand for English wool. The money they brought was the lifeblood of this kingdom of pastures, providing peasants with the cash to pay their rents, entrenching their liberties.

But the social changes were not all benign. Later the great trade was to bring misery and starvation in its wake. Land would finally cease to be a common resource for the benefit of all. It would become merely a form of private capital from which peasant farmers would be shut out. The practice of enclosure was to blight English rural society for generations. Among the victims would be the shepherd.

In the small Hampshire hamlet of Martin – where the medieval peasants reared their flocks – sheep are now as scarce in the fields as in its sister parish of Damerham, a couple of miles down the road. But in the churchyard beneath the downs a small ewe flock grazes among the moss-covered tombstones. A length of wire netting keeps them off a neatly mown patch of turf beside the church path. In the centre of the little lawn an old headstone has been re-erected in a position easily visible to worshippers walking towards the church porch. Though the letters are worn and smudged with lichens, it is possible to make out the words.

Shepherd of the Wiltshire Downs
William Lawes
Died December 14 1886

William Lawes was the inspiration for Isaac Bawcombe in W. H. Hudson's *A Shepherd's Life*. Close by, sheep tug at the churchyard grasses in the early evening light. Beyond the village the first mists of autumn settle on the high downs.

9 *Summer Pastures*

Life in the medieval village of manor and church was settled and confined. Villagers were bound to their own corner of the kingdom by the ties of common right and obligations to the lord. But in the wilder uplands of western Britain an older tradition flourished, a way of life inherited from the Neolithic herders who once walked these rugged hills. It was the custom of the shielings.

Each year part of the rural community – often the girls and young women – would leave their family homes to live in rudimentary huts high in the hills, close to the upland grazings. There they would pass the summer months milking the cows and making the butter and cheese that would help feed their families through the winter. In the long, sunlit evenings they would spin flax or carve wooden spoons as they told each other stories.

Sometimes they would be joined by boys from the village for a night of music and dancing. But there were many more days passed in solitude among the crags and stony outcrops, where red kites and buzzards drifted on summer winds and the mountain mist could slip over the landscape as easily as the closing of an eyelid.

From the old Scots and Middle English word *schele*, the term shieling was used both for the summer pastures and the simple dwellings that were built on them.[1] The shieling system – the summering of cattle on mountain grazings – was part of a livestock-herding culture dating back to the Neolithic nomads. It was practised in high country right across Europe, and still survives in parts of Norway, Sweden and the Alps. It was a way of life centred on grass and with its roots in an ancient freedom. Across a dozen generations it became, for many women, the gateway to adulthood and understanding.

In those days the summers were very good. When summer came there was a summer. Honey would fall on the grass . . . There was nothing but honesty then. Nobody did treachery or harm to another, and they lived as Christians should, with nothing between them but what was right and just . . . I often heard my mother talking about the fine girls who were her companions in the shieling. There was in her company a fine woman from Feann-a-Bhuidhe above there, called Úna Mícheáil Síle . . . When she and my mother were in the shieling in their youth they always were close friends . . . I heard say that she was as strong as a stag. There was no man in the glen as strong and as active as she was when she was young . . . The summer pasturing continued in this district until my mother was twenty years old or more. That was about ninety years ago. I heard her say that the last summer was the most beautiful and pleasurable they ever had. They were a band of young, spirited girls with little to trouble them.

Niall Ó Dubhthaigh, 1943[2]

From the beginnings of settled agriculture, summer pasturing was an integral part of the rural economy in the hill country. Much of the land close to the main holdings in the more fertile valleys was sown to cereals. In the absence of proper fencing it was necessary to move the cattle away during the spring and summer to stop them straying on to crops. It was also an opportunity to leave the lowland meadows ungrazed so they could be cut for hay, the fodder for the forthcoming winter.

The seasonal use of mountain pastures meant that more cattle could be kept than the main holding alone would support. In the autumn the surplus animals could be slaughtered and their meat salted down, or handed over to drovers for sale in the markets of the south and east. The mountain pastures were usually in areas of good quality vegetation, where bent grasses and fescues flourished rather than the fibrous and unpalatable heather and *Molinia caerulea*, purple moor-grass.

The presence of grazing animals trampling and dunging on the turf over the summer months gradually improved the pasture, making it more productive. Many locals believed the butter produced on the summer pastures was sweeter and tastier than that produced on the lowlands.

The girls who produced it lived during the summer months in huts or houses characteristic of the country and region. In the Scottish Highlands the most common of the summer dwellings were circular or ovoid in shape. The walls were constructed of dry stone, with a roof of turfs overlaid on timbers. One end was used as a fireplace, while a large section was separated by kerbstones and raised to form a low platform on which the heather bedding was laid.[3]

Some of the Scottish summer huts were made entirely of stone, the best-known being the characteristic 'beehive' huts on the island of Lewis. These circular structures were built up with overlapping layers of stones. Conical in shape, they were left open at the top to allow smoke out and light in, though they could be sealed off with a flat stone or turf.[4]

Professor Ronald Miller discovered the sites of almost 250 former shielings in the district of Assynt in south-west Sutherland, a loch-strewn stretch of lowland moor dominated by the mountains of Suilven and Quinag.[5] Some of the shielings contained the ruins of a dozen bothies, the small, rectangular buildings of turf and stone that housed the dairymaids and the herders. Smaller circular structures are believed to have served as stores for butter and cheese.

In Wales the lightly built summer dwellings were known as *hafodai* in the north and *hafodydd* in the middle and south of the country. Though none of these medieval structures has survived, they are likely to have been flimsy affairs made from a wattle of rods and twigs supported on a frame of trimmed tree boughs. The medieval Welsh Laws valued the *hafod* at just twelve pence compared with a value of fifty pence placed on the *hendref*, the main homestead.

The builders of the *hafodai* sometimes used a method of 'glazing' commonly found among the nomadic peoples of the Eurasian steppe grasslands. Window apertures in the stone dwellings were normally left open to the elements, to be filled with a turf or flat stone only at times of bad weather. But in the huts of the better-off residents, a rudimentary window was made from the placenta of a newly foaled mare, stretched tightly across a wooden frame. According to historians, the emergence of this technique in medieval Wales is further evidence that the origins of Celtic peoples lie in the steppes of Asia.[6]

The eighteenth-century geographer Thomas Pennant described the *hafodai* of Snowdonia. 'These houses consist of a long low-room, with a hole at one end to let out the smoke from the fire, which is made beneath. Their furniture is very simple: stones are the substitutes of stools; and the beds are of hay, ranged along the sides.'[7] The summer dwellings in the Galtee Mountains of Ireland were rectangular in shape and constructed of dry stone walls almost a metre thick. The roof of turf overlaid with rush thatch was supported on rafters made from tree branches. The residents slept on pallets of straw and heather, covered with blankets.[8]

In other parts of Ireland rushes were used as bedding material in the summer houses or *booleys*. A seventeenth-century letter from John Dunton describes a booley in Galway: 'We all lay in the same roome upon green rushes . . . and they assur'd me no man ever gott cold by lyeing on green rushes, which indeed are sweet and cleane, being changed everie day if raine hinders not; but though they have not lice among them, they are very full of white snayles . . .'[9]

The summer huts were built on dry, sheltered sites,

sometimes a grassy slope or hillock, but more often an outcrop of rock. The most important requirement was for a plentiful supply of clean water, essential in butter- and cheese-making and for washing the wooden utensils. Dairymaids in the Scottish Highlands were said to have been so particular 'that nothing but water from the coldest hillside springs would satisfy them, not even water from the purest looking streams'.[10] In Wales the waters used by women for washing butter became known as *ffynnon ymenin*, the butter well. Irish booleys were 'nearly always located near running water, usually near the headwaters of mountain streams, where patches of bright green grass and such characteristic flowers as tormentil may reveal their sites even when almost all trace has gone'.[11]

The place where most of the shielings were, long ago, was behind in the place called Na Trí Phíopaí between this parish and the parish of Gaoth Dobhair. There was a nice level place where no turf was cut. There was a stream coming down from a lake which is up on top of the hill, called Loch an Duine. The name of the stream is An Sruthán Geal. The water rushing down that stream would delight you. It is nice to see and healthy to drink. Beside that stream the shielings were sited.[12]

Some early writers – including Thomas Pennant – have suggested that the owners of cattle, 'with their families', resided in the *hafodai* during the summer months. Yet in much of Wales, Ireland, and the Scottish Highlands it was the custom for women to do the milking and the butter-making. Boys would often come to the shielings as herders of cattle, sometimes even taking a turn at churning. But they viewed milking as 'unmanly' and 'women's work'.[13]

In contrast to other forms of cattle herding and nomadism, the shieling system was geared to the processing of milk. This was a responsibility that had long rested with women. It was the practice for three or four girls – sisters or friends, usually unmarried – to live in each hut, often caring for the cattle of several families, and dividing up the work and produce between them. Families with no young girls arranged for their cows to be looked after by others, paying the dairymaids of their families for the service.

The dates for moving to and quitting the summer pastures varied around the country. Women were required to help with the spring sowing at the main home farm. They could not leave for the mountains until the job was complete. Nor could the cattle be run on the upland grazings until grass growth was well underway. Spring came late to the mountain pastures, particularly those on the highest slopes and in the far north. Each locality had its dates for arriving at and leaving the summer pastures, and these were rigorously adhered to.

In the west of Ireland the summer grazing period ran from early May to late October, traditionally from Bealtaine, May Day, to Samhain, November Day.[14] In the Hebrides the summer migration took place relatively late, in early June when the tillage work was complete, returning to the home farm when the corn was ripe and ready for harvest. In Wales the *hafod* season was set out in the ancient Welsh Laws. The traditional date for moving on to the summer pastures was, as in Ireland, *Calan Mai*, May Day, while the date for returning to winter quarters was *Calan Gaeaf*, All Saints' Day.[15]

The time of the annual migration was eagerly looked forward to, though it would be a time of hard work. The Welsh language contains a verb *hafota* (derived from the noun *hafod*), which means to work hard. Similarly the word *hendrefa* (from *hendref*, the home farm) means to rest. The months in the shielings would be a period of long days spent milking, butter-making, moving cattle to and from their grazings and keeping the huts clean and weather proof.

But for most it was a happy time, this season passed in the fresh, mountain air far from the squalid and sometimes disease-ridden conditions of the 'township'. For all the hard work it was a sort of holiday, an escape from the routine and the humdrum, a taste of freedom and self-reliance amid scenery of immense grandeur. For some it was a release from the constraint of organised religion. In the shielings of Finglen in the central Scottish Highlands, a woman voiced her own delight at being far from the sermons and catechising of the minister: *'Fionna Ghleann mo chridhe, far nach bitheadh Didomhnaich'* – Finglen of my heart, where there would be no Sunday.[16]

In the mountains there were wide skies, a scent of heather, and broad views across the hills with perhaps a glimpse of the shimmering sea and its islands hanging as ephemeral as mist on the far horizon. The food was good and plentiful. In the sixteenth century it was said of the Scottish herders that 'they make good cheer of every sort of milk, baith of cow milk and ewe milk, sweet milk and sour milk, curds and whey, sour kitts, fresh butter and salted butter, reyme, flotwhey, green cheese and kirn milk. They had no bread but rye cakes and fustean scones made of flour.'[17]

There were dangers in the mountains, too, some real, some imagined. Violent storms might threaten both people and livestock with lightning strikes. Cattle might stray in their search for better grass, perhaps tumbling off a rocky crag or getting sucked into a peat bog. There was a risk of disease and sickness, with young and weak animals threatened by foxes, hawks and kites. There was also a threat from supernatural forces – the fairies that were believed to shoot cattle with 'elfbolts', and the practitioners of black arts who could halt the flow of milk from an udder or prevent butter from 'coming' in the churn.[18] A traditional Hebridean herd blessing invokes protection for the cows:

> From rocks, from drifts, from streams,
> From crooked passes, from destructive pits,
> From the straight arrows of the slender ban-shee,
> From the heart of envy, from the eye of evil ... [19]

The Hebridean herd owners protected their herds from evil forces by eating special cheeses on May Day, the great Iron Age Celtic festival of Beltane. The cheeses were known as Beltane cheese. Their consumption was supposed to secure the safety and health of the animals while they grazed the summer pastures. Another protection against the supernatural was invoked by driving the cattle through the fire and smoke produced from the burning branches of the rowan tree, the mountain ash.[20]

The annual migration spawned many popular myths and legends. In Ireland a story of the attempted abduction of a girl from a summer pasture is told in places as far apart as Galway, Mayo and Donegal.[21] On the even of departure for the shielings it was the custom of many cattle owners to draw blood from the animals' tails. Afterwards they would bind a length of red thread into the tail hair of each beast. It was said that no evil eye or spell could affect the animal with thread on its tail.[22]

The day of the migration became something of a holiday occasion. The girls did not travel alone to their summer homes. Fathers, mothers and brothers went with them, returning to the main homestead that same day. The mountain tracks were too rough for wheeled vehicles, so food, clothing and equipment had to be carried by pack-horse or donkey, or on people's backs. Among the luggage that had to be transported to the shielings were clothing, bedclothes, cooking utensils, spinning wheels and all the necessary dairy equipment. The cattle were herded along gently by the boys and their dogs.[23] In the Hebrides people and animals travelled together:

> On the given day, they were all up early, like bees about to swarm; the summer of their joy was come. The sheep and cattle knew the day as well as did the men and women, and they were eager to start. Should a funeral or some other chance happening delay the departure, the animals had to be guarded night and day, or they would be off to the hills by themselves. All the families brought their stock together at a particular place, and there the procession was formed in order. The sheep led; the cattle followed, according to their ages, the youngest leading; then came the goats, and finally the horses. The men carried burdens of sticks, pins, heather-ropes, spades and other things needed to repair their summer huts. The women carried the bedding, meal, dairy-vessels, and cooking utensils. The horses, with creels slung over their backs, shared some of the burdens.

When the procession moved off, all was noise and

clamour. Sheep were bleating for their lambs, lambs for their mothers; cows and calves, mares and foals were calling for one another; and the men, several at a time, shouted directions and scoldings. Bare-headed and bare-footed boys and girls, assisted by barking dogs, tried to head off some bolting young animal that objected to leaving its home for the first time. The women were talking and singing, and knitting stockings as they walked ... All who met the procession on its way wished it a good day, much luck, and safe herding.[24]

Left to themselves on the shielings, the girls set about their main tasks of milking and butter-making. They would set the milk, skim off the cream, churn the butter, pack it in firkins and store it away until it could be taken to the butter market in the nearest market town. In many pastures, special huts or stone-lined cellars were built for use as butter stores. Sometimes one of the boys from the home community would arrive to collect a quantity of butter or milk, though the frequency of such visits depended on the distance between the farm and the mountain pasture.[25]

Writing of shieling life in the Scottish Highlands at the close of the eighteenth century, Duncan Campbell describes the meticulous care taken by the dairymaids, who considered it 'a sin to permit any suspicion of sourness about the dairy vessels'.[26] They were scrubbed and scalded with hot water, washed in splashings of cold water, and laid out to dry on thyme-covered banks. Two sets of vessels were required. While one was in use the other was left 'sweetening'. Though rotary barrel-churns were easier to work, the girls of the shielings preferred to use upright plunge-churns because they were more easily cleaned and purified in the sun and fresh air.

On the island of Lewis the cattle were led to the day's pasture at about six in the morning. At nine o'clock they were brought back to the huts for milking, after which they were left to graze close by until the afternoon. The head girl would then lead them to a pasture further away, where they would stay until it was time for the evening milking at around ten o'clock. The milk was kept in dishes which were placed in crevices in the walls for cooling. The dairymaids skimmed the milk morning and evening, and churned butter once a week.[27]

In Donegal the cows were tied to stakes for milking. The stakes were made from bog-pine and driven firmly into the ground close to the shieling huts. Niall Ó Dubhthaigh recalls the daily routine, as related by his mother:

> When evening came the girls drove the milking cows and tied them up with the tyings. They milked them and left them there until morning next day. They usually threw down a little bundle of coarse grass or the like, which they gathered along the edge of streams. This was called 'kindness' – anything which coaxed a cow to be more fixed in the place she was tied. When the cows had some practice of this, they returned by themselves in the evening, as they wanted to get a little kindness.
>
> Often when one of the cattle was missing from the milking, the girl would call out to it by name, when it was perhaps half a mile away: 'Benthorn' or 'Hoofy' or 'Spotty' or 'Brindle' or 'Bee', and that cow would walk directly to her at the shieling. Then she would give it a handful of oatmeal in warm water, and that would coax it next time it was called. Those cows were as clever as humans. So accustomed were they to being put out and in, there was no trouble or work with them. When they had been milked in the morning, all that was to be done was to drive them up the hill to where the young animals were, and they grazed there until evening.[28]

Unsalted butter produced on the shielings was often preserved by burying it in peat bogs. Finds of bog-butter have been made by peat diggers in both Scotland and Ireland. One explanation is that the bog-butter was buried simply to stop it becoming rancid. But some historians have suggested that these were ritual offerings. According to legend the burial of food was supposed to appease angry fairies.[29]

Despite the hard work of the dairymaids, they often found

time for social gatherings. In the Hebrides the festivities would go on all night, the youngsters dancing and singing on the soft, summer grass to the music of the pipes.[30] Often the people of widely separated home communities would meet together socially on the summer grazings they shared. On the Berwyn Mountains in north Wales people from the Dee valley in the north and the Tanat valley in the south made use of adjoining grazings. Each year the two communities would meet on the summer pastures, swapping invitations to each other's *hafodai*, exchanging stories and gossip.[31]

In Donegal the social life of the shielings was equally active:

When my mother was in the pastures, there were nine or ten shielings round about her own. The girls would all gather into one shieling, and the boys from their neighbourhood would occasionally go up on a summer evening to entertain them in their loneliness up on the hills. My mother had many sweet Irish songs. She would tell us that long ago in the shieling she heard the song from this one or that, some from fine boys who went to America and were killed in the Civil War and never more returned.[32]

After the festivities the dairymaids would return to their lives of solitude and toil amid the whirling mists, mountain rain and sudden storms, and the roaring streams to which they gave birth. The young male herders, alone with their cattle, felt the solitude deeply. 'The spirit of the hills lay like a spell on us.'[33]

Sometime in the seventeenth century, the shieling system began its long decline. Hill pastures that had long been communal grazings were enclosed and occupied by a single owner. In Wales it became the established practice for younger sons to carve homesteads for themselves and their families from the upland *hafodai*, building permanent dwellings and turning them into self-contained holdings.[34] Customary use of the same grazings fostered a sense of ownership among the users, and since many farmers were interested in enclosing their own upland *heaf* or *cynhefin*, the process took place without great rancour. Hill farms with names containing the words *hafod* or *hafoty* are today common throughout upland Wales.

The breakdown of summer pasturing coincided with the rapid spread of sheep farming. Sheep did not need the continuous attention demanded by dairy cows – they could graze the most far-flung and difficult pastures without supervision. Sheep farming became the dominant enterprise on the Welsh mountains, and by the close of the eighteenth century George Kay reported that he had been unable to find any trace of the shieling system in the whole of Caernarvonshire.[35]

By the same time most of the shielings in the central Scottish Highlands had been abandoned, though a naturalist on Lewis was able to write as recently as 1927:

> Shieling custom has been in existence in Lewis for four hundred years, and it is interesting to note that with few exceptions the institution is still preserved in all its ancient purity, and in no way tainted with modern ideas . . . I am writing this at the door of my lonely shieling hut which is built on a green knoll over-looking a fresh-water loch studded with islands.
>
> These islands are the abodes of nymphs which, however, are seen only by those who have a certain kind of eye to see them . . . one would need to be an earth-bound mortal who could not for the moment indulge in dreams of delight and beauty, and appreciate in spellbound bewilderment the dazzling glory of a perfect summer evening on a Lewis moor.[36]

For a way of life so central to the economy of the hill country, transhumance – the seasonal movement of livestock to a different area – has left remarkably little documentary evidence. The historian R. U. Sayce, researching the history of the old summer pastures in Montgomeryshire, wrote of 'the curious silence of contemporary records about everyday things'. What little is known about life on the summer pastures is mainly based on accounts written by eighteenth-century travellers to the British uplands. But while the documentary evidence may be scant, the shieling system left indelible marks on the landscapes and people of these harsh, highland places.

Some of the most vivid reminders are inscribed on the very mountain turf. Where once the people of the valley summered their cattle and goats, perhaps centuries earlier, the bright, green grass still stands out in sharp relief from the grey-brown of the surrounding vegetation. Summer grazing with cattle did a power of good to these bleak, upland swards. Cattle are the least selective of all farm livestock in their grazing habits. Unlike sheep, they will happily munch on the coarser, less palatable vegetation such as the tough mat grass and the wiry purple moor-grass, particularly at the start of the season when the leaves are young. In this way they check the spread of coarse species and encourage the more succulent and nutritious grasses such as sheep's fescue and bent-grass.

Their heavy, trampling hoofs also help to control bracken and gorse. And because, under the old shieling system, they were taken off in late October, when there was still growth left in the turf, there was a chance for the grasses to build up the root reserves that would get them off to a good start next year.

For more than two centuries mountain grasslands have been grazed mainly by sheep. In recent years the upland pastures have been dominated by ewes and lambs, put there by a subsidy system that cares little for working with the grain of nature. Suckling ewes and fast-growing lambs ignore the tough, fibrous grasses and graze the more succulent species so hard they become weaker year by year. Thus the turf gradually deteriorates as unpalatable clumps of mat grass and other coarse species take over.

The grazing system that improved the pasture also turned out healthy foods. The milk for today's butter and cheese comes mainly from cows grazing heavily fertilised grassland supplemented with a substantial amount of high-energy concentrate feed, the kind of ruminant diet that falls short of the ideal as far as human health is concerned.

Cows on the old shielings ate nothing but grass and other forms of vegetation, some of it coarse and fibrous. For ruminant animals like cattle this is the perfect ration – high in fibre and low in energy. It also happens to be the diet producing the healthiest milk from the consumer's point of view. Cows fed this forage-based ration produce milk that is rich in omega-3 fatty acids – the sort that stop you getting heart attacks – and in a lipid known to protect against a number of cancers. This may be one of the reasons why both cattle, and their female minders, usually returned from their summer in the mountains a lot healthier than they started out.

The other legacy of the shielings is seen in the character of the people they produced. In Scotland, the annual migration to the summer pastures created the distinct character of Highlanders with their own singular view of the world.[37] Scottish accounts refer to the Highlander's 'superior degree of fancy and feeling', which is attributed to the leisure of the pastoral life.

Like the Mongol nomads of the steppe grasslands and the Native American of the prairies, the Highlander had time for 'music, poetry and lounging in the sun'.[38] This was the eternal gift of grass, the freedom of the open sky, the freedom to be fully alive. It was a gift taken from the Highlander by the break-up of the clans and the 'clearances' that were to transform large tracts of the upland landscape into 'lonely sheep runs and sombre, empty deer forest'.[39]

On the island of Lewis, where the shieling system survived as late as the 1950s, the life of the summer pastures inspired many lyric songs. In 1984, Donald Macdonald of North Tolsta, Lewis, wrote: 'Life on the moors in summer was as idyllic as life could possibly be.'[40] Many see more than nostalgia in this attachment to a way of life now past. 'The people of Lewis are more tenacious of their Gaelic, more imperialistic than in the other Gaelic dialect areas . . . Very much alive in the memories of an older generation is the inherited and instinctive fondness for the notion of a freedom they enjoyed when they were young, or the frequently described holiday atmosphere, the change from the annual routine and round of tasks.'[41]

In seventeenth-century Wales, hill shepherds adopted the old custom of shieling.[42] These were independent and resourceful men, famed for their intimate knowledge of the mountain terrain. Each would be familiar with every crag, every rocky outcrop, every cluster of blackthorn trees in his hill domain.

Many upland shepherds milked the sheep they ran on the summer pastures, making cheese from the milk as generations of dairymaids had done before them. The legendary strength and stamina of the shepherds of Plynlimmon was put down to their lifelong diet of sheep's milk. They would stride like giants across the grey crags and high moorland, knitting wool as they went.

In a mellow stone farm building at the end of a long, high-banked lane in Pembrokeshire, Thelma Adams makes delicious cheeses. With names like Perl Wen, Caerffili, Ddraig Goch, and Lancych, they are as Welsh as the cloud shadows on the Brecon Beacons or the sparkling stream that tumbles from a high peak in Snowdonia. Such is the quality that they sell in London's top store, Harrods, as well as in independent shops all over Wales. Thelma Adams refuses to supply them to the big supermarket chains.

Caws Cenarth at Fferm Glyneithinog near Newcastle Emlyn is very much a family business. Thelma's husband Gwynfor, their son Carwyn, who takes care of the farm's sixty cows, daughter Caroline, and Carwyn's Russian-born wife, Susanna, all take a share in running the enterprise. As well as selling in Harrods, their cheeses have been enjoyed by the royal family and scooped major honours in the annual British Cheese Awards.

Beyond the farm's gently sloping pastures, wooded hills climb steeply to the high moors of the Preseli Mountains, whose purple peaks brood over this pastoral landscape. Half a millennium ago the young women from these lowland farm-steads took their cattle to summer on the same high pastures. At Fferm Glyneithinog the cows stay on the lowland. But the milk they give is from grass alone. And the cheeses made on the little farm are the same healthy, hand-made foods as the dairymaids produced on their windswept shielings centuries ago.

In the small cheese room Thelma Adams carefully cuts up the curd in a vat of what is destined to be a new blue cheese. She says: 'There's a long tradition of farmhouse dairy products in this part of Wales. A few generations back, many farms made butter and a few of them cheese. What we are doing is nothing really new. Small farms like this have always made wonderful foods – better than the modern factory products. Perhaps people are at last beginning to realise the value of what we had and have lost.'

High above, a chill breeze from the Irish Sea stirs the brown heads of wiry mat grass on a lonely Preseli hilltop. It is October. The summer is ended.

10   The Drowning Fields

E
ngland at the turn of the sixteenth century was a nation
stalked by hunger. The population had scarcely grown
above the level it reached before the Black Death. In the
countryside, where most people worked, grain yields rose and
fell like an ocean swell, making sickness and starvation the
constant companion of rural communities.

Arable lands were suffering a chronic loss of fertility.
Successive wheat and barley crops depleted soils of essential
plant nutrients, and remedies were limited. Since Saxon times
the land had been rested or fallowed after a couple of cereal
crops, allowing time for soil bacteria to work on plant residues,
converting organic nitrogen into nitrates which crop plants
could use. There was also the old expedient of dunging the
arable fields by grazing them or hauling manure out from the
cattleyard.

Neither method was particularly effective in keeping up
fertility. Livestock numbers were seldom high enough to meet
the demand for manure. As a result soil became exhausted and
people went hungry.

The country was caught in the classic trap identified by

Thomas Malthus: periods of famine and social unrest whenever population numbers outstripped the production of grain. But in a secluded valley close to the Welsh border an eccentric landowner had come up with a novel solution.

Rowland Vaughan, the second son of Watkyn Vaughan of Bredwardine in Herefordshire, had been destined for a life in Queen Elizabeth I's court. He had some useful connections: one of his cousins was groom of the royal chambers, while his great-aunt, Dame Blanche Parry, was chief gentle woman of the Privy Chamber.

But Dame Blanche's regime at court was a harsh one, tougher even than the life of a soldier. After a brief taste of court life the young Rowland couldn't wait to escape from his great-aunt's 'crabbed authority'. In desperation he signed on in the army, soon finding himself plunged into the Irish wars. After four years of poor diets and periods spent 'standing twist deep in bogs', he contracted a condition referred to as 'the country disease' and was invalided home to Bredwardine.

Having recovered his health he might well have returned to soldiering but for the intervention of romance. Elizabeth Vaughan was a 'fair and virtuous' woman, a near neighbour and the daughter of his cousin. The two were married and Rowland devoted himself reluctantly to the management of her property, she being 'seized of a manor and an over-shott mill'.

The manor was New Court, a large estate with land running alongside the River Dore in Herefordshire's 'Golden Valley'. In legend the river had been named by Saxon invaders following their capture of the valley from the Welsh. Demanding of some wretched prisoner the name of the little brook, they were told simply that it was *dwr*, the Welsh word for water. The Saxons took the name to be Dor, or gold. Centuries later the Cistercian monks, who built an abbey nearby, called the place Valle d'Oro.

Rowland Vaughan had little relish for the job of running his wife's estate. For a while he did his utmost to avoid the responsibility, preferring instead to go out on drunken bashes with his friends. But the 'fair Elizabeth' managed to put a stop to his carousing. He 'obeyed her will, as many doe, and many miseries do ensue thereby'.

There also seem to have been a number of benefits, not least a revolutionary idea that would transform the fortunes of the New Court estate, creating a thriving community in this remote valley. It was an idea that would be adopted by agricultural 'improvers' across Britain, boosting the output of their pastures and helping to rid the countryside of hunger.

Vaughan's big idea was to exploit the fertility carried in river water, particularly when it was in flood. He claimed to have had his inspiration from the activities of a mole. In his book, *Most Approved and Long Experienced Water-workes*, published in 1610, he recalls the moment of enlightenment:

> In the month of March, falling (with the streame) to the milne-ward within my meade . . . I happened to finde a mole or wants nest, raised on the brim of the brooke, like a great hillocke, from which . . . there issued a little streame of water, drawne by the working of the wante downe a shelving or descending ground, one pase broad and some twenty in length. The running of which little streame did . . . wonderfully content mee, seeing it pleasing greene; and that other on both sides full of mosse, and hide-bound for want of water.

Rowland Vaughan was an early pioneer of one of the great accomplishments of British agriculture – the floated water meadow. For three centuries landowners with low-lying pastures close to rivers and streams would 'drown' or 'float' them by diverting water across them. The idea spread to hill areas where farmers with steep fields would divert the tumbling streams to create 'catch meadows'.

Their aim was to cover the grassland with a thin film of flowing water, protecting the turf from winter frosts and fertilising it with deposits of silt. Floated pastures carried more stock and produced larger quantities of manure, which in turn lifted the yields of arable crops. In an age before nitrogen fertiliser, they were a means of raising the fertility of pasture land. But floating was not for the peasant farmer, nor for the faint-hearted rich. Construction of a network of channels and sluices to distribute water across the grass surface, and to drain it off afterwards, required a lot of capital. It is no coincidence that the first recorded water-works were designed and built by a well-off landowner.

Rowland Vaughan's own account of the construction gives no detailed picture of the lay-out or its cost, though the works are known to have irrigated all the land on the western bank of the River Dore from Peterchurch to New Court. He describes the excavation of a main channel – he calls it the Trench Royal – three miles long and so carefully levelled that by the judicious use of dams, or stanks, water could be made to flow in either direction.

From the main channel it was conducted across the grass surface via a network of smaller channels, variously described as 'counter trenches, defending trenches, topping or braving trenches, winter and summer trenches, double and treble trenches, a traversing trench with a point, an everlasting trench' together with sundry other 'troublesome trenches'.

At the time of its construction – in the closing decades of the sixteenth century – the water-works at New Court were not without their critics. As the scheme took shape Vaughan reports that a group of his neighbours 'summoned a consultation against mee and my man John the leveller, saying our wittes were in our hands and not in our heads'.

Nor was the Golden Valley pioneer free of dissent from within his own ranks. When John the leveller realised just how celebrated a task he had been employed on he demanded that he be given a grander title. From now on he wanted to be known as chief agent for the project. In his reply Vaughan tersely informed him that he had been employed for 'his hands and not his head'.

There followed a further 'brabble', this time with the carpenter employed to construct the weirs and sluices that would control the flow of the main river. When the soundness of his foundations was challenged, the craftsman grew 'teasty, hott and peremptory'. It was not 'the maister's manner to controule', he complained, 'but to examine'.

The carpenter assured his client that all his 'water-workes

were according to the Venetian foundation, built altogether uppon piles'. Vaughan wryly observed that the man's 'Venetian fashion' had cost him no less than 2,000 pounds.

Despite the setbacks, the irrigation system at New Court appears to have been a success, raising the rentable value of the pasture from forty pounds to three hundred pounds, an improvement that must have delighted the business-minded Elizabeth.

> As the River Nilus drownes Egipt from the Abissine Mountaines, enriching the countrey, to the wonder of the world, so doth the muddy-floudes from the upper part of the Golden Valley (as from a golden mountaine or fountaine) improove my estate beyond beleef . . . It's confessed by all in the Golden Vale that that little land which we have would be bettred fifteene hundred pounds a year. If the like were done through-out England, it would profit the kingdome in a yeare two millions, which would maintain an army-royalle, to the honour of Great Brittaine, and be most comfortable to all honourable souldiers, creste-falne for want of warre and military imployment.

Even as Vaughan proclaimed the benefits of his water-works on the borderlands, similar constructions were already in place elsewhere in England. In the Dorset village of Affpuddle on the River Piddle the lord of the manor, Sir Edward Lawrence, had long encouraged his tenants to irrigate their meadows.[1] An order of the Affpuddle manorial court shows that the practice of watering grassland was already well established by 1607.

> Whereas the water course is used to be turned into the meads by the tenants thereof and kepte theare longer than it hath been accustomed, yt is therefore ordered that the tenants of the meads shall use the same in noe other sorte than in ancient tyme it hath been used.[2]

In Dorset development of the new technology was a communal undertaking, driven by a small group of tenants with the encouragement of their landlords.[3] Not all were willing participants. Some farmers opposed the idea. Even so water meadows were constructed along the length of the Piddle, Frome, Cerne, Tarrant, Gussage and other chalkland streams. In 1629 pioneering tenants of Affpuddle agreed on a more general scheme for watering the meadows, even engaging a 'waterman' to run it. A rate was charged on the tenants to cover his wages.

The 'drowning meadows' were equally popular on the chalk streams of neighbouring counties. In Wiltshire floating began experimentally in 1616, and had become firmly established by the middle of the century.[4] In 1639 the constable of Shalbourne 'presented' Richard Clifford, gentleman of that place, at quarter-sessions for 'raysing up a new hatch in his meadow whereby the water is bayed back in such wise' that the pathway to the church is barred. In the same year Richard Constable, a gentleman of Broad Hinton, was 'presented' for turning an ancient watercourse to the annoyance of his neighbours.[5]

The court roll at Wylye contains a 1632 order for the general floating and watering of the meadows of the township.[6] Sir Giles Mompesson and Guy Everley, together with freeholders, tenants and 'customers' entered an agreement with John Knight of Stockton who undertook to float, manage and maintain the Marsh, Nettlemead and the Moors. For their part the people of Wylye undertook to make and maintain all the timber works, flood-hatches and bays, to allow John Knight and his workmen to dig trenches and conduits, and to pay him from the common purse 14s. for every acre floated plus 2s. per acre annually for maintenance.

In Hampshire water meadows had been built on all the major south-flowing rivers by 1686.[7] Drowning schemes included Sturbridge Mead at North Stoneham, constructed on a tributary of the River Itchen, How Park Meads near Kings Somborne on the River Test, and Gorley Meade on the River Avon. By the end of the eighteenth century, few sites remained to be exploited.

Floated meadows were constructed in many parts of the country, but they were nowhere more prized than in the chalk valleys of the southern counties. There the decaying remnants of sluice, ditch and drain are still discernible in riverside meadows. In this part of England they transformed the farming economy of the eighteenth and nineteenth centuries, playing an important part in Britain's farming revolution.

The value of flood water in stimulating grass growth was well known long before anyone thought of channelling it. For centuries farmers with meadows on the flood plains of major rivers had benefited from the fertility introduced by the annual inundation. In his 1652 volume, *The English Improver Improved*, Walter Blith had no doubt of the 'fruitfulness of water'.

A rich land-flood is ever the washing down of great road wayes, common fields, under tillage; or else from great townes, houses or dunghils; the riches whereof is unvaluable. Consider the goodnesse of thy water if thy water be a rich land-flood, or a lusty gallant streame, it will run further and wider upon thy land with life and fruitfulnesse.

John Worlidge, whose *Systema Agriculturae* appeared in 1687, urged the deliberate flooding of grassland when the flow and course of a waterway made natural inundation a rare event.

Other meadows there are, and those the most general in England, that border the lesser rivers and streams, and in many places are overflown or drowned, by diverting the water out of its natural and usual current over them. This art of diverting rivers and streams over dry lands, is much used through the world; rice, a more universal grain than wheat, being propagated for the most part in irrigated lands. And so long since as Virgil wrote of husbandry was this in use, as well for corn in those hotter parts, as here for grass, as he sings:

When his scorch'd fields with dying herbage burns,
Then may he conduct from some rising ground
Water, whose current makes a murm'ring sound
'Mongst polish'd pebles, and refreshment yields
From bubling rivulets, to thirsty fields.

In the floating meadow of the southern chalk country a weir

or hatch is first constructed across the main river to control the flow. From this hatch water is conducted down a main trench or duct to the meadow, and then down a network of smaller ditches or *carriages* across the 'pitch of work'. The flow through them is obstructed at intervals by 'stops', which keep the levels high enough to feed smaller carriages carrying water over the land surface.

Between each pair of peripheral carriages a drainage channel, or *drawn*, conducts the water to a main drain, which rejoins the river further downstream. In a well laid-out network the carriages and drains 'bring on and carry off the water as systematically as the arteries and veins do the blood in the human body'.[8] The water was said to come in 'at a trot' along the ducts and leave 'at a gallop' along the drains.

The main channels, both carriages and drains, had to be floored and walled with timber, with hatches, sluices and stops constructed of timber and iron. Finally grass had to be seeded over the meadow. Construction was not cheap. The cost of creating the floated meadows of south Wiltshire was estimated at between twelve pounds and twenty pounds an acre in the eighteenth century.[9] By the mid-nineteenth century landowners were spending as much as fifty pounds an acre to float their grassland.[10]

Once up and running, the water meadow was controlled and managed by a skilled 'drowner'. When autumn rains swelled the river, bringing with it village washings and nutrient-laden sediments from the soil, the drowner would pass the stream over his meadow in a sheet, keeping up the flow for as long as the frosts continued.[11]

The water provided a warm blanket for the grass, maintaining growth through the winter cold. As a result of the sediment, much of it from the chalk soils, this growth was often luxurious. After a couple of days' drying out, the meadow was ready for grazing by sheep, usually the ewes and their young lambs.

The floated meadows of downland England were crucial to characteristic 'sheep-and-corn' husbandry widely practised on the thin, chalk soils before the chemical age. The principal reason for keeping sheep was for the dung they supplied to the arable land. As Bishop Latimer observed: 'A plough land must have sheep; yea, they must have sheep to dung their ground for bearing corn; for if they have no sheep to help fat the ground, they shall have but bare corn and thin.'[12]

Without sheep the downland soils would have become exhausted and of no use for cropping. The usual pattern was to run the flock on the downland pastures during daytime. In autumn they would be confined at night on the wheat land or the land destined for spring barley, the 'Lenten corn'. The practice was known as folding and made use of portable wooden hurdles to form temporary pens. At lambing time the ewes – the favoured part of the flock – were run on the enclosed meadows and pastures, including the water meadows.[13]

The stimulus to grass growth allowed farmers to keep sheep in greater numbers, so boosting the supply of dung to the cereal crops. Floating had the additional benefit of providing an 'early bite', a grazing crop in the hungry month of April, that month 'between hay and grass' when, according to Thomas Davis, steward to the Marquis of Bath at Longleat, 'he who has not water meadow for his ewes and lambs, frequently has nothing at all'.

The ewes will bring a very good lamb with hay only; perhaps a few turnips are preserved for the lambs, which, in a very favourable season, may last them through March. But if they are obliged to go to hay again, the ewes shrink their milk, the lambs 'pitch and get stunted', and the best summer food will not recover them. To prevent this, recourse is had to feeding the grass of those dry meadows that are intended for hay, the young clovers, and frequently the young wheat; in fact, everything that is green. And who will pretend to estimate what is the loss a farmer suffers by this expedient?[14]

Sheep flocks throughout the southern chalk downland followed a regular seasonal calendar of grazing and folding devised to make the best use of the water meadows. At Winfrith Newburgh in Dorset, the meadow on the banks of the River Frome was floated from All Saints' Day (1 November) to St

Thomas's Day (21 December), to benefit from the silts and sediments brought down by autumn floods.[15] The hatches were then drawn, and the water was allowed to flow on to irrigate the meadows at Moreton and Bovington lower down the valley.

On some manors farmers and millers entered into complicated deals over the use of flood waters. The meadow at Waddock in Affpuddle was allowed to be watered 'from each and every Saturday night unto each and every Munday morning, and at all and every other tyme and tymes doing no prejudice unto the mill there'.

In a report to the Royal Society Robert Seymer described the practice of his own area: ' . . . the chiefest time they account for watering is to begin about All-hallows, and to continue until Candlemas and no longer, especially if the ground be naturally moyst; for they find by experience that if the water run any considerable time longer than this on their ground it breeds abundance of rushes, but all the winter it destroys them . . .'

The first grass crop from the floated meadow was up to six weeks ahead of the dry meadows. By the end of April the sheep would have grazed off most of the herbage, and after a few more days of floating the meadow was shut up for hay in July. The hay crops often amounted to two tons an acre, twice the yields of ordinary hay meadows. The very best floated meadows could produce three tons an acre or more.[16]

The irrigation of grassland transformed the economies of the chalkland counties, turning them into major producers of wheat. In south Wiltshire alone no less than 9,000 acres of grassland had become floated meadows by the mid-eighteenth century, most of them in the valleys of the chalk downs.[17]

They are thought to have been the reason for a near-doubling in size of the old Wiltshire sheep breed between the seventeenth and early nineteenth centuries. The Wiltshire, now extinct, was hardly the most attractive of sheep: it had a large, clumsy head, a long, arched face, horns that twisted back behind the ears, and awkwardly long but sturdy legs.[18] But the animal was agile and strong, ideally suited to its long morning climb to the downland grazings and its nightly return to the fold on the arable.

Following the development of floated meadows the breed went from strength to strength. Early nutrition was probably more influential than genetic improvement in the breed's rapid increase in stature. The milk produced from lush, irrigated grassland got the young lambs off to a good start.

While water meadows were popular with farmers, they failed to impress anglers on these celebrated chalk streams. They often caused catastrophic damage to fish populations.[19] Migrating parr and smolt lost their way in the rafts of weed cut adrift by drowners clearing their channels. Fish were also drawn into the network of channels where water levels might change rapidly, leaving them stranded.

The deposition of sediment and detritus on the meadow deprived fish in the main stream of food. Insects and plankton were filtered from the water as it passed over the vegetation, reducing the nutrient content of the returning stream. Fish were starved to feed the luxuriant growth of bankside meadows.

Despite the disadvantages, the general enthusiasm for water meadows grew throughout the eighteenth century. Water engineers entered into long debates over the finer points of their construction, while evangelistic landlords urged their tenants to embrace the wondrous new technology. By the end of the century any landowner with a parcel of low-lying land that seemed even remotely suitable had at least investigated the possibility of drowning it.

But the floated meadow only worked on relatively level land. Some alternative system was needed if landowners in the hills and uplands were to share the benefits of grassland irrigation. That alternative was not long coming. The *catch meadow*, developed in the English west country,[20] was particularly well suited to small parcels of grassland on steep slopes. The only requirement was that there should be a convenient spring or stream emerging at a higher level than the ground to be irrigated.

Water was first carried to the catch meadow by a canal 'of small gradient', and discharged into a trench or *conductor* running along the top of the area to be watered. Below the main conductor a series of small, parallel trenches traversed the meadow at regular intervals down to the bottom of the hill. When the conductor was full, water overflowed along its entire length, running down the slope in a uniform sheet to the next trench, which then began to fill up. In this way water flowed from trench to trench until, from the lowest gutter, it was returned to the river or channelled into another field. The entire meadow was covered by sheets of water cascading down from trench to trench.

The catch meadow brought a new fertility to grasslands far from the chalk streams of southern England. In Devon, birthplace of the new system, thousands of acres of hillside that were 'once mere furze-brakes, are now valuable grassland, owing to this watering, never having received a load of manure within the memory of man'.[21]

High on Exmoor, farmer Robert Smith transformed barren land – 'certainly not worth two-and-six in its natural state' – into valuable grassland, worth more than two pounds an acre for the summer grazing alone. He had made the change 'without a cart ever being led on the land, by the judicious use of large horizontal gutters, which have been made to carry down the washings of the hill, and so do the work of the cart by carrying earthy matter where it is required'.[22]

A few miles away on the banks of the River Barle, close to the stepping stones known as Tarr Steps, the Reverend Joseph Jekyll constructed both a catch meadow and a floated meadow for 'but a trifling cost'. The flat meadow was

> not long since a rough bramble-brake, the loss of which might be regretted by the lovers of the picturesque, if the smooth green velvet of the meadow had not its own charm ... The difference between the herbage on the higher part above the level of the sluice, which had been manured with dung, and that on the part which had been watered, was in favour of the latter; and the waters of the Barle are by no means of the first quality for irrigation.

Sometimes the extravagant claims of water meadow enthusiasts were more than the sceptics could stomach. In 1850 the agricultural writer James Caird visited the estate of Berkshire MP Philip Pusey, afterwards making reference to the productivity of the farm's newly constructed water meadows. Caird reported the owner's claim that the meadows had carried thirty-six sheep to the acre for five months. But he felt bound to add that 'some of the neighbouring farmers allege that the sheep were *kept*, not *fed*, and that it was marvellous to them how Mr Pusey managed to keep so many sheep, even alive, on this small space during the whole summer'.

Somewhat incensed, Pusey dashed off a letter to *The Times*, which had commissioned Caird's report.

This rumour, I beg to assure you, is utterly without foundation. The sheep left the field, after each time of eating it off, in thriving condition. The whole of my last year's lambs will at the end of seven days have left the farm for Smithfield to be sold, though but a year old, as mutton, and are this year unusually fat ... My flock of ewes also were never at any former lambing season in better order than now, after being kept on these catch meadows. The rumour therefore is one of those by which men endeavour to account for things which exceed their powers of belief, and appearing to them fabulous or mythical, seem to require a rational explanation ... The sceptics would do well to inquire whether irrigation does not at least double the yield of grassland.[23]

With the development of catch meadows the enthusiasm for irrigation spread around the country. During the nineteenth century, agricultural matters aroused interest among a wide cross-section of middle–class society, not just landowners. Everywhere there were heated debates about the mysterious power of flood water to stimulate the growth of grass, to splash the pastoral landscape with vivid green amid the winter's snow and frost, to change the very seasons themselves.

Irrigators disputed whether clear or cloudy water produced the more luxuriant growth. Some argued that the incoming stream should be 'thick' with sediment, leaving a rich deposit on the meadow surface and returning to the watercourse 'so clear a pike might be detected basking six feet deep'. Others argued with equal conviction for the growth-promoting properties of the clear chalk stream.

On the matter of water temperature there was more general agreement – the warmer the incoming stream, the better the result. Water meadows were widely thought of as 'a hot-bed for grass whose action excites fermentation'. The beneficial properties of the flood stream lay chiefly in the 'warmth it communicated to the soil, gently rousing the sleeping grass'.

There was debate about the grass varieties best suited to irrigated meadows. Sweet-scented vernal grass (*Anthoxanthum odoratum*), meadow fescue (*Festuca pratensis*) and perennial ryegrass (*Lolium perenne*) – all were found in abundance in Wiltshire water meadows. But in the best meadows the most plentiful species were timothy (*Phleum pratense*) and fiorin grass (*Agrostis stolonifera*). And for newly-sown water meadows a mixture of Italian ryegrass (*Lolium multiflorum*) was recommended.[24]

The excitement even infected public authorities. The engineer William Tatham called for convicts, vagrants and the 'disorderly classes' to be put to work on the construction of national irrigation schemes.[25] The Board of Agriculture wrote to the canal companies asking them to devise ways of using navigable waterways for land irrigation.

A number of town councils began to see water meadows as a promising outlet for sewage. Until the mid-eighteenth century most domestic and livestock waste was disposed of in open drains or cesspools. By surface flow and underground seepage it found its way into open ditches, giving off offensive odours and sometimes posing a disease hazard. But if the material were first passed across a field of growing vegetation, where the sediment would settle out to produce a useful plant food, the remaining liquid might be discharged safely into a river or the sea.

An early attempt at 'sewage irrigation' was carried out at Craigentinny Meadows on the sandy land between Edinburgh and the sea.[26] Edinburgh sewage was collected in ponds and allowed to settle for a short time before being passed down a wide open drain known as the Foul Burn, with an outfall in the Forth estuary. Farmers with land alongside the burn drew off agreed amounts of the slurry to irrigate their grasslands.

Most of the fertilised grass was cut for hay and fed to dairy cows housed in sheds in the nearby towns of Leith, Musselburgh and Portobello as well as in Edinburgh itself. Old grassland produced about forty tons an acre on the contents of Scottish water closets, ryegrass pastures as much as sixty tons. The milk from the cows went back on to the streets from where it had started.

The Craigentinny system was widely praised as an example of 'scientific agriculture', producing far more milk per acre than conventionally managed grassland. Public corporations and private individuals scrambled to copy the scheme. In Cheshire enterprising farmers built reservoirs to collect and store both farmyard waste and domestic sewage, along with surface water run-off. Then in dry weather they spread the liquor on their fields using the catch meadow principle.[27]

Sewage irrigation farms sprang up around the country. Run by councils and local health boards, they drew their raw material from the neighbouring towns and villages. By 1877 more than forty urban councils were disposing of at least part of their sewage on the land, most of it passing over catch meadows.

In farming circles the relative fertiliser values of sewages from different parts of the country became a matter for rational, scientific debate.

The results of many analyses by our leading chemists, whether of the food of a mixed population, or of the resultant sewage of a town supplied with water closets and well drained, teach that nitrogen equal to two hundred ounces of ammonia is voided annually in the urine and faeces of every individual ... equal to one part of ammonia in every ten thousand parts of the drainage water of our towns – the actual quantity varying with the water supply so much as to make a thousand tons of it worth as much as from six to sixteen hundredweights of guano (imported manure made from the excrement of Peruvian seabirds), or from one penny to two pence per ton.[28]

James Archibald Campbell, a Scot farming near Rugby in Warwickshire, had seen the Craigentinny Meadows for himself and applied the system on his own land. His report to the Bath and West of England Society cut through to the heart of the matter.

> The sewage farmer should keep cows himself. If the farm buildings are within half a mile of a large town, the sale of new milk will produce the highest profit ... There is no reason why the sewage of all our towns should not be utilised in this way, producing a larger supply of nutritious milk, and protecting the water of our rivers and streams from pollution.[29]

The most grandiose scheme of its kind was undertaken by the Duke of Portland on his Clipstone Park estate near Mansfield in the heart of the 'wild and barren' Sherwood Forest. The completed water meadows covered no less than 400 acres, stretching seven miles along one side of the valley of the River Maun. They cost the duke 40,000 pounds and returned an extra ten pounds an acre in produce each year.

Irrigation water was taken from the Maun as it left Mansfield, 'charged with the whole sewerage of the place'. The meadows were irrigated throughout the year producing a 'constant succession of green meadows glistening with the trickling water, or covered with flocks of ewes and lambs browsing on the luxuriant herbage'. It was 'the pride of Nottinghamshire, unrivalled as a work of art in irrigation, and in its cost worthy of the liberality of a wise and patriotic nobleman'.[30]

> The eye, after wandering through the glades of the forest, and resting on the brown carpeting of fern and heather with which it is clothed, is amazed on coming suddenly in view of the rich green of the meadows, extended for miles before it, laid in gentle slopes and artificial terraces, and preserved in

perpetual verdure by supplies of water continually thrown over their surface.[31]

Water meadows made grassland a proper subject for study and debate. In the new age of scientific agriculture the great farm 'improvers' had chiefly focused their attention on developments that might bring a clear cash benefit – heavier crops of wheat, flax and potatoes, or faster-maturing breeds of livestock. Grass was merely the vegetation they were fattened on. It was the product of rain and sunshine, the 'strength' of the soil and the porosity of the parent rock. There seemed precious little the farmer could do to enhance this most abundant of nature's gifts.

But the early enthusiasts and eccentrics who doused their meadows in running water and slopped out with the contents of a thousand water closets proved the very opposite. Grassland could be managed. And with the right management it would reward the farmer with as bountiful a harvest as the finest wheat land. This was a crop to be nurtured, a resource to be husbanded. It was a key component in the great agrarian cycle which sustained civilisation.

By the end of the nineteenth century British water meadows had entered their long, slow decline. Sheep farmers now grew turnips and the new fodder crops for rearing strong, healthy lambs. Besides, they could rely on artificial fertilisers to stimulate the growth of grass. Irrigation, with its high labour demand, was no longer worthwhile. As the old drowners retired, few were willing to replace them by learning the skills that would keep the rills and ripples dancing across the turf. The carriages and drains silted up while sedges grew tall and thick in the boggier parts.

The meadow now yields its abundance to the power of fossil energy. And nearby the river resumes its uninterrupted course carrying its riches to the sea.

11   *An End of Arcady*

It is hardly a battle of titans. The sleepy Wiltshire hamlet of Kingston Deverill is playing its annual fixture against nearby Fovant. The home side has knocked up an uninspiring 107. Now a workman-like third wicket partnership between Mike from the bookshop and Martyn the retired head teacher has put the visitors within sight of victory.

In the final over before tea the younger batsman lofts a loose ball over deep cover for six. A ripple of applause breaks out among his team mates relaxing in the late summer sunshine. 'Nice one,' observes the wicket keeper generously as four of his fielders head for the long grass to help look for the ball.

Modestly ignoring the acclaim, Mike steps from his crease to prod his bat at a section of the pitch. Three swallows swoop in low across the velvet turf in search of gnats. Somewhere in the village a lawn mower drones into life. The square-leg umpire glances at his watch and longs for his cup of tea.

This is English village cricket – polite, restrained, genteel; a ritual dance that is as formal as a Military Twostep; a set-piece encounter with as much passion and pace as a chess game. Yet the national summer game was not always like this. In its earliest form it would have been very different.

The origins of cricket lie somewhere among the mass of folk games played throughout Europe in the Middle Ages. Some – like folk-football – were savage affairs without written rules. The details of play varied from village to village and were passed to each new generation by word of mouth. The pitch might encompass an entire field, and the teams would include virtually all the able-bodied men in the community. The games were little more than ritual warfare between villages.

It may rather be called a friendly kind of fight than a play or recreation. A bloody and murderous practice than a fellowly sport or pastime. For does not everyone lie in wait for his adversary seeking to overthrow him and to pick him on his nose, though it be on hard stones, in ditch and dale, in valley and hill or what place so ever it be, he cares not, so he may have him down. And he that can serve the most of this fashion, he is counted the only fellow and who but he. So that by this means, sometimes their necks are broken, sometimes their arms, sometimes one part thrust out of joint, sometimes another, sometimes their noses gush out with blood, sometimes their eyes start out. But whosoever escapes away the best, goes not scot free, but is either sore wounded and bruised so he dies of it, or else escapes very hardly.[1]

The folk games which bear the closest resemblance to modern cricket were those in which a stationary player struck a ball or piece of wood away from himself, and scored by running between two or more fixed points.[2] Games of this sort included stool-ball, trap-ball, tip-cat and cat-and-dog. Like football, these were team games. But batsman and bowler confronted each other as individuals. Individual identity was not submerged in the roaring, brawling ruck of early football.

By Tudor times the sports of the common people were viewed by the state as a threat to civil order. The aristocracy would have nothing to do with them, preferring instead their own amusements of hunting, hawking and the martial arts.

Without the protection of the ruling class, folk games came under sustained attack from the Crown, Parliament and the Puritans.

Then in the mid-seventeenth century a remarkable transformation took place. The wild, lawless antecedent of cricket began to arouse the interest of the landed class. Before long they were arranging matches and betting on their outcome, standardising the rules and organising the game's administration. In less than a century cricket was being played and patronised by no lesser personage than the Prince of Wales. The wild, lawless pastime of the common people had been taken over and 'civilised' by the gentry.

It was a *coup* that mirrored a wider upheaval in Tudor society. Just as the people's sport had been usurped, so their rights to land were being taken away. By the expedient of enclosure, landowners had begun to deny peasant farmers their traditional access to common fields, ending the age-old pact between humans and the earth, and creating the class of landless labourers that would later operate the mills and factories of industrial Britain. Ideas of land as a shared source of life and well-being were giving way to notions of private property, of land as a mere factor of production, the locus of individual power and wealth.

It marked the beginning of free-market capitalism and the emergence of Britain as a powerful nation state. It also carried echoes of freedoms betrayed and innocence lost. And like the game of cricket it was a drama played out on grass.

Tudor Britain was still a predominantly pastoral society. In the later years of Elizabeth I an Italian visitor wrote of the English: 'They often eat mutton and beef, which is generally considered to be better here than anywhere else in the world. This is due to the excellence of their pastures . . .'[3] About those who created the pastures he was less than complimentary: 'The farmers are so lazy and slow that they do not bother to sow more wheat than is necessary for their own consumption; they prefer to let the ground be transformed into pasture for the use of the sheep that they breed in large numbers.'

The people of Britain were reliant on grassland both for their food and their livelihoods. This is not to deny the importance of tillage crops. When the harvest failed – as often happened in Tudor times – the poor went hungry. Even at moments of national emergency harvesting took precedence. With news of the Spanish Armada's defeat coming through, the Kentish militia were summarily disbanded 'to save their corn, for that otherwise it stood upon their undoing'. In the words of W. G. Hoskins, fluctuating harvests were 'the heart-beat of the whole economy'.[4]

But if harvests were the pulse, grasslands were the sinews of rural Britain. An acre or two of pasture would feed the house cow of the lowly peasant farmer or 'cottager', keeping the family supplied with milk, butter and cheese throughout the year, whatever the price of bread. For the emerging class of yeomen farmers, the group that would form the backbone of rural society for four centuries, grassland and its products of beef and wool were the route to prosperity, even to becoming part of the gentry.

Those already well advanced on the social ladder used grassland to consolidate their wealth and found great dynasties. By the middle of Elizabeth's reign the Spencers of Althorp, Northamptonshire, kept a flock of 14,000 ewes and lambs,[5] while one of the biggest sheep farmers of the age, the Duke of Norfolk, owned a flock of nearly 17,000 in East Anglia.[6]

Others used grassland simply for amusement. Merchants with fresh fortunes made from trading in cloth, wine or glassware were eager buyers of country estates, turning the tilled land back to pasture and stocking it with venison. The new 'parks' became centres for country sports – hunting, hare coursing and falconry.

Elizabethan grassland made fortunes for scores of graziers, those half-hearted farmers who lived by buying lean, young 'store' cattle from breeders in the hills and fattening them on lush, lowland pastures before selling them in the thriving market towns. Those with land close to London were especially fortunate, as the contemporary commentator John Norden observed in his county survey, *Speculum Britanniae*. Writing of Middlesex he says:

Another sort of husbandmen and yeomen there are, and that not a few in this shire, who wade in the weedes of gentlemen; these only oversee their husbandry, and give directions unto their servants, seldom or not at all putting their hand unto the plough, who having great feedings for cattle, and good breed for young, often use Smithfield and other like places with fat cattle where also they store themselves with lean. And thus they often exchange not without great gain, whereby and by their daily increase at home they commonly become very rich.

Also making money were the drovers, the roughneck bands who lived the travelling life herding cattle from grazing to grazing, from watering point to watering point, on the long journey to market. In the towns a growing army of craftsmen and traders were earning a living from the products of grass – cloth makers, clothiers, butchers, shoe makers, saddle makers, workers in horn and bone.

For holders of land with secure tenancies on fixed rents the opportunities for acquiring wealth seemed almost limitless, and nowhere more than in the counties surrounding London. Between 1582 and 1605 the capital's population more than doubled to one quarter of a million, leading Daniel Defoe to assert that the entire country was dependent on the city.

Livestock reached the capital from all over England, chiefly coming in on the hoof. Most had passed along a complex marketing chain on their journey to London. Lean cattle from Wales and the north were bought and sold by country drovers in the principal markets of the midlands – Shrewsbury, Coventry, Market Harborough, Northampton and St Ives. They were then fattened on the rich marshland grazings of Lincolnshire, Norfolk, Essex and Kent, before making the final journey to London.[7]

The Essex marshes produced much of the capital's meat and many of its dairy products. Marshland graziers supplying the city with mutton would buy wether lambs at Smithfield Market in the autumn and walk them back to the Essex coast. There the animals would grow to 'full flesh' on the marsh grasses. When the price rose in early winter they were driven back to Smithfield, earning a substantial profit for their owners.[8]

The bulk of the city's requirement for butter and cheese came from Essex and the wood-pasture region of central Suffolk, shipped from Ipswich and Woodbridge as well as from a score of villages fringing the wide estuaries of the two counties.[9] As many as 900 loads of butter and cheese were dispatched from a single Suffolk harbour in the course of a year.

Other counties shared in the lucrative business of provisioning London. In *Speculum Britanniae* John Norden wrote of the farm women of Middlesex who took to London 'twice or thrice a week so much milk, butter, bacon, cheese, ham, chicken, eggs, apples and pears that they made a goodly living thereby'. Further from home, the cattle farmers of the north-east built up a profitable business supplying butter to the expanding London market.

But it was not just the voracious appetite of the capital that brought prosperity to grassland farmers. Rising prices and a fast-growing population together generated an insatiable demand for pastoral products across the whole country. No longer were they merely the staples of a subsistence economy. These were the products of an infant capitalism.

Everywhere cattle fairs sprang up and thrived, aiding the flow of livestock from their breeding pastures on the high uplands of the west and north to the fattening areas of the south and east. Each region of the country had its own great centres of cattle trading – Preston, Burnley, Northallerton, Wakefield and Rotherham in the north; Coventry, Northampton and Market Harborough in the midlands; Rhos Fair, Eglwyswrw and Knighton in Wales.

Town markets were also prospering, many of them specialising in one or other of the products of pastoral Britain – cattle, sheep, horses, cheese, butter, wool, yarn and leather. Everywhere the countryside was traversed by cattle herds and sheep flocks, large and small, on their way to market.

In charge were the drovers, the disparate rural army of chancers and entrepreneurs who bought and sold the beasts, either on their own behalf or as agents for yeomen farmers and landowners. The meat they marketed was not bound for the households of labourers or small husbandrymen, but for the homes of the rich. For the new Tudor middle classes, who had made their money from trade, the law or court patronage, consumed meat in enormous quantities.

In 1590 the Earl of Derby and his family employed no fewer than 140 servants at their country house in Lathom. In one year they consumed a total of 56 oxen and 535 sheep, running up a household expense of nearly £3,000.[10] In the household of Sir William Fairfax at Gilling Castle, Yorkshire, meat consumption in 1579 accounted for 49 oxen and 150 sheep. In Scotland the Bishop of Aberdeen and his household managed to eat their way through the meat of 48 oxen, 160 sheep and 17 pigs.

Grassland powered the Tudor economy. Though the grain harvest was important in preventing hunger, much of the England of Shakespeare and Queen Bess was down to meadows and pastures. The antiquary William Camden embarked on a tour of Elizabeth I's kingdom and published his observations in *Britannia* in 1586. He wrote that Northamptonshire was 'very populous and everywhere adorned with nobleman's and gentlemen's houses; and very full of towns and churches. Its soil both for tillage and pasture is exceedingly fertile; but everywhere it is filled, and, as it were, beset with sheep.'[11]

Across the county boundary his impressions were similar. Leicestershire was a county 'rich in corn and grass, the east part hilly and feedeth a vast number of sheep. Melton Mowbray is a market town, the most considerable for cattle in this part of England.' Oxfordshire was 'a rich and fertile county, the lower parts cultivated into pleasant fields and meadows. But though most parts of it bear corn well, its greatest glory is the abundance of meadows and pastures, to which the rivers add pleasure and convenience.'

The counties so admired by Camden were areas of lowland mixed farming, or 'champion' countryside, where arable cropping took place alongside livestock husbandry. Here the common-field system remained widespread, with ploughland and meadow divided into unhedged strips, thrown open to communal grazing after harvest or during fallow seasons.

Villagers also enjoyed common grazing rights over pasture and forest wastes, the communal system being regulated by the time-honoured manorial court or village meeting.[12]

But there was a second important landscape type in lowland Britain – wood pasture. In these wooded areas the farmland was predominantly in pasture, with little or no arable cropping. Here dairy farming and cattle rearing were carried on alongside woodland crafts and part-time forestry enterprises. Wood pasture areas included 'high' Suffolk, Essex, the Kentish and Sussex Wealds, much of Dorset and Wiltshire and the Northamptonshire forests, together with parts of Derbyshire and the West Midlands.

In Warwickshire the two lowland landscapes were represented in a single county. To the south-east lay the open fields of the 'champion' country, the 'Feldon', lying between the River Avon and Edgehill. This was the granary of middle England, supplying wheat to the western towns. To the north-west of the Avon lay the Forest of Arden with its dark woodland heart and remote pastoral settlements.

> Thus the winding Avon, spanned by Stratford's famous bridge of 'fourteen arches of stone', divided the lonely forest from the populous cornlands. One born and bred in the town upon its banks saw, in his boyhood's rambles, what was best in wild nature on one side of the river, and what was most characteristic of man upon the other.[13]

The communities of wood-pasture areas were very different from those of the 'champion' country, with its nucleated villages and open fields. In 'champion' areas the social order was rigidly maintained, with the landed magnate firmly established at the top of the pyramid. These were stable, law-abiding communities, where labouring families remained rooted in the same district from generation to generation, often working on the same farms. Few were well off, and their common rights were meagre. Nevertheless they freely accepted their dependence on the squire and the parson.[14]

In woodland settlements, by contrast, the roots of society

were more shallow. The population was made up of a core of indigenous peasants with their own holdings and a growing number of poor squatters and wanderers. These were far from law-abiding communities. Here the authority of church and manor house seemed remote. According to Londoner John Norden they were 'living very hardly with oaten bread, sour whey, and goats' milk, dwelling far from any church or chapel, and are as ignorant of God or of any civil course of life as the very savages amongst the infidels. People bred amongst the woods are naturally more stubborn and uncivil than in the champion countries.'

It was in the wood-pasture areas that bat-and-ball games flourished. In the rigid societies of the 'champion' country football was the popular game. Players were prepared to submerge their own identities in the great tribal battle. But in the wooded, pastoral areas games such as stool-ball appealed to a greater spirit of individualism in the community.

The seventeenth-century writer John Aubrey identified the two cultures in Wiltshire, calling them the 'chalk' and the 'cheese' countries. The chalk downlands in the south of the county were the 'champion' lands, with arable cropping and distinct villages. Here football was the popular sport, ironically, since its disorderly violence was at odds with the ordered and authoritarian village communities. In the 'cheese' country – the pastoral landscape in the north of the county – stool-ball was the popular game.

According to Aubrey, on the downs 'where 'tis all upon tillage, and where the shepherds labour hard, their flesh is hard, their bodies strong; being weary after hard labour, they have not leisure to read or contemplate of religion'.[15] In the 'dirty, clayey country' to the north, by contrast, the people 'speak drawling; they are phlegmatic, skins pale and livid, slow and dull, heavy of spirit; hereabout is but little tillage or hard labour, they only milk the cows and make cheese; they feed chiefly on milk meats, which cools their brains too much, and hurts their inventions'.

Pastoral farming also dominated the highlands of Britain – chiefly those areas to the north and west. These were lands of open pastures: rough, communal grazings, with just enough corn grown on the lower ground to meet the local need.

Some among these remote hill settlements still clung to the custom of partitioning their land between sons,[16] a practice that produced uneconomic holdings but which kept families together, providing at least a fighting chance for the next generation. As in earlier times, the people of these pastoral lands were independent and resourceful, valuing their freedoms and resisting attempts by landlords to curtail their right to run their land as they chose.

Along with that spirit of independence went a sense of community. When it was in the interests of the group to enclose a piece of common land for arable cropping or as a hay meadow, it was usually achieved without rancour. And when the meadow needed manuring the community would be there with coaldust, wood ash or chimney soot, whatever was required.

During hard times, when returns from the sale of butter and cheese to the town were poor, or when lowland beef fatteners had driven a hard bargain for store cattle bred in the hills, there was money to be made from employment off the farm.

In the wood pasture regions of the lowlands the supplementary income might come from furniture-making or some other forest-based craft. In the English and Welsh uplands small tenant farmers worked at quarrying or down the mines to make ends meet.

The pastoral way of life had an inherent stability. To a large extent it was buffered against the economic and social upheavals that were shaking rural life in the mixed-farming regions. For the small tenants and cottagers of the 'champion' country there was no such shelter against the gathering storm. Many were to end up as dispossessed vagabonds in the Elizabethan 'golden age'.

Tudor society was being shaken by powerful economic forces. The rapid population growth of the second half of the sixteenth century had helped create a vigorous, mercantile economy. At the same time it produced a huge increase in the demand for food from a countryside still bearing the imprint of feudalism.

The Black Death and successive plagues had halved the population in the mid-fourteenth century. Two centuries later it had still barely recovered: in 1541 the population of England stood at less than three million.[17] But by the turn of the century it had leaped to more than four million. The impact on a society in which nine-tenths of the population lived in the countryside was momentous.

The demand for food was insatiable, particularly in the rapidly expanding towns. In years of poor harvest the demand often outstripped supply, leading to widespread hunger among landless people. An index of essential items such as food and textiles showed that in the century following Henry VIII's accession average prices rose fivefold.[18] A series of failed harvests in the late 1590s fuelled the inflationary spiral.

With demand for meat and dairy products powering the rural economy, yeomen farmers had a second reason to celebrate. The English wool trade had returned to its former prosperity, chiefly because of the supremacy of long wool in the manufacture of cloth. During Elizabeth's reign it became a penal offence for a male over the age of six to be out on Sundays and holy days without a cap made of English cloth.[19]

Sheep outnumbered people by almost three to one. With the woollen cloth industry booming, the spinners and weavers who worked mostly in their own homes found they could not obtain enough wool.[20] The local clothiers who controlled the industry were prepared to pay almost any price for their raw material.

This provided a powerful inducement to landholders facing ever rising costs. While the grain price looked attractive, and often reached dizzying heights in years of harvest failure, few of the rewards went back to those who had grown the crop. The grain trade was largely controlled by racketeers who creamed off much of the profit. For the farmer, oppressed by rising prices, wheat-growing was seldom an attractive option, with its endless cycle of planting, hoeing, reaping, ploughing and harrowing demanding a great deal of village labour.

Sheep farming, by contrast, could be carried out by just one

shepherd supported by casual labour at busy times such as
shearing and lambing. Not surprisingly, a growing number of
farmers opted for sheep, converting their plough lands back to
grass and depriving village labourers of the opportunity for
regular work.

Holders of land were constantly looking for ways to increase
their acreage of grass and cash in on the livestock boom. Some
landlords deliberately forced out tenants in order to enlarge their
own holdings, a process known as *engrossment*. It was not
unheard of for more prosperous yeomen to be equally ruthless
in exploiting their neighbours if they saw a chance to expand
their own farms.

The upsurge in free market capitalism, though distorted by
Henry VIII's manipulation of the currency, led to a widening
gulf between the 'haves' and the 'have nots'. The historian G.
M. Trevelyan ascribes the Tudor social *malaise* to the 'casual and
irregular' way price rises affected the different classes of
peasantry. Those lucky enough to have long-term leases or
copyhold tenures of the kind that were by law unbreakable
reaped the full advantage of soaring prices for their products.

Landlords, who were themselves hit by the general price
inflation, were able to recoup their losses by putting up the rents
of those unfortunate peasants and farmers whose leases were
renewable annually or after a period of years. So as one group of
peasants made fortunes from the products of their pastures while
paying no more in rent, another group – distinguishable only by
the date of their leases – were being hammered.

At the same time yeomen freeholders, who paid no more
than a nominal rent to the lord of the manor or, in many cases,
no rent at all, were selling their cattle and sheep for three times
more than their grandparents had been able to secure.

The yeomen, commented observer William Harrison, 'com-
monlie live wealthilie, keepe good houses and travell to get
riches'. Their houses were furnished with 'costlie furniture', and
they had 'learned also to garnish their cupboards with plate,
their joined beds with tapistrie and silke hangings, and their
tables with carpets and fine naperie'.[21]

Though rents had risen 'yet will the farmer thinke his gaines verie small toward the end of his terme if he have not six or seven yeares rent lieing by him, therewith to purchase a new lease, beside a faire garnish of pewter on his cupboard, three or foure featherbeds, so manie coverlids and carpets of tapistrie, a silver salt, a bowle for wine, and a dozzen of spoones to furnish up the sute'.

By the mid-sixteenth century the wealthier yeomen had begun to build themselves bigger and better houses.[22] Sometimes they merely built on to the ancestral home, but more often they demolished the old dwelling and rebuilt in free stone, where it was available.

As a class the yeomen farmers were advancing faster than any other landed group. Like the gentry they were building up their estates, taking advantage of what Hoskins termed 'the largest transference of land ownership since Domesday'.

Competition for land was not confined to those already prospering from farming. There were other bidders, outsiders, men who had made money from business. With wealth to spare they now wanted to share in the bounty being made from grasslands. Their numbers included 'merchant adventurers, clothmakers, goldsmiths, butchers, tanners and other artificers', those who would 'bie fermes out of the handes of worshypfull gentlemen, honest yeomen and pore laborynge husbandes'.[23]

Between 1540 and 1640, the aristocracy and gentry trebled in number while the rest of the population barely doubled.[24] This influx into the English ruling class was brought about chiefly by the release on to the land market of large areas previously owned by the Crown or the Church. The new landowners despised the tradition of subsistence farming. For them the soil had to yield profit as well as food, a return on capital as well as a harvest. Most were interested in the products of grass, substituting pasture for tillage, sheep for corn.

Typical of the new breed was Sir William Fermour, a London merchant who bought up a number of scattered manors in Norfolk, turning them over to pasture and building a huge flock of 17,000 sheep.[25] His magnificent house at East Barsham stands as testimony to the enormous wealth to be made from England's golden fleece. Another London merchant, Sir

Richard Gresham, the wealthiest of his time, bought extensive monastic estates including Fountains Abbey in Yorkshire. When he died in 1549 he owned three country seats and was worth 800 pounds a year in lands.

The English ruling class was no longer the homogenous entity it had been in the Middle Ages. The old aristocratic families had been too interested in military affairs and the prospect of life at Court to bother with the running of their estates. But the new landowners, with a background in trade and commerce, were more concerned to extract profits from the land. Before long the entrepreneurial outlook had spread to traditional landowners. By the early sixteenth century the older aristocracy and gentry had begun to dabble in speculative ventures.

The stage was set for the eviction of village people from their common lands. The spirit of capitalism was abroad. Custom and tradition would count for little when revenue was at stake. The peasantry were also to be robbed of one of their popular folk-games. In his book *English Cricket*, Christopher Brookes attributes the ruling-class adoption of the game to changing pattern of land ownership. Cricket offered 'gentlemen' a means of settling personal rivalries without resort to the duelling sword. It also provided them with a wonderful new vehicle for betting. The first references to 'gentlemen' watching the game also record the fact that large sums of money were usually at stake.[26]

Not all villagers were excluded from the pastoral boom, however. A few peasant labourers or 'husbandmen' prospered, particularly in areas where the grassland economy already flourished. An indication of peasant fortunes is contained in the inventories of goods drawn up for probate purposes after their deaths. These showed that most 'cottage farmers' kept at least one dairy cow or heifer supplying milk, cheese and butter to the family as well as a surplus that could be sold at the butter-cross in the nearest market town.[27] A number of resourceful individuals like Richard Gurleye of Knebworth, Hertfordshire, and Robert Wood of Nuneaton produced butter and cheese specifically for

the market. Others like Henry Joyce of Winwick in Northamptonshire and Thomas Hall of Fillongley in Warwickshire were
able to build up substantial cattle herds and sheep flocks on their
lush, green pastures.

But such people were exceptional. While the better-off
peasants continued to thrive, most became poorer, many sinking
to the level of a landless proletariat. Those with the best chance
of climbing the social ladder lived in wood-pasture areas where
the grassland economy was strong. They were able to build up
substantial numbers of livestock, subsidising them with part-
time work in wood-turning, carpentry, forestry and charcoal
burning. Others took work as gamekeepers and gardeners.

Over most of Britain, it was grassland that sustained the mass
of the people through the economic turbulence of the Tudor
years, just as it had done in an earlier age. For wheat was
unpredictable – despite the heavy labour demands of ploughing
and cultivating, sowing and hoeing, a wet summer could
destroy much of the crop and all of the profit. But the mild,
moist Atlantic climate that made arable farming an uncertain
enterprise kept the grass growing vigorously. In Tudor England,
as in modern Britain, a lush, green sward was almost as
predictable as the rising of the sun and the passing of the seasons.

Come rain or shine England's pastures fed the house cows of
the lowland peasant cottage and the remote hill settlement.
They built the noble houses that grew up everywhere across the
Tudor countryside. They put pewter plate on the sideboards of
prosperous yeomen and fat cheeses on the peasant carts
trundling along the lanes to market.

But for the peasants and small farmers of the 'champion'
country – the countryside of mixed farming, open fields and a
strong remnant of the old manorial tradition – the flowering of a
grass economy spelled misery and destitution. These were the
first victims of the long process of attrition that was to beset
British agriculture down the ages: the process of enclosure.

In the strictest sense, enclosure means the planting of a hedge
or ditch around an open field. But the term has become a
shorthand for the exclusion of poor people from the land, a

dispossession linked to the loss of common rights and the engrossment of scattered holdings into large blocks.

In Tudor times and even earlier, much enclosure took place without enmity. It had begun in the fourteenth century when new land was cleared for cultivation from forest and waste. The shutting up of pastureland was often in the interests of the whole village since it led to easier management. Groups of farmers sometimes got together to enclose common land by general agreement, using co-operative labour to carry out the job.

Contemporary farming writers had no doubts about the benefits. John Norden, an experienced surveyor, considered enclosure 'the most beneficial course that tenants can take . . . for one acre enclosed is worth one and a half in common, if the ground be fitting thereto'. In his opinion 'when feildes are inclosed every man will use a further trayvale and dylygence with his lande to converte yt to the best use and purpose, whiche before they coulde not'.[28]

In the *Five Hundreth Good Pointes of Good Husbandrie*, Thomas Tusser compares 'champion' or open country with 'severall' or enclosed land.[29]

> More profit is quieter found,
> Where pastures in severall bee;
> Of one seelie aker of ground
> Than champion maketh of three

But the popular sentiment in Tudor England was implacably opposed to enclosure. When carried out on a common field or pasture it cost the community their common rights. Labourers and small husbandmen lost the grazing for their household livestock, a catastrophe for the poor family on the very edge of survival.

Historians have argued that enclosure with its greater productivity was essential for the feeding of a fast-growing population. Yet many of the new landowners – the wealthy merchants and lawyers who bought up rural estates – had no interest in producing food for the teeming populations of the towns. What they wanted was a share in the returns from a profitable wool trade.

When they bought and enclosed arable land it was not to increase the output of grain or dairy products. Instead they turned the land over to pasture for stocking with sheep. The local villagers lost not only their common rights, but the wages from work in arable fields.

One such landowner was William Cope, former cofferer to the household of Henry VII, who bought an estate at Wormleighton in Warwickshire. In October 1498 he evicted the occupiers of a dozen small farms and three cottages and enclosed the land with hedges and ditches, allowing the buildings and dwellings to fall into ruin.

In evidence to Cardinal Thomas Wolsey's commission of inquiry into enclosures twenty years later, witnesses claimed that Cope had

> converted the aforesaid arable land from cultivation and arable into pasture for animals, and that land is still used as pasture for animals. And he still holds that land so enclosed in severalty, whereby twelve ploughs which were fully engaged in the cultivation of these lands are completely idle, and sixty persons who lived in the aforesaid houses while they were maintained and were occupied in cultivating the aforesaid land were compelled tearfully to depart, to wander and be brought to idleness and so presumably perished from want.[30]

Cases like this outraged Tudor society. Enclosures were vehemently denounced from the pulpit and in political pamphlets and popular ballads.

> The townes go down, the land decayes;
> Off cornefeyldes, playne layes;
> Gret men makithe now a dayes
> A shepecott in the church.
>
> Commons to close and kepe;
> Poor folk bred to cry and wepe;
> Towns pulled downe to pastur shepe;
> This ys the new gyse![31]

Popular anger was directed at the hedges and fences, outward symbols of injustice, along with the hated sheep which were seen as the main cause of destitution and depopulation.

> Sheepe have eate up our medows and our downes,
> Our corne, our wood, whole villages and townes;
> Yea, they have eate up many wealthy men,
> Besides widows and orphane childeren;
> Besides our statutes and our iron lawes,
> Which they have swallowed down into their maws;
> 'Til now I thought the proverbe did but jest,
> Which said a blacke sheep was a biting beast.[32]

Thomas More took up the lament of the common people, now dispossessed by the new, harsh law of the market.

> Therfore that on covetous and unsatiable cormaraunte and very plage of his natyve contrey naye compasse about and inclose many thousand akers of grounde together within one pale or hedge, the husbandmen be thrust owte of their owne, or els either by coveyne and fraude, or by violent oppression they be put besydes it, that they be compelled to sell all: by one meanes therfore or by other, either by hooke or crooke they muste needes departe awaye, poore, selye, wretched soules, men, women, husbands, wives, fatherlesse children, widowes, wofull mothers, with their yonge babes, and their whole household smal in substance, and muche in numbre, as husbandrye requireth manye handes.[33]

Fearful of social unrest, Tudor governments passed a string of acts and statutes to control enclosure and the amalgamation of holdings; legislation to counter the 'pullyng downe of tounes'. An act of 1515 declared that villages engaged in tillage were to continue with it, ruined buildings were to be rebuilt, and land newly turned over to pasture was to be restored to arable.

A further act of 1533 ruled that no one person was to keep

more than 2,400 sheep, or take up more than two farms or tenements. According to historian Joan Thirsk, the measure was 'a puppet wearing a bold face but stuffed with straw'. Amendments introduced following pressure from landowning Members of Parliament allowed them to evade the restrictions, though smaller farmers were caught.

Following the sharp price rises of the mid-sixteenth century, Parliament sanctioned a new tax on sheep and cloth. Though inflation had more to do with poor harvests and the king's debasement of the coinage, pasture farmers, and particularly sheep farmers, were seen as threatening the peace of the realm.

Henry VIII's currency debasement had made English exports – including cloth – more profitable. The economic choices of farmers were distorted because cloth could be freely exported while grain could not.[34] William Lane observed wryly:

> The exchange doth engendar dere clothe, and dere clothe dothe engendar dere wolle, and dere wolle dothe engendar many schepe, and many schepe dothe engendar myche pastor and dere, amd myche pastor ys the dekaye of tyllage, and owte of the dekaye of tyllage spryngythe ij evylls, skarsyte of korne and the pepull unwroghte, and consequentely the darthe off all thynges.[35]

The sheep and wool tax was repealed in 1549, the year of its enactment. By then rioting against enclosure had broken out in many parts of the country, sparked off, it seemed, by the sympathy shown by government. The most serious risings were in the south-west and in Norfolk.

None was solely concerned with enclosure. Rather the hated sheep and hedges became the focus for a host of rural discontents. Robert Kett, the leader of the Norfolk rebellion, included on his list of abuses the selfish lords who overgrazed the commons with their livestock, while allowing pigeons from their dovecotes and rabbits from their warrens to damage tenant crops.

During July and August 1549 Kett gathered as many as 20,000 dissenters 'with banners unfurled, swords, shields, clubs, cannon, halberds, lances, bows, arrows, breast-plates, coats of mail, caps, helmets and other arms offensive and defensive, armed and arrayed in warlike manner, traitorously did make an insurrection and levy war against the same lord King that now is'.[36]

Edward VI dispatched the Earl of Warwick to deal with the rising. The rebels were quickly put down and Kett, together with his brother William, was hanged, drawn and quartered at Tyburn.

Following the disturbances two reforms were quickly introduced. The first, in 1550, was designed to maintain crop-growing and help homeless cottagers find accommodation in the countryside.[37] The second act, two years later, had similar aims. But by the latter half of the sixteenth century the allure of sheep-keeping had waned. Cloth prices had slumped following the end of the Antwerp boom, and flock owners were no longer vilified as the source of the rural *malaise*. Instead attention focused on the growing army of graziers: those who produced meat by buying in 'store' cattle and fattening them on pasture.

This time discontent erupted in the English midlands. The first rising took place in Northamptonshire in 1607. It was quickly followed by violent disturbances at Hillmorton in Warwickshire and Cotesbach in Leicestershire, where 'there assembled of men, women and children to the number of full five thousand' to cast down the hedges.[38] Cotesbach, on the borders of Northamptonshire and Warwickshire, had been in ferment since the new owner of the estate, a London merchant called John Quarles, had enclosed more than 900 acres of the 'lordship', converting more than half to pasture.

He had previously tried to raise the rents of thirteen tenant farmers. When they refused to meet his terms, he bought out two of the estate's freeholders and applied for a royal licence to enclose. The tenants now had no option but to pay the higher rents or quit their tenancies.[39] Some took up less land than before, others rented cottages only. A number left the village altogether. The landlord's precipitate action effectively doubled the estate's income and halved the number of tenants.

It was the simmering resentment caused by this overthrow of the established village order that sparked the 1607 revolt.

Fearing a wider conflagration, the authorities erected a gallows in Leicester as a warning to wrong-doers. They were at once torn down by an angry crowd, but there was no further trouble. By the end of the Tudor period, the wide-scale conversion of arable land to pasture had ceased, and with it the depopulation of the 'champion' counties.

Britain's sixteenth-century pastoral revolution was unique in world history. Never before had arable land reverted to grassland on a substantial scale while remaining in private ownership. In the past it had always gone back to some form of common tenure.[40] Without a powerful Tudor state the revolution could not have taken place. Feudal kings had once introduced powers to curb the robber-barons and protect their subjects' property, but the English Tudors did the opposite: they protected predatory landowners from an outraged peasantry. It was not until the late Tudor and Stuart periods that monarchs tried to limit enclosures for grazing.

In Britain the pastoral revival laid the foundations of a great industrial state. Private landowners now held titles to the pastures which produced the wool for much of Europe's cloth. The country's grasslands attracted a significant part of Europe's total economic surplus, some of which provided the manufacturing capital to make Britain the world's leading nation for two centuries. At the time of the Black Death England had been an economic backwater. Within three centuries it had become the most advanced country in Europe, both politically and economically.[41]

The wealthy merchants and traders who bought the Tudor estates were the same group whose profits had prevented peasant farmers from building up capital. Now they were the owners of an asset more valuable than the entire stock of English capital.

The losers were peasant farmers and landless labourers who were forced to compete with grazing animals for land and work. They would go hungry. Their share of the national production had been cut almost overnight. Not until the industrial revolution of the eighteenth century would the mass of English people recover at least part of what they lost when their common lands were enclosed.

Many of the dispossessed tenants – the 'masterless' vagrants and vagabonds that so alarmed Tudor society – found their way to the wood-pasture areas where they stood a better chance of getting work. In the village England of manor and open field, the return of pastoral farming had destroyed their livelihoods. In desperation they sought a new life in those places where the pastoral tradition had never gone away.

In the 'champion' country, the new land-owning class settled down to enjoy their estates. Soon they were playing cricket, arranging matches and placing large wagers on the result. Before long they had re-invented the people's game, drawing up new rules, turning it into a pastime appropriate for 'gentlemen'. None could oppose them since now they owned the very grass it was played on.

In the 'chalk' country of the Wiltshire downs there are no more wild, tribal games of folk-football. But two or three times a week in summer, village cricket teams don their 'whites' and caps to play the 'great game'.

At Kingston Deverill, nestling beneath the surging chalk escarpment, the home-team's bowler finally retrieves the ball from the long grass. 'Well done,' says Martyn, the retired headteacher. And both sides amble in the direction of the village hall for their tea.

12   Roots of Revolution

Despite a flourishing overseas trade, Tudor farming remained stubbornly resistant to outside influences. The wool market was booming and a small army of merchants made regular crossings to the centre of European cloth-making in Flanders. But like many modern tourists they journeyed with their eyes closed.

Had they troubled to look at what was going on in the fields around them they might have stumbled on the techniques that were to revolutionise the British economy. Flemish farmers had discovered the secret of high-output farming. They had found that 'holy grail' of agrarian societies, a means of doubling production from nature's poorest soils, so banishing starvation and energising an economy heavily reliant on agriculture.

As it was, the travelling English merchants had little on their minds but the price of the staple. At home the farming revolution of the Low Countries went largely unnoticed. Among the new capitalists buying themselves extensive country estates were successful merchants, many of whom had plied the well-trodden wool roads to Flanders. Having turned themselves into minor gentry, they set about enclosing their fields and adopting farming patterns that were little different in their essentials from those of feudal times.

It would be another century before the secrets of the Flanders fields crossed the North Sea, and two centuries before they were widely taken up by the yeomen farmers of the island nation. In time they would feed a growing urban population, and help turn Britain into the manufacturing capital of the world. The seeds of Britain's industrial revolution lay not in her over-grazed pastures or impoverished arable lands, but in a dry, sandy plain in continental Europe.

Among the Flemish school of artists, Pieter Bruegel the Elder is generally considered the most humane. Though a cultured and cultivated man, he earned himself the nickname of 'Peasant Bruegel' because of his fascination for peasant life. An early biographer, Carel van Mander, relates that the young artist would sometimes put on peasant clothes in order to gatecrash a village wedding party. There he would claim to be some distant relative of the bride or groom, bringing gifts for the happy couple.

His later landscapes reveal his attachment to working people. They show a peasant people at one with the natural world. In such works as *The Corn Harvest, Haymaking, Hunters in the Snow*, and *Return of the Herd* – all painted in 1565 – nature is depicted as a benign, sometimes generous provider.

Seldom does he hint at scarcity or want. Corn crops are shown tall and thick, the hay crop so abundant that it spills over the edges of the cart. The returning cattle are healthy and well-fleshed. The picnic basket of the harvest labourers is full. The peasants themselves look stocky and strong. There is no suggestion here of the chronic hunger and sickness that disfigured many sixteenth-century communities. Nature generously provides for those who serve her.

Bruegel's landscapes are not meant to be an accurate representation of the Flemish countryside. They are curious hybrids which combine elements of Alpine and Italian landscapes with those of the Low Countries. But in their depiction of a peasantry living comfortably off the land do they reveal something of rural life in the countryside around Antwerp, the area their painter knew so well?

In Britain peasants still laboured in fields drained of essential plant nutrients and producing dismally small crops. During the final decades of the Tudors and the early years of the Stuarts population growth consistently outstripped food supply, leading to frequent famines, at least in some areas. Not until the mid-seventeenth century did news of the Flanders achievement begin to filter through to a sceptical farming community. One of the early messengers was, not a merchant with Flemish connections, but a catholic landowner, briefly choosing exile in order to escape from Cromwell's army.

Sir Richard Weston had been born into the minor gentry, inheriting the family estate on the death of his father in 1613. While indulging a lifelong passion for agriculture, or 'husbandrie', his main interest seems to have been the rendering of rivers and canals navigable by means of weirs and locks. In 1635 at the age of forty-four he was appointed to the royal commission charged with making the River Wey navigable from Guildford through to its junction with the Thames at Weybridge.

But the civil war presented Sir Richard with a new mission. Following the sequestration of his house and estate at Sutton in Surrey he was forced to flee England, taking refuge in the Low Countries. At some time during his exile he made the journey from Ghent to Antwerp where he was struck by the barrenness of the local heathland soils. They reminded him of the sandy heaths in his native Surrey.

In a later conversation with a Dutch merchant he discovered that those same heathland soils were among the most profitable in all Flanders. At first he took this to be a joke. He knew from the heathland on his own estate that such thin, sandy soils seldom retained moisture and provided few plant nutrients. How could such inherently infertile lands be made productive?

But the merchant was adamant. These meagre soils turned in greater profits than the best land in Flanders, making their farmers, or 'bores', among the wealthiest in all Europe. Sir Richard had chanced upon a system of husbandry which had helped turn the region into the economic hub of Europe. In a burst of enthusiasm he made up his mind to study the Flemish methods and, when it was safe to do so, take them back home.

A year later, in 1645, he wrote up his findings as a *Discours of Husbandrie used in Brabant and Flanders*, early copies of which were circulated in manuscript form. One of them fell into the hands of an unscrupulous publisher, Samuel Hartlib, who pirated the work in 1650, shamelessly including a dedication to 'the right honorable the counsel of state'.[1] The following year Hartlib wrote two letters to the author asking him if he would care to correct and enlarge the *Discours* and perhaps add a preview. Receiving no reply Hartlib went ahead and re-published the treatise anyway.

The little book did its work. The secret of Flemish agriculture was out. Across the light lands of Britain enthusiastic landlords, sceptical tenants and obdurate yeomen farmers began to take up the new methods. Output per acre started to rise along with labour productivity. The island nation had broken out of its Malthusian trap and was now on course for industrial greatness.

It is hardly surprising that Sir Richard Weston should have been so impressed with the farming he saw around Antwerp. Flemish husbandry in the seventeenth century was far superior to English agriculture which remained locked into the cropping patterns of the Middle Ages. By contrast the farmers of the Low Countries – that part of north-west Europe which included modern Belgium, French Flanders and the Netherlands – had been forced to innovate in order to feed a growing industrial population.

Since medieval times the region had been among the most densely populated areas of Europe.[2] Local cereal production was insufficient to meet the demand, so grain was regularly imported from the Baltic. Even farmers bought in grain, preferring to concentrate their own production on higher-value commercial crops such as flax, hops, madder and tobacco. At the same time increasing demand from the towns stimulated the growth of market gardens and fruit orchards.

Valuable crops like these required meticulous care. Deep digging and continuous weeding were common practices in horticulture, and wood ash, compost and sewage were applied liberally as fertilisers. Such intensive methods were possible because labour was plentiful and the value of the produce high.

Inevitably the techniques pioneered in horticulture produced a spin-off for mainstream agriculture. By the sixteenth century the traditional three-course rotation of winter corn, spring corn and fallow had been replaced by a system of 'convertible husbandry', in which tillage crops alternated with grass pasture producing meat and manure.[3] A century later the place of grass in the rotation had been usurped by the crop that was to power the English farming revolution − red clover.

When Sir Richard exiled himself to Flanders he took with him 'thirtie years experience of husbandrie'. Like many of his class he was deeply imbued with ideas of public service. Land ownership was the natural aspiration of the wealthy and industrious, whether that land was acquired through inheritance or by purchase. But ownership carried obligations. The owner of land had a duty to put it to good use.

It is a great shame to a man not to leav his inheritance greater to his successors then he received it from his predecessors; and that he despitheth the liberalities of God, who by slothfulness loseth that which his land may bring forth, as not seeming willing to reap the fruits which God hath offered him. Nay, he threatens the crime of high treason to those that do not augment their patrimonie so much as the increase surmounts the principal.

Though temporarily dispossessed, Sir Richard expected his estate to be restored to him once the ferment in England had died. He was determined to make good use of this enforced sojourn by learning the secrets of heathland agriculture so that he might one day apply them to the light, hungry soils of his native Surrey.

In conversation with Flemish merchants he found out that the local farmers had settled on a rotation of flax, turnips and then oats, 'undersown' with red clover. Once the oats had been harvested, the clover crop was grazed by cattle or mown for hay in the same way as a grass crop, staying down for four or five years. Finally the land was ploughed up and planted to flax once more.

In this wealthy cloth-making region flax was the most profitable crop in the rotation. It was the raw material for linen manufacture. Turnips were valued for different reasons. Though they might not return the cash of the flax crop, they provided useful fodder for cattle and sheep whose dung could be returned to the land, helping to raise the fertility of these thin, hungry soils.

But it was the prominent place of sown red clover in the rotation that had transformed these worthless heathlands into some of the richest and most productive soils in the Low Countries.

Clovers are leguminous plants – they have the ability to 'fix' nitrogen from the atmosphere and convert it into soluble soil nitrates which can be used by growing plants. This transformation of gaseous nitrogen into mineral nitrogen is carried out by symbiotic Rhizobia bacteria in the soil which form nodules on the clover roots. The bacteria use carbon compounds from the host plant as an energy source.

It was legumes, and in particular the clovers, which ended the fertility 'bottleneck' which had held back the productivity of medieval agriculture. In the Middle Ages crop yields were limited by levels of available soil nitrogen. The only remedy for farmers was the application of heavy dressings of sheep and cattle dung.

Unfortunately, manure always seemed to be in short supply. The number of livestock was itself limited by available fodder, particularly during the winter months. When human population numbers rose, farmers responded by ploughing up grassland and sowing more land to wheat and oats. But this meant there was less pasture land for grazing livestock and less meadow land for producing winter hay crops. So the numbers of cattle and sheep fell.

As a consequence there was less manure to return to overworked arable lands so that grain yields fell. Rarely in the Middle Ages did they exceed a meagre ten bushels an acre.

Hunger remained a dread if intermittent visitor. The population was held in check. Britain's economic development and growth as a world power were hobbled by the slow recycling of nutrients within a farming system hopelessly inadequate for an emerging capitalist economy.

Sir Richard saw in the husbandry of the Low Countries the seeds of rural renaissance. As he tramped the dusty highways of Brabant and Flanders, questioning farmers, inspecting their crops, studying the flax market by buying and selling samples, he grew more than ever convinced that this cropping pattern could be applied, with advantage, to the farms of his own country.

In Flanders the rotation of flax, turnips, oats and clover had made barren heathland more profitable than prime wheat land or the finest pastures. Sir Richard calculated that 500 acres of heathland, returning five pounds an acre under traditional management, might yield more than 7,000 pounds when converted to the new rotation. In seventeenth-century Europe this was little short of a fortune.

He saw no reason why the same cropping sequence should not prove equally profitable on the sandy heaths of Surrey since 'by their nature those seeds do delight to grow rather in a light and gentle land then in one too stiff and heavie'. English farmers adopting the system could be sure to harvest not just a sizeable profit, but the praise and honour of their neighbours.

Sir Richard wrote his *Discours* – an unqualified endorsement of the Flemish system – as a 'legacie to his sons'. He referred to them sombrely, as 'precepts from a dying father'. He urges his sons to try the methods he has set out without eloquence, but as 'a true story plainly set forth'.

> You will find this husbandrie . . . to bee very pleasing to you, and so exceeding profitable, that it will make you diligent; for no man of any art or science (except an alchimist) ever pretended so much gain any other way, as you shall see demonstrated in this ensuing treatise. The usurer doubles but his principal, with interest upon interest, in seven years, but by this little treatise you shall learn how to do more than treble your principal in one year's compass . . . Besides the

excessive profit you shall reap by sowing these commodities, imagine what a pleasure it will be to your eies and sent, to see the russet heath turned into greenest grass, which doth produce most sweet and pleasant honie-suckles [Dutch clover]; and what prais and reputation you will gain by your examples, first introducing that into your countrie, which beeing followed by others, must needs redound to the general benefit of the whole common-wealth.

But the value of clover was not unknown in Britain. While Sir Richard was among the first to advocate the sowing of it as a crop, the plant's virtues were well established. The local term for wild white clover had cropped up in Northamptonshire field names since the fourteenth century – Cleuerslade in 1345, Claversbalke in 1437, Clevrehill in 1512 and Claverefurlong in about 1600.[4] The writer Barnaby Googe, translating the farming advice of the German Conrad Heresbach, commended the use of 'trefoil or Burgundian grass', assuring English farmers that 'there can be no better fodder devised for cattell'.[5]

Writing in the early sixteenth century, John Norden urged farmers to reseed bare patches in their meadows with 'some hay seede, especially the seede of the Clauergrasse, or the grasse honcy-suckle and other seedes that fall out of the finest and purest hay; and in the sowing of it, mingle it with some good earth. But sow not the honey-suckle grasse in too moist a ground, for it liketh it not, therefore you must drain the place before you sow it.'[6]

Almost a century later Trifolium or three-leaved grass is mentioned by George Owen in his *Description of Pembrokeshire*, published in 1603. He tells of a land covered with both white and red clover whose flowers emitted 'a most pleasant sweet smell'.

By the time Sir Richard Weston had made his momentous discoveries about Flemish agriculture a few English farmers had already begun to experiment with clover as a sown crop. Seed had been imported into Norfolk from Holland since 1620,[7] and by 1650 seed of 'the great clover of Flanders' was being sold at the shop of Mr James Long at The Barge, Billingsgate.[8] Much of this imported seed was of poor quality, and the contemporary writer Walter Blith was probably not alone in suspecting a foreign plot to prevent English farmers reaping the benefits of the new husbandry.

> Much that is sold in the seed-mens shops in London was either corrupted by the Dutch before it came thence, or else parched by over-drying, or else by the shop-keepers, either mingling old and new, or keeping it another year, and then selling it for new . . . And I have heard that the Dutch out of an evill spirit, lest we should have the same benefit they have, have kiln-dryed it. Therefore my advice is to send over a knowing man that hath had experience of it, and knows the right coloured seed to buy, and search all the country and buy the best and choicest seed he can possibly buy for silver . . . [9]

Despite the difficulties Walter Blith remained an enthusiast for the crop that would 'grow upon the barrenest ground as on Windsor Forrest'. An acre, he reckoned, might keep 'four coach horses and more all summer long'. But even if it supported only two cows 'it is advantage enough upon such lands as never kept one'.

Among the early pioneers was the engineer and agriculturalist Andrew Yarranton. Although he had started life as an apprenticed linen-draper, he later took up farming at Ashley in Worcestershire where he spent more than twenty years growing and experimenting with clover. His little book, *The Great Improvement of Lands by Clover*, published in 1663, was described by a later biographer as 'the most truly practical' work of its time.[10]

Yarranton's influence led to the wider adoption of the crop, at least among the gentry. In his book he tells of sixty acres sown with clover seed by his neighbour, the former High Sheriff Sir John Winford, on 'barren, gravelly land; which land if laid down to bear natural grass is not worth above four shillings and six pence the acre at most . . . and I know there hath been made of it at least forty five shillings per annum upon each acre by clover'.

Another neighbour, a grazier called Thomas Hill, who frequented the fairs in Worcestershire, Staffordshire and Shropshire, had also grown the crop and was ready to give 'an account of the profit from it'. One local farmer was so impressed that he put his feelings into verse.

> With what delight and pleasure have I seen
> The barren pastures clothed all in green!
> Where neither grass nor corn would grow before
> It hath of honeysuckles planted store.
> It brings us store of butter and of cheese,
> It feeds our sheep, our turkeys and our geese;
> It feeds our horses, oxen and our kine
> (and that with speed) our pigs do feed like swine.
> Fat beef and bacon now shall be our fare
> And with Westphalia gammons we'll compare.
> The milk maid hath her wish, her pails it fills
> Just at the dayry door, such store it yields.
> The land that once we thought not worth our sowing
> For three years time stands to with six times mowing.
> Three-leaved grass soon yields a threefold profit
> Three volumes may be writ in praises of it.
> But to conclude; thy purse will ne'er run over
> Till thou hast got the art of sowing clover.[11]

Through experiment and propaganda Andrew Yarranton is credited with making Worcestershire and its neighbouring counties the first region of Britain to grow the crop on any scale. But in the words of farming historian Lord Ernle, 'it was long before clover emerged from the fields of gentlemen into common use'. The revolution, when it came, was to take place not in these midland counties, but far to the east, in Norfolk.

When the 36-year-old Captain Yarranton left the Parliamentary army in 1652 few friends would have predicted that he would make his name as an agricultural 'improver'. Though all thoughts of becoming a linen-draper had vanished, he was now set on a career in 'ironworks'. With his contemporary Sir Richard Weston he shared a passion for water transport, involving himself in a number of waterway navigation schemes, most of which seem to have been dogged by financial setbacks.[12] At some time in his career he surveyed the three great English rivers – the Thames, Humber and Severn.

His political life was colourful throughout. Following the Restoration he was compromised by the discovery of letters linking him to a planned Presbyterian rising. A later warrant for his arrest described him as being 'as violent a villain against the king as any in those parts'.

Yarranton's own account of the affair is the stuff of fiction. It includes his denunciation of the letters as 'fraudulent', his arrest on no fewer than three occasions, and allegations that he had spoken treason against the king.[13] After a full jury trial he appears to have been acquitted.

In less turbulent times he was sent by a group of English industrialists to learn the secrets of the tin plate trade in Saxony. He found his Saxon hosts surprisingly open. They seemed more than willing to show him round their factories and explain their production methods. He went back to his sponsors with a working knowledge of the tin plating process. But before they could set up their own factory, a rival group started production using a 'trumpt up' patent.

Many of Yarranton's adventures are set out in his work *England's Improvement by Sea and Land*, published in two parts between 1677 and 1681. Like other 'gentlemen' of his time he was motivated by a strong desire to serve his country. Though he cannot have known it when he died, his lasting legacy to the nation was to be a little book about clover.

The work is primarily a practical guide for farmers. He recommends sowing the crop on dry, well-limed soil, using a seed rate of twelve pounds to the acre. Ideally it should be sown under a 'nurse crop' of barley. His advice to farmers cutting a clover crop for hay includes the warning: 'Do not shake your swathes as you do other hay, onely turn it with as much tenderness as may be until it is for to cock, for the leaves of it are too apt to fall.'

The book contains advice on how to prevent grazing cattle going down with bloat, a constant risk with clover. The author suggests they should be allowed a quarter of an hour only on the first day, a half-hour on the second day, an hour on the third day, and so on until the seventh day when they might be allowed to graze continuously.

'Also have a care that your kine [dairy cows] or oxen drink not of two hours after they come out of the clover, for this grass is so sweet a feeding for them that drinking immediately after it they are in danger of swelling.'

Despite the hazards Yarranton is convinced of the feeding value of clover. Just six acres of the crop, he claims, will support as many cattle as thirty acres of 'natural grass'. And dairy cows grazing clover will give better milk, butter and cheese than those raised on 'ordinary grass'.

Yarranton ends his treatise with an unusual invitation. Anyone wishing to know more about the cultivation of clover is asked to call at his home where they will be shown evidence 'that may convince the most incredulous'. He adds: 'In my absence Mr Robert Vicaris, my next neighbour, will be ready to perform what I have here promised.'

How many local yeomen beat a path to his door at Ashley we have no way of knowing, but he seems to have become a clearing house for the exchange of information on clover culture. A certain 'J. B.' wrote to him in December 1662, taking him to task for proposing spring as the best time to sow the crop. As far as 'J. B.' was concerned autumn was the best time to sow it, particularly on heavier clay soils currently cropped with wheat.

They are fain to sow a great part of their land with horse-meat [grain for draught horses], and that at a great charge; which the team devouring next winter, and the family most or all the bread corn, the poor farmer can hardly pay his rent, and is always kept necessitous. For such lands clover is the greatest, if not the only improvement; for sowing clover either with or without his winter corn, the year after the fallow, he shall that year not onely have excellent fodder far beyond what ordinarily comes from barley or oates, but also the clover will have gotten so good rooting, that the next winter's grazing shall not destroy so much, as it does usually that which is sown in spring; so that without further charge, he shall have second year's profit to be imployed either for hay or grazing, as his occasions best serve.[14]

However attractive the crop may have looked to the gentry, tenant farmers were slow to take it up. Like poor farmers everywhere they were unwilling to chance failure. The larger landowners and yeomen freeholders had capital enough to invest in untried crops. But for small farmers there were real risks whatever the promised benefits.

Clovers are susceptible to pests and diseases, notably stem eelworm and clover rot, both of which are likely to have been endemic in soils where the pioneer crops were grown. Farmers who ignored the dangers of bloat and skimped on the prudent rationing suggested by Yarranton were likely to find their animals down, gasping for breath, and blown up like billowing breeches on a washing line.

This was the fate that overtook Bathsheba Everdene's sheep flock in *Far From the Madding Crowd* when they broke into a field of young clover and grazed on it until they 'blasted themselves'.

Quite apart from the hazards there were those who rejected the three-leaved grass simply because it was new. In Yarranton's words they clung to methods that had been introduced for no better reason than that 'men were most ignorant' at the time, methods that had now acquired the 'venerable name of antiquity'. Lord Ernle refers to the 'round-frocked' farmers of Surrey, who prided themselves on preserving the practices and dress of their forefathers, men of 'inflexible honesty', enemies equally of agricultural improvements and the new commercial morality.[15]

But there were also people of capital and adventurous spirit prepared to follow the enthusiasts. In Kent landowner Nicholas Toke bought clover seed in 1653, his farm accounts showing that the crop was regularly grown from that time.[16] Both red and white clover were known to have been cultivated on land around Ashford, probably from seed imported through one of the Channel ports.

By 1681 clover was regularly grown in Staffordshire though it seems the farmers in nearby Cheshire and Lancashire had yet to discover the secret.[17] The crop was also known in Cambridge-shire where farmers were said to have sown very small quantities of seed. And in 1686 an early reference to the growing of clover in Norfolk appeared in the estate book of the Townshends of Raynham.[18] Dutch woollen merchants living at Topsham on the Exe estuary in Devon regularly imported clover seed for distribution at markets throughout the West Country.[19]

In 1707 John Mortimer, author of *Whole Art of Husbandry*, wrote that clover was commonly grown in the southern counties. Fifty years later market gardener Richard North spoke of meeting Somerset farmer Jonathan James of Chilcompton, near Wells, whose father had been the first in the county to grow and market perennial red clover, locally known as Marl-grass.

> The farmer observing a great deal of this wild clover growing about his farm, and thriving exceedingly in such places as had been mended with deep blue, or what they call black marl; where it was convenient he let it stand, and ripen the seed, which was gather'd and clean'd out from the husks and sown the spring following. From this beginning, Farmer James went on with cultivating this kind of clover, from time to time, increasing his quantity, and supplying his neighbours and others with the seed; so that at this time, the present Farmer James, and many other farmers and gentlemen in Somersetshire, Gloucestershire and the contiguous counties, raise great quantities of this grass for pasture, for hay, and for seed, which seed is frequently sold at Bristol, and other market towns in the west country by the name of Marl-grass; and for two or three years past has been sold in London at a very extraordinary price, by the name of Perennial red-flowering Clover.[20]

This was no headlong rush into a new venture; rather the

cautious edging towards it by a few brave souls over a span of nearly two centuries. It was not yet the revolution. That would have to wait until the nineteenth century. But it was a preparation for revolution; a marshalling of arms, a stiffening of the sinews.

Clover was grown not in the predominantly pastoral areas of Britain – the hills and vales of heavy clay which remained in permanent pasture – but in the tillage areas, particularly on light, sandy soils. It marked the start of a new form of farming, the so-called 'up-and-down' or 'convertible' husbandry in which arable and clover were alternated on the same piece of land. Sometimes a 'catch crop' of turnips was included in the rotation just as Weston had seen in Flanders.

The effect on soil fertility was dramatic. As in Flanders the new crops meant that cattle and sheep could be carried in greater numbers, especially through the winter. The manure they produced enriched the soil and raised the yields of cereal crops in the rotation. Farmers were able to eliminate the fallow altogether while harvesting bumper crops of grain.

Sometimes farmers sowed clover not on its own, but mixed with grass seed. In the early eighteenth century John Mortimer described a rotation worked out by farmers on the clay lands of the Sussex Weald.[21] The traditional system of two crops and a fallow, still popular in the common fields of many neighbouring counties, was replaced by a rotation of two corn crops followed by a three-year 'ley' of clover mixed with 'ray grass'.

English seed was considered the best. The Sussex improvers sowed ten pounds of clover to the acre in a mixture with eight pounds of ray grass, the old term for a collection of grasses which included not just ryegrass, but meadow fescue, meadow foxtail, crested dog's-tail, cocksfoot, tall oatgrass and even herbs like yarrow, burnet and ribwort plantain.

Fifty years later, Edward Lisle, author of *Observations in Husbandry*, reported that farmers on the chalk downland near his home at Crux Easton, Hampshire, had been sowing mixtures of clover and ryegrass since the turn of the century. Lisle stated his own preference for ryegrass grown on its own.

The vogue for exotic crops among the better-off and more

adventurous farmers of the age led to the proliferation of unfamiliar forage crops in the new rotations. Among them were the 'French grasses', the legumes St Foyn, or holy-hay (sainfoin), and La Lucerne (lucerne), which, like clover, were able to fix atmospheric nitrogen and make it available to plant roots.

Writing in 1669 John Worlidge advised 'timorous rusticks' not to plant the new seeds on land that already grew profitable crops, but to choose some small, forgotten corner and 'bestow a little seed on it'. The experiment might prove highly profitable.

> In Wiltshire in several places there are presidents of *St Foyn*, that hath been there twenty years' growing on poor land, and hath so far improved the same, that from a noble per acre, twenty acres together have been constantly worth thirty shillings per acre, and yet continues in good proof . . . This plant *La Lucerne* is commended for an excellent fodder. It is good for all kind of cattle; but above all, it agreeth best with horses; it feedeth much more than ordinary hay, that lean beasts are suddenly fat with it; it causeth abundance of milk in milch-beasts . . . By eating this grass in the spring, horses are purged and made fat in eight or ten days time. One acre will keep three horses all the year long.[22]

As in Flanders the new alternate husbandry made light, sandy soils more valuable than the heavy clays. Until now these heavier soils had been the chief producers of wheat. They were far from easy to manage. Working the land when it was too wet was likely to turn it into the consistency of lumpy porridge, though the farmers who timed their cultivations right could expect a decent yield. But the new rotational forage crops so raised the fertility of the light lands that they began to yield serious wheat crops for the first time. And because these soils were more easily worked, growing costs were usually lower than on traditional wheat land. Arable production began to shift from heavy soils to the light land areas.

One contemporary observer noted that 'the dry grounds in Hertfordshire, which formerly were lett for a trifling rent, are now lett at twenty shillings per acre, since the introduction of clover and turnips into their poor and barren hills; while the low lying stiff grounds pay only ten shillings, which is the rent they gave near a century ago'.[23]

Under the new husbandry the light lands also began to increase their output of livestock, much to the chagrin of meat producers in the traditional grassland areas of the north and west. A group of northern graziers lobbied Parliament for a law to suppress the new grasses in southern England. They feared that grazing might become as plentiful there as in other areas, thus harming the traditional producers of hay and livestock.

According to the lobbyists, it is because of

a plentiful stock of hay and grass in that fatal winter of 1673, that it preserved almost all those cattle in those countries, or places where these grasses were most grown; and hay at no great price, when in the western and northern parts of England, through the defect of hay and the scarcity of pasture, the greatest part of their cattle perished, and were forced to seek a supply from those parts, whose markets they used to furnish.[24]

There would be no curbs on the new grasses. And as writers such as Blith and Worlidge proclaimed their benefits, a growing number of farmers adopted the technology. As a result the average wheat yield had doubled to twenty bushels an acre by the close of the eighteenth century.[25]

But it was in Norfolk that the new husbandry made its greatest impact. The very term 'Norfolk four-course' – the rotation of wheat, turnips, barley and clover – has become synonymous with the agricultural revolution. In 1769 the farming writer Arthur Young observed: 'Half the county of Norfolk, within the memory of man, yielded nothing but sheep feed; whereas those very tracts of land are now covered with as fine barley and rye as any in the world – and great quantities of wheat besides.'[26]

The new clover leys were also producing a great deal of beef. By 1705 at least 30,000 cattle were being driven each year from

Scotland to England. Most went to Norfolk to be fattened on grass and clover in the summer, and turnips and hay in the winter.[27] During the month-long journey the cattle lost one-eighth of their bodyweight and sold in Norfolk for two pounds a head. The returning drovers took back to Scotland their own travellers' tales of wondrous green pastures on the poor, sandy soils of north-west Norfolk, just as Sir Richard Weston had returned with stories of the heathlands of Flanders.

Leading exponents of the new farming became national heroes, among them Thomas Coke of Holkham. When in 1776 he came into the family's north Norfolk estate at the age of twenty-two he was already the county's Member of Parliament. His management of the estate over the next thirty years was praised as 'exemplary', with The Park at Holkham being hailed by contemporary observers as a model of the best farming practice.[28]

In fact 'artificial' grasses and clover had been regularly sown at Holkham long before 1776. When Arthur Young praised Coke's farming in 1784 he noted that it cannot have been easy for the young landowner to make his farm outstanding 'in the midst of the best husbandry in Norfolk, where the fields of every tenant are cultivated like gardens'.[29]

While convertible farming reached its zenith in eastern England, the techniques were applied on lighter soils almost everywhere in the country. During the seventeenth century clover leys were being sown from the south coast to Sherwood Forest, and from East Anglia to the Welsh border. By the end of the following century the farmers of Britain and Ireland were effectively feeding an extra seven million people as the UK population soared.[30]

In the century and a half to 1850 the output of animal products from English farms increased by two-and-half times.[31] Along with a doubling of grain yields, the four-course rotation produced 80 per cent more food than the traditional three-course arable rotation of wheat and oats followed by a fallow.[32]

It was a remarkable achievement; a flowering of agrarian culture before the coming of the chemical age, and historians continue to seek explanations for it. Enclosure may have played a part. During the eighteenth century most of the remaining open fields were enclosed by Act of Parliament. At the same time major structural changes were taking place, with peasant holdings becoming amalgamated into large, capitalist farms. The population was rising again, and by the middle of the century enough farmers seem to have adopted the new crops and techniques to create a 'critical mass': an explosion in its uptake. Farming and food production could now make their great advance.

The real improvement of convertible husbandry was the transformation of the nitrogen economy in agriculture. Throughout the Middle Ages wheat yields had been held in check by low levels of soil fertility, in effect a shortage of nitrogen. The great builder of fertility was grassland, the meadowlands and the pastures, the community's stock of old permanent grasslands on to which went the manure of cattle and sheep. Medieval farmers were well aware of the yield-boosting potential of grass. They knew that when they ploughed an old pasture and sowed it with wheat or barley, they could expect to harvest double the grain yield of crops grown on the arable land.

The ploughing-up of permanent pasture in the late sixteenth century amounted to a 'cashing in' of fertility built up since the land had been laid down to grass in the fourteenth century. Grassland represented a reserve bank of nitrogen locked up in foliage and soil organic matter until released by the plough.

The new alternate husbandry brought the fertility-building power of grassland on to the cultivated land. Grasses and livestock rearing were no longer separated from crop growing. For the first time both activities were to be carried out alternately on the same ground, speeding the cycling of nitrogen and dramatically improving productivity per acre. Flemish genius had spawned an English farming renaissance.

Part of the genius had been to include clovers in the system. Nitrogen-fixing legumes had been grown on English farms since the Middle Ages, among them peas, beans and vetches. But with clovers the transformation of nitrogen is carried out faster. In northern Europe the introduction of clover is estimated to have raised the total nitrogen supply to the land by as much as 60 per cent.[33]

Convertible husbandry brought something else to England's overworked crop lands – the culture of pastoralism. The growing of crops is essentially an extractive process. The farmer plants a crop. The crop draws nourishment from the earth. The farmer harvests the crop, consuming it himself or selling it. The land is left the poorer. Though the farmer may try to put something back by fallowing, the overall effect has been one of nutrient loss, of impoverishment.

By contrast, the growing of grass enriches the earth. The farmer still gets a return in meat, or milk, or wool. But the land gains something as well. Grassland returns nutrients to the soil, particularly when it is rich in clover plants. A healthy pasture nourishes the earth even as it feeds the animals grazing on it. The livestock farmer has taken part in a process, not of extraction, but of renewal.

Through early history the culture of grassland was relegated to the margins of agrarian activity – to the wastes at the forest edge, to marshy grazings by the stream, to the hills and uplands, to far-flung places. At the heart of village life lay the arable land, constantly tended, coaxed and sweated over. And still it had failed to deliver what the community expected from it.

But alternate husbandry, with its grasses and clovers, brought the process of renewal to the very centre of agrarian life. Land that had provided arable crops was now to be rested under pasture. Farming had been reborn as a continuous cycle of depletion and restoration, of loss and renewal. The age-old union of plant and grazing beast – the union that had created the endless prairie and the sun-dappled forest glade – had been rebuilt in microcosm here on the English and Scottish lowlands. A new harmony had been restored and nature gave of her bounty.

13   *The Improvers*

Like a column of roaring bull elephants the forty-tonners thunder down the straight stretch of Roman road that forms part of the trunk route from Huntingdon to the east coast. This is no place to linger and gaze at the countryside. But then this is not a countryside that expects to be gazed upon. Bleak and featureless, it lies at the edge of fenland, the great low-lying plain to the south and east of the Wash.

In the Middle Ages this land was a wilderness of marshes, reed-shoals and wet grasslands; a landscape of open skies and slow, meandering rivers where the people walked on stilts and made their living by fishing, wild-fowling and pollarding the stark outcrops of willow trees. In the seventeenth century, despite fierce opposition from local commoners, the area was drained. Like much of East Anglia it is now devoted to arable crop production on an industrial scale. In summer broad swathes of ripening wheat stretch away to the far horizon, with only the march of power pylons to break the dreary pattern.

From the roaring highway a minor road winds its way across the fields. It is empty like the endless stretches of ripening grain, twitching in the summer breeze like an ageing skin soon to be shed. Fenland countryside has an air of business-like efficiency about it. This is an agriculture that is lean and bent on profit; an agriculture conducted from glass enclosures perched high on the backs of great machines. Up here sit the operators, air-conditioned and bathed in surround sound, controlling some vast spray boom or the whirling pick-up reel of a combine.

Every so often the little road passes an industrial shed, the home of a small-scale factory operation that has been plucked from the town and dropped in this open landscape. Somehow it does not look out of place. Like the edge-of-town industrial park, this is an area dedicated to production. A group of ramblers would look as incongruous around here as a family of picnickers in a builder's yard.

Six hundred years ago this landscape was filled with people – commoners herding their geese between marsh grazings, and fenmen striking out in flat-bottomed punts to net a fish-filled pool. In medieval fenland people were as plentiful as the larks that filled the summer sky and the waders that flocked to the waterlogged grasslands.

Then the drainers came. The first was John Morton, Bishop of Ely, later Archbishop of Canterbury in the reign of Henry VII. A deep cut forty feet wide and twelve miles long, designed to speed the flow of the River Nene between Peterborough and Guyhirn, still bears the name Morton's Leam. The next major work, Popham's Eau, carried water from a tributary of the Nene to the Ouse, a prologue for the ambitious schemes of the fourth Earl of Bedford and Cornelius Vermuyden – later Sir Cornelius Vermuyden – the great drainage engineer from Zealand.

Making use of Dutch engineers and labourers, Vermuyden was responsible for draining large areas of southern fenland, cutting new channels, scouring and straightening existing drains, raising embankments, building sluices and dams, and creating outfalls to the sea, finally producing a new landscape for agriculture. As he reported to his backers: 'Wheat and other grains, besides unnumerable quantities of sheep, cattle and other stock were raised, where never had been any before.'[1]

Most of the livestock have vanished from the landscape that still bears Vermuyden's imprint. Many field levels have sunk as the peat soils dried out and oxidised under the new regime of cultivation. Pumps are now widely used to lift water from the ditches into the artificial drains that will carry it away. To deliver up its annual harvest of grain the reclaimed marshland must be kept in intensive care.

In the village of Over – as in many fenland communities – some of the older houses are of Dutch design, with shutters and stylish red-brick façades. Originally thatched, they date back to the seventeenth century when they were built to house the engineers who worked on the fenland reclamation. These Protestant workers from across the North Sea aroused a great deal of anger among the native villagers, who viewed the project as a threat to their livelihoods, as indeed it was. Today the people of the fenland villages must commute to Cambridge and other towns to find work. There are precious few jobs in the highly mechanised business of arable farming.

To get to farmer Les Cook's yard you turn opposite Over's village green into a lane signposted Fen End, passing a row of modern, up-market houses. Almost at once the village is behind you and the lane narrows to a single track, overhung with tall hedges, itself a rarity in this part of Britain. The farm entrance opens into a concrete yard with a heap of round straw bales and a collection of farm machines. Les Cook emerges from a barn, his hands black with grease, some of which has transferred to his shirt. There has been a minor emergency – the clutch has failed on the farm's ageing International tractor, and before the maintenance firm will come along and replace it the front-end loader must be removed.

Since the machine hasn't been off the tractor for years, shifting it has proved a tough job. Les and a neighbour have just about managed it after two hours, a big expenditure of muscle power and a few choice expletives. This is no mechanised agribusiness with a shed-full of modern machines. Albany Farm is one of those rarities in eastern England – the small family farm. There isn't much more to it than a couple of hundred acres or so of rented land, some well-worn items of farm machinery and a newish-looking bungalow where Les lives with wife Anna and their three young daughters. There's something else rather special about the place. It has a herd of pedigree Hereford cattle of the kind experts would call 'traditional'.

Britain once supplied the world with farm livestock. The very names of the great breeds proclaim their island roots: Aberdeen Angus, Devon, Sussex, Scotch Shorthorn, Lincoln Red, Gloucester, Galloway, Ayrshire, Welsh Black and, of course, the Hereford. They arose from a frenzy of activity by groups of dedicated enthusiasts, each out to secure a place in history for their own cherished breed. Many succeeded. In the eighteenth and early nineteenth centuries British breeds – the Hereford included – stocked the grasslands of five continents. The island kingdom, with its natural capacity to grow grass, became for a brief period stud farm to the world.

Most of the great breeds emerged from the ferment that was the industrial revolution. They played a part in feeding the towns and cities that were everywhere expanding in the youthful industrial economy. They marked the pinnacle of the pastoral achievement; a parting gift from an old and declining culture to a brash and confident new one. And in the flick of a cow's tail their time had gone.

Long before the tragedy of BSE the world's raisers of cattle and sheep had stopped coming to Britain for their breeding stock. The traditional breeds were no longer seen as suited to the modern consumer taste. They were too small, too prone to over-fatness. Thus the traditional British breeds, once the crown jewels of her livestock empire, went the way of Sunbeam cars and Norton motorbikes.

Les Cook steers his Land-rover between the ruts and potholes of the lane leading to his grazing pastures. The rented fields border the River Ouse and are often flooded in winter. They form part of the natural flood plain. When the river runs high it spills over the banks just as it has done for a thousand years. The low-lying grassland acts as a natural sponge, temporarily holding excess water when the river is in spate and protecting the valuable arable crops on the drained land next door. Some of the grasses in this flood pasture are coarse and stemmy. But the Herefords seem to thrive on it.

We park in a field gateway and walk to where a group of about thirty cows are lying contentedly with their calves. As we approach they struggle to their feet and watch our approach with mild interest. They have no fear of humans. They seem merely curious as Les Cook walks among them pointing out some particular breed feature such as the slight ridging at the base of a cow's horn that reveals the number of her calvings as surely as the rings of a felled tree denote the seasons of its life. Viewed up close these animals appear surprisingly small. In early oil paintings the Hereford is depicted as a massive beast with a deep covering of flesh.

In an attempt to revive demand for the breed, some enthusiasts are trying to breed bigger animals. It is not a strategy that appeals to Les Cook. In his own breeding programme he is determined to retain the size and shape of the traditional Hereford, the beef breed that almost all dairy farmers once bought to cross with their black and white cows. Even in the 1960s the Hereford remained the most popular beef breed in the land. Les Cook believes its popularity will return as a new generation of beef farmers discovers its merits – chiefly its unrivalled ability to convert grass into tasty beef.

He explains: 'In good pasture the Hereford will put on flesh quickly and efficiently. And on poorer grazing it will retain that flesh. If necessary the Hereford can thrive on next to nothing. Some of the big continental breeds may grow to an enormous size, but only when fed a lot of expensive grain. And then there's the taste. Nothing can compare with the taste of Hereford beef. It is well-marbled so it cooks wonderfully; a delicious healthy meat. One day people will start to wake up to these qualities. In the meantime it is up to us, the breeders, to pass on this magnificent animal unspoiled to a future generation.'

In the warm summer sunshine these cattle certainly look magnificent with their rich red coats and elegantly bowed horns. Standing quietly in the small grass field with its towering, unshorn hedges and a distant view of Swavesey Church, they complete a picture that might have come from a Constable oil painting. Like many traditional cattle breeds they were once regarded as an icon of pastoral plenty, a natural adornment to the grand country house. Many early breeders were as concerned with the way an animal would look in a manicured parkland setting as with its ability to produce meat.

A census of pedigree cattle in 1919 showed a surprising concentration around London, even though the home counties were birthplace to no native breeds.[2] Pedigree cattle were firmly linked with landscaped parks and the nineteenth-century squirearchy, both of which were found in abundance close to London. The breeding of fine livestock was a popular interest with the landed aristocracy whose fascination with genealogy had already found expression in the breeding of foxhounds and horses. Published in 1791, the first thoroughbred stud book was a full thirty years ahead of *Coates's Herdbook* for Shorthorn cattle, its livestock equivalent.

By the early eighteenth century dogs, gamebirds and vegetables were all being subjected to selective breeding, though the process was directed as much by 'fancy' as a wish to enhance some worthwhile attribute. Contemporary society saw the natural world as a strict hierarchy with human beings at the apex, free to intervene and manipulate all within their dominion. A prosperous bourgeoisie had the time and money to take up the noble task of perfecting nature. Those with fortunes made in commerce or industry bought landed estates on which to pursue their passion to 'improve'. They held an unshakeable belief in the idea of 'progress' and saw it as their duty to play a part.

The origins of British livestock breeding go back at least as far as the Middle Ages and probably earlier. But it was not until the eighteenth century that Britain took on the role of stud farm to the world. The epicentre of the revolution was Dishley Grange near Loughborough in Leicestershire, the home of Robert Bakewell. Born in 1725 Bakewell began his experiments in livestock breeding at the age of twenty, taking over the running of his father's farm when he was thirty-five. A stout, red-faced character in a scarlet waistcoat, leather breeches and top boots, he has been likened to the archetypal English yeoman as depicted through the ages on Staffordshire jugs.[3]

Bakewell was a bold and innovative farmer, which is probably why he went bankrupt at least once in his life. Even so, he was skilled enough in his chosen profession to be celebrated throughout the country for his water meadows and root crops. But it was the Dishley Grange livestock that brought visitors flocking to this little corner of Leicestershire, particularly his famous black stallion, his bull 'Twopenny' and his ram 'Two-pounder'.

Bakewell was a great self-publicist as well as an astute businessman. To impress visitors, he reconstructed the skeletons of some of his more successful animals in the hall of his house. From the walls he hung preserved joints of meat to illustrate such breed points as smallness of bone and thickness of fat. But any visitor wishing to pick up some clue to his stock-breeding methods was likely to go home disappointed. He is said to have confided business secrets to no one but an old shepherd.

Not all Bakewell's secrets can have been worth very much. His attempts at cattle breeding seem to have ended in failure. He had tried to improve the 'beefing' qualities of his favourite breed, the Lancashire or Craven Longhorn, named after its home in that corner of Yorkshire's West Riding which borders Lancashire and Westmoreland. In late-nineteenth-century England Longhorns of various types were the one truly national breed. They were milky enough to supply cheese-makers from Lancashire to Wiltshire, while the beefier types fattened moderately well on good pasture. But as Bakewell's methods began to produce a fleshier animal, they also reduced its ability to produce milk, a weakness that didn't much impress Britain's army of farmhouse cheese-makers.

He was scarcely more successful in his bid to improve the famed Berkshire pig. The progeny from his breeding experiments were described by contemporary critics as 'all rickety' and 'all fools'. But his great triumph, the single noble achievement which secured his place in farming history, was the Improved Leicester sheep. His raw material had been the local longwool, a large-framed, long-legged animal with 'a rump as sharp as a hatchet' and a skin 'that might be said to rattle upon his ribs like a skeleton wrapped in parchment'.[4]

Out of this unprepossessing beast Bakewell constructed the New Leicester, a compact, early-maturing sheep with a lighter fleece than its longwool forebears. The breed was an instant success. Sheep farmers across the county used the animal as a mutton producer either on its own or by crossing with their own flocks, thus 'up-grading' the stock. Soon New Leicester rams were being used to improve the meat-producing potential of a range of longwool types.[5] In 1750 Bakewell had been hiring out his rams for sixteen shillings a season, but by 1789 he would let none go for less than twenty guineas. His total fees for the season amounted to 3,000 pounds.[6] In less than thirty years his improved sheep had become world famous.

Even then he was not without his critics. On fertile land the New Leicester was said to produce too much fat, 'that which cannot be eaten, but which is good for the manufacture of soaps and candles'. John Lawrence once dined on a seventeen-pound leg of Dishley Grange mutton: 'The fat which dripped in cooking was measured and it amounted to between two and three quarts; besides this, the dish was a mere bag of loose, oily fat, huge deep flakes of which remained to garnish that which we called, by courtesy, lean.'[7] However, most people recognised his achievement. He became a celebrity, entertaining 'Russian princes, French and German royal dukes, British peers, and sightseers of every degree'.

Bakewell's success resulted from his bold use of inbreeding: the crossing of an animal with a close relative. First he would select an outstanding individual with the qualities he was interested in – usually its ability to put on flesh. Having found his champion he would then cross it repeatedly to close relatives so as to 'fix' the desired characteristics. At that time inbreeding was the only way of preserving the qualities of a champion. Without it the genetic contribution of a good bull or ram would have been halved at each generation. Today a good bull can be made to sire thousands of offspring through artificial insemination and the use of frozen semen. In the nineteenth century inbreeding was the sole means of hanging on to genetic excellence.

Nevertheless there were risks attached. Inbreeding might

expose serious genetic defects normally masked in the *genotype*. If these were numerous the breed might even die out, there being too few healthy individuals born to sustain it. Bakewell took plenty of jibes about his 'incestuous' practices. References to his 'foolish' pigs suggest that the critics might not have been entirely wrong. Nevertheless he stuck to his methods despite the setbacks. And in the end they paid off.

Bakewell had sensed that times were changing. He had anticipated the momentous social upheavals that were to follow the first stirrings of industrialisation – an explosive urban growth and a rise in living standards that would together boost the demand for meat. Until now cattle had been kept mainly for their milk or for pulling a plough. Similarly sheep had been valued chiefly as wool producers. In future both would be sought for their meat. But for this to happen the tough, rangy beasts of his time would need to be transformed into efficient growers of flesh. His gift to a nation on the threshold of urbanisation was the means of securing this metamorphosis.

Following Bakewell's success with the New Leicester a host of other breeders adopted his methods. Among them were the Colling brothers, Robert and Charles, who farmed close to each other near Darlington in County Durham. As a young man Charles had been sent by his father on a study visit to Dishley Grange. The prime motive seems to have been to end the boy's infatuation with one Mary Colpitts, a woman considered 'unsuitable'. The strategy failed spectacularly. Charles returned to marry Mary, and together the pair laid the foundations of a cattle breed that was to dominate British livestock farming for two centuries and influence beef production all over the world.

The starting point was a type of cattle found principally in the north-east of England and described variously by eighteenth-century writers as Teeswaters, Holderness cattle, Durhams, or simply the 'Dutch kind', their ancestors having been introduced via the east coast ports and crossed with native cattle. Their colours varied though most were mixed red and white, or 'flecked' as the breeders called them. Apart from their short horns they were noted for their heavy build and capacity to produce milk, though the milk was not regarded as the highest quality.[8] From this raw material the Colling brothers founded the Shorthorn.

In an early stroke of either genius or good fortune they managed to obtain for just eight pounds a small bull they had seen grazing in a roadside field. There was little certainty about his pedigree, though he appeared to carry Dutch blood on the male side and Highland blood on his dam's side. This was the famous bull Hubback, who turned out to be highly potent, well able to bring a compact, beefy shape to these large, clumsy north-country cattle.

A squabble between the brothers led to a second stroke of luck. Mary sent her cow Phoenix to the home of brother-in-law Robert for service by one of his bulls. Testy Robert refused to oblige, and in pique Mary mated the animal with one of her own bulls, Lord Bolingbroke, who was both nephew and half-brother to the cow. Out of that union came the handsome bull Favourite. Much encouraged Mary and Charles resolved to pursue the policy of inbreeding, mating Favourite 'to his own get' into the sixth generation. It was a policy that paid off handsomely. Among the offspring was the legendary bull Comet which, when sold as a six-year-old at a herd dispersal sale in 1810, realised the fabulous sum of 1,000 guineas.

Comet was a light roan, sired by Favourite out of Young Phoenix, who was herself a daughter of Favourite having been mated to his own mother.[9] A nineteenth-century observer wrote: 'He was not very large, but with that infallible sign of condition, a good wide scorp or frontlet, a fine placid eye, a well-filled twist, and an undeniable back.'[10] Charles Colling had another calf of Favourite fattened until it reached the extraordinary weight of one and one-third tons as a five-year-old. He had a special railway car constructed to carry the famous 'Durham Ox' up and down the country, generating much publicity for its owners. Not to be outdone, brother Robert went on the stump with his own beast, 'The White Heifer That Travelled', weighing in at a more modest one ton.

In the early nineteenth century it became fashionable to promote breeds by feeding individual animals until they reached vast proportions. A painting of Robert Colling's White Heifer by the artist William Ward portrays a beast with a grossly distended body perched on four spindly legs that must surely have buckled under the strain. A contemporary livestock painter, Thomas Bewick, was angered by the pressure from breeders to exaggerate the size of their animals: 'I objected to putting lumps of fat here and there when I could not see it . . . Many of the animals were, during this rage for fat cattle, fed up to as great a weight and bulk as it was possible for feeding to make them; but this is not enough, they were to be figured monstrously fat before the owners of them could be pleased.'[11]

Some of the Colling brothers' stock passed to a contemporary Shorthorn breeder, Thomas Booth, who ran herds at Studley Park, Killerby and Warlaby in Yorkshire. Booth founded some of the best-known Shorthorn families, and by the 1870s, when his grandson was running the Warlaby herd, other breeders were having to pay up to 300 guineas for one season's hire of a bull. At Kirklevington in Yorkshire Thomas Bates, a younger contemporary of the Colling brothers, was concentrating on the milk-producing qualities of the breed. Two distinct types of Shorthorn began to emerge, one with superior beef qualities and the other renowned for its milkiness. A popular slogan of the day recommended: 'Booth for the butcher, Bates for the pail.'[12]

In Scotland the Shorthorn was developed by breeders with little interest in pedigree. They merely wanted an animal of the right shape that looked as though it might thrive in the harsher climate of the north. The best known of the Scottish breeders was a shy farmer from Aberdeenshire, Amos Cruickshank of Sittyton. With the financial backing of his brother Anthony, Cruickshank made regular buying trips to England where he bought hardy, compact cattle with 'meat in the best places'. For a long time he rejected the strategy of inbreeding, choosing instead to 'cross the best with the best'.

In 1859 he bred a bull calf that seemed to have the qualities he was looking for. He named it 'Champion of England' and embarked on a programme of intense inbreeding. Now was the time to 'fix' those qualities into his herd. The bull and its progeny are said to have exercised a greater influence on the Shorthorn than any other animal since the Collings. By such means a breed is made, not through the creation of a single, superior strain, but by the parallel actions of a number of enthusiasts, each pursuing some personal idea of excellence.

By the late nineteenth century the Shorthorn had become the most populous cattle breed in Britain. A census in 1908 revealed that more than four million of Britain's seven million cattle belonged to the breed. It had also become popular around the world. Shorthorns were able to thrive in a wide range of climatic conditions, from the harsh winters of the Canadian prairies to the hot, dusty summers of the South American pampas. The breed was highly prepotent – it had the capacity to pass on many characteristics to its progeny. Dozens of breeds around the world were built on a first cross with the British Shorthorn. So great was its contribution to meat and milk production that it acquired the title 'universal provider'.

A handful of other breeds contributed to Britain's dominance in livestock breeding. Among them was the Hereford with its characteristic white face and body of rich red. The breed had begun as a draught animal, yoked to the plough for five or six years, then sold to graziers who would fatten it for the London market. Its chief qualities were docility and an ability to fatten on grass. Among pioneer improvers of the breed were the Tomkins family, four generations beginning with the yeoman farmer Richard Tomkins of the New House, King's Pyon, who had built a reputation for breeding draught oxen with a great capacity for laying down meat.[13]

In his will, drawn up in 1720, Tomkins bequeathed to his fourth son Benjamin a cow called Silver, together with her calf. From this line Benjamin went on to build a herd of cattle famed for their beefing qualities. The perfected breed quickly gained a reputation for thriving under poor conditions as well as maturing at an early age. It was particularly popular with graziers buying store cattle to fatten for the London market.

By the mid-nineteenth century graziers were flocking to Hereford for the annual Michaelmas Fair at which hundreds of cattle were bought and sold in the city's streets. The fair 'was not exceeded by any show of beasts in good condition in the kingdom'.[14] Each year on the third Tuesday and Wednesday of

October 'the parade begins at Hereford Station and extends right through the heart of the town' so that 'windows are barricaded against them and trap doors burst in by them'.[15]

In Scotland breeders were developing the famous Aberdeen Angus from Buchan Humlies, the hornless local cattle, and Angus Doddies from Forfar, another local type with an unusually long coat. The race that was to make the Angus world famous was bred by Hugh Watson, the tenant of Keillor, close to the border of Forfarshire and Perthshire. Watson pursued a policy of inbreeding more relentlessly than either the Colling brothers or Bakewell. But it seems to have set off no genetic time bombs. His most celebrated bull, Old Jock, born in 1841, took the sweepstakes at the Highland Society's Perth Show in 1852, while his cow, Old Grannie, produced twenty live calves and continued breeding until her twenty-ninth year.[16]

The bloodline of Old Jock was later used by William McCombie, tenant of Tilleyfour, near Aberdeen, who built up the breed's popularity just when its future seemed threatened by the Scottish Shorthorn. The Aberdeen Angus became widely known for the quality of its beef – lightly marbled, succulent and well-flavoured.

By the late nineteenth century British breeds were gaining a world-wide reputation. British Shorthorns and Herefords dominated the vast cattle herds of the American prairies and the South American pampas, where they were used to grade-up the native cattle. The two great breeds then spread across the Empire from the dry South African veld to the Australian savannahs and the tussocky grasslands of New Zealand's Canterbury Plain.

Smaller breeds have also shared in this global advance of British cattle. Large numbers of Devons, or 'Red Rubies', stocked the great *estancias* of Brazil, their success emulating earlier triumphs in the United States and New Zealand. In South Africa and Argentina hardy Welsh Blacks were winning new converts. British pedigree cattle were transported to every continent, and with them the pastoral tradition of the 'old country'. Wherever they encountered unimproved grassland the newcomers grazed selectively, as they had on the American prairies. Quickly stripping out the more palatable species, they destroyed age-old plant communities, opening them up to invasion by coarser species.

On Argentina's rolling plains, the 'campo' – a waving ocean of bunch grasses that had once made up the pampas – followed America's prairie grassland to extinction. The endless tussock grasslands of Canterbury Plain met with a similar fate. Wherever they went British cattle recreated British pastures, or some facsimile of them. From the Americas to the Antipodes ranchers and cattle farmers buying British livestock imported with them an entire pastoral tradition. It was a package developed on the island of bright, green pastures and warm summer rain. And that's where many of the progeny returned.

The carcasses that filled the new refrigerated dockside storage chambers at British sea ports were not those of hardy native cattle. They were the progeny of British bulls, bred to fatten on rolling English downlands, damp Welsh hillsides and cool Scottish moors. While British beef farmers resented the competition, the imports were warmly welcomed by working people in the towns. Demand for red meat was growing so fast that home producers were unlikely to have kept pace whatever the price on offer. The UK population was expanding fast. During the years of rural depression it rose by no less than ten million. Many left the depressed countryside for jobs in the expanding industrial towns.

Life was better in the towns, at least for those in work. Wages were rising quickly. In the boom years between 1880 and 1896 they almost doubled.[17] For working families there was now a little money to spend on butcher's meat, a rare treat on a farm labourer's wage. It was the rapid rise in demand from a better-off working class which brought the refrigeration ships steaming across the Atlantic with the frozen and chilled bounty of the American prairies. Though British farmers were horrified, imports led to no wholesale price collapse. Meat prices slipped a little, but demand remained keen enough to prevent the kind of seismic fall that had occurred in the grain market.

By exporting its prize cattle to the world Britain had overcome the challenge of feeding a fast-growing population from a relatively small land area. International capital – much of it British – flowed into new, big-scale ranching businesses wherever there were large stretches of unimproved grassland. In effect the country had hired pastures overseas to produce the meat and dairy products demanded by working people as well as a prosperous middle class. With their famed Hereford and Shorthorn, Sussex and South Devon, the cattle breeders had created small corners of England on the grassy plains of five continents.

The global advance of British livestock was not confined to cattle. Bakewell's success at Dishley Grange had set off a boom for British sheep. The New Leicester might have been prone to put on fat, but when crossed with unimproved sheep it transmitted the qualities of fleshiness and early maturity. One of the breeds to benefit was the old Lincoln Longwool, which in earlier times had been one of England's great wool producers. The New Leicester gave it a new lease of life as a dual-purpose animal, producing both meat and wool.

Sheep breeder John Ellman of Glynde was even more successful with his improved Southdown sheep. He took the leggy animal of the downland and started the metamorphosis that was to change it into a compact meat animal with a fine fleece. Crossed with a number of local breeds, the improved Southdown gave birth to a clutch of new meat breeds, among them the Hampshire Down, the Suffolk and the Oxford Down. Like the great beef breeds, all have been exported around the world.

At the time when Bakewell's attempts at inbreeding were bearing their first fruits, industrialism had already transformed the British economy. Between 1780 and 1850 the population doubled. With the rapid rise of the manufacturing town, capital flowed from industry to the land, just as it had in Tudor times. The inevitable consequence, according to Thomas Malthus, whose *Essay on the Principle of Population* had been published in 1798, was famine, war and death. Population growth, he claimed, would always outstrip production.

Spurred by such sentiments, livestock breeders strove to produce animals that would put on meat more efficiently. From large-boned, slow-maturing draught cattle they created thoroughbreds that would fatten younger, mainly by laying down fat within muscle tissue, the marbling that is said to improve both flavour and succulence. But consumer tastes can change as rapidly as the shape of cattle. Today the meat eaters of the western world want lean beef. As a result farmers have turned from the traditional British breeds and adopted bulls from continental Europe: large, slow-maturing breeds like the Charolais, Simmental and Limousin, breeds that will grow to heavy weights without laying down fat.

The famous old British breeds that once dominated the world are consigned to the obscurity of the rare breeds park, to be preserved like museum pieces, curiosities washed up by the tide of consumer preference. Most still survive, thanks to the loyalty of a few dedicated enthusiasts. Each year they bring their best animals to the Royal Show in Warwickshire, setting up their tents, awnings and publicity boards, and hoping that this year will see the start of a renaissance for their particular breed.

The true contribution made by the legendary breeds to food production remains a contested issue. Shorthorn enthusiast Robert Bruce was in no doubt that 'the universal provider' had played a crucial role in raising the productivity of native breeds around the world. While the mighty Shorthorn was at its zenith he wrote: 'Having had practical experience of mating the veriest of scrub Mexican cattle – degenerate remains of what were originally Spanish cattle – with Shorthorn bulls, I can confidently say that the value of the produce of native dams was increased at least one hundred per cent over that of the native sires.'[18]

Others thought the claims of the pedigree breeders much overblown, more concerned with petty breed points such as the shape of horn than with valuable commercial qualities. 'It would be as sensible to go in for breeding Gloucester Old Spot pigs because you are fond of *noir et blanc* whisky as to keep many of the anti-milk and anti-beef creatures that one sees so often fetch large prices . . . solely because they have pedigrees as long as the Trans-Siberian Railway.'[19]

Pedigree breeders always exaggerate the importance of

genetics. The way livestock are fed and looked after has more influence on their output than their breeding. In this sense the decline of some famous native breeds is of little consequence. Even so their loyal supporters who still await the trumpet call to herald a new golden age may yet have cause to smile. There is one quality of the traditional breeds that could soon reawaken the interest of fickle consumers.

Les Cook's battered Land-rover moves slowly along a pitted lane to where another herd grazes the river pastures. But these are not the rich, red Herefords. Their coats are mostly white with here and there a few dark flecks that match the black of their noses, ears and feet. All are polled or hornless. They are British Whites, an ancient breed of cattle descended from the Middleton Park herd in Lancashire, and possibly related to the white cattle that were feral in Britain 1,500 years ago.

Les Cook leans on a field gate to watch them as they range slowly across the field, a designated nature reserve. The flood-plain species they graze on are not the nitrogen-enriched, broad-leaved grasses of the modern, intensive livestock farm, but finer, coarser plants – tufted hair-grass and Yorkshire fog, with occasional patches of red fescue and meadow foxtail. These wet grasslands are also the nesting place of snipe and the feeding grounds of wigeon, mallard and goldeneye. The drainage channel that flows by harbours water voles in its banks and sticklebacks and smooth newts in its dark waters. Yet on these unpromising pastures the British White cattle – like the Herefords – seem to thrive, remaining healthy, contented and well-nourished.

Many of the traditional British breeds are efficient converters of grass into beef and milk. After all, they have been bred in a country with an rare capacity to grow the green gold. The bigger continental breeds, while putting on weight quickly, need a forage diet supplemented by energy-rich cereals to grow to their potential. There is mounting scientific evidence that beef from grain-fed animals is less healthy than beef produced on grass, the standard fare of the older British breeds.

Central to the new theory are fats. About 10 per cent of beef fats are in the form of polyunsaturates, with the rest divided equally between saturates and monounsaturates. Most of the monounsaturated fat is oleic acid, the major component of olive oil and thought to be beneficial to human health. Among polyunsaturates, the fatty acids known as omega-3 and omega-6 are of greatest significance to human health. A high ratio of omega-3 to omega-6 fatty acids has been found to reduce blood lipid concentration, and with it the incidence of thrombosis and coronary heart disease.[20] A range of inflammatory diseases including asthma and rheumatoid arthritis have been linked to high intakes of omega-6 fatty acids. Beef from cattle fattened on grass contains four times as much omega-3 fatty acid as beef from cattle fed on concentrates, or grain. It also contains four times the conjugated linoleic acid, or CLA, a lipid known for its protective action against a number of cancers.

Traditional British beef – the roast beef of old England – was predominantly of the beneficial, grass-fed variety. The nine-teenth-century tide of cattle from the upland grazings of Scotland and Wales were 'finished' on Essex grazing marshes or Middlesex meadows before making their final journey to the London market. For centuries grasslands have produced British beef, with its rich marbling and distinctive taste. But the economics of modern industrial agriculture are fast turning a healthy, natural food into yet another degraded factory product. Increasingly beef animals are finished not outdoors on pastures, but inside sheds where they are fed on grain or maize.

In Britain the decline started with 'barley' beef in the 1960s. Farmers in the main cereal growing areas found they could add value to their grain by 'processing' it through cattle – turning it into meat. Across the broad, open acres of arable country sheds sprang up to house the new animal production lines. The system mirrored that of the American feedlot, the highly automated beef plants that were expanding across the mid-west.

A large proportion of American beef now comes out of the feedlots, many of them holding tens of thousands of animals in open compounds. Most of the cattle are of beef breeds. They are brought in as well-grown calves or older yearlings and fed on a 'complete' ration containing a high proportion of grain or maize. Some of the larger units are vertically integrated with their own, computer-controlled feed mills to prepare and mix the carefully formulated rations, and, at the other end, abattoirs and meat-packing plants. This young, grain-fed beef is said to suit the American palate. While American citizens cherish their myths of cowboys and the open range, their steaks and burgers are of beef from vast 'flesh factories' running on raw materials of corn or cereals.

Though the feedlot system is not widely applied in Britain, the practice of grain finishing is almost universal. About half of all British beef is from animals bred on dairy farms, principally from black-and-white Holstein-Friesian cows. Most are crosses with large, slow-maturing European breeds. These are the animals favoured by the big meat processors and supermarket buyers. On a high-energy, grain based ration they will put on weight quickly without getting over-fat. A large, lean animal produces industrial-scale efficiencies throughout the food chain from slaughter to retail pack. According to Les Cook, it is a carcass bred 'to fit in a box'.

The other half of Britain's home-produced beef comes from dedicated beef breeds. Few finished animals are of the traditional breeds. Most are crosses of one sort or another. As with 'dairy' beef, the most popular sires for producing the final, 'terminal' cross are the big European breeds. And like 'dairy' beef animals, most are fattened on high-energy diets rich in cereals. The old-style beef raised gently on rain-washed pastures is now a rare and expensive commodity. The steak and topside cuts that fill supermarket chilled cabinets have the bright red flesh and dazzling white fat characteristic of grain-fed meat. Like the beef that fills the burgers, it is fast, cheap and probably less healthy than the old beef from pasture and hay.

The entire economic system now militates against the raising of healthy beef. Subsidised grain from the pesticide-ridden arable areas is more likely to turn in a profit for the fattener than the fine grasses and herbs of an unspoiled pasture, not yet overdosing on chemical fertilisers. Even health regulations favour poor-quality, industrial beef. As part of the BSE-control measures, no beef animal over thirty months old may be sold for human consumption. Few beef animals will 'finish' off grass in that time. For centuries the finest British beef came from animals four or five years old. Nowadays beef farmers are obliged to hasten the finishing process by feeding their cattle an industrial ration high in cereals. The irony is that had all beef continued to be raised on grassland and forage, the BSE tragedy would not have occurred.

Les Cook's traditional Herefords are among the finest converters of grass into beef. But because they do not produce the large, lean carcasses sought by the profit-centred meat trade they are no longer in vogue. Thirty years ago breeders of pedigree Hereford cattle earned a fair slice of their income from sales of breeding stock. Not so today. Most are now sold for beef, with just a few being retained for breeding. The cattle from Albany Farm go to a butcher with a reputation for supplying high-quality meat. But there is no real premium for producing a food that is healthy and humanely reared. Nor is there a pay-off for producing a landscape of stunning beauty amid an endless vista of cereal monoculture.

Some might be depressed by the consumer's willingness to buy inferior beef when the real thing is available for just a little more. Not so Les Cook. He remains philosophical. Like most breeders who have stayed true to the traditional breeds he is content to play the long game. He says: 'We have a great national asset here. This is a breed that can convert the grass of our hills and valleys into tasty, succulent, healthy beef. Hopefully in the future we'll start to value it again – perhaps when the oil runs out.

'Until that day I see it as my role to maintain this wonderful animal and its genetics for future generations that will need it. The fact that it doesn't make a lot of money now is not that important. This is a great national treasure. I'm happy to play my part in safeguarding it.'

In the gathering twilight his dark red and white beasts graze contentedly on the herbs and grasses of the flood meadow. It is hard to believe they have had their day.

14 _Invasion_

The early years of Queen Victoria's reign were a good time for British agriculture. The population was rising fast, always a happy statistic for farmers. And the surging industrial economy had put more money into people's pockets and purses. In the grim manufacturing towns factory workers and their families could afford a little meat and cheese to go with their bread and potatoes. The powerful middle classes could afford more of everything.

This was farming's golden age. The feared deluge of imported grain that was expected to follow the ending of the Corn Laws had so far failed to materialise. As the wheat price soared to seventy shillings a quarter, its highest level since 1813, farmers scrambled to plough up old pastures and sow them to corn, just as they had in the earlier boom years during the wars against Napoleon. With cash crops offering a quick return it was easy to forsake the long, slow promise of the pastoral economy. Now was the time to cash the fertility invested in grass.

Farming had gone through a long period of expansion lasting almost a century. The new crops and rotations from the Low Countries had made broad stretches of formerly worthless

244

heathland profitable. Thousands of acres had been brought into production, particularly during the French wars. Sir George Sinclair, president of the Board of Agriculture, had made it a national campaign. 'Let us not be satisfied with the liberation of Egypt or the subjugation of Malta, but let us subdue Finchley Common; let us conquer Hounslow Heath, let us compel Epping Forest to submit to the yoke of improvement.'[1]

But even as farmers prospered, the advance of a vibrant, young capitalism was unleashing forces that were soon to plunge them into crisis. In 1846, the year the Corn Laws were abolished, the American John Deere Company patented the steel plough that would strip the age-old turf from the prairies as carelessly as the rattlesnake sheds its skin. As British farmers rushed to turn their pastures over to arable crops, the new transcontinental railroads had begun threading their way across America's heartland, taking barbed wire and homesteaders to the rich, virgin lands and carrying back the truckloads of cheap wheat that were eventually to collapse prices in Liverpool and London. Farmers would come to rue the easy abandonment of their pastoral traditions.

The period of 'high farming' – a euphemism for intensive farming – was a time when good husbandry gave way to the pursuit of maximum production. Alternate husbandry or mixed farming – the system in which grass and clover leys were included in the arable rotation – had brought the fertility-building benefits of grassland on to the cropping area.

The mixed farm was largely self-sufficient, generating 'wealth' from the natural recycling of nutrients in a healthy and vigorous soil. It was a system rooted in the pastoral tradition. Its return was the ageless gift of grassland – liberty and independence. Farmers who continued to practise it remained secure and self-reliant, largely immune to the fluctuations of international markets, in greater control of their destiny.

Two centuries earlier the farming writer Walter Blith had prescribed the fertilisers that might be applied to the land when a pasture was ploughed up for an arable crop. He had recommended 'Liming, marling, sanding, earthing, mudding, snayle-codding, mucking, chalking, pidgeons-dung, hens-dung, hogs-dung, rags, coarse wooll, pitch-markes and tarry stuffe, and any oyley stuffe, salt ... and almost anything that hath a liquidnesse, foulnesse, saltnesse or good moysture in it.'[2]

These were mostly local materials. They represented the fertility of the muck heap, the river bank and the bottom of the pond, free supplements to enhance the nutrients built up under grass. In the era of high farming farmers increasingly ignored them, preferring to apply more exotic materials. In the new industrial economy fertilisers came from far and wide. And they had to be paid for in cash.

One of the most popular was guano, 'wizard of the Pacific': the accumulated droppings of seabirds mined from islands off the coast of Peru. Guano had been highly prized by the Incas, reports of it first reaching Europe via the Spanish explorer Pizarro in the sixteenth century.[3] Three centuries later this early form of 'compound' fertiliser, containing as it did nitrogen, phosphate and potash, suddenly found favour with Britain's prosperous farmers. Imports rose from two thousand to almost three hundred thousand tonnes in the early 1840s.[4]

One of the first importing companies, Antony Gibbs and Sons, made a fortune from the trade.[5] Henry Huck Gibbs went on to become Lord Aldenham, and was the first merchant banker to be appointed Governor of the Bank of England. However, the company was always known as:

> The House of Gibbs that made their dibs
> By selling the turds of foreign birds.

Others were making money from the growing international trade in bones. The value of imports rose sixteenfold to more than £250,000 over a fourteen-year period. In the early part of the century they had been crushed into two-centimetre slivers or ground to a fine dust, but by the 1850s most were destined for sulphuric acid vats where they were converted into superphosphate.[6]

The Doncaster Agricultural Association observed that 'one ton of German bone dust saves the importation of ten tons of German corn'. Some years later the German chemist Justus von

Liebig remarked wryly that English merchants were rifling the battlefields of Europe and ransacking the catacombs of Sicily, adding that the proceeds were largely squandered down sewers to the sea.[7] Soldiers and saints apart, it seems that most of the bones came from South American cattle.

To match their penchant for exotic fertilisers the high-flying Victorian farmers developed a fondness for novel feeding stuffs, notably the 'cake' remaining as a residue when oilseeds such as linseed and rape seed were crushed for their oil. By 1856 home production of cake from imported seed had risen to eight times the level of 1815.[8] Annual imports of manufactured oilseed cake rose from one thousand to eighty-three thousand tonnes over the same period. Maize was also popular as an animal feed. By the 1880s farmers were spending £10 million a year on imports.

Spurred on by high prices, they had abandoned the pastoral tradition of self-sufficiency and were riding the tidal forces of international commerce. Their total spending on purchased inputs rose from £3 million a year in the late 1830s to £17 million a year in the early 1870s. At the Great Exhibition of 1851 farmers queued up to place orders for the horse-drawn Virginia Reaper from McCormicks of Chicago.[9] The machine was based on a design by Northumberland millwright John Common of Denwick, who had entered a gold medal competition run by the Society of Arts. But he had been unable to develop it himself in the face of strong opposition from local farm labourers who feared for their summer employment harvesting corn with scythes.

The McCormick reaper overshadowed another innovative machine at the 1851 exhibition, this one designed to carry out land drainage.

> But for the American reapers, Mr Fowler's drainage plough would have formed the most remarkable feature in the agricultural department of the exhibition. Wonderful as it is to see the standing wheat shorn levelly low by a pair of horses walking along its edge, it is hardly, if at all, less wonderful, nor did it excite less interest or surprise among the crowd of spectators when the trial was made at this place, to see two

horses at work by the side of a field, or a capstan which, by an invisible wire-rope, draws towards itself a low framework, leaving but the trace of a narrow slit on the surface. If you pass, however, to the other side of the field, which the framework has quitted, you perceive that it has been dragging after it a string of pipes, which, still following the plough's snout, that burrows all the while four feet below ground, twists itself like a gigantic red worm into the earth, so that in a few minutes, when the framework has reached the capstan, the string is withdrawn from the necklace, and you are assured that a drain has been invisibly formed under your feet.[10]

Farmers were adopting the methods of the factory, using purchased raw materials and machines to boost labour productivity. In place of the elegant symmetry of the self-sustaining mixed farm, they were building rural replicas of the industrial mills and workshops that were springing up in Britain's manufacturing cities.

But in the final quarter of the century the price-led expansion of agriculture went into reverse. Boom turned to bust. In 1879 the wheat price collapsed. A run of wet seasons and ruined harvests should have led to shortages and rising prices. Instead the shortfall in supply was made up by low-priced American wheat pouring off the grain ships. This was the first harvest of the pioneer settlers; an early pay-out from the age-old fertility bank that had been the prairie grassland. In the third quarter of the century wheat production from the new croplands west of the Mississippi went up thirtyfold to almost four million tonnes.

On land they had bought for a dollar or two an acre the pioneer settlers could grow wheat for twenty shillings a quarter and ship it across the Atlantic for another seventeen.[11] So great was the competition for freight among the new railroad companies that in 1879 the charge for transporting a barrel of flour from St Louis to New York – a distance of 1,000 miles – plunged from forty-six cents to just eight. American farmers found they could profitably sell their wheat in Liverpool for as little as forty shillings a quarter, a price that spelled ruin for British growers with their high land-rental costs.

The same economic forces that had swelled the market for bread among Britain's industrial workers were now mining the ancient fertility of the prairies to meet that demand, and in the process driving British growers to the wall. William Sturge, president of the Institution of Surveyors, voiced the frustration of arable farmers:

> Three thousand miles of ocean and one thousand miles of inland carriage formed, until recent years, a formidable protective barrier, which has now succumbed to the railway and the steamship; and fertile land of boundless extent, genial climate and nominal value, is brought into direct competition with the expensively cultivated farms of this country.[12]

While American homesteaders enduring drought and wind storm might have challenged his reference to a genial climate, they could hardly have faulted his analysis. The ferment of rising prices in the Old World had awakened a sleeping giant in the New. A hidden powerhouse of energy, trapped by ancient sunlight and locked away in the organic matter of soil, was now being freed from its subterranean store to fuel an explosion in global wheat production. The accumulated energy of a great grassland was about to shake the world.

As the slump continued year after year, a mood of despondency settled over British agriculture. Apart from a few brief periods when the wheat price rallied – including the years of the Great War – the depression lasted for almost sixty years, finally coming to an end with World War Two. Farmers responded by taking the course they had always followed in hard times: they returned to their pastoral roots. They began converting their arable fields back to grassland just as their medieval ancestors had done in the years following the Black Death. Suddenly the brash new world of industrial agriculture seemed cold and merciless.

Many regretted their haste in abandoning pastoral production for the promise of instant riches from wheat. Old and valuable pastures had been ploughed up in the rush to arable; productive grasslands that might take decades to replace. Even grass-draped downlands that had once produced the finest wools had felt the sharp bite of the plough.[13] With hindsight it all seemed to have been a terrible blunder. The anticipated riches had failed to materialise.

Writing before the great depression, James Caird, the leading farming commentator of his day, had concluded that even during the years of expansion most farmers would have been better off sticking with the products of grassland. He calculated that over the seventy years to 1850 the prices of butter and wool had doubled while the price of meat had increased by 70 per cent. By contrast the price of bread – that 'great staple of the food of the English labourer' – had scarcely risen at all since 1770. According to Caird these price differentials were reflected in the value of land.

> The great corn growing counties of the east coast are thus shown to yield an average rent of 23s. 8d. an acre; the more mixed husbandry of the midland counties, and the grazing green crop and dairy districts of the west, 31s. 5d. This striking difference, being not less than thirty per cent, is explained chiefly by the different value of their staple produce. That the large capitalist farmer of the east coast, possessing the most cheaply cultivated soil, and conducting his agricultural operations with the most skill, should not only pay the lowest rent, but be the loudest complainer under the recent depression of prices, is to be accounted for by his greater dependence on the value of corn.[14]

As far as James Caird was concerned, the brightest future for Britain's agriculture lay in her grasslands. Demand for dairy products, meat and fresh vegetables was rising in the fast-growing manufacturing towns. In the past these markets had been supplied principally by farmers in the immediate neighbourhood, but as the population increased and industrial earnings rose these foods were being drawn in from an ever-widening catchment area. These were the markets that would keep farmers profitable in the long term, not the volatile and chancy business of wheat production they had become so enamoured by.

Caird was over-optimistic in expecting dairy farmers and meat producers to stay free of foreign competition. He could not have anticipated the rapid development of refrigerated shipping. But he had read the signs of change. He had looked beyond the wild swings of the grain market to the social revolution that was going on in the back-to-back houses of the factory workers and the comfortable villas of the rising middle class.

In the manufacturing districts where wages are good, the use of butcher's meat and cheese is enormously on the increase; and even in the agricultural districts the labourer does now occasionally indulge himself in a meat dinner, or season his dry bread with a morsel of cheese. In a gentleman's family consisting of himself, his wife, six children and ten servants, the average expenditure for each individual per annum, for articles of food produced by the farmer, is nine pounds and ten shillings for meat, butter and milk, and one pound, two shillings and fourpence for bread. In a large public establishment containing an average throughout the year of 646 male persons, chiefly boys, the expenditure per head for meat, cheese, potatoes, butter and milk is four pounds, ten shillings and sixpence, and for bread two pounds, one shilling and sixpence.

The first example shows an expenditure in articles the produce of grass and green crops nearly nine times as great as in corn; and the second, which may be regarded as more of an average example, also shows an outlay two and one-quarter times greater on the former articles of produce than the latter. Here we see not only the kind of produce most in demand, but the direction in which household expenditure increases when the means permit. It is reasonable to conclude that the great mass of the consumers, as their circumstances improve, will follow the same rule . . . The only species of corn which has risen materially in price since 1770 is barley, and that is accounted for by the increasing use of beer, which is more a luxury than a necessary of life.

Every intelligent farmer ought to keep this steadily in view. Let him produce as much as he can of the articles which have shown a gradual tendency to increase in value. The farms which eighty years ago yielded one hundred pounds in meat and wool, or in butter, would now produce two hundred pounds, although neither the breed of stock nor the capabilities of the land had been improved. Those which yielded one hundred pounds in wheat then, would yield no more now, even if the productive power of the land had undergone no diminution by a long course of exhaustion.[15]

In their haste to cash in on the wheat boom farmers had been chasing fool's gold. Their real wealth had lain where it always had – in the green turf of lowland meadows and fellside grazings. Now the corn price 'bubble' had burst and British agriculture faced a lean and uncertain future. At the same time the nation's grasslands were suffering from severe neglect (if they had not actually been destroyed). Like her armed forces at the start of World War Two, Britain's pastoral assets had been allowed to run down just at the time they were most needed.

At a meeting in Gloucestershire in 1862 farmer Owen Wallis declared the poor state of the country's grasslands 'a national disgrace'. While Britain's croplands were considered worthy of care and thoughtful management, her pastures were assumed to have some mysterious recuperative powers of their own, so that they would go on producing milk and meat without fertiliser, cultivation or even proper drainage. Fields once said to have 'fed off two lots of beasts in a season' were now barely able 'to make one lot fat'.

A correspondent to the Royal Bath and West of England Society claimed that the great majority of British pastures 'yield year after year just what the rain and sunshine cause them to bring forth, not merely without the aid of artificial stimulant or assistance, but in spite of many artificial drawbacks and disadvantages placed in their way'.[16] He urged that 'their character and habits, wants, and modes of growth, should be studied and accommodated, just like those of wheat or mangold-wurzel'.

In a paper to the Royal Agricultural Society's journal the Reverend W. R. Bowditch of Wakefield, Yorkshire, railed against the 'plunder' of meadows and pastures, with the 'spoils' being lavished on the 'petted tillage lands'.[17] While France had half its cultivated land in corn, England devoted just one-quarter of its croplands to cereals. Yet both countries produced the same quantity of wheat per head of population, a little over five bushels. The higher productivity of the English arable was derived from its pastures and meadowland. In England each acre of corn land was spread with the manure from three acres of grass. In France the dung from an acre of grass was spread across more than two acres of cropping land.

As the Neolithic herders had discovered more than 4,000 years earlier, bumper grain crops were a gift of the pastoral world, a bequest from the kingdom of grass to the kingdom of the plough. The neglect of Britain's grassland was a tragedy for the nation, claimed the Reverend Bowditch, since the people were 'obliged to spend enormous sums of money with the foreigner for meat and wool, which, under a better system, might be spent upon their neighbours at home'. The West of England correspondent warmed to the same theme.

If a man mows his poor, wet pasture every year, and hardly dresses [manures] it at all . . . he will very soon find it full of yellow rattle, sedge, hawk-weeds, purging flax, devil's bit, and other weeds; fescue, poas and clovers will dwindle and almost disappear. If he drains it and gives up mowing it, dresses it with farmyard dung and bone-dust, if he pulls up thistles and docks and the larger weeds, feeds sheep on it, folding them upon the land if necessary, and foddering them with hay in winter, giving also roots and cake, he will soon have good grazing grounds, and meadows full of clovers and grasses.[18]

There remained a few productive pastures in Britain, pastures capable of fattening grazing bullocks in a season without additional food. The famed midland fattening pastures of Northamptonshire and Leicestershire came into this category, as did the prized pastures that line the rivers Axe, Brue and Parrett in Somerset. In 1871, as the depression began to bite, a farmer near the Yorkshire town of Settle refused to accept the princely sum of 3,000 pounds for a ten-acre field said to produce grass 'of the best quality', and to grow 'whenever the thermometer is above freezing point'.[19] But there were many more grasslands across the length and breadth of Britain that 'only began to grow on Midsummer Eve, and gave up growing on Midsummer Day'.

With corn prices on the floor, farmers felt a new urgency to revive neglected pastures and worn-out meadows. If grasslands were to save British agriculture from bankruptcy they would need some of the care and attention currently devoted to arable land. While farmyard manure was the usual remedy for infertile soil, bones became the fashionable tonic for rejuvenating an exhausted turf. They had been popular since the boom times of the 1840s, and plenty of farmers were ready to sing their praises as providers of essential phosphates.

Edward Billyse, a tenant farmer in Nantwich, Cheshire, declared bones to be the cheapest of all manures for hay meadows.[20] He preferred fresh bones to boiled bones, though he admitted they were hard to come by. In the same county Captain De Hollenworth of Hollenworth Hall spent no less than £1,500 on boiled bones over a period of three years, applying them chiefly to old turf.[21] So great were the benefits that land which had been let for thirty shillings an acre was soon worth twice as much.

The demand for bones became so strong that a trade grew up in bone sawings, the remnants and offcuts of bones used in the manufacture of buttons, combs and knife handles, though they were frequently adulterated with sand by unscrupulous merchants.[22] In the little township of Minshull, whose wealth was derived mainly from dairying for cheese, scarcely a square metre of farmland remained untreated with bone dust.

Though they relied heavily on the manure of their livestock, hard-up farmers continued looking for new ways to boost the fertility of their overworked grassland. Shoddy, the woolly waste product of the Lancashire and Yorkshire cloth mills, provided a cheap alternative to Peruvian guano. These woollen remnants, liberally coated in oil and grease from the manufacturing process, were applied to grassland at the rate of four tons an acre. A single dressing was said to improve grass growth for several years afterwards.

A number of prominent farmers advocated the use of human excrement or 'night soil' as a fertiliser, though there is little evidence that it was used on any scale outside those towns with sewage irrigation schemes.

Moveable boxes should be attached to every house, and removed weekly in summer, fortnightly in winter. A cistern filled with dry, pounded clay would be placed overhead, and a simple mechanical contrivance would throw down a measured quantity of this every time the handle was raised, as water is now let down a closet. Nature's deodoriser and disinfectant would prevent the escape of injurious exhalations, and the refuse would be removed by water or other carriage some miles into the country, to await under shed the farmer's season of use . . . Every element of grass is contained in this manure in large abundance, and while its preparation formed a sanitary improvement of much value to the town, its use would be a boon of enormous value to the country.[23]

In addition to its chronically low fertility, grassland suffered badly from poor drainage. No matter how plentiful the essential plant nutrients, they were of little value if the roots were often too waterlogged to take them up. During the period of high farming major advances had been made in drainage technology. John Reade had developed a permeable tile drain, and within a few years pipe-making machinery had brought down the cost.[24] John Fowler's steam-powered mole plough – the machine that had been so praised at the 1851 Great Exhibition – transformed the farming of heavy clay land, providing a cheap alternative to the old ridge-and-furrow.

A handful of enthusiasts threw themselves into improving

their pastures. A particularly heroic attempt at grassland renovation was made by one Edmund Ruck at Manor Farm, Braydon, on the clay land between Swindon and Gloucester, where pastures were said to be little but sedge and moss, and where livestock appeared 'only half alive, stunted and ill-shapen'.[25] An early visitor described the cart ride along the farm track as 'like a stormy day afloat'. He commented that 'the slush and water everywhere were beyond description'.

But the resourceful Edmund Ruck had the entire farm drained using Mr Fowler's celebrated steam plough, following up the treatment with liberal dressings of guano, superphosphate and a home-made compost. The transformation was striking. Within three years the rushes and sedges had gone and the unproductive grasses such as crested dog's-tail and quaking grass had been largely replaced by the more nutritious fescues, meadow grasses and timothy. The rental value of the pasture rose from twelve shillings to thirty shillings an acre. On a return visit the earlier critic remarked: 'The change of colour, from a dull brown to a lively green, was most remarkable. The livestock looked healthy and thriving; and altogether the face of the country was altered.'

While the collapse in grain prices led some to renovate old grasslands, others attempted to sow new meadows and pastures on land exhausted by years of corn growing. It was no easy task. The impoverished soils needed a period of fertility-building before they would sustain productive turf. The grass mixtures being sold by commercial seed companies were of low quality, containing too many poor species and too few productive ones. A Kent farmer with the unlikely name of C. De Laune Faunce-De Laune wrote in the Royal Agricultural Society's journal: 'However careful I was in my orders, and from whatever seed merchant I ordered my seed, the percentage of ryegrass, soft woolly grass and other bad grasses and weeds, was beyond all belief.'[26]

He identified five coarse grasses that were 'valuable beyond all others' for permanent pasture – cocksfoot, meadow fescue, tall fescue, cat's-tail or timothy and meadow foxtail. The grasses most pernicious to newly formed grassland were annual ryegrass and Yorkshire fog, also known as soft woolly grass. Both grew rapidly and 'made a great show'. They also produced copious amounts of seed – hence their popularity with seed merchants. 'Enormous profits are made by the sale of them, and, what is worse, incalculable loss is entailed upon those who sow them for permanent pasture.'

Some farmers dispensed with commercial seed mixtures altogether and sowed their new grassland by the system known as 'innoculation', as practised by a Hertfordshire farmer in the 1850s. Narrow ribbons of turf were stripped from an old pasture with a plough and cut up into small squares. These were laid out in lines across the ground to be trodden in by a gang of men, a job that 'must be done in damp weather in September or October'. In spring the ground was rolled and allowed to seed itself. In the autumn livestock were run on the new grass. 'By this process a fine pasture is rapidly formed, and on that portion where the strips of turf had been cut out, the ground soon covers itself from the adjoining rows of grass.'[27]

Despite the difficulties, many arable farmers made the transition back to a fully pastoral economy. Across Britain wheat land was sown down to pasture, with two million acres added to the stock of permanent grassland in the decade from 1877, an increase of 14 per cent.[28] Those hardest hit by the slump in grain prices had been farmers on heavy clay land, where cultivation costs were high and harvesting risky. They were joined in the 'flight to grass' by wheat growers on the chalk soils of the southern downlands, where yields had always been low.

On better soils many farmers stuck to the old arable rotation which had been so rewarding in the past. While there was precious little money to be made out of wheat, even for the efficient producer, cultivation costs were lower than on the heavy lands so there was at least some prospect of a profit. The old four-course rotation still persisted on the chalk wolds of Lincolnshire and Yorkshire.[29] But for others the traditional products of grassland – meat, wool, butter and cheese – appeared to offer an economic bolt-hole from the ruinous tide of American wheat. Yet even this refuge was coming under pressure from the seemingly limitless production of the New World.

On 12 February 1874, the *Liverpool Daily Post* carried a short news story under the less-than-riveting headline: 'Interesting to beef consumers'. It was also of some interest to farmers:

> For the last few days, and especially on Saturday, a curious sight has been seen at the bottom of Mount Pleasant, opposite to the Adelphi Hotel. There have been crowds around the wholesale provision shop of Mr William Brittain, engaged in inspecting the cutting-up of sides of prime beef, and afterwards in purchasing pieces for consumption. On inquiry, it was found that Mr Brittain had received by the Allan Steamer 'Caspian', which arrived in Liverpool last week, a very considerable consignment of fresh Canadian beef, which was being disposed of at the moderate prices of sixpence and seven pence per pound for the prime parts . . . The writer had the opportunity of testing a piece of sirloin, which was in all aspects equal to ordinary English sirloin at eleven pence and one shilling per pound.

Farmers on the virgin soils of north America had realised that it made more sense to export meat than grain. The freight charge for 'shipping' a railroad car full of beef cattle from the Mississippi Valley to the Atlantic coast was little different from that of a carload of corn. But in New York and Philadelphia the cattle were worth almost four times as much. Not surprisingly the farmers of the mid-west were choosing to add value to their corn by 'processing' it into beef.

Early ship-born cooling systems were simple but effective. On the first transatlantic meat ships air was blown by a steam-driven fan through an ice-bank and then over the hanging carcasses. By variations in the flow rate, temperatures in the chilled compartment could be maintained a few degrees above freezing point. Soon the new compressed-air refrigeration systems would be introduced on meat ships. But the ice-bank seems to have been effective enough at keeping meat in prime condition during its Atlantic crossing.

I purchased in Manchester a piece of standing-ribs of the beef which had come over in the 'Celtic', taking pains to assure myself that it has formed part of the cargo I had inspected the day before. This piece of meat was several days in 'muggy' weather before being cooked, and the signs of decay in it then were very slight. We ate a portion of the meat warm and the remainder cold; I had several friends in to taste it, and they all pronounced it as good as very fair English beef. This was my opinion of it, too. I gave ninepence halfpenny a pound for it.[30]

The beef of the great American grassland began to appear in British shops alongside the meat of the Scottish glen and the English meadow. This beef had been raised on the tall-grass prairies of Kansas and the short-grass ranges of Texas, Colorado and Wyoming, then fattened on corn from the broken prairies further east. It was America's best. No mere 'beeflings' of two and three years old, these were mature animals of four and five years, hardy native breeds softened by the early-maturing shorthorn bulls imported from English stock.

Let it be remembered that the whole country from the Rio Grande, the southern boundary of Texas, to the British boundary in the north, 1,500 miles in extent; and westward from the Missouri for from 500 to 1,000 miles, is either one grassy plain or luxuriant, grass-covered valleys . . . By and by all this vast pasture will be occupied by graziers with their herds of grade shorthorns. This is the competition that English graziers and farmers must inevitably meet.[31]

The first American beef imports arrived in Britain in 1873. In autumn 1875, the first shipment refrigerated by the new Bates Process arrived, a trial consignment of sixteen tonnes.[32] Within a year the amount had risen to more than one thousand tonnes a month, and by 1881 shipments were running at fifty thousand tonnes a year. Soon the beef import tide would be swelled by supplies from the grasslands of South America and Australia. Though long anticipated by British farmers, the new trade deepened their mood of despondency. They had seen their cattle herds devastated by the cattle plague rinderpest which had swept through the country in the 1860s. But they had held on to the hope that shortage might lead to higher prices. With mounting despair they now watched those prices undercut by imports from a continent where land was cheap and soils gave up their bounty without being coaxed by fertilisers.

The early meat imports arrived at a time when Britain's pastoral interests had already taken a battering from overseas. For some years butter and cheese from France, Holland and Denmark had been steadily eroding the market for British farmhouse produce, whose quality, it must be admitted, had been variable. In 1851 the first American cheese 'factory' was opened by farmer Jesse Williams of Rome, Oneida County, New York, and within twenty years there were 500 such plants in New York State alone. In Britain cheese-making was still a farm enterprise, employing old wooden vats and brass cheese kettles, 'polished until they dazzled the eye'. The job was mostly carried out by dairymaids whose talent was as variable as their products.

The new American factories – chiefly located in the great dairying states of New York, Pennsylvania, Ohio and Illinois – employed metal cheese vats, vast curing rooms and managers with 'character to force obedience from others'. Their early products failed to win many devotees in Britain. But the American innovators worked hard to improve the taste and textures of their cheeses, so that by the 1870s they had won a significant share of the British market, including that of the most English of cheeses, Cheddar.

In 1868 the Royal Agricultural Society instructed their journal editor to investigate the American cheese factory system and advise on its suitability for English dairying regions. In his report he quoted from cheese-maker John R. Chapman of Madison County, New York:

All the trouble with the English counties in making cheese is 'they don't know how'. If they would use American vats, and adopt the American system in making, they would fully equal the famed Cheddar cheese. A Scotchman of the name of McAdam made cheese last season in Herkima County, New York, on the Cheddar plan, and was beaten by a neighbouring factory in sale of cheese. If you wish to put up a model factory I can send you next year a first class cheese-maker.

Dairies supplying the American cheese-makers were also linked to butter factories. American butter swelled the substantial tonnage already entering Britain from the European continent. English farmhouse butter was a poor product, often over-churned and seldom produced with any precision or care. Thermometers were unknown in most farm dairies, and the standard advice to the dairymaid was that she should 'use a cold hand'.[33]

The best British butter was able to hold its own against imported competition. But there was too little of the 'best' around. In the latter decades of the nineteenth century the market came in for yet more punishment as the new butter substitute, butterine – later called margarine – began to find favour with consumers.

By the 1870s the British farmers' traditional shelter in hard times – the products of their neglected grasslands – had been demolished, first by the 'fertility mining' of the American prairies, and then by the avalanche of chilled meat from Argentina, Australia and New Zealand along with dairy products from continental Europe. In the words of agricultural historian Robert Trow-Smith: 'Henceforth for nearly seventy years, and with one brief interval, British farming was to be an unwanted creature, wandering in an economic maze which yearly became more tortuous and impossible to escape, and the exit to which not even agriculture's few friends knew.'[34]

British farmers had fallen victim to an explosion of free-market capitalism. New railroads had opened up the prairies to global capital markets, bringing in the homesteaders and ranchers to exploit these rich, fat lands, and hauling out their tribute of corn and beef. Powerful shipping companies extended the market from thriving east coast cities across the Atlantic to the old world.

In Britain those same economic forces had driven the masses from the countryside, breaking their link with the land, and concentrating them in new industrial cities. Traditional food chains linking farmers with village markets and market towns were weakened or broken. Torn from their agrarian roots, the people were now to be fed by the industrial leviathan they served.

Free-market capitalism openly raided the fertility bank built over aeons beneath the ancient prairie grassland and used it to undermine the farms and food markets of the old world. For British farmers slipping ever deeper into recession there was just one bright spot – the growing consumer demand for liquid milk. And it was those same capitalist forces that delivered up this buoyant new market to the ailing rural economy.

In the mid-nineteenth century the taste for fresh milk among the working poor was met chiefly by 'town dairies', small herds of cows housed in the dark, dreary cellars of industrial towns and cities, and fed chiefly on oilseed 'cake' and hay hauled in from farms in the surrounding countryside. In former times the peasant family had kept their cow on the common pasture or the village green. Now as urban labourers they relied on a small army of town milk producers, selling their product to town shops or dispensing it direct from churns hauled by horse and cart around the mean streets.

The quality of town milk was poor. Much of it had been adulterated by watering down, and hygiene conditions were non-existent. The milk supplied to most town shops was held to be nutritionally worthless or, worse, downright dangerous. With 'little more than a thick curd remaining, the delicate stomach of a child cannot digest it; and hence the diarrhoea, atrophy and the multitudinous diseases which tell so terribly on infant life in towns'.[35] But the coming of the railway returned dairy farming to the countryside. Farmers who could somehow get their milk to a railway station or halt might begin to win a share of the one expanding market. Not even the Americans could take advantage of the growing British appetite for fresh milk.

Hundreds of grassland farmers from Scotland and the English

west country moved to the home counties of Hertfordshire, Essex and Buckinghamshire, taking over ruined arable farms and seeding them down to pasture. The growing network of branch railway lines meant they could sell their milk on the London market, offering a better-quality product than the grim town dairies at a comparable price. The Duke of Buckingham even laid an eight-mile private railway to carry the milk and butter from his tenant farms on the Wootton Estate to Quainton Station, part of the national rail network.[36]

Contemporary observers were amazed by the transformation of dairy farming and the rise of the milk trade. John Sheldon described it as 'the most remarkable phenomenon which can be found in the history of agriculture'[37] The industrial workers and their families wanted milk not from a dingy city cellar, but from 'country-fed cows, clean and fresh from hedge or wall-encircled pastures'. To meet this demand farms in almost every cow-keeping parish within reasonable distance of a railway station switched from making farmhouse butter and cheese to selling fresh milk. The British people had drunk an average of nine gallons a head in 1861. By the end of the century they were consuming fifteen gallons.[38]

During the Great War the flight to grassland and milk faltered. Grassland was ploughed up and more land sown to cereals in aid of the war effort. For British agriculture it was only a temporary respite from the general fall of prices. Between 1920 and the early 1930s a new and severe depression gripped farming. Once more the strong market for home-produced fresh milk shone as a ray of light in an otherwise gloomy agricultural landscape. Between 1907 and 1929 British milk production rose by almost a quarter.[39] The iron heart of capitalism had returned something to the landscape it had plundered.

While the farming depression was reaching its nadir towards the end of the nineteenth century, a former Indian tea planter, now farming on the edge of the Cheviot Hills in Roxburgh-shire, came up with a sure-fire remedy. He urged British farmers to reject the chemical fertilisers and imported animal feeds that were being thrust at them by brash commercial companies. On a poor Scottish hillside he had proved it was possible to make profits during lean times simply by rebuilding soil fertility. This was best done not by buying expensive chemicals, but by laying down a good turf.

Robert Elliot first published his book, *Agricultural Changes*, in 1895. Later, under a new title – *The Clifton Park System of Farming* – it ran to four editions and became a minor classic. In it he told of his experience of running a landed estate during hard times. On his return from India he had changed the crop rotation on one of the estate farms. Instead of following the local pattern of a two-year grass ley followed by two or three cereal and root crops, he switched to a system based on four-year grass leys. The accumulated fertility built up under grass was enough to grow four cereal and root crops, usually without any additional fertiliser.

The four years of grass was a key feature of the system. According to Elliot, it takes four years for newly sown grass to develop a deep-rooted, fertility-building turf. The plant species in the turf are also important. As well as productive grasses such as cocksfoot, tall fescue, *Festuca arundinacea*, and tall oat-grass, *Arrhenatherum elatius*, there must be deep-rooting herbs like chicory and burnet, together with nitrogen-fixing legumes such as red clover and kidney vetch. Grazed by the farm's Galloway cattle and Cheviot cross ewes, this botanically rich pasture fertilised and aerated the soil, building up reserves of organic matter and humus.

Elliot claimed that the natural wealth of the soil would see farmers through tough times. It would provide cheap, nutritious feed for their cattle and low-cost nutrients for growing healthy crops. They had no need to spend money on artificial fertilisers and imported feedstuffs. A good turf would keep them profitable and independent even when the country was being flooded with imported food.

High farming on the old lines is no remedy for low prices . . . In the face of foreign competition we must look to an economy of production which will carry with it, with the smallest possible expenditure on commercial fertilisers, an increasing fertility of soil ... The Clifton Park system will arrest the steady decadence of all British arable soils ... Yet with liming and a freer and freer use of artificial manures, the decadence is steadily continuing. And the farmer expects that foreign competition may be met by ever augmenting bills for purchased fertilisers, which will cause the soil still further to decline in fertility, while the agricultural chemist, aided by the manure [fertiliser] merchant, is emptying his pockets.[40]

At the opening of the twenty-first century British farming is again beset by falling prices and fierce competition from imported foods. Robert Elliot's farming system might have kept many more farmers in business. But by now few were in a position to adopt it. On many farms the grass leys and livestock had gone completely. These had become arable 'factories', totally dependent on agrochemical companies.

The wealth of grass had been squandered, and with it the health of the planet.

15 The Whirling Blade

The new town of Milton Keynes stretches out across the flat, Buckinghamshire countryside like a rumpled woolly blanket. Its planners conceived it as a bold, assertive, post-industrial city. Its critics slate it as boring and bland, an endless gridiron of suburbia, neither town nor country, recklessly dependent on the car. Its residents see it as neither of these things. To them it is a collection of villages wrapped in parkland and clustered around 'the city' which is Central Milton Keynes.

Whatever else it may be, this town is defiantly green. Everywhere the commercial and residential areas are enfolded in the foliage of trees, shrubs and especially grasses. Without grasslands this place would have no meaning. They line its broad boulevards and flood the land between adjoining woods and shrubby areas. They are the setting for its architecture, both the grandiose and the drab. They cover much of its 4,000 acres or so of parks.

They are the mortar that binds together the disparate elements of this adventurous and innovative settlement. Without grasslands the idea that is Milton Keynes might never have been conceived. And but for one man's inspired invention it would never have been built.

Milton Keynes Museum is housed in a beautiful Victorian farmstead situated on the north-western outskirts of the city. The museum includes some impressive Victorian room settings as well as vintage farm machinery and a transport collection. Tucked away at the edge of the grounds, beneath a spreading oak tree, stands a modest wooden hut with a green corrugated roof. This inauspicious building contains part of the museum's collection of early lawn mowers.

Among them is a cumbersome-looking machine with a large, cast-iron roller and a cutting reel turned by a crude arrangement of cogs and wheels. Pushing this weighty contraption would be a daunting prospect. Lifting it would be out of the question. Yet the inventor and builder of this unwieldy device was to transform urban landscapes around the world.

In any list of nineteenth-century inventors the name of Edwin Beard Budding would be unlikely to figure prominently. This was no Thomas Edison or Alexander Graham Bell. Yet his contribution to the social and cultural life of the West has been little short of immense.

Without his big idea the national games of cricket, soccer and rugby might never have achieved their popular appeal nor become the great spectacles of skill and entertainment they are today. Instead they would have been confined to a few enthusiastic amateurs stumbling around in tussocky meadows. Other games like golf, bowling and lawn tennis might never have acquired a mass following, remaining instead the preserve of the rich.

Edwin Budding's invention gave outdoor sport to the masses and made possible the greening of Britain's industrial areas. Thanks to him the Victorians were able to develop their vision of grand urban parks – those 'green lungs' of the city – together with the distinct landscape of the English suburbs, that characteristic blend of redbrick villas and green lawns which followed the expanding metropolitan railway network out from the city's edge. It had become possible to recreate the country meadow in miniature within the town, a development that would transform the urban environment and win for its author a small but enviable place in Britain's social history.

Budding's big idea led to the cylinder lawn mower. At the time of his inspiration in 1830 he was working at iron foundries near Stroud in Gloucestershire, where he had shown a talent for overcoming engineering problems. The young engineer had become intrigued by the carding machine used in textile mills to trim the nap from newly woven cloth, thus giving it a smooth finish.

The heavy bench machine incorporated a revolving metal cylinder on which were mounted a series of angled blades. Budding devised a way of transferring this simple mechanism on to a wheeled frame so the rotating blades would come into close contact with the grass. In a cutting action like that of garden shears, the grass would be trapped between the moving blade and a fixed bottom blade or 'bed knife'.

This basic cutting mechanism was to be incorporated into lawn mowers for the next century and a half. The only serious challenge came with the introduction of rotary mowers in the mid-1930s. But even today the cylinder mower survives, a testament to the soundness of Budding's original idea.

Before the invention of the mower, lawns, at least those of any scale, were the preserve of the landed rich. Under the influence of Capability Brown and others the broad mantle of grassland had become a popular garden design feature, but its maintenance was troublesome and expensive. Across rolling acres of parkland the task could be left to some suitably decorative grazing animal – the rich, red Hereford or Devon, the shaggy Highland, or the jet-black Angus. But inside the ha-ha maintenance became more problematical. There was no practical alternative to scything.

The eighteenth-century scythes-man was a highly skilled operator. He – for the scythes-man was invariably a male – was not matched to his implement until he had reached physical maturity. Scythes, like suits, were made-to-measure. An ill-fitting tool would result in a jerky action and produce an uneven cut. Fine adjustments to grass-cutting height were made

by strapping wooden blocks of varying thickness to the scythes-
man's boots.

In large country houses teams of scythes-men, or mowers,
were permanently employed to keep lawns in shape through the
summer months. Working in line abreast, a skilled team might
achieve a tolerably even cut. Behind them a small army of
women and children would be employed to gather up the
mowings.

In his Georgian treatise on gardening John Abercrombie has
advice for the concerned landowner:

> Let the grass be regularly mown; cut it always close and as
> even as possible. This should be particularly regarded; for
> when the lawns and walks are so mown that every stroke of
> the sithe appears, they make very disagreeable appearance. To
> keep short grass lawns in good order, they should be mown
> sometimes once a week, but not less than once a fortnight, or
> three weeks at the farthest; generally taking opportunity of
> dewy mornings, as early as possible, while the dew remains,
> which should be particularly regarded in mowing of short
> grass, otherwise it will be impossible to mow it short and
> even.[1]

Such prescriptions were fine when labour was cheap and
plentiful, but by the nineteenth century the proliferation of mills
and factories was drawing rural workers into the towns. The
owners of country estates found it less easy to spare skilled
scythes-men for the purely cosmetic task of maintaining the
lawns around the great house.[2]

At the same time the countryside was attracting a new breed
of landowner, the successful industrialist. The new landowners
scorned the old ways of carrying out routine tasks. For them this
was the age of the machine.

It was into this fast-changing world that the self-taught
engineer and former carpenter Edwin Budding launched his
lawn mower. The 1830 patent document described the device
as 'a new combination and application of machinery for the
purpose of cropping or shearing the vegetable surfaces of lawns,

grass-plats or pleasure grounds, constituting a machine which may be used with advantage instead of a scythe for that purpose'. The patent concluded that 'grass growing in the shade, too weak to stand against the scythe to cut, may be cut by my machine as closely as required, and the eye will never be offended by those circular scars, inequalities and bare places so commonly made by the best mowers with the scythe, and which continues visible for several days. Country gentlemen may find in using my machine themselves an amusing, useful and healthy exercise.'

The 35-year-old Budding formed a partnership with John Ferrabee who owned the Phoenix Iron Works at Thrupp Mill in Stroud. Ferrabee agreed to cover the development costs, and in return would have the right to manufacture, sell and license other manufacturers to produce lawn mowers. One of the early Budding and Ferrabee mowers was used at Regent's Park Zoological Gardens in 1831. The foreman, a Mr Curtis, declared himself entirely satisfied with the machine. 'It does as much work as six or eight men with scythes and brooms,' he reported, 'performing the whole so perfectly as not to leave a mark of any kind.'[3]

The first machine produced at the foundry had a cutting width of forty-eight centimetres and was built on a frame of wrought iron. The cutting cylinder was driven by a set of cast-iron gears connecting it to a large rear roller which provided the motive power. A smaller, adjustable roller between the cylinder and the rear roller enabled the operator to alter the cutting height. Lawn clippings were hurled forward on to the grass box, a horizontal tray at the front.

While the Budding design may have been revolutionary in concept it had a number of defects in operation. For a start the sheer mass of iron work made the machine impossibly heavy to operate. Even for a gardener used to hard toil the mowing of a sizeable patch of grass became a Herculean task. An extra handle was quickly added to the front of the machine so an assistant could be employed to help pull it along.

The ill-fitting gears of cast iron were noisy and easily damaged by stones. Many gardeners were forbidden to use their machines early in the morning or at times when residents and their guests might wish to enjoy the peace and tranquillity of the garden. Another fault arose from the small, wooden roller that Budding had placed behind the cylinder, close to the rear drive roller. This made the cutting cylinder difficult to control so the cut was rough and uneven. Sometimes the cylinder even dug itself into the ground. To correct the fault Ferrabee adopted the idea of a rival manufacturer, putting the wooden roller in front of the cylinder. This simple change produced a more even cut and became the standard configuration for roller mowers up to the present day.

Despite its faults the Budding machine enjoyed a modest success through the middle decades of the nineteenth century. By 1862 Ferrabee was making eight models in a range of sizes up to ninety centimetres' cutting width at prices from four pounds ten shillings to twenty pounds. When production ceased in the mid 1860s more than 5,000 machines had been sold. Another 1,500 had been built by the great Ipswich plough manufacturers J. R. and A. Ransome, who made the machine under licence.[4]

The Budding idea had its imitators. One of the first mowers from the Stroud foundry was bought by a Scot named W. F. Carnegie, who wished to keep his extensive lawns in trim without employing a team of scythes-men. When the Gloucestershire machine proved inadequate for the job Carnegie engaged a local engineer, James Shanks of Arbroath, to construct something a little bigger. The brief was for a sixty-eight-centimetre machine capable of being pulled by two men or a pony.[5] The pony won by a short head, and in 1842 Shanks applied for a Scottish patent. In the same year he went into the production of horse-drawn lawn mowers.

One early user of the Shanks machine, a grounds-man at Nottingham's Clumber Park, commented: 'The mower has been in constant use in the gardens for upwards of three months. Though constructed on the same principle as Budding's patent mowing machine, it is altogether stronger and less liable to go out of repair. Drawn by one horse it requires a boy to lead the horse and a man to direct the machine. The saving in labour has amounted to seventy per cent.'[6]

The next great advance in lawn mower technology was to come from south of the border. In 1855 Thomas Green, a former blacksmith and maker of wrought-iron gates, began manufacturing mowers to a design based on the Budding machine. Four years later his Leeds-based company astonished the gardening world with a revolutionary chain-driven machine, the oddly named Silens Messor, the Latin for 'silent operation'. Out had gone the cumbersome gears. In their place Green had introduced a chain to transmit power from the rear roller to the cutting cylinder.

The combination of sprocket and open chain was far less prone to damage from small stones and garden débris, making the machine more reliable in operation. Other innovations included a reversible reel or cutting cylinder. With a chain sprocket at each end, the cylinder could be detached from the frame and put back the other way round. There were now two sharpened faces on the edge of the blade. Both could be used before the cylinder needed to be reground.

But it was the mower's quiet running that caught the imagination, not least of the company's sales staff. For the first two decades of Queen Victoria's reign demand for mowing machines came mainly from the wealthy, particularly those with country houses. Despite the ending of the Corn Laws agriculture remained buoyant. Landowners both large and small could afford to indulge their appetite for broad sweeps of ornamental lawn. To them this relatively noiseless new machine held a definite appeal.

However, the more astute manufacturers were shrewd enough to spot a far bigger market in the making – the market of the middle classes. In the early part of the century the middle class had largely comprised the wealthier merchants and traders together with a professional class made up of doctors, lawyers and engineers. But as industry prospered, their ranks were swelled by a new group, those who would be known today as white-collar workers. These were the chief clerks and managers of the thriving new factories, and the leading officers of fledgling local authorities, the 'upwardly mobile' of Victorian society.

They took the metropolitan railway routes out to the city suburbs where they snapped up the solid, redbrick villas that seemed to be sprouting up everywhere. Out here they planted up their plots and dreamed of Arcadia, a new Arcadia in which the ornamental trees and flower-strewn borders might be separated by little parcels of neatly shorn grassland, just as grassy meadows separated the woods and hedgerows of the country-side. But first they would need an artificial grazing machine, compact, manageable and affordable.

The Silens Messor spawned a clutch of chain-driven mowers adapted for a range of users other than the callused gardener in the grand country house. Ransomes, who had returned to mower manufacture in 1867 with the first of their successful Automaton range, unashamedly designed models to suit the power of the user. An 1883 sales leaflet lists a twenty-five-centimetre model 'for use by a lady or boy', a thirty-five-centimetre machine 'for a man', a forty-five-centimetre model 'for a man and a boy', and a fifty-five-centimetre mower 'for use by two men'.[7] The largest machine in the range was a horse-drawn mower priced at thirty-two pounds. Leather boots were provided for the horse at an additional charge of thirty shillings per set.

Despite the undoubted advance of the chain drive, it took another great innovation to make the lawn mower a truly universal tool, to give it a place in the garden shed of the suburban semi as well as in the coach house of the grand country manor. In 1869 the Manchester engineering firm of Follows and Bate took out a patent on a mower that dispensed with the heavy iron roller that had characterised all earlier machines. The drive was transferred to wheels set on either side of the cutting cylinder and linked to it by a system of internal gears. The grass box – for fitting at the front or the rear – came as an optional extra.

The new Climax mower was light, manoeuvrable and cheap. Gone were the heavy external gears and the complicated chain-drive mechanism. For a pound or two the proud owner of a new suburban villa could buy a machine that would make easy work of the front lawn and follow the curve of the most intricate flower bed. By 1871 Follows and Bate had sold more than 4,000 mowers and induced a dozen other firms to adopt the side-wheel design.

US manufacturers were quick to spot the potential of the new style mower. The lightweight, side-wheel design was particularly well suited to American lawns with their coarser grasses and more erect growth pattern. Elwood McGuire of Richmond, Indiana was first on to the grass, but within fifteen years the US was manufacturing 50,000 lawn mowers annually, many of them for export.

Because of their longer production runs, American machines were often cheaper than their British equivalents. This made them great favourites with the UK ironmongery trade. In the latter years of the nineteenth century an ironmonger ordering a sizeable quantity could have the company name or badge cast into the base of the handle.[8] Suitably branded, the mower could then be included in the firm's annual gardening catalogue, a practice which led to American machines manufactured specifically for this trade being given the name 'catalogue mowers'. One of the biggest importers was the Birmingham firm of Hoods who sold their popular Premier model for forty years, from 1885 to 1925.

But British manufacturers did not stand helplessly aside in the face of this US invasion. With the new suburbs already ringing to the sound of the American 'reel' mowers, Ransomes introduced their Anglo-Paris range of side-wheel machines while Thomas Green brought out its Multum in Parvo (the Latin for 'With little, much') range of mowers designed for small plots. James Shanks of Arbroath followed the American lead with a machine called the Yankee.

John Post Lawrence, a Somerset businessman visiting the 1878 Chicago World Fair, was introduced to the US firm Lloyd, Suplee and Walton, makers of the successful Pennsylvania range of mowers. Back in Britain he set up an agency to import the machines, whose improved gearing made them easier to push than the innovative Climax of Follows and Bate.

By 1913, a record year for sales of the Pennsylvania, a total of almost two million machines had been sold. So successful were the American models that in 1920 the agency, then known as Lloyds and Company, set up a UK manufacturing plant, the Pennsylvania Works, at Letchworth.[9]

A handful of British manufacturers managed to compete with American side-wheel machines on price. The Gripper, made by Alex C. Harris of Leicester, sold for just ten shillings and sixpence in 1909, a pound or more below the price of most competitors.

The new middle classes of late Victorian and Edwardian Britain took to the cheap, lightweight machines with enthusiasm. At the turn of the century families often posed around the mower for group photographs. Possession of a mower proved not only that they were wealthy enough to live in houses with gardens, but that they did not need to devote their entire plots to growing food. The mower set their homes apart from the back-to-back terraces or the mean farm labourers' cottages their parents had grown up in. Owning a mower confirmed their new middle-class status – it marked them out as little landowners.

Magazine advertisements for lawn mowers around the turn of the century showed them being used by well-to-do women in expensive dresses and fine bonnets. In 1904 the music hall star Marie Studholme, wearing an elegant dress and bonnet, posed with a Ransomes Automaton mower. A Ransomes poster of the same period shows the rather grand lady of the house, complete with ribboned hat and parasol, effortlessly pushing the mower while the unhappy gardener stands watching, hat in hand. A 1906 magazine advert for the Philadelphia lawn mower features a chic young woman in a long dress and extravagant bonnet.

The choice of subject was doubtless meant to demonstrate the ease with which the machines might be operated. But the publicity material was also giving out a subtler message. The mower had become a symbol of social status. Once the well-tended lawn had been the preserve of the gentry in their fine country houses. Now this emblem of affluence could be attached to even the modest suburban villa. With the arrival of grassland in the town the middle classes might become the gentry. Like the Daimler and Mercedes of later generations, the lawn mower had become an object of aspiration.

The simple side-wheel machines held an enduring appeal for British gardeners as they did for home-owners throughout the US. To this day tens of thousands of them still gather dust and cobwebs in the dark corners of garages and garden sheds. The vogue for houses with small gardens fuelled the demand for push mowers for a century.

While World War One halted the expansion of the middle-class suburbs, the end of hostilities triggered a rash of council-house building.[10] Radiating outwards from the fringes of older towns, the new estates, with their bathrooms and gardens, appeared as a new Arcadia to a generation brought up in smoky back-to-backs with just a yard and an outside privy. Later the 'ribbon development' of middle-income housing snaked out along the main roads from towns and cities, taking suburbia deeper into the countryside. In the home counties thousands of tiny plots were sold to Londoners over a glass of bubbly, giving rise to what were known as 'champagne estates'.

While such unplanned urban sprawl may have horrified the aesthetes, it was good news for the makers of small mowers. New houses with small gardens set the cash tills ringing in ironmongers' stores. By the early 1920s the flow of side-wheel machines from the US had dried to a trickle, chiefly as a result of uncompetitive tariffs, but mowers from Germany and Sweden had quickly filled the gap in the market.

Following World War Two social housing again became the priority, with ever bigger areas of land being covered with council estates and new towns. Then as social housing declined in the 1960s, another round of speculative house building began, this time with even smaller gardens. Once more there were healthy profits to be made on the basic side-wheel mower, which had altered little over decades. Only when cheap, electrically powered mowers became available in the 1970s did sales of side-wheel machines grind to a halt.

The side-wheel was the Model-T Ford of small-scale grass cutting, seemingly simple, yet near-perfect in function. Thus it remained a favourite across the generations. But for all its lightness and manoeuvrability it retained one serious drawback – users still had to push it. This is why resourceful engineers had been searching for an alternative power source ever since Victorian times.

In 1893 Lancashire blacksmith James Sumner took out a patent for a steam-powered lawn mower. The production model, when it finally arrived, was cumbersome and unwieldy. A large metal boiler sat perched on a platform above the rear roller while a water tank was slung under the handle arms. The paraffin fired boiler took ten minutes to get up to operating pressure.

The operator walked behind, steering it with two handles while opening and closing the large steam regulator. It could hardly have been a relaxing job. The machine weighed a ton and a half and was hard to control, especially on corners. Trundling along at four miles an hour, the machine produced an unremitting din.

Rival steam mowers were quickly brought out by Alexander Shanks and Thomas Green. But in the world of grass cutting the flirtation with steam was to be a brief one. In a working trial at Eaton Hall near Chester, Sumner's mower – marketed by the Leyland Steam Motor Company, later to become British Leyland – was pitched against a revolutionary machine from Ransomes. Developed by James Edward Ransome, the founder's youngest grandson, it had a cutting width of more than a metre and was propelled by a cast-iron roller placed behind the cylinder. The operator sat above a smaller, rear-mounted roller which steered the machine.

The chief distinguishing feature of the Ransomes machine was the four-stroke Simms petrol engine which drove it. In competition with the steam mower it proved a runaway winner. King Edward VII was so impressed that he ordered a demonstration in the grounds of Buckingham Palace, as a result of which he bought two machines. That same year the legendary cricketer W. G. Grace gave the machine his full endorsement, having seen it perform on the London County Cricket Ground at Crystal Palace.

'Every ground should have motor mowers and rollers as, early in the season, whenever the ground is soft, you can get on with a motor machine when it would be impossible for a horse machine to be used without doing harm to the ground.'[11]

By 1906, four years after bringing out their first petrol-driven mower, Ransomes were producing three different models, the smallest costing seventy-five pounds and the largest twice as much. In the years leading up to World War One the company produced eighty machines a year, many of them for export. Ransomes motor mowers clipped the lawns of Government House in Calcutta, the cricket ground of the Hurlingham Club in Buenos Aires, and the tracks of the Victoria Racing Club in Melbourne.

Once more Ransomes' two great rivals, Greens and Shanks, introduced their own versions of the petrol-driven mower. But until the First World War such machines were beyond the reach of most lawn owners. They were principally aimed at the well-off, the landed classes, those with sizeable grounds and the staff to maintain them. Others went to professionals, the ground staff and green-keepers employed in public parks or private institutions.

The people who used these early petrol-driven machines had first to be trained in the necessary skills. Many of them were chauffeurs. Hand-pushed and horse-drawn machines continued to account for the bulk of lawn mower sales. But at the end of the war things began to change.

In 1920 Charles H. Pugh, who ran a Birmingham foundry making parts for the textile and cycle trades, entered the lawn mower market with a pedestrian machine powered by a Villiers engine. He named the chain-driven mower Atco after the Atlas Chain Company which he owned. The cast-iron frame of the early production models was made by the Derwent Iron Foundry which had registered the name Qualcast to mark the quality of its castings.

Pugh ignored the traditional market for motor mowers: the well-to-do in their large, well-staffed houses. His marketing was directed at middle-income earners, those buying up the speculative houses springing up in the suburbs and snaking out into the country alongside the main trunk roads. He set up a chain of service depots across the UK, the first company to attempt this, introducing hire-purchase arrangements for cash-strapped customers. More significantly, he adopted a rigorous pricing policy in his drive to win new customers at a time when the country was slipping ever deeper into recession.

A company sales leaflet of the early 1930s proclaims:

The famous twenty-one guinea Atco is now eighteen guineas, or five pounds down and twelve monthly payments of one pound seven shillings and sixpence. Thousands of people who used to think their lawns too small for a motor mower are buying the famous Atco mower to enjoy the effortless efficiency of motor mowing at little more than the price of a push mower.

During the inter-war years dozens of other companies followed Pugh into the powered mower market. Many of them were engineering companies seeking new lines to keep their factories busy during the dark years of depression. Dennis Brothers of Guildford came in with a singularly unsuccessful machine. Later models fared better and the company eventually gained a considerable reputation for larger, heavy-duty mowers aimed at local councils and institutions.

JP Engineering produced a powered lawn mower with a petrol engine that could be detached and used for other jobs around the garden. The Enfield Cycle Company launched a range of machines with a trademark echoing its origins in arms manufacture. 'Made like a gun' read the slogan beneath a picture of an artillery field piece.

Early users of motor mowers might have considered the association apt as they coaxed temperamental machines, popping and spluttering, across their treasured turf. Most of the smaller machines were fitted with two-stroke engines which have to be turned over fast before they fire. It was not uncommon for a mowing session to begin with a long and frustrating struggle with flywheel and starter rope before the engine finally sprang into life and allowed the real work to get underway.

Through the 1930s the new breed of motor mower filled the gardening catalogues and ironmongery showrooms, standing alongside the push mowers, the side-wheels and the roller mowers. While they varied in their width of cut, transmission and power sources, they all shared the same cutting action. A century after Edwin Budding's invention of the cutting cylinder or reel, its use on domestic lawns remained almost universal. The principle had also been adopted for the maintenance of parks and public gardens.

From Victorian times civic leaders in the burgeoning industrial towns and cities had dreamed of broad expanses of greensward; places to walk, or sit, or play games, places to breathe out the acrid air of the foundry and mill. The first machines for cutting large areas of grass were the pony mowers, broad-width versions of Budding's roller mower. Later came the wider, horse-drawn versions of the side-wheel mower.

In the US the American Worthington Mower Company of Stroudsburg, Pennsylvania, patented a system in which three side-wheel mowers were linked by a frame, the whole unit being pulled by a horse. In Britain Ransomes began making these 'gang mowers' under licence in 1921, and soon the horse-drawn triple mower became a familiar sight on the golf course. One delighted green-keeper wrote to the Ipswich company: 'The turf is generally improved since using the triple. Hills and hollows are closely and evenly cut. The turf is beautifully springy in the driest weather and drains much more quickly in wet. The ball sits up and asks to be hit.'[12]

By the end of the decade the company's catalogue featured five-mower and seven-mower combinations, and by the outbreak of the Second World War Ransomes had introduced the Nonuple gang mower with nine cutting units and a cutting width of more than six metres. Old cars were often adapted to pull gang mowers. Their forward speeds were limited and much of their bodywork stripped away to provide a load-carrying space. The largest units were pulled by farm tractors.

By the close of the 1930s grass everywhere in urban Britain was being cut by Budding's method – in the parks, in domestic gardens, in sports fields, around public buildings. In one form or another the cylinder mower was to remain dominant for another forty years. But in the Berkshire town of Slough an alternative system was under development, one which would eventually topple the Budding system from its lofty pinnacle.

A company called Power Specialities developed a motor mower which cut grass with a horizontal blade rotating at high speed.. Driven by petrol engine, the blade was covered with a hood below which the spinning blade created a vacuum. Within it the cut grass was sucked up and propelled into a collector behind. Following a company takeover the machine was marketed as the Shay Rotoscythe and became quite popular. But it was not until Flymo introduced the first hover mower in the 1960s that the rotary system acquired a mass market.

Today rotary mowers abound in a variety of forms. There are wheeled types and hover types, petrol-driven machines and electrically powered mowers. Many tractor mowers also cut by rotary action. Yet the demand for cylinder mowers remains strong, particularly from lawn connoisseurs. They are still believed to give the best and cleanest cut, though the dominance of a system dreamed up in a Gloucestershire textile mill more than a century and a half ago has clearly ended.

Each year in May members of the Old Lawnmower Club gather at the Milton Keynes Museum for a weekend rally. They bring along mowers from their own collections of vintage machines, and for two days the talk is of flywheels, crankshafts and epicyclic clutches. There is great admiration for a well restored Silens Messor or an unusually well-preserved example of the Follows and Bate Speedwell with rear-mounted grass box. A certain amount of trading takes place though the mowers themselves rarely attract more than a few pounds.

To the visitor it looks like a harmless piece of eccentricity, this fascination with an article so mundane and workaday. Could any object be less inspiring than the garden mower? Yet the club members are tapping into something more profound. They are celebrating a technology whose impact has been almost entirely beneficial and whose effect on civilisation has been immense.

Edwin Budding and his successors have greened the urban

environment. They have helped to make the city a tolerable, even a pleasant place to live. His invention opened up the possibility of bringing the country meadow into the town. We could now trim it, parcel it up and fit it into any space we chose. In the suburbs or the city centre we could construct great grassy plains for street-locked youths to play soccer on at weekends. Or we could create a rug-sized turf in the back yard for the toddlers to scamper around on.

Thanks to the humble lawn mower we are able to transform our grey urban landscapes into the Elysian Fields of our fantasies. We can re-create the woodland glade in the garden of our three-bedroomed semis, there to lie on it, dream on it, and experience the primitive freedom of a barefoot walk on it.

The lawn gives root to the desire deep within us to throw off our twenty-first-century shackles and engage with the planet at a more elemental level. The mower in the garage gives us the means to do so in safety. What else can account for the peculiar satisfaction that comes with a couple of hours on the ride-on or even with the hover?

In part it is, of course, a matter of utility. Nothing so instantly improves the appearance of a garden as a quick whisk round with the mower. But the appeal seems to work at a deeper level, too. There is a sense of engaging with the natural world, of shaping it for our own purpose. For a time we are people of the Neolithic turning our cattle on to a woodland pasture. Or with the smell of new mown grass in our nostrils we are Saxon farmers swinging scythes in a summer meadow.

On a summer Sunday afternoon a dozen or so members of the Old Lawnmower Club watch as an ageing Atco motor mower is put through its paces on a patch of rough grass outside the museum building. Its newly restored paintwork gleams in the bright sunshine. In Milton Keynes city centre a cricket team is taking to the field in Campbell Park. In the parkland beyond groups of early sunbathers are stretched out on the turf. Some are reading books, but most just lie in the sunshine and ponder the meaning of things.

16 Breathing Space

A biting April wind, scudding in from the north Atlantic, shakes the bright yellow heads of early cowslips. Richard Scott pulls up the collar of his overcoat, thrusts his hands deep into the pockets and gazes intently across the short grass turf. He has the barely suppressed excitement of a Klondike prospector who knows there is gold in this land.

Soon he finds what he has been looking for – a cluster of low-growing plants whose leaves are made up of separate leaflets arranged in parallel rows on either side of the stalk. 'Kidney vetch,' he announces with a note of triumph. 'Give it another couple of weeks and this whole area will be ablaze with yellow and orange. They're really thick around here. Further up we'll see a block of devil's-bit scabious, and beyond that it'll be yellow rattle. They've done really well here. We've even seen a few orchids.'

His enthusiasm is infectious as he recites the flowers of the meadow, flowers that once festooned the turf of every lowland parish in Britain until farm subsidies and cheap artificial fertilisers put an end to them. Yet this is no remnant hay meadow in the heart of rural Britain. Just metres away are the back gardens of urban terrace houses, while beyond them a cluster of high-rise blocks stands stark against the grey sky. Driven from the countryside, meadow flowers now thrive in the grassland of a northern city.

Richard Scott is in the business of getting meadow flowers to grow in unexpected places. Landlife, the charity he works for, is dedicated to doing just that – helping city landscapes to bloom. The group describes the work as 'creative conservation' – finding new places for wildlife in a heavily populated island.

This patch of amenity grass, part of a 'green corridor' in the Liverpool borough of Knowsley, is one such place. A decade ago the rank grasses went largely uncut, growing waist-high unless they were 'torched' by local youngsters. Now the rank, coarse grasses have been edged out by fine, low-growing species, flecked with the flowers of summer.

Bringing about the change was simple enough for the designers of this new urban landscape. First they brought in bulldozers to strip away the fertile topsoil and its reservoir of seeds. With the fertile topsoil removed, the tall, aggressive grass species that had dominated the turf no longer held sway. Slower-growing plants would be able to find a niche and establish themselves. The sandy subsoil now exposed was an ideal growing medium for species-rich grassland.

Into this impoverished ground the Landlife team sowed seeds for a brighter, more colourful turf – the slow-growing grasses, crested dog's-tail and browntop, together with a small number of wildflower species such as oxeye daisy, greater knapweed and field scabious. Their aim was not to re-create the complex botanical mix of an ancient, species-rich hay meadow. They were looking for a simple, open sward, dominated in season by blocks of kidney vetch or cowslips, but into which other species might colonise. There was to be room for the timeless dance of evolution.

Ten years on, the transformation has been spectacular. The once dreary green turf is now a vibrant flower meadow, filled with life. Of the sown species devil's-bit scabious and kidney vetch have spread to form dense, colourful stands. Other species like the pinked-flowered common centaury and the delicate bee orchid – sown by the scattering of tiny amounts of seed – have established strong and growing communities.

Colonists have moved in, invasive plants taking advantage of the opportunities offered by the slower-growing grasses. Among the incomers are both red and white clovers. And as the plant life has grown more diverse, so the variety of insect life has soared. Grasshoppers, leaf beetles and butterflies are now plentiful in this modern meadow, while skylarks pour out their silver sound from the skies above.

But for Landlife success is not simply measured by the number of species the new sward attracts. Equally important is the verdict of Knowsley residents. The field may look stunning in early summer with its banks of purple scabious and yellow hay rattle. But if it fails to make an impact on the local community it will be deemed a failure. Unlike the grasslands of the countryside, these urban fields are intended to enrich the lives of people – to waken a cold city landscape with the beat of the natural world.

Richard Scott wanders across the four-acre meadow looking for signs of community approval. The early spring is cold. Most plants have barely emerged from their winter dormancy. Even when the soil has warmed these fine grasses will grow only slowly. In a dry summer they may burn brown, so poor is the moisture-retaining capacity of this light, sandy subsoil. But the temporary loss of grass vegetation will do the deeper-rooting flowering plants no harm at all. Some will exploit the short-lived advantage by spreading to fill the vacant site.

He picks up an empty crisp packet, a reliable indicator of local approval. Nearby a large patch of scorched earth is evidence of a less welcome form of human activity – car burning. The local borough council, which owns the field, has promised to close off vehicle entry with barriers.

'It's important that we keep the area looking tidy and well-cared-for,' he says. 'It must feel like a safe, unthreatening place for families to use. We want children to play here. We want parents to bring them here for summer picnics. We want them to enjoy it, to pick the flowers even. This is not meant to be a nature reserve. It's a local amenity, a resource for people to use.

'More than anything we want the local community to feel a sense of ownership. This is their meadow. It should be a place of fun, of celebration. A place for enjoyment.'

He points out a pathway, worn bare of grasses, which follows a meandering line across the field. It may have been made by joggers, dog walkers, even mountain bikers. There is no way of knowing. But to Richard Scott it is a welcome development whoever its unwitting creators. 'It shows the place is being accepted and used,' he says. 'People are starting to feel they own it.'

A geographer by training, he is refreshingly free of conventional ideas about wildlife management. In a recent project he investigated alternatives to soil as a growth medium for wildflowers. Waste materials such as brick rubble, crushed concrete, motorway scrapings, cockle shells and pulverised fuel ash from coal-burning power stations are low in plant nutrients and so make ideal substrates for species-rich grasslands. All have been used by Landlife in the creation of new habitats.

It is an imaginative approach to wildlife restoration, one that is light years from the usual preoccupation with preserving ancient habitats like chalk grasslands. Richard Scott has little interest in habitat creation as a numbers game. He is unimpressed by the purist argument that a re-created chalk grassland should have the forty or so plant speeies to the square metre of the original. Here the aim is to design new, durable landscape features, not to protect museum pieces. The habitat and its wild species are not ends in themselves. They are there to enhance the urban landscape and enrich the lives of those who live in it.

Scott works from an office in a converted stable block at the nearby Court Hey Park. Formerly the home of the Gladstone family, it is now the headquarters of Landlife and location of Britain's new National Wildflower Centre, created with the support of the Millennium Commission. From this parkland centre in Liverpool a small team works to advance a bold mission – nothing less than the revitalisation of Britain's towns and cities through the power of nature.

With its clutter of desks, files, books and wildflower packs, the Landlife office has an air of purposeful chaos about it. From its centre Chief Executive Grant Luscombe spreads his vision of an urban renaissance. He aims to bring the experience of nature to the places where most people live, to link city dwellers with the natural world in all its glorious diversity.

He believes that green spaces play an important part in enriching city life. To planners and politicians they are often seen as expendable. While the green fields of the countryside must be protected from development, the city's small fragments of green space are swallowed up by brick and concrete, often without protest. Yet their power to enhance community life is far greater than that of some far-flung hay meadow in the depths of rural Britain.

The Landlife team is bent on changing attitudes to the small, green places of the city – the patch of grass around the block of flats, the square of turf in the middle of a housing estate, the green corridor that links two neighbouring boroughs. Usually they are little more than green deserts, these unloved pockets of urban space, bleak stretches of open grassland clipped short by the council's gang mowers, silent, devoid of colour and life. The charity's aim is to re-awaken them, to release the bound forces of evolution, to recut these diamonds of the city landscape so they flash and sparkle with the hues and tints of the universe.

Grant Luscombe sees the work as a form of impressionism, an attempt to evoke the natural environment, though not to replicate it. The process begins with a simple seed mixture and a soil stripped of its fertility. Into this basic ecosystem the forces of evolution intervene, adding new species, introducing complexity. Over the years the artificial becomes the wild. Nature reclaims the city landscape.

It is a model Grant Luscombe wants to see applied across the length and breadth of urban Britain. He says: 'In the past our cities had a village feel to them. There were pockets of wild land even in the city centres. Unfortunately no one realised their intrinsic value, and they were easy prey to development. We now have the techniques to put wild lands back, to give urban people the chance to see wildlife from their doorsteps. Conservation is a creative force that can inspire the way we live.'

This is not the first time that Liverpool has been at the heart of a movement aimed at bringing elements of the rural landscape into the city. In the mid-nineteenth century, when the north-west seaport was still prosperous and strong, Britain's politicians were seized with the idea of creating spacious municipal parks in the nation's fast-growing towns and cities. In part they were motivated by altruism. But with it went an anxiety about political unrest in overcrowded, disease-ridden housing areas. For a hundred years the urban population had been growing at an unprecedented rate. In England and Wales alone the numbers living in towns rose from just over one million to a staggering nine million.

Across the country the remorseless rise of industrialism had created mile upon mile of dismal back-to-back houses and crowded tenements. Inside these purpose-built slums, with their maze of dark alleys and grimy courtyards, daily life was grim. Most people lived in terrible poverty. Diseases like typhoid and diphtheria were rampant, snatching tens of thousands each year and reducing the average age at death to a little over thirty. Adults sought escape in the street corner ale-houses and gin palaces that flourished in the morass of human misery. Outside in the damp, sunless streets children grew up wheezy and rickety, seemingly born to be old.

As working-class political movements like Chartism gained in support and influence, the prospect of unrest and revolution became a nagging fear of the ruling classes. Everywhere the tinder of discontent seemed to be piling up in chill and cheerless streets, waiting only for the inconsequential spark to sweep away the entire social order in one huge inferno.

In 1833 the Parliamentary Select Committee on Public Walks proposed that public parks in towns would exert a 'civilising influence' on those urban citizens in greatest need of improvement.[1] There would be contact with nature and the chance to meet people of other classes, so reducing social tensions. Moreover, parks would provide an alternative recreation to the tavern. As if to amplify the point, the Select Committee on Drunkenness later provided evidence from a Liverpool iron merchant who stated that on Sundays 'all the public houses are open and all the public walks, cemeteries, zoological gardens and botanical gardens, where people might amuse themselves innocently, are closed'.[2]

The first town to use public funds for creating a municipal park lay on the other side of the Mersey in Birkenhead. These early providers of public green space seem to have been motivated as much by personal greed as concern for the down-trodden poor or fear of revolution. Development of the new town was controlled by sixty commissioners, half of them Liverpool businessmen.[3] In 1842 they were persuaded by Liverpool merchant Joseph Harrison – an early settler of Birkenhead – to seek the necessary Parliamentary powers for creating a public park.

When the time came to purchase land earmarked for the project its ownership had quietly changed. The new owners were a consortium of landowners including Joseph Harrison. They had also bought land surrounding the park, an area scheduled for development as suburban housing, to include villas, terraces and crescents. Even before the park had opened the value of the building land had risen by seven times.

Design of the park was placed in the hands of Joseph Paxton, the former garden boy from Woburn who had later come to public notice as head gardener to the sixth Duke of Devonshire at Chatsworth. In his plan the park was to be divided by a main road linking the dock area with Manor Hill, the home neighbourhood of one of the commissioners, William Jackson. The park would be laid out in the new *gardenesque* style, with undulating ground, winding paths and curved wedges of tree plantation.

In a new innovation, each half would include broad expanses of open grassland with areas laid out for cricket and archery. Until Birkenhead, parks had been thought of solely as places for gentle walks. Now there was to be provision for more vigorous exercise and greater freedom of expression. While the creators of public parks may have been motivated by self interest, the places they created were soon to become the realm of the people. Municipal parks were a recognition of the urban public as a body politic.

Joseph Paxton was also the designer of an early park in Liverpool. In a plan drawn up in 1842, and now surviving as a lithograph in Liverpool Record Office, he is described as 'Garden Architect and Landscape Gardener, Chatsworth'. The design was for Prince's Park, an eighteen-hectare site in the south of the city, the property of Richard Vaughan Yates, a Liverpool landowner. The project was purely speculative. A central park – simply laid out to grass, trees and a lake – was to be surrounded by a residential development of villas and terraces, a combination first employed successfully at Regent's Park in London.

But the city corporation was slow in taking a lead from the private sector. It would be twenty-six years before Liverpool followed the example of Birkenhead and applied for powers to spend ratepayers' money on the creation of urban parks. Throughout this time new blocks of poor, insanitary housing spread outwards in an ever-widening arc from its focus at the docks. A census of 1841 showed that 56,000 people lived in the city's overcrowded courts while 20,000 more lived in cellars.[4]

The Irish potato famine of the mid-1840s further swelled the city's population as impoverished families arrived by ferry in search of a better life. The thriving port of Liverpool was gateway to the United States, making it a magnet for the destitute and defeated. Healthy, young males who failed to secure an Atlantic berth found ready work as 'navvies' building canals and later the railways. For the rest it was a life of squalor on the damp and airless streets of the city.

In the 1850s the borough surveyor, Mr Newlands, proposed that the city build a *cordon sanitaire* of parks and boulevards linking the outer suburbs. By the time the council got round to taking action the outward advance of the developers had ruled out any such grand scheme. But in the 1860s the city obtained Parliamentary powers for the purchase of land and the creation of three new parks, Newsham, Stanley and Liverpool's great green jewel, Sefton Park.

Lying to the south-east of the city, the park was laid out on a 150-hectare site bought from the Earl of Sefton in 1864. Two years later the corporation announced a public competition for the design of the park with a first prize of 300 guineas.[5] The prize went to a joint submission from Liverpool architect Lewis Hornblower, who had designed many of the features in both Birkenhead and Prince's parks, and French designer Édouard André, gardener-in-chief to the city of Paris. André brought Parisian design ideas to Liverpool, the sweeping circles and ellipses of path and driveway echoing those in the Jardin d'Acclimatation in the Bois de Boulogne.

The Sefton site included a steep valley around which André created cascades leading down to a lake. The skilful distribution of trees in small clumps and mass plantings added grandeur to the scene, providing long, uninterrupted vistas and adding to the illusion of space and distance. Within the framework of looping paths and driveways were extensive grassy areas for sports and recreation, each separated and enclosed by inspired planting, yet all bound within a grand unity by the swirling circles of the design.

Sefton Park was completed and officially handed over to the people of Liverpool in 1872 when the Duke of Connaught drove in procession from the town hall and was greeted by cheering crowds, including 5,000 seated in a specially built grandstand in front of the park gates. Across the country the park movement gathered momentum, spurred by a public health act giving local authorities the general right to buy land for public recreation. Land was donated by wealthy industrialists and entrepreneurs seeking to improve the miserable conditions in the industrial cities they had built. But as the century advanced most of the initiatives came from civic leaders and city corporations who began to see public parks as tools of social engineering.

In the Victorian view parkland was the place where 'nature could be viewed in her loveliest garb, the most obdurate heart may be softened and gently led to pursuits which refine, purify and alleviate the humblest of the toilworn. It has been firstly observed that in the same proportion as sources of innocent amusement and healthy recreation are provided for a people, so in the same proportion do they become virtuous and happy.'[6]

'The first great industrial city to open municipal parks had been Manchester in 1846, where the money had been raised by public conscription. A little over fifty years later every local authority, big or small, felt the need to provide at least one public park. By the end of the century parks had become a source of civic pride, an essential element in the urban fabric, an integral part of town life along with the public library, the municipal baths and the museum.

The earliest parks represented idealised landscapes set within the squalor of industrial development. Their designers brought to them ideas formed in the landscaping of the country estates. There were *gardenesque* features – the detailed, intricate planting of beds and borders, a celebration of the exotic to mark a growing knowledge of horticulture. Beyond these intimate areas were the broad sweeps of turf and timber, with lakes, streams and waterfalls to add movement and change.

Victorian parks were intended for spiritual improvement. As the family strolled starch-collared and corseted around the criss-cross network of paths and walkways, their minds were meant to soar above the grime and filth to find eternal verities. The healing power of nature would sooth all passion, blunt all discontent. This was the conviction of the city dignitaries and rich philanthropists as they melded that uniquely Victorian amalgam of civic duty and self-aggrandisement.

The reality was rather more complex. Soon the park creators were forced to shift the emphasis from spiritual improvement to physical recreation. People whose lives were bounded by dark, dingy courtyards and grimy machine-shop walls craved, more than anything, for space – space to run, or roam, or sit apart with a lover or the family. The park was a place to kick a ball, to enjoy a picnic, or simply to lie full-length on a green sward allowing yells and shouts of others to drift away harmlessly to the ether.

Town dwellers made parks their own. These were the only green spaces the ordinary citizen had an absolute right to occupy. The mills and factories, slums and sweatshops had been built for occupation by the labouring poor, the landless peasants whose livelihoods had been snatched away over centuries of commons' enclosure. Now they had their common acres back, if not to graze and till, then at least to enjoy some new sense of ownership.

For generations the park became one of the sunlit rooms of fond-remembered childhood. Almost everyone growing up before World War Two retained affectionate memories of visits to the local park. For the child they were a first glimpse of the vastness of the world beyond the garden and the street. They opened a window on to the wild and untamed. They provided an early experience of freedom in a setting that was safe.

As a youngster, I and my friends . . . spent nearly all the school holidays there . . . There was a café in the park . . . Beyond this there were sixteen tennis courts, where as a teenager I played tennis three or four times a week . . . Two bowling greens lay behind the tennis courts where some sunny evenings we would sit and watch older people bowling . . . Evenings, weekends and school holidays the park would be busy, and parents used to take the young children to paddle or play there. It was like a great picnic. Everyone was safe.[7]

Town parks are considered safe no longer. They have ceased to be objects of civic pride. Cash-strapped local authorities, under pressure to make efficiency savings, view them as a prime target for cuts. Manchester, the city that first pioneered urban parks by organising voluntary subscriptions to pay for them, cut its spending on them by 40 per cent in the final quarter of the twentieth century.[8] The government's own estimate of spending on parks showed a 16 per cent cutback over the last decade.[9]

Budget pressures tear the soul from public parks. Dedicated gardeners, with pride in their particular parks, are transferred to anonymous labour pools, sometimes known as 'leisure services departments', where initiative and commitment go unnoticed and unrewarded. Sometimes the work is contracted out to private companies, an arrangement that may prove adequate for routine jobs such as grass mowing, but seldom succeeds for the small, intricate tasks that once depended on the caring attention of the gardener-in-residence.

The flower beds and borders – with their rituals of planting, separating and weeding – are the first to go. There is no room for horticultural curiosities in the hard-headed world of competitive tendering. Shrubberies become overgrown through lack of trimming; streams silt up; tree plantings grow dense and dark, shading out the lower-growing flowers and shrubs, and blocking the broad vistas envisioned by the designer. The park takes on an air of neglect. And finally the vandals move in.

Statues and ornaments are smashed, trees are damaged, shelters and pavilions are smothered in graffiti. Permanent park keepers have long since vanished. In their place are park rangers – seldom assigned to any particular site – or at worst the mobile security guard. An occasional patrol by a guard in a dog van is scarcely a substitute for a regular park keeper and a team of permanent staff.

With the rise in car ownership city dwellers prefer to drive out of town for their fresh air and exercise. Why run the gauntlet of park-bench drunks and aggressive youths when the ordered world of country parks offers easy parking, unvandalised toilets and an unthreatening environment?

To Ken Worpole, a park enthusiast, the falling standard of the nation's urban green spaces reflects a wider fear. 'Is the "keeper-less park", along with the unstaffed railway station, the poorly lit underground car park, the unsupervised playground, and the deserted, night-time town centre, to become another ghost zone of modern Britain?' he asks.

The decay of the structural fabric in Britain's parks is revealed in an analysis carried out by the Heritage Lottery Fund. It shows that the rot began with the removal of metal railings and gates for the war effort. Since then the process of decay has accelerated, reaching a crisis in the final two decades of the old century. 'This period saw the loss of a huge number of bandstands, fountains, shelters, play equipment and paddling pools. Where features were not completely lost they were often abandoned, vandalised, boarded-up or rotting away.'[10]

On a cold spring morning of the new millennium a large clump of yellow daffodils are coming into flower on a grassy bank close to Sefton Park's great lake. A flotilla of ducks glides across the glassy waters, watched intently by a small child and his mother. A nearby shelter is boarded-up though it bears no stain of graffiti. André's broad, undulating landscape still looks impressive, though some of the finer details of his canvas – the flower borders, the small shrubs – are gone.

Further into the park, in one of the designer's wide, elliptical plains, a trio of dog owners try to extricate their animals from a whirling, yelping mêlée of tails and tongues and flapping ears. The owner of a boisterous English sheepdog seems especially agitated. 'Dougal, come here . . . Dougal . . . DOUGAL . . .' His frantic shouts bounce across the grass, percolate through a streamside copse where a willow stands draped in a mist of early leaf, and are lost in a denser shrubbery beyond.

In the little park café all is quiet. The sole customer of the morning – a young mountain biker – swigs his drink from a bright orange can and gazes out at the still-leafless trees. Around him the walls are hung with faded photographs of more glorious moments in the park's life: of sunlit Edwardian days when the paths were thronged with women in long skirts and men in high, starched collars and coats; of warm, summer evenings when the lights burned brightly through the glass of Henry Yates Thompson's magnificent, three-domed Palm House, now newly restored.

Steve Perkins, who runs Liverpool's parks, is hopeful there may be more glory days to come for Britain's parks. The years of cutbacks and neglect could be over, he says. A new generation of civic leaders is rediscovering the social and economic value of these grassy oases at the heart of a modern city. Their renewal can spread benefits beyond the park boundary and out into the streets. The rebirth of a great park can lead to the re-awakening of the entire city.

City parks arouse this sort of enthusiasm in those who get to know them. Perkins has worked for Liverpool's parks since he joined the council as a horticulture apprentice in the mid-1960s. Now he plans their future from a bright, spacious office in the rambling Mansion House of Calderstones Park, just east of Sefton Park. He has no doubt about their value to the community, nor about their power to catalyse social change.

'First you take a city that has hit rock-bottom economically,' he says. 'You could say that about Liverpool a few years back. Then you restore the parks and maintain them to a high standard. The neighbourhoods around them become desirable places to live, so property values start to rise. People then become protective of their local park – they take ownership of it. In this way the park becomes the focus of urban regeneration. We've seen it over and over again – in Barcelona, Boston, Chicago, New York – the same story.'

It is a story that may be repeated in Liverpool. Under a parks restoration scheme financed by the Heritage Lottery Fund, plans were drawn up to replace the neglected trees of Sefton Park. A planting programme aimed to restore the species structure and age profile of the original design. But when local residents heard rumours of change in the park, they feared it was about to be closed or zoned for development. At an impromptu protest meeting almost 200 people turned up.

All age groups were represented – from young students to octogenarians. The protestors included business people, manual workers, retired people and the unemployed. All were united in opposition to what they saw as a threat to their beloved park. They made it clear to councillors and politicians alike – there were to be no changes without their approval.

Steve Perkins remembers the stormy meeting with some satisfaction. 'It's great,' he chuckles. 'It shows people have started to take ownership of their park. It's exactly what we want to happen.'

The text-book tale of park transformation is the story of New York's Central Park. Opened in 1859, Central Park was the first landscaped public park in the United States. Its designers, Frederick Law Olmsted and English-born architect Calvert Vaux, were attempting to recreate a pastoral landscape in the English romantic tradition, including open, rolling meadows. In his search for ideas Olmsted visited Birkenhead Park twice during the 1850s, incorporating some of its features in his successful design.[11]

Like many city parks, Central Park went into a decline during the 1970s, a victim of New York's fiscal crisis which almost led to the city's bankruptcy. Many of the park's original features suffered from damage and neglect, while almost anything that did not move collected graffiti. In the public mind the park had become the haunt of vandals and muggers, and most New Yorkers gave it a wide berth. According to Timothy Marshall, the park's former deputy administrator, 'Most of the public felt that if you visited the park and got out safely you should go and buy a lottery ticket. This was your lucky day.'[12]

In a bid to restore this neglected jewel, the city authority formed a partnership with the non-profit-making Central Park Conservancy, an organisation dedicated to improving the park. Using a small army of professionals and volunteers, the conservancy cleaned off the graffiti, fixed the broken benches, cleared away rubbish and smashed glass, and repaired the land drains so that the lawns would no longer flood after heavy rain. The police agreed to step up their patrols and to use bicycles and scooters in place of the usual patrol cars, thus putting officers in closer contact with park visitors.

At the same time the conservancy embarked on a mammoth fund-raising campaign, persuading corporate and private donors to contribute almost two hundred million dollars towards capital reconstruction and maintenance. There were special family- and youth-centred activities to encourage New Yorkers to make greater use of their park, while park staff worked with teachers to extend its role as an educational resource.

The entire programme was aimed at returning the 340-hectare site in the heart of Manhattan to the people. And it worked. Over the last two decades of the century visitor numbers doubled to twenty million a year, while the crime rate dropped dramatically. As the park began to look cared-for the citizens came back and the hoodlums stayed away. New Yorkers had reclaimed their park. Now a new generation has discovered the healing power of the green sward. Central Park has returned to being what its creators intended – a pastoral retreat, a place of calm to act as an antidote to urban stress and frenetic activity.

Similar tales of park rehabilitation have been repeated across America. In Britain, too, a renaissance of municipal parks has begun. Among a handful of sites to win big grants from lottery funds was the model for the New York venture, Birkenhead Park, with its lakes, summer houses, grottos and romantic bridges. The social and health benefits of these lush, green islands set amid the constant swell of city life are again becoming recognised.

Studies have shown that human stress levels – measured by heart rate, blood pressure and excess muscle tension – are reduced within minutes of entering a park.[13] This phenomenon, known by psychologists as the 'biophillia effect', links health and social behaviour to the quality of the environment. The walk in the park is both calming and restorative. In the densely populated centre of London's Camberwell district, people have been observed to slow their walking pace as they crossed Camberwell Green.[14]

Urban parks produce a battery of environmental benefits. These green spaces act as the city's 'lungs', contributing to its ecological health, trapping dust particles and filtering out pollutants. During hot weather evaporation of moisture from the leaves of trees and grasses helps to cool the air. The turf of a football field has the cooling capacity of a large, industrial air conditioner.[15] But while the machine may be run on fossil energy, adding to the atmospheric greenhouse effect, turf takes in carbon dioxide from the air and stores it harmlessly in soil organic matter. A hectare of urban park, with its trees, grass and shrubs, is estimated to remove 600 kilograms of carbon dioxide from the air over a twelve-hour period, returning a similar amount of oxygen.

But more important than the environmental improvements are the social benefits of parkland. Inside these boundaries stressed-out city dwellers can experience a closeness to the elements, what Ken Worpole calls the 'unharmed world'. Liz Greenhalgh sees parks as places for social display just as they were in Victorian times. They are, she says, 'open public places which strangers share. They are common ground where competing groups have to find ways of coexisting. Parks are valued as places of freedom where playing, resting, running and sitting in public are all normal. Public parks can add to the mix of moods and pace of a city ... A good public park works because it is a social place, not just a green one.'[16]

The park is the place where people of all races and beliefs, of all classes and incomes, can meet on common ground. It is a unifying place, a place of encounter, adjustment and tolerance. It lies at the heart of urban life just as the green was at the heart of village life. When the working people of Britain moved from the countryside to the towns they brought their beloved grasslands with them.

The park is the common pasture set down within the built environment. When the residents of town and suburb flock to the neighbourhood park for a brass band concert or a rock music festival, they are following a pattern established centuries ago when villagers congregated on the green for fairs and markets. The soccer-playing youngsters who turn up at the local 'rec' for their weekly Sunday league fixtures would have been playing their matches on the common pasture in medieval times.

Grassland has never been solely the provider of our food. Through the ages it has been the hub of our leisure and cultural life, too. In the age of multi-screen cinemas and the worldwide web, those small squares of community turf still seem to be essential for our happiness and well-being.

17 *The Dance of Life*

In 1880 Charles Darwin – by now an honoured and respected scientist – approached his publisher, John Murray, and asked him to accept what was to be his last book. He was somewhat hesitant about it. He feared the book would be of little interest to the public. But the research had preoccupied him for many months and he wanted to see it published.[1]

Whatever Murray's reservations, he agreed to take the book. It appeared in the shops the following year, and proved surprisingly popular given the subject matter, though it failed to make the impact of *Origin of Species*. Had it done so, the British countryside might now be a very different place.

The worst excesses of intensive agriculture with its wholesale destruction of wildlife habitats might have been avoided. Brightly coloured butterflies would still flicker over flower-strewn meadows, while above them larks soared heavenwards to pour out their liquid notes on the summer air.

Darwin's final book was about earthworms. He had carefully studied their activities in the soil, particularly their ability to undermine objects placed on the ground. At Down House, his home in Kent, he had constructed a 'worm-stone' on the lawn to measure the rate at which it was drawn into the ground as a result of worm activity. He had even visited Stonehenge to inspect the great ring of monumental stones erected by the people of the Neolithic period. Many were overturned and had become imbedded in the ground like his worm-stone. He was able to demonstrate that the collapse and partial burial of these mighty stones had been caused by earthworms burrowing in the soil over many centuries.

But more important than the creature's ability to level great monuments was its role in enriching the soil and making it fertile for farming. Earthworms carry decaying leaves and other plant débris deep into the ground. There they consume it together with particles of soil, excreting a mixture of finely blended humus and mineral matter. Worms are natural agents at mixing plant residues with rock particles and converting the whole lot into fertile soil.

In his book Darwin wrote:

> The plough is one of the most ancient and valuable of man's inventions. But long before he existed the land was regularly ploughed, and still continues to be thus ploughed by earthworms. It may be doubted whether there are many other animals which have played so important a part in the history of the world as have these lowly, organised creatures.[2]

At the time of Darwin's last book British agriculture was in the process of being re-invented by chemists. Throughout history the productivity of the land had depended on the continuous return of organic matter in the form of animal dung and plant residues. The secret of fertility had been learned and protected by the Neolithic herders as they moved their cattle across the open grassland they had wrested from the forest.

In the soil organic matter is converted into humus through the activities of organisms large and small. The subsequent breakdown of humus by a different group of organisms releases nitrogen, phosphorus and other essential plant elements in a slow, steady stream through the growing season. But by the middle of the nineteenth century agricultural scientists had begun to question the need for humus and other organic matter in crop growth. Farming was on the verge of a revolution that would sweep away the traditions of 6,000 years and recreate it as an industrial activity.

The opening shots had been fired by the distinguished German chemist Baron Justus von Liebig, professor of chemistry at the University of Giessen. Liebig had become interested in the science of farming and in 1840 published the monograph *Chemistry in its Application to Agriculture and Physiology*, a report to the British Association which laid the foundations of agricultural chemistry, particularly the study of fertilisers and manures.[3]

Liebig poured scorn on the plant physiologists of his day who held that plants obtained their carbon from the soil and not from the carbonic acid of the air. Their experiments were 'fitted only to awake pity', he railed, going on to demolish the role of humus in maintaining soil fertility. What good were plant nutrients when they remained 'locked up' in a complex of organic compounds? Until they were released in soluble form they were of no use to the crop. They might as easily be added to the soil in a form that was directly available to the plant, that is, as simple inorganic fertilisers.

The exact amount of each of the major nutrients removed in a crop at harvest could be estimated from an analysis of its ash, reasoned Liebig. After that it became a simple matter to calculate the amounts of fertiliser nutrients needed to replace them. The rhythms and cycles of nature, the very dance of life, had been all but reduced to a chemical balance sheet.

> The farmer will thus be enabled, like a systematic manufacturer, to have a book attached to each field, in which he will note the amount of the various ingredients removed from the land in the form of crops, and therefore how much he must restore to bring it to its original state of fertility. He will also be able to express in pounds weight how much of one or other ingredient of soils he must add to his own land in order to increase its fertility for certain kinds of plants.[4]

The recycling of nutrients in organic form – the central process of agriculture down the ages – was now unnecessary. In essence farming was to be conducted by the application of chemical fertilisers rather than by manipulation of biological cycles. Many farmers took to the new methods with enthusiasm. This was the age of science and reason. The old truths of fertility based on natural processes had been subjected to the same penetrating logic that had spawned a new industrial society and a dynamic economy. The spirit of change was in the air, liberally charged with a non-conformity, and the larger farmers wanted to be a part.

Had Darwin's book on earthworms received more attention it might have provided a counterbalance for the confident urgings of the chemists. By drawing attention to the soil's biological activity it exposed the shortcomings of the view that crop growth was nothing more than a simple chemical process. But the book arrived too late. As an academic discipline, chemistry was in the ascendancy. The science of ecology had not yet staked its ground. The battle for humus was already lost under the crushing onslaught of hard science.

Following publication of Liebig's monograph, the fertiliser manufacturer John Bennet Lawes (who later became the founder of the Park Grass Experiment) set up the first long-term experiment on his Rothamsted estate in Hertfordshire. In a field known as Broadbalk he grew a series of wheat crops year after year, treating them with a range of fertilisers from traditional farmyard manure to artificials.

In 1881 he appeared before a Royal Commission to argue that the debate about the relative merits of organic and chemical fertilisers was meaningless. There was no difference. They merely supplied the required plant nutrients in different forms.[5] By the time of his death the Broadbalk field had produced fifty-seven consecutive wheat crops, some of which had been grown solely with artificial fertilisers.

But many farmers believed that muck was the only lasting source of fertility. They condemned the new chemicals as 'no more than whips and spurs wherewith the bad farmer might urge the soil to special efforts and drive it the more rapidly to exhaustion'.[6] One worried correspondent wrote to *The Times*:

> In the poorer soils, which include a great proportion of the more level cultivable portion of the globe, the vegetable mould [humus] is fast suffering exhaustion under the present system . . . In the case of a heavy crop being produced by the artificial small manures so much vaunted by Liebig and his followers, there results a great exhaustion of the other components of the soil not easily to be recovered.[7]

But the chemical revolution seemed unstoppable, partly because of the powerful commercial forces driving it. In just twenty years the manufacture and sale of artificial fertilisers had, in the words of Augustus Voelcker, consulting chemist to the Royal Agricultural Society, risen from 'a venturous speculation' to 'a legitimate, well-regulated business' of huge proportions.[8]

In the decade to 1870 the number of fertiliser factories had risen from twenty to eighty at sites all over the country.[9] Most were in the business of manufacturing 'superphosphate', made by dissolving naturally occurring nodules of calcium phosphate – known as coprolites – in sulphuric acid, in the same way as bones.

Not that the new 'scientific agriculture' was without its pitfalls. One early pioneer of chemical farming wrote of his first experience with nitrate of soda as a top-dressing for his grassland.

> This salt had been only recently introduced to the notice of agriculturalists, and I watched the result with considerable interest. The field soon assumed a deep green colour, and showed unmistakable signs of vigorous growth. It was stocked with sheep which, coming from turnips, ate it well; but, to my surprise, they were seized with scour, and did not thrive. I had not then become aware that agricultural products raised by heavy dressings of nitrogenous manure are always of inferior quality and unwholesome for stock . . . if ammonia, which is extremely soluble, be presented in excess

when compared with the other elements of their growth, the result is that sap is circulated through the plant of too stimulating character. This produces in the vegetable organisms results somewhat similar to those too often observed in the human subject who imbibes too much soluble matter of a stimulating kind: viz., high colour and vigorous vitality, but with a tendency to premature decay. In short, plants so treated are on the high-road to gout.[10]

Despite its limitations, chemical agriculture was given a boost by the tide of American imports flowing in during the final quarter of the nineteenth century. As prices fell and farming slipped deeper into depression, thousands of acres of crop land were sown down to grass. A growing number of farmers chose to fertilise it with the cheap, new products of the chemical companies. Those who opted to persevere with arable farming turned to artificials to reduce their production costs. Some went wholeheartedly into industrial wheat growing, taking their lead from Lawes and his results at Rothamsted.

They abandoned the old crop rotations, the grass leys and the root crops grown for feeding livestock whose dung then restored the fertility of the crop land. Instead they relied on chemical fertilisers to maintain the yields of their wheat crops, now grown year after year without a break. At the same time they brought in steam-powered ploughs and threshing machines to replace regular staff, turning their farms into highly mechanised 'wheat factories'. In Berkshire George Baylis found it so profitable to fertilise his cereal crops with chemical compounds in place of livestock manure that he built up enough cash to rent or buy more than twenty farms totalling 9,000 hectares, and this at a time of depression.[11]

The new philosophy took root among an influential group of innovative, mostly large farmers, though it would take a century to achieve total dominance, helped by the largesse of a bountiful European state. Those farmers who held to the view that fertility was the culmination of natural processes were stigmatised as backward-looking and anti-scientific. Farming was no longer an art to be learned at a parent's knee and perfected over a lifetime's acquaintance with the local soil and landscape. Now it could be conducted from a blueprint, a standard prescription that might be applied anywhere in the land. The culture had gone from agriculture.

Among the first casualties was the grass ley, that gift of the pastoral kingdom to the world of tillage and crops. The mainspring of the eighteenth-century farming revolution, the ley had been for generations the bringer of fertility to overworked crop lands. Farmers no longer needed it. They could restore their arable land to good heart by applying a cocktail of chemical fertilisers, or so they believed.

But while the new scientific agriculture produced an early crop of 'wheat factories' in the arable areas of eastern England, it had an even bigger impact in the grassland areas of the west and north. On the permanent grazings of the heavy clay country, and on the high pastures of the hills and uplands, flowers and slow-growing grass species began to disappear. Soluble forms of nitrate and potash create the conditions in which a few aggressive species come to dominate the turf, crowding out the less competitive species and drastically reducing botanical diversity.

Edmund Ruck, the Wiltshire farmer who had drained his land with the Fowler steam plough, was delighted with the effect of a couple of dressings of 'artificials' on the quality of his hay crop. Before the improvement his meadow had been filled with 'filth of all kinds', including knapweed, *Centaurea nigra*, spiny restharrow, *Ononis spinosa*, and the purple devil's-bit scabious, *Succisa pratensis*. Now such unproductive species had gone, together with slow-growing grasses like crested dog's-tail and quaking-grass. Faster-growing grasses such as smooth-stalked meadow grass and timothy had taken over, the herbage becoming 'more simple in character'.

The chemical habit did more than drive wild flowers from the fields. It eroded the soil's organic matter and humus, the age-old repository of wealth and fertility. The chemical balance sheets of the nineteenth century gave birth to modern agribusiness, with its monocultures, livestock factories, giant machines and addiction to pesticides. By the close of the twentieth century industrial agriculture had begun to alter global weather systems and heighten the risk of an environmental cataclysm.

But the innovators of chemical farming did not get their way without a struggle. In the years leading up to World War Two the chorus of protest against it was swelled by many influential voices, including those of the writer H. J. Massingham and Richard de la Mare, son of the poet Walter de la Mare.

The most informed objections came from an agricultural scientist, Sir Albert Howard, who had spent much of his early career in India. A former president of the Indian Science Congress, Howard had been director of the Institute of Plant Industry in the state of Indore. There he had applied modern scientific knowledge to the ancient practice of composting, subsequently developing the 'Indore process', which mimicked the natural process of humus formation taking place on the forest floor.[12]

Animal and vegetable wastes accumulate under forest trees where they are exposed to air and water filtering down through the leaves. Howard felt that farmers ought to imitate this natural process, producing soils rich in humus. In these soils plants were nourished by the direct absorption of soluble nutrients through their roots, and also through a symbiotic association with certain soil fungi. Only when plants were nourished in this dual way, he argued, were they healthy enough to resist disease and produce wholesome, health-giving foods.[13]

In marked contrast, plants grown in infertile soils, which had been 'stimulated' with chemical fertilisers, were only partially nourished. As a result they suffered more disease so that their produce was of impaired quality. Animals and human beings eating this produce would be less than healthy in their turn.

Fired by such ideas Howard returned from India in the early 1930s to mount an energetic campaign against what he considered to be a hazardous and short-sighted system of agriculture. He accused farmers of 'robbing the future' in their desperate pursuit of higher yields. Like the homesteaders on the American prairies, they had cashed in the future fertility of their land.

Agricultural science has been based on premises which are, to say the least of it, incomplete. The results have been disastrous. Undue emphasis has been laid on the maintenance of the soil solution and the use of artificial manures, which history will condemn as one of the greatest misfortunes to have befallen agriculture and mankind. We have now to retrace our steps, to jettison the theories and practice based on the work of the disciples of Liebig and of experiment stations like Rothamsted. We have to go back to nature and to copy the methods to be seen in the forest and prairie.[14]

Heartened by Howard's strong advocacy, the opponents of chemical farming grew in strength and confidence. In the autumn of 1943 the 'great humus controversy' reached the House of Lords. Under spirited attack the Duke of Norfolk, joint Parliamentary Secretary to the Minister of Agriculture, was forced to deny any government connivance with an influential chemical industry: 'I wish to deprecate any suggestion of antagonism between chemical fertilisers and humus. There is no evidence that a balanced use of fertilisers has a harmful affect on soil, crops or man, or, I might add, on the influence and profits of ICI.'[15]

By the close of World War Two, opposition to the chemical orthodoxy had hardened into a strong organic lobby from which arose the Soil Association. However, it failed to deflect mainstream agriculture from its headlong rush toward industrialisation. Charles Stewart Orwin, a leading land agent and director of Oxford University's Agricultural Economics Research Institute, replied to farming's critics:

Do we want 'to secure a healthy race of people by feeding them on healthy crops grown on healthy soil', to quote the *cliché* which is heard so often nowadays? Do we want, in other words, to forget all that the agricultural chemists have taught us, and to return to the 'balanced agriculture', a simple crops–and–livestock economy, of a hundred years ago? This is not rural reconstruction, it is reaction and prejudice.[16]

A return to 'balanced agriculture' might have been a good deal healthier for agriculture and the nation. In a Somerset wheat field, soil fertility consultant Robert Plumb crouches in the short trench he has dug in the autumn stubble. He is about to make a close inspection of the soil profile, the exposed cross-section of earth down to a depth of a metre and a half. At the start of a new millennium he spends a considerable part of his working life looking at agricultural soils. He is not happy about what he has found.

For a few moments he looks intently at the exposed surface. The colour is far from uniform. Distinct 'horizons' or layers are visible, each easily distinguishable by subtle changes in colour. The upper few centimetres are dark brown shading into a narrow grey band at a depth of twenty centimetres. At the very centre of this band runs a dark seam, like the stripe running through toothpaste. Below this the soil is brown but of a lighter shade than the topsoil.

Robert Plumb picks at the dark seam with a penknife. It is soft and slimy with blackened fragments of straw clearly visible, the undecomposed remnants of an earlier harvest. He has seen this many times before. It is a classic sign of compacted soil. 'There's no air getting through,' he explains. 'That means you have anaerobic conditions with formaldehyde produced. That'll pickle anything in sight. It's what they used on Egyptian mummies. Not many plant roots would have made it through a layer like that.'

He studies the exposed surface, looking for some sign of life – an invertebrate such as springtail or one of the larger soil nematodes; a worm channel, or a plant root that has managed somehow to get through the compacted layer and reach the lower horizons. In a healthy soil, roots will stretch down four metres or more, threading their way through the fissures and air channels in their quest for nutrients. But this is not a healthy soil. Most of the roots left from the crop now harvested are bunched up in the top few centimetres.

The grain yield from this soil will have been low, probably no more than eight tonnes a hectare. This would scarcely cover the farmer's input costs – the seed, pesticides, herbicides, fertilisers, growth regulators and all the other chemical aids most cereal growers rely on. Back in the 1960s this land would have been in a rotation which included a grass ley to break up the run of arable crops and put organic matter back in the soil. But this farm, like many others, has long abandoned mixed farming. Now the land must produce arable crops year after year without a break, urged on by a cocktail of chemicals. Not surprisingly, it is becoming exhausted and sick.

'There's one that's made it.' Robert Plumb has found a lone fragment of plant root near to the base of the trench. There are no others. The life has gone out of this soil. A healthy soil would be teeming with life – bacteria and microscopic protozoa; moulds and algae, and the larger soil fauna, including slugs, caterpillars, centipedes, millipedes, spiders, beetles, mites and springtails. And, of course, there would be earthworms. A soil in good condition would support a couple of dozen worms to the spadeful, burrowing deep into the subsoil, opening up air channels, carrying down organic matter, creating humus.

This soil appears to have none. Under an annual deluge of agrochemicals and fertilisers its structure has all but collapsed. To provide a healthy growing medium for plants, soils need a good crumb structure, produced when clay particles aggregate together, or *flocculate*. Clay particles are able to do this because they carry negative electrical charges to which plant nutrients such as calcium, potassium and magnesium become bound.

But this healthy condition is easily disturbed when the soluble nutrients in the soil become imbalanced. The ratio of calcium to magnesium is particularly important in maintaining a sound soil structure. Many chemical fertilisers supply soil nutrients in forms which damage soils by disrupting their essential mineral balance. The crumb structure breaks down, the mineral particles collapse into a dense mass, air spaces disappear, anaerobic organisms take over, producing diseased plants. Healthy soil life is extinguished. At that point the farmer calls in a soil fertility expert.

For many years Robert Plumb worked in the conventional fertiliser business. Then he began to discover how, wrongly used, these products could do great damage to the planet and its life systems. He began to read the scientific literature, particularly research done on the prairie states in America, where modern, industrial farming methods have taken a heavy toll on a once-fertile landscape. Now, in middle age, he has re-invented himself as a healer of sick soils, a restorer of healthy life to farmlands ailing from decades of chemical abuse.

Working from a Norfolk base, his company will carry out a full health check on a problem soil, analysing mineral levels and assessing the degree of biological activity, a key indicator of its ability to grow good crops. There will follow a programme of remedial action designed to restore structure and vitality to the soil. Nutrient imbalances will be corrected and a humus supplement may be recommended to liven up moribund organic cycles. Special cultivations may be necessary to open up heavily compacted soils.

Robert Plumb's services are much in demand these days. For all their spending on chemicals, farmers are not harvesting the heavy crops they expect. Often their yields are no higher than they were twenty years ago, despite better crop varieties and heavy inputs of sprays and fertilisers. Robert Plumb knows the reason. The soil – starting point for life on the planet – has been exploited to the point of exhaustion. The age-old secret of fertility is no longer understood by farmers. The lesson of grassland is easily forgotten.

At Rothamsted – now a publicly funded farm research institute – the Broadbalk experiment set up by John Bennet Lawes still continues after more than 150 years. The plots fertilised by artificial fertilisers during this period now have an organic matter content of less than 2 per cent, little different from the plots that have received no fertilisers for over a century and a half. But the organic matter content of plots receiving traditional farmyard manure is more than twice as high and rising, despite producing a cereal crop every year. Though not the equal of a grass ley, animal manure provides some of the benefits of mixed farming.

The ultimate destination of all soil organic matter is the family of complex organic compounds known collectively as humus. Some are remarkably durable. Some may have been formed in

Neolithic times when the nomadic herders followed their cattle across the open downland. Other humus molecules break down almost as soon as they are formed, releasing their store of nutrients for the roots of growing plants to take up.

Humus is at the heart of a productive soil. Like clay particles it forms aggregates, helping to give the soil a crumb structure, the perfect growing medium for crops. And, like clay particles, its electrically charged surfaces enable it to bind nutrients so they are not leached from the soil in rainwater. Humus has another useful characteristic: by creating a crumb structure it opens up air spaces, allowing the soil to hold water, to soak it up like a sponge. Soils rich in humus and other organic materials are able to support growing plants even in times of drought. Soils whose organic matter has been depleted by years of chemical farming need constant irrigation in dry weather.

Soil is not an inert material. Its mineral particles are enmeshed in a teeming mass of life forms whose myriad activities provide the starting point for life on earth. Humus is the hub of a whirling, rhythmic dance, an explosion of living energy which regulates the health of the planet. And chemical farming is steadily destroying it.

Chemical companies claim their fertilisers supply essential plant nutrients in soluble forms that are readily accessible to crops. But many artificial fertilisers have another effect. They fracture and destroy humus molecules, allowing the instant release of nutrients that would otherwise have been made available to plants over a long period. While plant roots may capture some of this sudden flush of nutrients, most are washed away with the drainage water. Meanwhile the breaking up of humus molecules will have damaged the soil structure and made it less productive, even when bombarded with chemical fertilisers. It is because farmers have begun to notice these effects that soil fertility experts like Robert Plumb are kept busy.

It is the nature of life on this planet that all things are connected. The decline of a species here will have its knock-on effects elsewhere, perhaps in ways that are unpredictable. In the 1980s, when subsidised, high-input farming was powering ahead, ornithologists began to notice an alarming fall in the numbers of many farmland birds. Once-common species such as the tree sparrow, bullfinch, song thrush, spotted flycatcher, linnet, lapwing and skylark had all gone into a steep decline. They were victims neither of disease nor climatic change. They were early casualties of the slow destruction of soil fertility.

The loss of humus and organic matter diminishes the life of the soil. The run-down begins with microscopic inhabitants – the protozoa, bacteria, fungi and algae which make up the base of the food chain. Next to be affected are the micro-fauna – the rotifers and nematodes living in water films, and the mites, springtails and small insects living in soil air spaces. Then the larger invertebrates go into a decline – the enchytraeid worms and earthworms, the millipedes and centipedes, the dipterous flies and the beetles.

Insect-eating birds are the next to be hit – lapwings, grey partridges, corncrakes and skylarks – along with the small mammals, the shrews and voles. Finally the larger carnivores are affected, the stoats and weasels, the kestrels and the barn owls. And so the landscape falls silent. The health of countryside is sustained by the life of the soil, the ceaseless pulse of decay and renewal that beats in a fertile earth. As chemical farming clogs the soil channels, the pulse is weakened and all life suffers. And there is no reason to suppose that human beings escape the consequences.

The early pioneers of the organic movement were concerned less with the damage to wildlife than with the effects of industrial agriculture on human health. In 1942 Lord Teviot wrote a strongly worded letter to the press demanding government action:

I am convinced from my own studies of the experiments, tests and experiences of many learned men in medicine and agriculture, that the chief cause of disease in man, plant and animal is due to their food. There is outstanding evidence . . . that food produced from soil deficient in rich, healthy humus is a source of ill health. The tests which have been made demonstrate that food grown from fertile soil, rich in humus, means good health and happiness, while the same food produced from soil impregnated with chemical artificial fertilisers causes bad health and sterility.[17]

Some of the evidence had come from the work of Robert McCarrison – later Major-General Sir Robert McCarrison – who joined the Indian Medical Service in 1901. During his time in India he had encountered a tribal people known as Hunzas, whose country lay close to the north-west frontier. He was struck by their extraordinary health and vitality, a quality he attributed to their diet and to their system of farming. The Hunzas returned every scrap of organic matter to the land, including animal wastes, plant wastes and human sewage. All were carefully mixed and composted before being spread on to the fields.

It was a system that seemed to emulate the natural processes taking place in forest and prairie soils, and it had been practised for thousands of years by many ancient peoples including the Chinese and Japanese. In the Hunza people it produced a strength and stamina that amazed British colonialists like McCarrison. The encounter inspired him to abandon the conventional approach of medical science and study instead the life styles of healthy human beings. How was it, he wondered, that some peoples could become such impressive physical specimens while others – notably those of western industrial countries – battled constantly with illness?

Writing of McCarrison's work, Dr Guy Theodore Wrench concludes that western medicine has looked for its solutions in the wrong places:

The prevention and banishment of disease are primarily matters of food; secondarily, of suitable conditions of environment. Antiseptics, medicaments, inoculations and extirpating operations evade the real problem. Disease is the censor pointing out the humans, animals and plants who are imperfectly nourished. Its continuance and its increase are proofs that the methods used obscure, they do not attack, the radical problem.[18]

The destruction of farmland fertility – principally by the replacement of grass leys and manure with chemical fertilisers – has had an equally damaging impact on the health of the planet. When the Earth was young its atmosphere contained too much carbon dioxide for human existence. But the activities of plants and animals slowly reduced the atmospheric load, locking it up in the biosphere, the territory of living organisms. Much of it is now held in the great fossil deposits of coal and oil, and the limestone deposits of fossil bone.

There are other 'active' carbon sinks, constantly being replenished with carbon from the atmosphere or giving it back in the form of carbon dioxide. The oceans act as a major carbon 'store', holding huge quantities as dissolved carbon dioxide and methane. Forest lands make up another important sink, the leaves taking in carbon from the air and locking it up as woody biomass. A third major instrument of planetary carbon regulation are the world's cultivated lands, the fifteen million square kilometres of the Earth's surface that is under the plough.

A fertile soil may easily contain 10 per cent organic matter in the top thirty centimetres, a total of about 400 tons of soil organic matter in every hectare of land. But with their battery of artificial fertilisers and agrochemicals arable farmers have waged a ceaseless war on soil organic matter for decades. As a result the bank of fertility – a legacy of the generations who farmed the land before them – has been virtually exhausted.

Many soils under continuous cultivation now contain less than 1 per cent organic matter, amounting to just forty tonnes per hectare. The lost organic matter has not simply disappeared. The carbon it held has been released back into the atmosphere as carbon dioxide, adding to planetary warming. The deliberate squandering of soil fertility by intensive agriculture has been a major cause of the greenhouse effect. At the same time the chemicals used to replace the soil's real fertility – the vast armoury of chemical fertilisers and pesticide sprays – all consume large quantities of fossil fuel energy in their manufacture, adding to pressures on global life-support processes. Not only does industrial agriculture degrade the quality of food and obliterate wildlife, it is a direct and major cause of disruption to the Earth's weather patterns.

The extra atmospheric load of carbon that is the cause of global warming is not large. Throughout history the carbon dioxide content of the atmosphere remained at around 280 parts per million. With the widespread burning of fossil fuels it has now risen to 350 parts per million. This additional carbon load of just seventy parts per million is responsible for the droughts and cyclones, the floods and hurricanes that have so alarmed climate scientists. The total amount of carbon released annually by the burning of fossil fuels amounts to less than one half per cent of the carbon locked up in soil organic matter.

A return to sound husbandry in agriculture would end global warming without the need for motoring cuts. Simply by raising the organic matter content of cultivated land by a percentage point or two – returning them to the levels of thirty years ago – we would go a long way towards solving the problem. The techniques for achieving it are well known. They are the techniques practised by farmers through all history until Liebig debunked them in the nineteenth century.

While crop lands could play a part in cleaning up the world's atmosphere, grasslands could do the job at a stroke. In 1954 at a long-defunct research station near Maidenhead in Berkshire, a team of scientists embarked on a thirty-year experiment to compare soil conditions under grazed pasture and continuous cultivation for crops.[19] Each year they ploughed, sowed and harvested their arable plots, putting on the same chemical fertilisers that farmers were using across Britain. They also applied fertilisers to the adjoining grassland plots, though they were receiving dung from the cattle and sheep that grazed them.

At the time the experiment ended in the mid-1980s, British farmers had embarked on a new round of intensification, enticed by the tempting subsidies on offer from the European Community. Specialism was the new creed. Every farmer with land good enough to grow a half decent cereal crop abandoned mixed farming, sold off the livestock, ploughed up the grass leys and sowed the whole lot to grain crops. Of course, to make the system work they had to become even more dependent on chemical fertilisers and pesticides, driving tramlines through their crops so they could go in with the sprayer or the fertiliser spreader at any time in the growing season.

In the fevered climate of state-driven expansion, the results from the Berkshire experiment attracted little attention. But they revealed clearly the damage caused by modern industrial agriculture. After thirty years of continuous cropping the level of soil organic matter had fallen by a third, even from its low starting point. The soil now contained little more than 1 per cent organic matter, a condition that had left the upper layers compacted, seriously prone to drought and incapable of producing a healthy crop without an annual fix of chemicals. This over-exploited soil had lost most of its earthworms, even developing a plough pan – a solid layer without cracks or air spaces – through which no plant root can penetrate.

By contrast the soil under pasture showed a steady rise in fertility. It contained four or five times as many earthworms as the arable plots, and since they were bigger, the combined weight of worms under grass was at least ten times higher than the total under cereals. The action of earthworms in creating a well-aerated surface layer, rich in soil nutrients, produced a steady increase in grass growth year by year. More important, the level of organic matter increased by 55 per cent in the first ten years, equivalent to an annual increase of one tonne of carbon to every hectare.

Grasslands are the unsung purifiers of the earth's atmosphere. Everyone acknowledges the role of forests in cleaning up the air and stabilising climatic systems, but grasslands store as much carbon in the organic matter of their soils as temperate forests and far more than tropical rain forests. Every acre of park, every patch of green space between city buildings, every sunlit meadow is contributing to the survival of the planet, taking in carbon from the atmosphere and locking up some of it safely in the soil.

Many of the earth's grasslands are now threatened by the plough, or by the remorseless loss of their fertility to chemical fertilisers. Rangelands are equally threatened by overgrazing, the slow obliteration of fragile ecosystems by overstocking with too many cattle and sheep. If somehow we can manage to protect it, this vast kingdom of grass will save the polar icecaps and restore disrupted weather patterns. At the same time it will provide a healthier food supply. The only losers will be those with shares in the chemical industry. The winners will be everyone else on earth.

In the war-troubled winter of 1941 Newman Turner, a university-trained agriculturalist, took over the running of Goosegreen, a low-lying mixed farm on Somerset clay land in the village of Sutton Mallet, near Bridgwater. The farm had been neglected and run down, though the cows milked well enough on their diet of imported concentrate feeds. And the arable fields seemed to produce reasonable crops with the aid of artificial fertilisers. Turner set out to run the farm on 'orthodox' lines, buying all the chemical fertilisers that were available in a war-time economy.

His reward, as he later related in his book *Fertility Farming*, was a hefty trading loss, a dairy herd riddled with contagious abortion and tuberculosis, and a corn crop ruined by the diseases smut and take-all. When he got the chance to buy the farm he decided to run it differently.

I would manure the fields as nature intended; I would stop exhausting the fertility of my fields and give them the recuperative benefit of variety. My cows would no longer have to act as machines, with compound cakes going in at one end and milk and calves coming out at the other. I would return them as nearly as possible to their natural lives . . . All the food would be home-grown on land filled with farmyard manure, compost and green crop manure. Artificial fertilisers, which had left my soil solid and impossible to live in for almost any form of soil life, were dispensed with entirely. Not only because I was at last convinced of the disaster they had brought upon me, but because I could no longer afford to buy them . . . This kind of farming restored life to a dying farm. Everything on the farm, from the soil teeming with life and fertility, to the cows all pregnant or in full milk, and to the farmer and his family full of energy and good health, acclaim the rightness of this policy.[20]

The unorthodox approach brought the farm to profit. With the herd now free of disease there were big savings on veterinary and medicine bills, plus cuts in feed and labour costs. At the same time yields went up, exceeding those of neighbouring crops still grown with the aid of artificial fertilisers.

From a herd riddled with abortion and tuberculosis, in which few calves were born to full time, and those few that reached due date were dead, I can now walk around sheds full of healthy calves, and cows normally sterile now heavy in calf or in milk ... Cows that have been sterile for two and three years have given birth to healthy calves. On the orthodox farm there is no hope for these cases, and the animals are slaughtered as 'barreners'. But nature intended the cow to continue breeding into old age, and if treated as nature intended there is every chance that her breeding capacity can be restored.

Turner claimed that the farming methods he advocated were 'simple and effective' – they could be applied on the poorest of farms by the poorest of farmers. Success was 'within the reach of any farmer who will turn back to fertility farming, and eschew the "get-rich-quick" methods of commercialised science, which are in fact a snare'.

18   *The Dying of the Green*

E ven before the scourge of foot-and-mouth disease, rural grassland had been under savage and sustained attack. It is as if the nation of pasture and meadow were bent on obliterating all traces of its pastoral heritage.

For decades farm subsidies have provided farmers with a powerful inducement to abandon crop rotations based on the fertility-building grass ley, and rely instead on chemical fertilisers to maintain crop yields. Ever since the agricultural revolution of the eighteenth century, mixed farming has been the prime source of village wealth and prosperity. Now rural Britain has staked its future on tiny white nuggets of ammonium nitrate, the explosive gift of a strong and persuasive chemical industry.

During the final quarter of the twentieth century farmers abandoned livestock in their droves, ploughing up their pastures, grubbing out hedges, and sowing the land to cereal monocultures. Compared with the rigours of livestock keeping this was easy, 'office-hours' farming. Suddenly they were freed from the ceaseless round of care and devotion to animals. They were no longer 'tied to the cow's tail'. Once the harvest was in and the autumn crop sown, the new wheat lords could jet off in search of winter sun.

The endless expanses of cereals that resulted from the changes presented a perfect target for crop pests and diseases. But an innovative agrochemical industry was ready with a battery of chemical weapons to spray across the crop-land war zone. In the ten years to 1980 the area of cereal crops treated with fungicides rose from virtually zero to almost three million hectares, chiefly because increasing levels of artificial nitrogen had made the plants more susceptible to disease, particularly mildew.[1]

With the grass ley gone, farmers were now wholly dependent on the chemical industry for fertility and disease control. They had replaced age-old biological cycles with an agriculture powered and sustained by fossil fuels. The fertilisers and pesticides on which they relied were produced with vast inputs of oil. The cost was largely borne by taxpayers through the farm-subsidy system.

As the remnants of a pastoral culture were stripped from Britain's arable areas, so the permanent grasslands of the west came under their own attack. Livestock displaced from the former mixed-farming areas became concentrated in the wetter areas of the west and north. Here herds and flocks grew ever larger as specialist meat and dairy producers expanded with the aid of their own generous subsidies.

To feed their expanding herds livestock farmers adopted their own form of intensive cropping – the monoculture of grass. Traditional species-rich meadows and pastures have all but disappeared from the British countryside. In their place are the seemingly endless expanses of single-species grassland. Most contain the aggressive perennial ryegrass, goaded into ever higher levels of production by constant applications of chemical fertiliser.

During World War Two the average application of nitrogen fertiliser to grassland amounted to just five kilograms per hectare. By the 1980s the average had risen by more than a hundredfold.[2] Some farmers were driving their pastures by applying annual nitrogen doses of more than 600 kilograms a hectare.

This was no longer pastoralism. It was a form of green industrialism – production by attrition. Under the weight of this sustained chemical assault the natural, humus-building processes of the soil collapsed. The wild herbs and flowers disappeared from the turf along with the fine, slow-growing grass species. With them went a myriad of other life forms – beetles and butterflies, small mammals and songbirds. The green clad hills of the west became as silent and lifeless as the arable monocultures of eastern Britain.

The new lords of the land were executives of the major chemical companies – Bayer and Monsanto, UKF and ICI. The successors of Von Liebig had become inheritors of the earth. This is not what the scientist and visionary George Stapledon had envisaged when he set out to revitalise the nation's pastoral economy at the start of the century. He had dreamed of a rural renaissance built upon the exploitation of grassland. What followed was a relentless process of industrialisation that cost a million rural jobs and drove thousands of family farms out of business.

George Stapledon – the greatest champion of British grassland in modern times – was born in 1882 into a family that had once produced a Lord Chancellor of England.[3] His father, a master mariner, had married into the family that built the last wooden ships at Appledor in north Devon. Then, at the age of forty, he had gambled everything on the success of the newly constructed Suez Canal, opening up a shipping agency in Port Said.

After taking a science Tripos at Cambridge, the young George spent a year working in his father's business at Suez. There he glimpsed the frenetic world of international trade, the 'hurried toiling of our age of smoke and light-hearted squandering of the patient labouring of natural forces . . .'[4]

For all its restless energy, the world of international commerce seemed to Stapledon a precarious foundation for a nation's health and prosperity. Even as he watched the great steamships discharging their cargoes and coaling for the next sailing, he dreamed of a society based on the natural bounty of the soil, and particularly on the productivity of its grasslands. A quarter of a century later he would write: 'Grassland, especially with the sea, is to be regarded as one of the corner stones on which the greatness of the British Empire has been built.'[5]

Stapledon returned to Cambridge to take a Diploma in Agriculture, and in 1910 joined the staff of the Royal Agricultural College in Cirencester. On the bare Cotswold hills he witnessed the consequences of an untrammelled free trade, given form in the feverish comings-and-goings of Port Said. This was a countryside brought close to ruin by neglect and under-investment.

Five centuries earlier the same Cotswold landscape had been enriched by international trade. Then the grass-covered hills had been peppered with sheep whose fleeces had built the great wool churches and the stately houses of merchants.

Now the fickle benefactor of free capital had bestowed its favours elsewhere, and the once-comfortable villages had slipped into decay. Around them the pastures had become worn-out and unproductive. Many had been re-sown with cheap imported seed, ill-suited to the local conditions. The great Cotswold estates were chiefly concerned with country sports. Farming was considered of secondary importance.[6]

It was while walking these forsaken hills that Stapledon formulated his ideas on ecology. For him no single organism spoke with an individual voice. Instead each contributed to a great natural chorus, sometimes discordant, sometimes sweetly harmonic, yet always under the influence of those around it. In the scorched summer days of 1911 he watched the sown grass leys turn brown and wither, while the wild grasses of the hedgebank and roadside verge remained green and vigorous. Nature seemed to have laid on a vast experiment for the benefit of the young grassland biologist.

In 1912 Stapledon joined the staff of the University College of Wales in Aberystwyth. In upland Wales he found another landscape wrecked and depopulated by economic neglect. As on the Cotswolds, the grass seeds sown by local farmers produced thin, poor pastures, unproductive and lacking in persistence.

Stapledon resolved to bring prosperity back to rural Britain by unlocking the wealth of her grasslands, that ancient treasury first opened by the Neolithic herders of the high country. But it would take two world wars to produce the political will for such a 'green revolution'. During World War One the country's grasslands were ploughed up on a vast scale as part of the national drive to grow more wheat. With the coming of peace it became apparent, even to politicians, that the nation's stocks of grass seed were too poor to produce the productive pastures now badly needed. So the Welsh Plant Breeding Station was established in Aberystwyth, with Stapledon as its first director.

He surrounded himself with a team of imaginative and committed scientists whose very names have passed into the folklore of Welsh agriculture – T. J. Jenkin, William Davies, Gwilym Evans, E. T. Jones and R. D. Williams. Together they embarked on a great crusade – to rebuild the nation's pastoral wealth.

Stapledon had long realised that the native or indigenous strains of grasses and clovers were far superior to the 'commercial' varieties sold by seeds merchants, chiefly because they were better adapted to the local environment. The Aberystwyth team spent their early years building up a collection of grasses from sites all over the country. Back at the station these were planted out and assessed for such useful qualities as growth rate, leafiness, frost hardiness and longevity.

The more promising individuals were incorporated into breeding programmes from which emerged the famous 'S' varieties: a family of grasses and clovers bred at Aberystwyth. They included the cocksfoot, S26, bred from a clutch of plants gathered on a gorse brake in Devon; the clovers S100 and S123, developed from the local strains Montgomery Red and Cornish Marl; and the legendary perennial ryegrass, S23, which was to make up many of the early grass monocultures of the 1960s, the beginnings of industrial agriculture.

In the evaluation of wild strains from around the country, Stapledon urged his colleagues to seek out the exceptional. He was interested in every single plant since its progeny might reveal some quality of use to humanity. Within what appeared to be uniform races of plants and animals there were huge differences, even 'contraries'. Through interbreeding and the combining of such differences, breeders might create exciting new varieties, grasses that would bring productivity back to meadows and pasture-land, and prosperity back to village Britain.

> When I was a student cocksfoot was just cocksfoot, and red clover just red clover. For several years I taught students and lectured to farmers on this fantastically false foundation. Then I had the shock of my life . . . I realised that living things, if at all highly organised – are true to a pattern, yes, but only within limits . . . within themselves they are unique, individualistic, and, one might almost say, egotistical in all their subtle and vital characteristics.[7]

With a clutch of new pedigree grasses and clovers to his credit, Stapledon set out to show how grassland improvement might bring prosperity back to the impoverished Welsh hills. His first field-scale experiments began in the early 1930s on the land of one Captain Bennett-Evans of Llangurig, an eccentric farmer who was conducting a protracted and acrimonious campaign against the Forestry Commission.[8]

Using their new Caterpillar tractor, the Aberystwyth team cultivated or ploughed large tracts of steep hill grassland, sowing the land with the new grass and clover varieties. Stapledon carefully monitored the productivity of the re-sown swards at different levels of fertiliser and grazing. Years later he wrote a moving tribute to his former partner in hill land reclamation.

> I remember motoring into Aberystwyth from Stratford-on-Avon on a dull and cold winter morning, and suddenly being roused from my apathy by the sight of Bennett-Evans's green patches, vibrant against the lowering background of dark and forbidding hills, the first green to meet my eyes since I had bundled myself into my car early that morning. I wondered rather morosely as I drove on, who cared? Who of the thousands who passed over that road in a normal summer gave those patches a moment's thought, or even noticed them?
> Were there any who had been suddenly thrilled; who

wished to know what like of man lived in that bleak, isolated spot in that strange home built of stone and railway carriages? What sort of man was this who, single-handed and of his own initiative, was waging war against the elements and the Forestry Commission? On the one side of the road trees, trees, thousands of trees planted at public expense; on the other turnips and grass, the raw materials of food, brought into being by the sweat and faith and enterprise of a private individual – of a farmer, of a man who lived on his hill and loved it. Who cared?[9]

Stapledon had brought the bright green oases back to the upland landscape just as the village girls had done when they moved their cattle up to the summer pastures centuries earlier. He had proved scientifically what mountain people had known for centuries – that hard grazing and fertility could transform mountain vegetation into lush and bountiful grassland. Fertility could make the barren hill country fruitful, just as irrigation made the deserts bloom.

But the great grassland crusader was not to be satisfied by a handful of green patches at Llangurig. His ambition was to work his transformation across a far larger canvas. He longed for the chance to demonstrate landscape change and rural revival across a truly extensive tract of hill country, a project he estimated might cost 20,000 pounds in land and machinery.[10] In the straitened times of the early 1930s the government was in no mood to shell out the money.

Undeterred, Stapledon appealed directly to the public. On 11 July 1932, *The Times* carried a letter pointing out the great benefits to the Empire that would flow from such an experiment, conducted with the assistance of 'progressive landowners and farmers'. The letter was seen by wealthy philanthropist Sir Julian Cahn, a man whose fascination with farming was matched only by his love of cricket. That same day he pledged the necessary funds, and the project – subsequently known as the Cahn Hill Improvement Scheme – was launched.

The land chosen for the experiment lay near the Cardiganshire town of Devil's Bridge. It extended to 2,000 hectares, rising at its highest point to more than 500 metres above sea level. Known as the Hafod Estate, it had been an area of summer pasturing in the distant past.

This was a bleak, heartbreaking landscape, as a former owner, Thomas Johnes, had discovered more than a century earlier. The turf was dominated by coarse mat-grass and purple moor grass, with rushes proliferating in the marshy areas. Stapledon was delighted with it. If this unprepossessing countryside could be made green and productive, it would stand as a visible reproach to those politicians and landowners who had allowed their grasslands to tumble into decay.

Work started on the Cahn Hill scheme in March 1933, under the direction of the redoubtable Moses Griffith.[11] Using rape and Italian ryegrass as pioneer crops, the Aberystwyth team quickly achieved a remarkable improvement in the stock-carrying capacity of these inhospitable hills. By 1936 Stapledon was able to report to the Royal Society of Arts that the re-seeding and fertilisation of poor hill pastures could increase their output of edible dry matter fivefold.

But it was not merely the greening of the hills he sought. To him pasture improvement was a way of bringing wealth into these remote upland communities, as the summer grazings had done centuries earlier. Productive pastures had the power to revitalise rural economies and boost village populations, putting new life into country businesses and expanding village schools. Once again grasslands might become the engine of economic growth as they had in the Middle Ages.

In the years leading up to World War Two Stapledon embarked on a nationwide crusade against the 'scandal' of derelict and wasted land. At the same time the Ministry of Agriculture commissioned his colleague William Davies to survey the state of the nation's grassland. Davies reported that in England and Wales no fewer than three-and-a-half million hectares of pasture lands were 'a standing reproach', fit only for the plough. The result was a great, war-time ploughing-up campaign in which vast tracts of worn-out and neglected grassland were cropped with wheat, their accumulated fertility being mobilised to help feed a hungry nation.

After the war Stapledon urged farmers to put grass leys back at the heart of their crop rotations on the newly ploughed lands. He called for a return to mixed farming – the rotation of grass leys and arable crops over the same land. 'Ley farming', as it was now known, was simply a form of 'alternate husbandry', the system that had so enriched the country in the eighteenth century. Though it had remained popular with farmers in parts of the north and west, decades of rural recession had led to its abandonment over much of lowland Britain.

In the post-war climate of public support, Stapledon's revolution took root. A wave of optimism swept through Britain's farmsteads. This time the government would not abandon agriculture as they had at the end of World War One. From now on more of the nation's food was to be grown at home.

For the first time in a century, farming's contribution to national life was to be recognised and rewarded. And at the very heart of this rural revival were the country's neglected grasslands. With the support of cash from taxpayers, mixed farming based on grass leys spread rapidly across lowland Britain as it had in the eighteenth century. At the height of the ley farming boom in the early 1960s, the area of land under 'temporary' grass was double the level of the depressed 1930s.

Under grasses and clovers, fertility began to build in soils impoverished by the war-time ploughing-up policy. When, in due course, the ley was ploughed for another sequence of arable crops, 'mineralisation' of the accumulated organic matter provided the necessary nutrients. It was a largely self-sustaining system that kept the land in good heart while returning wealth to the rural community. It seemed that the dreams of the Welsh grassland pioneers were to be fulfilled.

Stapledon had never intended that his pastoral revolution should be solely about making more money for farmers. His ultimate aim was to bring town and country closer together in a new, post-industrial landscape. He dreamed of a prosperous countryside, revitalised by a thriving agriculture, and supporting a growing population. Manufacturing industry would be encouraged to open new, decentralised factories in this dynamic rural community, so that industrial workers might themselves share in the delights of country living.

In his book *The Land, Now and Tomorrow*,[12] Stapledon outlined his vision for rural Britain, an all-embracing plan that would encompass farming, forestry, leisure and education. He viewed the land as a great unifying factor in national life. In his new order, farmers would enjoy state support in return for improving their land, while industrial workers would see their lives enriched through contact with rural values and ideas.[13]

Stapledon believed that everyone needed regular access to wild and open countryside if they were to remain healthy. It was their very detachment from the countryside and country life that accounted for much contemporary neurosis, he argued. If industrial workers could be as free to enjoy the countryside as the people of medieval Britain, then a healthy national psyche might be restored. The renewal of the pastoral economy would produce a happier society.

Yet even as ley farming advanced across lowland Britain, Stapledon's utopian dreams were being dashed. The growing productivity of agriculture led not to a thriving community of small farms as he had hoped, but to the emergence of large, predatory holdings which began swallowing up their weaker neighbours. The subsidy system showered rewards on those who produced the most. These were chiefly the farmers who grubbed out hedges and drained marshlands, who overstocked their grasslands or ploughed them up so as to put the land down to cereals.

They were also the farmers who relied most heavily on artificial fertilisers and pesticides, maintaining a relentless chemical assault on meadow and cropland ecosystems. The more intensive the farm, the more its owner was able to claim in public subsidy. British taxpayers were being asked to finance the laying waste of their own countryside.

It was a process that would have saddened Stapledon had he lived to see its inexorable advance through the final decades of the twentieth century. Though not committed to organic agriculture, he strongly opposed the rise of the monoculture and the specialist farm. He feared that the abandonment of rotations and mixed farming would lead ultimately to disaster.[14]

Yet the rules of the European Union's common agricultural policy, which the UK signed up to in the early 1970s, made specialisation inevitable. Farmers were paid on a commodity basis. To survive they had to choose between intensive arable farming or intensive livestock production. Following the so-called 'reforms' of 1992 they were even obliged to register their land for one or the other. Mixed farming – the source of rural health and prosperity throughout the country's history – became virtually impossible.

To maintain crop yields, arable farmers now relied on artificial fertilisers instead of the traditional grass 'break'. When pests and crop diseases began to take their toll, it was the crop sprayer they turned to. From now on they were totally reliant on a cocktail of chemical sprays to ensure a good harvest.

Specialisation proved equally damaging in the production of meat and milk. In the major grassland areas, inputs of fertiliser nitrogen soared to new heights, 'forcing' grass plants into the extravagant production of leafy growth, and destroying the natural, fertility-building rhythms of the soil. For the first time in all history, Britain's pasturelands had been made 'chemical junkies'. In the uplands, EU subsidies rewarded farmers for overstocking their pastures, weakening root systems and driving out clover along with all but the most aggressive grass species.

In little more than a generation Britain had turned its back on a pastoral tradition tried and tested over centuries. Instead the health of its people was to be entrusted to a new, industrial-style agriculture powered not by the natural fertility cycles of the soil, but by fossil fuels in the form of chemical fertilisers and sprays. Stapledon's great grassland revolution had been hijacked by a handful of large chemical companies. The cost to the country may be high.

In his later years Stapledon became more than ever convinced that mankind's reliance on simple, industrial farming systems would lead to some great catastrophe. As a scientist he was only too aware of the limitations of the scientific method, particularly when applied uncritically to agriculture. Life was maintained by the subtle interaction of millions of factors. Yet modern science pulled out a mere handful to look at in isolation.[15] Its findings were partial. They gave a distorted and fragmented view of the real world. Their unthinking application to the real world carried risks.

There are latent in all the facts and assumptions of biology . . . . seeds of lethal consequences to mankind and man's domesti-cated animals and plants. Further than this, lethal consequen-ces are all too likely to follow from the unguarded and wholesale application of the most tried and trusted facts of biology to man and the higher organisms generally, unless we are prepared to pay great deference to what we do not know . . .

Such lethal consequences as may lie latent in some of the current facts and assumptions of biology are likely to act rapidly, but if false facts and assumptions are long retained as authoritative biological dicta and generally acted upon, then the consequences might well be lethal in the extreme, and culminate in the premature extinction of man, or of his domestic animals and plants, or of all three together.[16]

While the nature and origins of the cattle plague bovine spongiform encephalopathy – BSE – remain obscure, it is hard to imagine that the disease could have posed a serious threat to human health without an industrial agriculture. BSE spread among dairy cows bred so ruthlessly for milk production that many had become little more than walking milk factories, with grossly enlarged udders and the capacity to 'milk off their backs'. To express what the breeders euphemistically termed their 'genetic merit' the poor creatures had to consume vast quantities of energy-rich and high-protein feeds. Recycled animal remains were one of the few foods to provide protein in a sufficiently concentrated form.

The breeders had produced a cow that was virtually obliged to feed on the flesh of other animals. They had turned a herbivore into an obligate carnivore. A food system constructed on an industrial model of centralised processing and mass distribution ensured that the contaminated meat was fed to much of the human population.

BSE was surely one of Stapledon's 'lethal consequences'. It was the harvest of betrayal – the betrayal of a gentle, long-suffering creature that had been the servant and companion of mankind down the ages. Whatever the true nature of the mysterious prion at the heart of the sickness, it would surely not have afflicted the hardy, unimproved cattle of the Tudor grazing marshes or the herb-rich summer pastures of the high mountains.

As Stapledon warned, the ill-considered application of scientific results to living processes is risky. Yet modern industrial agriculture commits this error constantly. The old pastoral culture contained its own system of checks and balances, its own protection against collapse and catastrophe. Modern industrial Britain has turned its back on such outdated concepts. It has abandoned a tradition that fashioned the character of this island people as surely as it shaped the landscape.

It is high-risk strategy. In denying the pastoral culture with its roots in the natural, fertility-building processes of the soil, the British people have embarked on a hazardous, uncharted journey. It may yet lead to destruction.

But the ways of grass are not irretrievable. There is still time to return to an older, safer road, the road travelled by the very first Britons. Consumers could fulfil George Stapledon's great vision simply by buying foods grown without the aid of chemical stimulants such as artificial fertilisers and pesticides; foods produced by the natural cycles of fertility that have been a repository of Britain's wealth throughout history. We could savour again the succulent beef of river meadow and salt-marsh; the sweet lamb of flower-filled chalk downland; the golden butter churned from milk produced on a fertility-building grass ley.

A wide-scale switch to organic foods would ensure that the land returned to mixed farming, with arable crops and grass leys alternating in the same fields. In absolute terms it might appear a little more expensive. But in relation to its nutritional quality it would represent far better value.

'Fertility farming' would deliver healthier foods from a healthier countryside, rich in the diversity of its wildlife and the beauty of its landscape. In real terms they would be far cheaper than the products of an impoverished and polluted countryside, a countryside of mass production and tastelessness and diets that make people ill.

At the start of the twenty-first century grasslands everywhere are in retreat. Both government and the governed have failed to understand them and the wealth they bring. To restore them – to value them afresh together with the way of life they engender – would be to return an island people to the path of prosperity and health. In the ancient green mantle of field and hillside lies the hope of the nation's redemption.

Notes

1 THE ENDURING PASSION

1 S. R. Eyre, *Vegetation and Soils*, Edward Arnold, 1963, pp. 240–1.
2 Richard Manning, *Grassland: The History, Biology, Politics and Promise of the American Prairie*, Penguin, 1997, p. 71.
3 Ibid.
4 E. D. Phillips, *The Mongols*, Thames and Hudson, 1969, pp. 21–2.
5 Robert Marshall, *Storm from the East*, BBC Books, 1993, p. 16.
6 Bruce Chatwin, 'Nomad Invasions', in *What Am I Doing Here*, Jonathan Cape, 1989, p. 216.
7 Richard Manning, op. cit. p. 75.
8 Bruce Chatwin, 'Heavenly Horses', op. cit., p. 203.
9 Ibid. pp. 195–205.
10 G. Catlin, *Manners, Customs and Conditions of North American Indians*, Vol. II, Chatto and Windus, 1844.
11 Lee Miller, *From the Heart: Voices of the American Indian*, Pimlico, 1995, p. 227.

12 Bruce Chatwin, 'Nomad Invasions', op. cit., p. 226.
13 James Shreeve, *The Neandertal Enigma*, Viking, 1995, pp. 8–25.
14 Ibid.
15 R. D. C. Evans (ed.), *Winter Games Pitches*, Sports Turf Research Institute, 1994, p. 31.
16 Ibid., p. 35.
17 Stephen Baker, 'Research on winter games pitches', in *Turfgrass Bulletin*, 204, April 1999, pp. 14–16.
18 Richard Manning, op. cit., p. 51.
19 *Town and Country Parks*, House of Commons Select Committee on Environment, Transport and Regional Affairs 20th Report, 1999, para. 38.
20 T. Bedford Franklin, *British Grasslands*, Faber and Faber, 1953, p. 26.
21 Brian Bailey, *The English Village Green*, Robert Hale, 1985, p. 37.
22 Trefor M. Owen, *Welsh Folk Customs*, Gomer, 1959, p. 96.
23 Brian Bailey, op. cit., p. 49.

2 PEOPLE OF THE GRASS

1 Konrad Spindler, *The Man in the Ice*, Weidenfeld and Nicolson, 1994, p. 80.
2 Peter Fowler, 'Wildscape to landscape: Enclosure in prehistoric Britain', in Roger Mercer (ed.), *Farming Practice in British Prehistory*, Edinburgh University Press, 1981, p. 39.
3 David Harris, 'First farmers were colonists after all', *British Archaeology*, No. 27, September 1997.
4 Julian Thomas, 'Neolithic Explanations Revisited: The Mesolithic-Neolithic Transition in Britain and South Scandinavia', *Proceedings of the Prehistoric Society*, 54, 1988, pp. 59–66.
5 Barry Cunliffe, *Wessex to A.D. 1000*, Longman, 1993, p. 38.
6 Roger Mercer, 'Introduction', in Roger Mercer (ed.), op. cit., p. x.
7 Barry Cunliffe, op. cit., p. 42.

8 Michael Parker Pearson, *Bronze Age Britain*, Batsford/English Heritage, 1993, p. 15.

9 Barry Cunliffe, op. cit., p. 44.

10 Michael Parker Pearson, op. cit., p. 26.

11 Barry Cunliffe, op. cit., p. 32.

12 Alasdair Whittle, 'When did Neolithic farmers settle down', *British Archaeology*, July 1996, p. 7.

13 Barry Cunliffe, op. cit., p. 78.

14 Roger Mercer, *Causewayed enclosures*, Shire Archaeology, 1990, p. 39.

15 A. J. Legge, 'Aspects of Cattle Husbandry', in Roger Mercer (ed.), op. cit., 1981, p. 179.

16 Julian Thomas, *Rethinking the Neolithic*, Cambridge University Press, 1991, p. 24.

17 Michael Parker Pearson, op. cit., p. 28.

18 Roger Mercer, op. cit., 1990, p. 51.

19 Julian Thomas, op. cit., 1991, p. 31.

20 Joshua Pollard, *Neolithic Britain*, Shire Archaeology, 1997, p. 50.

21 Timothy Darvill, *Prehistoric Britain*, Batsford, 1987, p. 70.

22 J. M. Coles and B. J. Coles, *Prehistory on the Somerset Levels*, Somerset Levels Project, 1989, p. 38.

23 Andrew Sherratt, 'Flying up with the souls of the dead', *British Archaeology*, June 1996, p. 14.

24 Merryn Dineley, 'Finding magic in Stone Age real ale', *British Archaeology*, November 1996, p. 6.

3   TRAVELLERS ON THE WIND

1 W. G. Chaloner, 'Plants, animals and time', *The Palaeobotanist*, Vol. 32, 1984, pp. 197–202.

2 G. P. Chapman, *The Biology of Grasses*, CAB International, 1996, p. 1.

3 R. N. Rudmose Brown (1912), in Agnes Arber, *The Gramineae: A Study of Cereal, Bamboo and Grass*, J. Cramer: Weinheim, 1934, repr. 1965, p. 332.

4 J. D. Hooker (1854), in Agnes Arber, op. cit., p. 351.

5 D. Griffiths (1912), in Agnes Arber, op. cit., p. 333.

6 J. J. Parsons, 'The Africanisation of New World tropical grasslands', *Tubinger Geographische Studien*, 34, pp. 141–3, in G. P. Chapman, op. cit., p. 8.

7 H. N. Ridley (1923, 1926, 1930), in Agnes Arber, op. cit., p. 333.

8 H. N. Ridley (1930), in Agnes Arber, op. cit., p. 334.

9 G. P. Chapman and W. E. Peat, *An Introduction to the Grasses (Including Bamboos and Cereals)*, CAB International, 1992, p. 66.

10 Carol C. Baskin and Jerry M. Baskin, 'Ecology of Seed Dormancy and Germination in Grasses', in G. P. Cheplick (ed.), *Population Biology of Grasses*, Cambridge University Press, 1998, pp. 30–83.

11 Ibid., p. 58.

12 Agnes Chase, 'The Meek That Inherit the Earth', *Grass: The Yearbook of Agriculture*, United States Department of Agriculture, 1948, pp. 8–15.

13 Agnes Arber, op. cit., p. 349.

14 Ibid., p. 350.

15 Ibid., p. 351.

16 Ibid., p. 352.

17 Ibid., p. 353.

18 O. Stapf (1917), in Agnes Arber, op. cit., p. 353.

19 J. E. Malo and F. Suarez, 'Herbivorous Mammals as Seed Dispersers on a Mediterranean *dehesa*', *Oecologia*, Vol. 104, 1995, pp. 246–55.

20 Agnes Arber, op. cit., p. 351.

21 Everett E. Edwards, 'The Settlement of Grasslands', *Grass: The Yearbook of Agriculture*, United States Department of Agriculture, 1948, pp. 16–25.

22 Agnes Arber, op. cit., p. 357.

23 G. P. Chapman, op. cit., 1996, p. 87.

24 G. P. Chapman and W. E. Peat, op. cit., 1992, p. 3.

25 W. L. Crepet and G. F. D. Feldman, 'The earliest remains of grasses in the fossil record', *American Journal of Botany*, 78, 1991, pp. 1010–14.

26 G. O. Poinar Jnr. and J. T. Columbus, 'Adhesive grass spikelet with mammalian hair in Dominican amber – first fossil evidence of epizoochory', *Experientia*, 48, 1992, pp. 906–9.

27 Richard Milner, *The Encyclopedia of Evolution*, Facts-On-File, 1990, p. 307.

28 G. P. Chapman and W. E. Peat, op. cit., 1992, p. 62.

29 Richard Milner, op. cit., p. 200.

30 S. A. Renvoize and W. D. Clayton, 'Classification and evolution of the grasses', in G. P. Chapman (ed.), *Grass Evolution and Domestication*, Cambridge University Press, 1992, pp. 1–37.

31 G. P. Chapman, op. cit., 1996, p. 19.

32 Elwyn Hartley Edwards, *The Encyclopedia of the Horse*, Dorling Kindersley, 1994, p. 10.

33 Stephen Budiansky, *The Nature of Horses*, Free Press, 1997, pp. 1–23.

4 A PLOT OF DREAMS

1 Gordon Strachan, 'Mud, Morton and my missing boot', *Observer*, 7 March 1999.

2 R. D. C. Evans (ed.), *Winter Games Pitches: The Construction and Maintenance of Natural Turf Pitches for Team Games*, Sports Turf Research Institute, 1994, p. 32.

3 Ibid., p. 33.

4 Ibid., p. 37.

5 Ibid., p. 39.

5 TURF DOCTORS

1 Simon Wilde, 'Two magical days herald new dawn', *Sunday Times*, 20 August 2000.

2 Michael Atherton, 'The day England turned the world upside down', *Sunday Telegraph*, 20 August 2000.

6 BATTLEGROUND

1 D. J. Harberd, 'Observations on Population Structure and Longevity of *Festuca rubra L.*', *New Phytologist*, Vol. 60, 1961, p. 184.

2 David D. Briske and Justin D. Derner, 'Clonal Biology of Caespitose Grasses', in G. P. Cheplick (ed.), *Population Biology of Grasses*, Cambridge University Press, 1998, pp. 106–35.

3 Ibid.

4 Richard Jefferies, *The Story of My Heart: My Autobiography*, Longmans, 1883.

5 H. J. Massingham, *Wold Without End*, Cobden Sanderson, 1932, p. 177.

6 Richard Mabey, *The Common Ground*, Hutchinson, 1980, p. 150.

7 R. G. Jefferson and H. J. Robertson, *Lowland Grassland: Wildlife Value and Conservation Status*, English Nature Research Reports, No. 169, 1996, p. 19.

8 R. M. Fuller, 'The Changing Extent and Conservation Interest of Lowland Grasslands in England and Wales: A Review of Grassland Surveys 1930–1984', *Biological Conservation*, Vol. 40, pp. 281–300.

9 K. Stephen, *Worcestershire Grasslands 1992: Report of a Botanical Survey for English Nature*, Worcestershire Nature Conservation Trust, 1993.

10 R. D. Porley and P. F. Ulf-Hansen, 'Unimproved Neutral Grassland in Dorset: Survey and Conservation', *Proceedings of the Dorset Natural History and Archaeological Society*, 113, 1991, pp. 161–5.

11 L. J. Redgrave, *Berkshire Unimproved Neutral Grassland Survey*, Newbury: English Nature, 1995.

12 R. G. Jefferson and H. J. Robertson, op. cit., pp. 4–6.

13 J. B. Lawes and J. H. Gilbert, 'Agricultural, Botanical and Chemical Results of Experiments on the Mixed Herbage of Permanent Meadow, Conducted for more than Twenty Years in Succession on the Same Land. Part 1: The

Agricultural Results', *Philosophical Transactions of the Royal Society*, 171, 1880, pp. 289–415.

14 D. Tilman et al., 'The Park Grass Experiment: Insights from the Most Long-term Ecological Study', in R. A. Leigh and A. E. Johnston (eds), *Long-term Experiments in Agricultural and Ecological Sciences*, CAB International, 1994, pp. 287–303.

15 M. Dodd et al., 'Application of the British National Vegetation Classification to the Communities of the Park Grass Experiment Through Time', *Folia Geobotanica and Phytotaxonomica*, 29 (3), 1994, pp. 321–4.

16 A. Hopkins and J. J. Hopkins, 'UK Grasslands Now: Agricultural Production and Nature Conservation', in *Grassland Management and Nature Conservation*, Occasional Symposium No. 28, British Grassland Society, 1993, pp. 10–19.

17 J. Philip Grime, 'The C-S-R Model of Primary Plant Strategies – Origins, Implications and Tests', in L. D. Gottlieb and S. K. Jain (eds), *Plant Evolutionary Biology*, Chapman and Hall, 1988, pp. 371–93.

7 THE ENDLESS PLAIN

1 R. A. Rees and S. J. Styles, *Longman History Studies in Depth: The American West 1840–1895*, Longman, 1986, p. 58.

2 Quoted in Richard Manning, *Grassland: The History, Biology, Politics, and Promise of the American Prairie*, Penguin Books USA, 1995, p. 84.

3 Ibid., p. 149.

4 John Ernest Weaver, cited in William Least Heat-Moon, *Prairy Erth*, Houghton Mifflin Company, 1991, p. 95.

5 William Least Heat-Moon, op. cit., p. 77.

6 David F. Costello, *The Prairie World*, David and Charles, 1971, p. 46.

7 Ibid., p. 40.

8 Charles Darwin, *On the Origin of Species by Means of Natural Selection*, John Murray, 1859, p. 85.

9 Douglas H. Chadwick, 'The American Prairie: Roots of the Sky', *National Geographic*, October 1993, pp. 90–119.

10 David F. Costello, op. cit., p. 129.

11 Ibid., p. 138.

12 Richard Manning, op. cit., p. 93.

13 R. A. Rees and S. J. Styles, op. cit., p. 75.

14 Tenth Census of the US, 1880, cited in R. A. Rees and S. J. Styles, op. cit., p. 66.

15 Mari Sandoz, *The Cattlemen*, University of Nebraska Press, 1958, p. 239.

16 Ibid., pp. 244–7.

17 Richard Manning, op. cit., p. 167.

18 Shepard Krech III, 'Ecology, Conservation, and the Buffalo Jump', in Marsha C. Bol (ed.), *Stars Above, Earth Below: American Indians and Nature*, Roberts Rinehart/Carnegie Museum of Natural History, 1998, pp. 139–64.

19 Richard Manning, op. cit., pp. 79–80.

20 Quoted in James Wilson, *The Earth Shall Weep*, Picador, 1998, p. 249.

8   THE GOLDEN FLEECE

1 *The Victoria History of Wiltshire*, Vol. 4, Oxford University Press, 1959, p. 28.

2 G. W. Morris and L. S. Wood, *The Golden Fleece*, Oxford University Press, 1922, p. 21.

3 Eileen Power, *The Wool Trade in English Medieval History*, Oxford University Press, 1941, p. 17.

4 M. M. Postan, *The Medieval Wool Trade*, The Wool Education Society, London, 1952, p. 4.

5 G. W. Morris and L. S. Wood, op. cit.

6 H. E. Hallam (ed.), *The Agrarian History of England and Wales*, Vol. 2, 1042–1350, gen. ed. Joan Thirsk, Cambridge University Press, 1988, p. 409.

7 Edward Miller (ed.), *The Agrarian History of England and Wales*, Vol. 3, 1348–1500, gen. ed. Joan Thirsk, Cambridge University Press, 1991, p. 190.

8 David H. Williams, 'Tintern Abbey – Its Economic

History', in *The Monmouthshire Antiquary*, Vol. 2, Part 1, 1965, p. 10.

9 T. Bedford Franklin, *British Grasslands*, Faber and Faber, 1953, p. 61.

10 Edward Miller (ed.), op. cit., p. 395.

11 Ibid., p. 396.

12 Eileen Power, op. cit., p. 43.

13 H. J. Massingham, *The English Countryman*, Batsford, 1942, p. 106.

14 E. Lamond (ed.), *Walter of Henley's Husbandry, Together with an Anonymous Husbandry, Seneschaucie and Robert Grosseleste's Rules*, Royal Historical Society, 1890.

15 Lord Ernle, *English Farming Past and Present*, 5th edn, Heinemann/Cass, 1936, p. 16.

16 Edward Miller (ed.), op. cit. p. 294.

17 Ibid., p. 235.

18 *The Victoria History of Wiltshire*, Vol. 4, p. 25.

19 Ibid.

20 Ibid., p. 23.

21 H. J. Massingham, op. cit., p. 26.

22 Ibid., p. 28.

23 Francis Duckworth, 'The Story of the Cotswold Wool Trade', in Adelaide L. J. Gosset, *Shepherds of Britain*, Benjamin Blom, 1972, pp. 229–32.

24 John Aubrey, *The Book of Days*, quoted in Adelaide L. J. Gosset, op. cit., p. 38.

25 W. H. Hudson, *A Shepherd's Life*, Macdonald Futura, 1981, p. 219.

26 Eileen Power, op. cit., p. 38.

27 Lord Ernle, op. cit., p. 46.

28 Eileen Power, op. cit., p. 40.

29 Robert Trow-Smith, *English Husbandry*, Faber and Faber, 1951, p. 77.

30 Ibid.

31 Eileen Power, op. cit., p. 18.

9 SUMMER PASTURES

1 Hugh Cheape, 'Shielings in the Highlands and Islands of Scotland: Prehistory to the Present', *Folk Life*, Vol. 35, 1996–7, pp. 7–24.

2 Niall Ó Dubhthaigh, 'Summer Pasture in Donegal', translated by C. O. Danachair, *Folk Life*, Vol. 22, 1983–4, pp. 42–54.

3 Hugh Cheape, op. cit., p. 10.

4 R. U. Sayce, 'The Old Summer Pastures. Part 2: Life at the Hafodydd', *The Montgomeryshire Collections*, Vol. 55, 1957–8, pp. 37–86.

5 Roy Millward and Adrian Robinson, *Upland Britain*, David and Charles, 1980, p. 142.

6 Cledwyn Fychan, personal communication.

7 Thomas Pennant, 1778, quoted in R. U. Sayce, 'The Old Summer Pastures', *The Montgomeryshire Collections*, Vol. 54, 1955–6, pp. 117–45.

8 Captain Caomhghin Ua Danachair, 1945, cited in R. U. Sayce, op. cit., 1957–8, p. 40.

9 E. Maclysaght, 1950, quoted in R. U. Sayce, op. cit., 1957–8, p. 40–1.

10 Duncan Campbell, *Transactions of the Inverness Scientific Society and Field Club*, 1895–9, in R. U. Sayce, op. cit., 1957–8, p. 44.

11 R. U. Sayce, op. cit., 1957–8, p. 44.

12 Niall Ó Dubhthaigh, op. cit.

13 R. U. Sayce, op. cit., 1955–6, p. 132.

14 Caoimhin Ó Danachair, 'Summer Pasture in Ireland', *Folk Life*, Vol. 22, 1983–4, pp. 36–41.

15 Elwyn Davies, 'Hafod and Lluest', *Folk Life*, Vol. 23, 1984–5, pp. 76–96.

16 Duncan Campbell, 'Highland Shielings in the Olden Time', *Transactions of the Inverness Scientific Society and Field Club*, 1895–9, p. 87.

17 Adelaide L. J. Gosset, *Shepherds of Britain*, Benjamin Blom, 1972, p. 94.

18 R. U. Sayce, op. cit., 1955–6, p. 138.

19 *Carmina Gadelica*, quoted in R. U. Sayce, op. cit., 1955–6, p. 138.
20 Roy Millward and Adrian Robinson, op. cit., p. 150.
21 Caoimhin Ó Danachair, op. cit., p. 39.
22 Niall Ó Dubhthaigh, op. cit., p. 47.
23 Caoimhin Ó Danachair, op. cit., p. 38.
24 R. U. Sayce, op. cit., 1955–6, p. 143.
25 Caoimhin Ó Danachair, op. cit., p. 138.
26 Duncan Campbell, cited in R. U. Sayce, op. cit., 1957–8, p. 48.
27 R. U. Sayce, op. cit., 1957–8, p. 49.
28 Niall Ó Dubhthaigh, op. cit., p. 50.
29 R. U. Sayce, op. cit., 1957–8, p. 72–3.
30 Ibid., p. 75.
31 Ibid., pp. 74–5.
32 Niall Ó Dubhthaigh, op. cit., p. 57.
33 Duncan Campbell, cited in R. U. Sayce, op. cit., 1957–8, p. 76.
34 W. G. Hoskins, *Royal Commission on Common Land 1955–8*, quoted in R. U. Sayce, op. cit., 1957–8, p. 85.
35 R. U. Sayce, op. cit., 1957–8, p. 83.
36 Norman Morrison, 'Shieling Life in Lewis', in John MacDonald (ed.), *Voices from the Hills*, Glasgow, 1927, pp. 206–7.
37 Roy Millward and Adrian Robinson, op. cit., p. 142.
38 Ibid.
39 Ibid.
40 D. Macdonald, 'Lewis Shielings', quoted in Hugh Cheape, op. cit., 1996–7, p. 23.
41 Hugh Cheape, op. cit., p. 23.
42 Cledwyn Fychan, personal communication.

10   THE DROWNING FIELDS

1 J. H. Bettey, 'The development of water meadows in Dorset during the 17th century', *Agricultural History Review*, Vol. 25 (1), 1977, pp. 37–43.

2 Dorset R. O.: D29/M1 Court Book of Affpuddle 1589–1612; J. Brocklebank, *Affpuddle in the County of Dorset*, Bournemouth, 1968, pp. 22, 54–6.

3 J. H. Bettey, op. cit., p. 38.

4 Eric Kerridge, 'The floating of the Wiltshire water meadows', *The Wiltshire Magazine*, Vol. 55 (199), December 1953, p. 113.

5 Ibid., p. 112.

6 Ibid., p. 113.

7 G. G. S. Bowie, 'Watermeadows in Wessex – a re-evaluation for the period 1640–1850', *Agricultural History Review*, Vol. 35 (2), 1987, p. 154.

8 T. Davis, *General View of the Agriculture of the County of Wiltshire*, 1794, cited in Eric Kerridge, op. cit., p. 106.

9 T. Davis, *General View of the Agriculture of the County of Wiltshire*, 1794, p. 34.

10 Sir Stafford Henry Northcote, 'A few words on water meadows', *Journal of the Bath and West of England Society*, Vol. 3, 1855, p. 113.

11 Eric Kerridge, 'The sheep-fold in Wiltshire and the floating of the water meadows', *Economic History Review*, 2nd series, Vol. 6, 1953, p. 287.

12 Latimer, *Sermons*, cited in Eric Kerridge, 'The sheep-fold in Wiltshire . . .', op. cit. p. 282.

13 Eric Kerridge, 'The sheep-fold in Wiltshire . . .', op. cit., p. 284.

14 Thomas David, 'Water meadows', *Bath and West of England Society Letters and Papers*, Vol. 7, 1795, p. 139.

15 J. H. Bettey, op. cit., p. 41.

16 John Combes, 'Irrigation as practised in south Wiltshire', *Journal of the Bath and West of England Society*, Vol. 9, 1861, p. 413.

17 Ibid., p. 410.

18 Eric Kerridge, 'The sheep-fold in Wiltshire . . .', op. cit., p. 283.

19 John Sheail, 'The formation and maintenance of watermeadows in Hampshire, England', *Biological Conservation*, Vol. 3, No. 2, January 1971, pp. 101–6.

20 Sir Stafford Henry Northcote, op. cit., p. 112.

21 T. Barker, 'On water meadows as suitable for Wales and other mountain districts', *Journal of the Bath and West of England Society*, Vol. 6, 1858, pp. 267–82.

22 Ibid.

23 James Caird, *English Agriculture in 1850–51*, 2nd ed, Kelley: New York, 1967, p. 110.

24 John Combes, op. cit., pp. 410–14.

25 William Tatham, *National Irrigation*, London, 1801.

26 E. H. Carrier, *The Pastoral Heritage of Britain*, Christophers, 1936, p. 126.

27 Ibid., p. 128.

28 J. Chalmers Morton, 'Agricultural experience of town sewage in 1867', *Journal of the Bath and West of England Society*, Vol. 15, 1867, p. 22.

29 James Archibald Campbell, 'Application of sewage', *Journal of the Bath and West of England Society*, Vol. 14, 1866, pp. 141–59.

30 James Caird, op. cit., p. 206.

31 John Evelyn Denison, 'On the Duke of Portland's water-meadows at Clipstone Park', *Journal of the Royal Agricultural Society of England*, Vol. 1, 1840, p. 359.

11 AN END OF ARCADY

1 Philip Stubbes, *The Anatomie of Abuses*, 2nd edn, 1583, quoted in J. Dover Wilson, *Life in Shakespeare's England*, 2nd edn, 1913, pp. 18–19.

2 Christopher Brookes, *English Cricket*, Readers Union, 1978, p. 13.

3 'Impression of England by an Italian visitor', in David C. Douglas (gen. ed.), *English Historical Documents*, Vol. V, Eyre and Spottiswoode, 1967, p. 190.

4 W. G. Hoskins, 'Harvest fluctuations in English economic history, 1480 1619', *Agricultural History Review*, xii, 1964.

5 Penry Williams, *The Later Tudors: England 1547–1603*, Clarendon Press, 1995, p. 204.

6 D. M. Palliser, *England under the Later Tudors: 1547–1603*, Longman, 1983, p. 169.

7 John Charles (ed.), *Agricultural Markets and Trade, 1500–1750: Chapters from The Agrarian History of England and Wales*, Vol. 4, gen. ed. Joan Thirsk, Cambridge University Press, 1990, p. 58.

8 Robert Trow-Smith, *English Husbandry*, Faber and Faber, 1951, p. 119.

9 John Charles (ed.), op. cit., p. 59.

10 T. Bedford Franklin, *British Grasslands*, Faber and Faber, 1953, p. 70.

11 William Camden, *Britannia*, cited in T. Bedford Franklin, op. cit., p. 70.

12 D. M. Palliser, op. cit. p. 165.

13 G. M. Trevelyan, *English Social History*, Longmans, Green, 1942, p. 144.

14 Joan Thirsk (ed.), *The Agrarian History of England and Wales – Volume IV: 1500–1640*, gen. eds H. P. R. Finbery and Joan Thirsk Cambridge University Press, 1967, p. 462.

15 John Aubrey, *Nat. Hist. Wilts.*, quoted in David Underdown, *Revel, Riot. and Rebellion*, Clarendon Press, 1985, p. 73.

16 David Underdown, op. cit., p. 14.

17 E. A. Wrigley and R. S. Schofield, *The Population History of England, 1541–1871*, London, 1981.

18 John Guy, 'The Tudor Age', in Kenneth O. Morgan (ed.), *The Oxford Illustrated History of Britain*, Oxford University Press, 1984, p. 227.

19 Lord Ernle, *English Farming Past and Present*, 6th edn, Heinemann/Cass, 1961, p. 79.

20 Derek Wilson, *England in the Age of Thomas More*, Granada, 1978, p. 136.

21 Cited in Lord Ernle, op. cit, p. 83.

22 W. G. Hoskins, *The Making of the English Landscape*, Hodder and Stoughton, 1955, p. 155.

23 Thomas Lever, *Sermons*, cited in Lord Ernle, op. cit., p. 57.

24 Christopher Brookes, op. cit., p. 26.

25 Derek Wilson, op. cit., p. 137.

26 Christopher Brookes, op. cit, p. 33.

27 Christopher Clay (ed.), *Rural Society: Landowners, Peasants and Labourers 1500–1750, Chapters from the Agrarian History of England and Wales*, Vol. 2, gen. ed. Joan Thirsk, Cambridge University Press, 1990, p. 178.

28 John Norden, *The Surveyor's Dialogue*, cited in D. M. Palliser, op. cit., p. 179.

29 Thomas Tusser, *Five Hundreth Good Pointes of Good Husbandrie*, cited in Lord Ernle, op. cit, p. 66.

30 The Commission of Enclosures 1517, Pat. Roll, 9 Hen. VIII, pt 2, mbd., in David C. Douglas (gen. ed.), op. cit., p. 933.

31 'Nowe-a-dayes', cited in Lord Ernle, op. cit., p. 62.

32 *Bastard's Chrestolerus*, 1598, bk iv, epigram 20, cited in Lord Ernle, op. cit., p. 63.

33 Thomas More, *Utopia*, cited in Derek Wilson, op. cit, p. 129.

34 D. M. Palliser, op. cit, p. 182.

35 R. H. Tawney and E. Power (eds), *Tudor Economic Documents*, cited in D. M. Palliser, op. cit, p. 182.

36 Official Record of the Trial of Robert and William Kett, 1549, cited in David C. Douglas (gen. ed.), op. cit., p. 939.

37 Joan Thirsk (ed.), *Agricultural Change: Policy and Practice, 1500–1750, Chapters from the Agrarian History of England and Wales*, Vol. 3, gen. ed. Joan Thirsk, Cambridge University Press, 1990, p. 78.

38 Ibid., p. 88.

39 L. A. Parker, 'The Agrarian Revolution at Cotesbach 1601–1612', in W. G. Hoskins (ed.), *Studies in Leicestershire Agrarian History*, Transactions of Leicestershire Archaeological Society, 24, 1948, pp. 41–76.

40 R. Crotty, *Cattle, Economics and Development*, CAB, 1980, p. 23.

41 Ibid., p. 26.

12 ROOTS OF REVOLUTION

1 Lord Ernle, *English Farming Past and Present*, 6th edn, Heinemann/Cass, 1961, p. 108.

2 B. H. Slicher van Bath, 'The rise of intensive husbandry in the Low Countries', in J. S. Bromley and E. H. Kossman (eds), *Britain and the Netherlands*, 1960.

3 G. E. Fussell, 'Low Countries' influence on English farming', *English Historical Review*, Vol. 74, 1959, pp. 611–24.

4 T. Bedford Franklin, *British Grasslands*, Faber and Faber, 1953, p. 86.

5 Barnabyy Googe, *Foure Bookes of Husbandrie*, 1577, cited in Lord Ernle, op. cit., p. 100.

6 John Norden, *The Surveior's Dialogue*, 3rd edn, 1618, p. 208.

7 G. E. Fussell, 'Adventures with clover', *Agriculture*, 62 (7), October 1955, pp. 342–5.

8 Samuel Hartlib, *Samuel Hartlib His Legacie; or An Enlargement of the Discourse of Husbandry used in Brabant and Flanders*, 1651.

9 Walter Blith, *The English Improver Improved*, 3rd impression, 1652.

10 John Donaldson, *Agricultural Biography*, 41, 1854.

11 'Folium in Trifolium Encomasticon', in Andrew Yarranton, *The Great Improvement of Lands by Clover*, 1663.

12 *Dictionary of National Biography*.

13 Andrew Yarranton, *Full Discovery of the First Presbyterian Sham Plot*, 1681, cited in *Dictionary of National Biography*.

14 In Andrew Yarranton, op. cit.

15 Lord Ernle, op. cit., p. 202.

16 Eleanor C. Lodge (ed.), *The Account Book of a Kentish Estate, 1616–1704*, 1927, cited in G. E. Fussell, op. cit., p. 344.

17 G. E. Fussell, 'Pioneer farming in the late Stuart age', *Journal of the Royal Society of England*, Vol. 100 (3), March 1940, pp. 13–19.

18 T. Bedford Franklin, op. cit., p. 91.

19 Charles Wilson, *Holland and Britain*, Collins, n. d., p. 108.

20 Richard North, *Account of the different kind of grasses propagated in England, for the improvement of corn and pasture lands, lawns and walks*, 1759, quoted in G. E. Fussell, 'Grassland advice in

the mid-eighteenth century', *Journal of the Ministry of Agriculture*, 38 (6), September 1931, pp. 607–12.

21 G. E. Fussell, op. cit., March 1940, p. 14.

22 John Worlidge, *Systema Agriculturae: The Mystery of Husbandry Discovered*, 4th edn, Thomas Dring, 1687, pp. 29–31.

23 J. H. Smith, *The Gordon's Mill Farming Club, 1758–1764*, Oliver and Boyd, 1962, p. 149.

24 John Worlidge, op. cit.

25 Robert C. Allen, 'The two English agricultural revolutions, 1450–1850', in M. S. Campbell and Mark Overton (eds), *Land, Labour and Livestock – Historical Studies in European Agricultural Productivity*, Manchester University Press, 1991, pp. 236–54.

26 Arthur Young, *The Farmers' Letters*, cited in R. A. C. Parker, *Coke of Norfolk*, Oxford, 1975, p. 73.

27 T. Bedford Franklin, op. cit., p. 92.

28 R. A. C. Parker, op. cit., p. 71.

29 Ibid., p. 73.

30 J. D. Chambers and G. E. Mingay, *The Agricultural Revolution, 1750–1880*, Batsford, 1966, p. 3.

31 Mark Overton, *Agricultural Revolution in England*, Cambridge University Press, 1996, p. 115.

32 Ibid. p. 118.

33 Ibid. p. 110.

13 THE IMPROVERS

1 Lord Ernle, *English Farming Past and Present*, 6th edn, Heinemann/Cass, 1961, p. 118.

2 John R. Walton, 'Pedigree and the National Cattle Herd Circa 1750–1950', *Agricultural History Review*, Vol. 34 (II), 1986, pp. 149–69.

3 Lord Ernle, op. cit., p. 184.

4 William Marshall, cited in Lord Ernle, op. cit., p. 186.

5 Allan Fraser, *Animal Husbandry Heresies*, Crosby Lockwood, 1960, p. 27.

6 R. B. Greig, 'The Improvement of Cattle', in prof. C.

Bryner Jones (ed.), *Livestock of the Farm Vol. 1*, Gresham Publishing, 1920, p. 195.

7 Quoted in Robert Trow-Smith, *English Husbandry*, Faber and Faber, 1951, p. 164.

8 Robert Trow-Smith, *A History of British Livestock Husbandry 1700–1900*, Routledge and Kegan Paul, 1959, p. 90.

9 Stephen J. G. Hall and Juliet Clutton-Brock, *Two Hundred Years of British Farm Livestock*, British Museum, 1989, p. 50.

10 H. H. Dixon, cited in Stephen J. G. Hall and Juliet Clutton-Brock, op. cit., p. 50.

11 Thomas Bewick, quoted by Basil Taylor, *Animal Painting in England*, Penguin, 1955, pp. 41–2.

12 Robert Trow-Smith, op. cit., 1959, p. 239.

13 E. Heath-Agnew, *A History of Hereford Cattle and Their Breeders*, Duckworth, 1983, p. 17.

14 William Youatt, *Cattle*, 34, cited in Robert Trow-Smith, op. cit., 1959, p. 253.

15 H. H. Dixon, 'Rise and Progress of Hereford Cattle', *Journal of the Royal Agricultural Society of England*, Vol. 4, p. 286.

16 James Wilson, 'Aberdeen-Angus Cattle', in Professor C. Bryner Jones, op. cit., p. 34.

17 Kenneth O. Morgan (ed.), *The Oxford Illustrated History of Britain*, Oxford University Press, 1984, p. 481.

18 Robert Bruce, 'Shorthorn Cattle', in C. Bryner Jones, op. cit., p. 156.

19 H. Harmsworth, 'The 2,500 Gallon Dairy Shorthorn', *Live Stock Journal Almanac*, 1919, pp. 56–7.

20 Raymond Steen, 'Beef: A Naturally Healthy Product', *Beef Farmer*, Spring 2000, pp. 17–18.

14 INVASION

1 Quoted in Mark Overton, *The Agricultural Revolution in England*, Cambridge University Press, 1996, p. 92.

2 Quoted by Robert Trow-Smith, *English Husbandry*, Faber and Faber, 1951, p. 109.

3 Diane Montague, *Farming, Food and Politics*, Irish Agricultural Wholesale Society, 2000, p. 218.

4 J. D. Chambers and G. E. Mingay, *The Agricultural Revolution 1750–1880*, Batsford, 1966, p. 174.

5 Diane Montague, op. cit., pp. 218–19.

6 F. M. L. Thompson, 'The Second Agricultural Revolution 1815–1880', *Economic History Review*, 2nd series, Vol. 21, 1968, pp. 62–73.

7 Quoted in J. Hendrick, 'The Growth of International Trade in Manures and Foods', *Transactions of the Highland and Agricultural Society of Scotland*, 5th series, Vol. 29, 1917, p. 16.

8 F. M. L. Thompson, op. cit., p. 67.

9 Robert Trow-Smith, op. cit., p. 203.

10 'Machinery and Implements Displayed at the Great Exhibition', *Journal of the Royal Agricultural Society of England*, Vol. 12, 1851, pp. 638–9.

11 William Sturge, 'On Some of the Causes of Agricultural Depression', *Journal of the Bath and West of England Society*, Vol. 11, 1879, pp. 168–85.

12 Ibid.

13 Joan Thirsk, *Alternative Agriculture*, Oxford University Press, 1997, p. 151.

14 James Caird, *English Agriculture in 1850–51*, 2nd edn, Kelley: New York, 1967, p. 480.

15 Ibid., pp. 484–5.

16 J. C. Morton, 'On the Management of Grass Lands', *Journal of the Bath and West of England Society*, Vol. 13, 1865, pp. 61–73.

17 Rev. W. R. Bowditch, 'On the Manuring of Grassland', *Journal of the Royal Agricultural Society of England*, Vol. 19, 1858, pp. 219–50.

18 J. C. Morton, op. cit.

19 H. S. Thompson, 'On the Management of Grass Land, With Special Reference to the Production of Meat', *Journal of the Bath and West of England Society*, 3rd series, Vol. 4, 1872, pp. 109–36.

20 Edward Billyse, 'On the Application of Bones to Grass Lands on Lord Combermere's Estate', *Journal of the Royal*

Agricultural Society of England, Vol. 2, 1841, pp. 91–2.

21 J. Dixon, 'Manuring of Grass Lands', *Journal of the Royal Agricultural Society of England*, Vol. 19, 1858, pp. 204–18.

22 Ibid.

23 Rev. W. R. Bowditch, op. cit.

24 Robert Trow-Smith, op. cit., p. 179.

25 Dr A. Voelcker and Professor Coleman, 'Improvement of Grassland on the Manor Farm, Braydon, Wiltshire', *Journal of the Bath and West of England Society*, Vol. 14, 1866, pp. 127–41.

26 C. De Laune Faunce-De Laune, 'On Laying Down Land to Permanent Grass', *Journal of the Royal Agricultural Society of England*, 2nd series, Vol. 18, 1882, pp. 229–64.

27 James Caird, op. cit., pp. 457–8.

28 Joan Thirsk, op. cit., p. 152.

29 Ibid., p. 153.

30 J. P. Sheldon, 'Report on the American and Canadian Meat Trade', *Journal of the Royal Agricultural Society of England*, 2nd series, Vol. 13, 1877, pp. 295–374.

31 Henry Stewart writing in the *Chicago Tribune*, quoted in J. P. Sheldon, op. cit.

32 Mari Sandoz, *The Cattlemen*, University of Nebraska Press, 1958, p. 235.

33 Ernest Mathews, 'The Revival of the Butter Industry', *Journal of the Bath and West of England Society*, Series 4, Vol. 10, 1899–1900, pp. 9–19.

34 Robert Trow-Smith, op. cit., p. 175.

35 John Chalmers Morton, 'Town Milk', *Journal of the Royal Agricultural Society of England*, 2nd series, Vol. 4, 1868, pp. 69–77.

36 'Secondary or Narrow Gauge Railways for Agricultural Purposes', *Journal of the Royal Agricultural Society of England*, 2nd series, Vol. 17, 1881, pp. 391–6.

37 J. P. Sheldon, 'Dairy Farming: Fifty Years Ago and Now', *Journal of the Bath and West and Southern Counties Society*, 5th series, Vol. 2, 1907–8, pp. 86–101.

38 Cited in Joan Thirsk, op. cit., p. 169.

39 Ruth L. Cohen, *The History of Milk Prices*, Oxford

University Agricultural Economics Research Institute, 1936, p. 188.

40 Robert Elliot, *The Clifton Park System of Farming*, Faber and Faber, 1908, pp. 28–9.

15   THE WHIRLING BLADE

1 John Abercrombie, *Every Man his own Gardener*, in Chris Thompson, 'From Castle to Council House – British Lawnmowers in their Social Context', The Old Lawnmower Club, Milton Keynes, October 1998.
2 David G. Halford, *Old Lawn Mowers*, Shire Publications, 1982, p. 4.
3 Ibid.
4 Carol and Michael Weaver, *A Bicentennial Celebration – Ransomes 1789–1989*, Ransomes Sims and Jefferies, 1989, p. 107.
5 Andrew Hall, 'The History of the Lawnmower: Part One 1830–1900', *Farm and Horticultural Equipment Collector*, No. 18, Jan/Feb 1995.
6 Ibid.
7 Carol and Michael Weaver, op. cit., p. 109.
8 Andrew Hall, 'The History of the Lawnmower: Part Three 1830–1900', *Farm and Horticultural Equipment Collector*, No. 20, May/Jun 1995.
9 David G. Halford, op. cit., p. 15.
10 Chris Thompson, op. cit.
11 Carol and Michael Weaver, op. cit., p. 114–15.
12 Ibid., p. 117.

16   BREATHING SPACE

1 Hazel Conway, *Public Parks*, Shire Publications, 1996, p. 5.
2 Ibid., p. 7.
3 George F. Chadwick, *The Works of Sir Joseph Paxton*, Architectural Press, 1961, pp. 49–50.

4 Margaret Jackson, 'The Competition', in *Sefton Park*, Sefton Park Civic Society, 1984, p. 47.

5 Ibid., p. 49.

6 Ibid., p. 13.

7 Miss Hargreaves, a Manchester resident, in evidence to the Select Committee on Environment, Transport and Regional Affairs 20th Report, *Town and Country Parks*, 1999, House of Commons.

8 *Town and Country Parks*, op. cit., para. 82.

9 Ibid., para. 81.

10 Memorandum of the Heritage Lottery Fund, in evidence to the Select Committee on Environment, Transport and Regional Affairs 20th Report, *Town and Country Parks*, op. cit.

11 Hazel Conway, op. cit., p. 17.

12 Timothy Marshall, Memorandum to the Select Committee on Environment, Transport and Regional Affairs 20th Report, *Town and Country Parks*, op. cit.

13 Bernard Sheridan of Stockport Metropolitan Borough Council in evidence to the Select Committee on Environment, Transport and Regional Affairs 20th Report, *Town and Country Parks*, op. cit.

14 Liz Greenhalgh, 'Greening the Cities', in Anthony Barnett and Roger Scruton (eds), *Town and Country*, Jonathan Cape, 1998, pp. 253–66.

15 Mike Canaway, 'The Environmental Benefits of Turfgrass', *Turfgrass Bulletin*, No. 204, April 1999, pp. 28–30.

16 Liz Greenhalgh, op. cit., p. 264.

17 THE DANCE OF LIFE

1 Arthur S. Gregor, *Charles Darwin*, Angus and Robertson, 1967, p. 158.

2 Charles Darwin, *The Formation of Vegetable Mould through the Action of Worms, with Observations on Their Habits*, John Murray, 1881, p. 148.

3 Philip Conford (ed.), *The Organic Tradition*, Green Books, 1988, p. 4.

4 Justus von Liebig, *Liebig's Chemistry*, pt 1, 3rd edn, 1856, pp. 212–14.

5 John Sheail, 'Elements of Sustainable Agriculture: The UK Experience, 1840–1940', *Agricultural History Review*, Vol. 43 (2), 1995, pp. 178–92.

6 J. A. Scott Watson and May Elliot Hobbs, *Great Farmers*, Selwyn and Blount, 1937, p. 79.

7 Cited in Charles Daubeny, 'On the Supposed Deterioration of the Soil of Great Britain, through the Exhaustion of its Vegetable Mould', *Journal of the Bath and West of England Society*, Vol. 12, 1864, pp. 129–48.

8 John Sheail, op. cit., p. 183.

9 Diane Montague, *Farming, Food and Politics*, Irish Agricultural Wholesale Society, 2000, p. 222.

10 H. S. Thompson, 'On the Management of Grass Land, with especial Reference to the Production of Meat', *Journal of the Bath and West of England Society*, 3rd series, Vol. 4, 1872, pp. 109–36.

11 C. S. Orwin, *A Specialist in Arable Farming*, Oxford, 1930.

12 Philip Conford (ed.), op. cit., p. 115.

13 Sir Albert Howard, *England and the Farmer*, Batsford, 1941, pp. 48–50.

14 Ibid.

15 Philip Conford, 'A Forum for Organic Husbandry: The *New English Weekly* and Agricultural Policy, 1939–49', *Agricultural History Review*, Vol. 46 (2), 1998, pp. 197–210.

16 C. S. Orwin, *Speed the Plough*, Penguin Books, 1942, p. 62.

17 Lord Teviot, cited in Lady Eve Balfour, *The Living Soil*, Faber, 1943, pp. 159–61.

18 G. T. Wrench, *The Wheel of Health*, Schocken Books, 1972, p. 130.

19 K. C. Tyson et al., 'Comparison of Crop Yields and Soil Conditions During 30 Years Under Annual Tillage of Grazed Pasture', *Journal of Agricultural Science*, Vol. 115, 1990, pp. 29–40.

20 Newman Turner, *Fertility Farming*, Faber and Faber, 1951, pp. 18–19.

18 THE DYING OF THE GREEN

1 Diane Montague, *Farming, Food and Politics*, Irish Agricultural Wholesale Society, 2000, p. 358.
2 Roger J. Wilkins, 'Grassland in the Twentieth Century', in *IGER Innovations*, No. 4, Institute of Grassland and Environmental Research, 2000, pp. 25–33.
3 Robert Waller, introduction to Sir George Stapledon's *Human Ecology*, Soil Association Edition, 1964, p. 23.
4 Ibid, p. 29.
5 Sir George Stapledon, *A Tour in Australia and New Zealand: Grassland and other Studies*, cited in Richard J. Colyer, *Man's Proper Study*, Gomer Press, 1982, p. 98.
6 Robert Waller, op. cit., p. 33.
7 Sir George Stapledon, *The Way of the Land*, Faber and Faber, 1943, cited in Robert Waller, op. cit., p. 46.
8 Richard J. Colyer, op. cit., p. 99.
9 Robert Waller, *Prophet of the New Age*, Faber and Faber, 1962, pp. 162–8.
10 Richard J. Colyer, op. cit., p. 100.
11 Ibid., pp. 101–2.
12 Sir George Stapledon, *The Land, Now and Tomorrow*, Faber and Faber, 1935.
13 Richard J. Colyer, op. cit., p. 98.
14 Sir George Stapledon, op. cit., 1943, p. 181.
15 Sir George Stapledon, *Human Ecology*, revised 2nd edn, Charles Knight, 1971, pp. 55–7.
16 Ibid.

Index

Index

Index